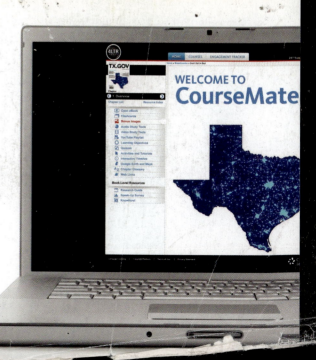

WADSWORTH
CENGAGE Learning™

TX.GOV First Edition

William Earl Maxwell

Ernest Crain

Adolfo Santos

Senior Publisher: Suzanne Jeans

Executive Editor: Carolyn Merrill

Developmental Editor: Rebecca Green

Assistant Editor: Scott Greenan

Editorial Assistant: Eireann Aspell

Brand Manager: Lydia LeStar

Market Development Manager: Kyle Zimmerman

Media Editor: Laura Hildebrand

Production Manager: Suzanne St. Clair

4LTR Press Project Manager: Kelli Strieby

Senior Content Project Manager: Ann Borman

Print Buyer: Fola Orekoya

Copy Editor: Jeanne Yost

Proofreader: Pat Lewis

Indexer: Terry Casey

Art Director: Linda May

Interior Design: RHDG

Cover Design: PHodepohl Design

Cover Images: Stock Trek/Getty Images;
skvoor/Shutterstock

Compositor: Parkwood Composition Service

For product information and technology assistance, contact us at
Cengage Learning Academic Resource Center
1-800-423-0563

For permission to use material from this text or product,
submit all requests online at
www.cengage.com/permissions

Further permissions questions can be emailed to
permissionrequest@cengage.com

Library of Congress Control Number: 2012952539

Student Edition, package
ISBN-13: 978-1-133-96441-4
ISBN-10: 1-133-96441-9

Student Edition, book only
ISBN-13 978-1-133-96442-1
ISBN-10: 1-133-96442-7

Wadsworth Political Science
20 Channel Center
Boston, MA 02210

Cengage Learning is a leading provider of customized learning solutions with office locations around the globe, including Australia, Brazil, Japan, Korea, Mexico, Singapore, Spain, and the United Kingdom. Locate your local office at **www.cengage.com/global.**

Cengage Learning products are represented in Canada by Nelson Education, Ltd.

To learn more about Wadsworth, visit **www.cengage.com/Wadsworth**

Purchase any of our products at your local college store or at our preferred online store **www.CengageBrain.com**

Printed in the United States of America

1 2 3 4 5 6 7 16 15 14 13 12

TX.GOV BRIEF CONTENTS

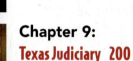

TX.GOV CONTENTS

A Note from the Authors

We know that you need something exceptional to keep you excited about a Texas politics textbook. So that is why we have created *TX.GOV*. If you have to learn how your state government works, why not make the job a little more fun? Working with instructors and students like you, we have created what we think is the most engaging Texas government book that exists today. This visually appealing, succinct textbook—along with its built-in and digital study tools—were designed to accommodate your busy lifestyle, enhance your learning experience, and improve your grades. *TX.GOV* also highlights how this subject surrounds and affects your life every day and why Texas government matters to you. This approach makes a required course a lot more interesting.

We have added a little spice to the subject matter through intriguing boxed features that deal with issues you care about. One of them is entitled *How Texas Compares*. You might be surprised at where your state stands relative to the other forty-nine states in terms of spending on education, crime, and energy production—just to name a few. You will also discover *Texas Political Social Media* boxes in each chapter. In other words, you can also learn about Texas politics by using Facebook and Twitter.

Throughout its text, *TX.GOV* employs a lively debate theme that focuses on the current hot-button topics and historical conflicts and controversies that define Texas politics. This will prepare you to speak intelligently about your state, understand today's issues, and join in the discussions around you.

You live in a unique state, but like other states, it faces many challenges—perhaps more than some states face. Yet, it also has so many positive qualities that we are all proud to be Texans.

William Earl Maxwell
San Antonio College

Ernest Crain
San Antonio College

Adolfo Santos
University of Houston, Downtown

Acknowledgments

A number of political scientists have reviewed *TX.GOV*, and we are indebted to them for their thoughtful suggestions on how to create a text that best suits the needs of today's students and faculty.

Mark Arandia
North Lake College

Robert Ballinger
South Texas College

Brian Bearry
University of Texas at Dallas

David Birch
Lone Star College–Tomball

Gary Brown
Lone Star College–Montgomery

Michael Campenni
McLennan Community College

John Carhart
Texas A&M University–Galveston

Kevin Davis
North Central Texas College

Henry Esparza
Northeast Lakeview College

Bonnie Ford
Grayson College

Steve Garrison
Midwestern State University

Theodore Hadzi-Antich
Austin Community College

Jeff Harmon
University of Texas at
San Antonio

Tiffany Harper
Collin College

Virginia Haysley
Lone Star College–Tomball

Donna Hooper
North Central Texas College

John Jordan
Frank Phillips College

Joe Jozwiak
Texas A&M University–
Corpus Christi

WooJin Kang
Angelo State University

Sharon Manna
North Lake College

Michael McConachie
Collin College

David McCoy
Cedar Valley College

Elizabeth McLane
Wharton County Junior College

Michael McLatchy
Clarendon College

Vinette Meikle
Houston Community
College–Central

Patrick Moore
Richland College

Mark R. Murray
South Texas College

Sharon Navarro
University of Texas at
San Antonio

Paul Phillips
Navarro College

Renato Ramirez
Del Mar College

Ryan Rynbrandt
Collin College

David Smith
Texas A&M University–
Corpus Christi

David Smith
University of Texas at Dallas

Suzie Smith
Trinity Valley Community College

Jeff Stanglin
Wharton County Junior College

Gabriel Ume
Palo Alto College

Linda Veazey
Midwestern State University

M. Theron Waddell
Galveston College & Texas A&M
University–Galveston

David Watson
Sul Ross State University

Kierah Weber
Stephen F. Austin State University
and Lone Star College System

Robert Webking
University of Texas–El Paso

Kevin Wooten
Angelia College

Tyler Young
Collin College

We would like to extend a special thanks to the authors of the supporting materials for *TX.GOV*. David McCoy of Cedar Valley College created the end-of-chapter quizzes, Chapter in Review cards, and Instructor Prep cards. Patrick Moore of Richland College wrote the Test Bank. Jeff Stanglin of Wharton County Junior College created the Instructor's Manual. These instructors' hard work and attention to detail is evident in the quality of these supplements.

SKILL PREP
A STUDY SKILLS MODULE

Welcome!

With this course and this textbook, you've begun what we hope will be a fun, stimulating, and thought-provoking journey into the world of Texas government and politics. In this course, you will learn all about the foundations of Texas government, Texas culture and diversity, interest groups, political parties, campaigns, elections, the media, our governing institutions, public policy, and local government. Knowledge of these basics will help you think critically about political issues and become an active citizen.

To help you get the most out of this course, and this textbook, we have developed this study skills module. You may be a recent high school graduate, or a working professional continuing your education, or an adult making your way back to the classroom after a few years. Whatever type of student you are, you want RESULTS when you study. You want to be able to understand the issues and ideas presented in the textbook, to be able to talk about them intelligently during class discussions, and to be able to remember them as you prepare for exams and papers.

This kind of knowledge doesn't just come from natural talent. Instead, it comes from the use of good study skills. This module is designed to help you develop the skills and habits you'll need to get the results that you want from this course. With tips on how to be more engaged when you study, how to get the most out of your textbook, how to prepare for exams, and how to write papers, this guide will help you become the best learner you can be!

STUDY PREP

What does it take to be a successful student? Like many people, you may think that success depends on how naturally smart you are, that some people are just better at school than others. But in reality, successful students aren't born, they're made. What this means is that even if you don't consider yourself naturally "book smart," you can do well in this course by developing study skills that will help you understand, remember, and apply key concepts.

READING FOR LEARNING

Your textbook is the foundation for information in a course. It contains key concepts and terms that are important to your understanding of the subject. For this reason, it is essential that you develop good reading skills. As you read your textbook with the goal of learning as much of the information as possible, work on establishing the following habits:

FOCUS

Make an effort to focus on the book and tune out other distractions so that you can understand and remember the information it presents.

TAKE TIME

To learn the key concepts presented in each chapter, you need to read slowly, carefully, and with great attention.

REPEAT

To read for learning, you have to read your textbook a number of times. Follow a preview-read-review process:

1. **Preview:** The first time you read a section of the book, you should preview it. Look over the chapter title, section headings, and highlighted or bold words. This will give you a good preview of important ideas in the chapter. (Notice that each major section heading in this textbook has a corresponding Learning Outcome. By turning headings or subheadings in all of your textbooks into questions or learning objectives—and then answering them—you will increase your understanding of the material.) Note graphs, pictures, and other visual illustrations of important concepts. Pay special attention to the first and last sentence of each paragraph. First sentences usually introduce the main point of the paragraph, while last sentences usually sum up what was presented in each paragraph. For each section, try to answer the question "What is the main idea?" The point is to develop some general ideas about what the section is about so that when you do read it in full, you can have a guide for what to look for.

2. **Read:** After the preview, read through each passage in detail. During this phase, it is important to read with a few of questions in mind: What is the main point of this paragraph? What does the author want me to learn from this? How does this relate to what I read before? Keeping these questions in mind will help you to be an attentive reader who is actively focusing on the main ideas of the passage.

    It is helpful to take notes while reading in detail. You can mark your text or write an outline, as explained below. Taking notes will help you read actively, identify important concepts, and remember them. Then when it comes time to review for the exam, the notes you've made will make your studying more efficient. After you have completed a detailed read of the chapter and taken a break, try writing a brief summary or paraphrase of what you read, identifying the most important ideas.

3. **Review:** After you've finished a detailed reading of the chapter, you should take the time to review the chapter at least once (but maybe even two or more times) before your exam. Review each paragraph and the notes you made, asking this question: "What was this paragraph about?" You'll want to answer the question

in some detail, readily identifying the important points.

A reading group is a great way to review the chapter. After completing the reading individually, group members should meet and take turns sharing what they learned. Explaining the material to others will reinforce and clarify what you already know. It also provides an opportunity to learn from others. Getting a different perspective on a passage will increase your knowledge, since different people will find different things important during a reading.

ASK QUESTIONS

If you are really engaged in your Texas government course, you will ask a question or two whenever you do not understand something. You can also ask a question to get your instructor to share her or his opinion on a subject. However you do it, true engagement requires you to be a participant in your class. The more you participate, the more you will learn (and the more your instructor will know who you are!).

TAKE NOTES

Being *engaged* means listening to discover (and remember) something. Not only do you have to hear what the professor is saying in class, you have to pay attention to it. And as you listen with attention, you will hear what your instructor believes is important. One way to make sure that you are listening attentively is to take notes. Doing so will help you focus on the professor's words and will help you identify the most important parts of the lecture.

The physical act of writing makes you a more efficient learner. In addition, your notes provide a guide to what your instructor thinks is important. That means you will have a better idea of what to study before the next exam if you have a set of notes that you took during class.

MAKE AN OUTLINE

As you read through each chapter of your textbook, you might want to make an outline—a simple method for organizing information. You can create an outline as

part of your reading or at the end of your reading. Or you can make an outline when you reread a section before moving on to the next. The act of physically writing an outline for a chapter will help you retain the material in this text and master it, thereby obtaining a higher grade in class.

To make an effective outline, you have to be selective. Your objectives in outlining are, first, to identify the main concepts and, then, to add the details that support those main concepts.

Your outline should consist of several levels written in a standard format. The most important concepts are assigned Roman numerals; the second most important, capital letters; the third most important, numbers; and the fourth most important, lowercase letters. Here is a quick example:

I. The Struggle for Equal Rights
   A. African Americans in Texas
      1. The White Primary
      2. Making the Right to Vote Effective
      3. Chipping Away at Segregation
         a. Smith v. Allwright (1944)
         b. Brown v. Board of Education (1954)

MARK YOUR TEXT

Now that you own your own textbook for this course, you can greatly improve your learning by marking your text. By doing so, you will identify the most important concepts of each chapter, and at the same time, you'll be making a handy study guide for reviewing material at a later time. It allows you to become an active participant in the mastery of the material. Researchers have shown that the physical act of marking, just like the physical acts of note-taking during class and outlining, increases concentration and helps you better retain the material.

WAYS OF MARKING The most common form of marking is to underline important points. The second most commonly used method is to use a felt-tipped highlighter, or marker, in yellow or some other transparent color. Put a check mark next to material that you do not understand. Work on better comprehension of the checkmarked material after you've finished the chapter. Marking also includes circling, numbering, using arrows, jotting brief notes, or any other method that allows you to remember things when you go back to skim the pages in your textbook prior to an exam.

IMPORTANT

TWO POINTS TO REMEMBER WHEN MARKING

Read one section at a time before you do any extensive marking. You can't mark a section until you know what is important, and you can't know what is important until you read the whole section.

Don't overmark. Don't fool yourself into thinking that you have done a good job just because each page is filled up with arrows, circles, and underlines. The key to marking is *selective* activity. Mark each page in a way that allows you to see the most important points at a glance. You can follow up your marking by writing out more in your subject outline.

TRY THESE TIPS

With these skills in hand, you will be well on your way to becoming a great student. Here are a few more hints that will help you develop effective study skills.

- As a rule, do schoolwork as soon as possible when you get home after class. The longer you wait, the more likely you will be distracted by television, video games, phone calls from friends, or social networking.

- We study best when we are free from distractions. Set aside time and a quiet, comfortable space where you can focus on reading. Your school library is often the best place to work. Set aside several hours a week of "library time" to study in peace and quiet. A neat, organized study space is also important. The only work items that should be on your desk are those that you are working on that day.

WWW

- Reward yourself for studying! Rest your eyes and your mind by taking a short break every twenty to thirty minutes. From time to time, allow yourself a break for surfing the Internet, going for a jog, taking a nap, or doing something else that you enjoy. These interludes will refresh your mind, give you more energy required for concentration, and enable you to study longer and more efficiently.

- Often, studying involves pure memorization. To help with this task, create flash (or note) cards. On one side of the card, write the question or term. On the other side, write the answer or definition. Then, use the cards to test yourself on the material.

- Mnemonic (pronounced ne-mon-ik) devices are tricks that increase our ability to memorize. A well-known mnemonic device is the phrase ROY G BIV, which helps people remember the colors of the rainbow—Red, Orange, Yellow, Green, Blue, Indigo, Violet. You can create your own for whatever you need to memorize. The more fun you have coming up with mnemonics for yourself, the more useful they will be.

- Take notes twice. First, take notes in class. Then, when you get back home, rewrite your notes. The rewrite will act as a study session by forcing you to think about the material. It will also, invariably, lead to questions that are crucial to the study process.

2x

winterling/iStockphoto.com

TEST PREP

You have worked hard throughout the term, reading the book, paying close attention in class, and taking good notes. Now it's test time, when all that hard work pays off. To do well on an exam, of course, it is important that you learn the concepts in each chapter as thoroughly as possible, but there are additional strategies for taking exams. You should know which reading materials and lectures will be covered. You should also know in advance what type of exam you are going to take—essay or objective or both. Finally, you should know how much time will be allowed for the exam. By taking these steps, you will reduce any anxiety you feel as you begin the exam, and you'll be better prepared to work through the entire exam.

FOLLOW DIRECTIONS

Students are often in a hurry to start an exam, so they take little time to read the instructions. The instructions can be critical, however. In a multiple-choice exam, for example, if there is no indication that there is a penalty for guessing, then you should never leave a question unanswered. Even if only a few minutes are left at the end of an exam, you should guess on the questions that you remain uncertain about.

Additionally, you need to know the weight given to each section of an exam. In a typical multiple-choice exam, all questions have equal weight. In other types of exams, particularly those with essay questions, different parts of the exam carry different weights. You should use these weights to apportion your time accordingly. If the essay portion of an exam accounts for 20 percent of the total points on the exam, you should not spend 60 percent of your time on the essay.

Finally, you need to make sure you are marking the answers correctly. Some exams require a No. 2 pencil to fill in the dots on a machine-graded answer sheet. Other exams require underlining or circling. In short, you have to read and follow the instructions carefully.

OBJECTIVE EXAMS

An objective exam consists of multiple-choice, true/false, fill-in-the-blank, or matching questions that have only one correct answer. Students usually commit one of two errors when they read objective exam questions: (1) they read things into the questions that do not exist, or (2) they skip over words or phrases. Most test questions include key words such as:

- all
- never
- always
- only

If you miss any of these key words, you may answer the question wrong even if you know the information.

Whenever the answer to an objective question is not obvious, start with the process of elimination. Throw out the answers that are clearly incorrect. Typically, the easiest way to eliminate incorrect answers is to look for those that are meaningless, illogical, or inconsistent. Often, test authors put in choices that make perfect sense and are indeed true, but they are not the answer to the question under study.

If you follow the above tips, you will be well on your way to becoming an efficient, results-oriented student. Here are a few more that will help you get there.

- Instructors usually lecture on subjects they think are important, so those same subjects are also likely to be on the exam. Therefore, be sure to take extensive notes in class. Then, review your notes thoroughly as part of your exam preparation.
- At times, you will find yourself studying for several exams at once. When this happens, make a list of each study topic and the amount of time needed to prepare for that topic. Then, create a study schedule to reduce stress and give yourself the best chance for success.
- When preparing for an exam, you might want to get together a

7. Proof.

As you ease down the home stretch, read your revised paper one more time. This time, go for the big picture and look for the following:

Proofreading checklist

- A clear thesis statement.
- Sentences that introduce your topic, guide the reader through the major sections of your paper, and summarize your conclusions.
- Details—such as quotations, examples, and statistics—that support your conclusions.
- Lean sentences that have been purged of needless words.
- Plenty of action verbs and concrete, specific nouns.
- Finally, look over your paper with an eye for spelling and grammar mistakes. Use contractions sparingly if at all. Use your word processor's spell-check by all means, but do not rely on it completely as it will not catch everything.

ACADEMIC INTEGRITY: AVOIDING PLAGIARISM

Using another person's words, images, or other original creations without giving proper credit is called *plagiarism*. Plagiarism amounts to taking someone else's work and presenting it as your own—the equivalent of cheating on a test. The consequences of plagiarism can range from a failing grade to expulsion from school.

To avoid plagiarism, ask an instructor where you can find your school's written policy on this issue. Don't assume that you can resubmit a paper you wrote for another class for a current class. Many schools will regard this as plagiarism even though you wrote the paper. The basic guidelines for preventing plagiarism are to cite a source for each phrase, sequence of ideas, or visual image created by another person. While ideas cannot be copyrighted, the specific way that an idea is *expressed* can be. You also need to list a source for any idea that is closely identified with a particular person. The goal is to clearly distinguish your own work from the work of others. There are several ways to ensure that you do this consistently:

- **Identify direct quotes.** If you use a direct quote from another source, put those words in quotation marks. If you do research online, you might copy text from a Web page and paste it directly into your notes. This is the same as taking direct quotes from your source. Always identify such passages in an obvious way.

- **Paraphrase carefully.** Paraphrasing means restating the original passage in your own words, usually making it shorter and simpler. Students who copy a passage word for word and then just rearrange or delete a few phrases are running a serious risk of plagiarism. Remember to cite a source for paraphrases, just as you do for direct quotes. When you use the same sequence of ideas as one of your sources—even if you have not paraphrased or directly quoted—cite that source.

- **Note details about each source.** For books, details about each source include the author, title, publisher, publication date, location of publisher, and page number. For articles from print sources, record the article title and the name of the magazine or journal as well. If you found the article in an academic or technical journal, also record the volume and number of the publication. A librarian can help identify these details. If your source is a Web page, record as many identifying details as you can find—author, title, sponsoring organization, URL, publication date, and revision date. In addition, list the date that you accessed the page. Be careful when using Web resources, as not all Web sites are considered legitimate sources. Wikipedia, for instance, is not regarded as a legitimate source.

- **Cite your sources as endnotes or footnotes to your paper.** Ask your instructor for examples of the format to use. You do not need to credit wording that is wholly your own. Nor do you need to credit general ideas, such as the suggestion that people use a to-do list to plan their time. When you use your own words to describe such an idea, there's no need to credit a source. But if you borrow someone else's words or images to explain the idea, do give credit.

Texas Culture and Diversity

© JAMES S. SOUTHERS/DEMOTIX/CORBIS

★ LearningOutcomes

The **Learning Outcomes** labeled 1 through 5 are designed to help improve your understanding of the chapter. After reading this chapter, you should be able to:

1–1 Analyze the relationships among political culture, public opinion, and public policy in Texas.

1–2 Distinguish among moralistic, traditionalistic, and individualistic political subcultures.

1–3 Discuss the distinctive social, economic, and political characteristics of major Texas regions.

1–4 Trace the struggle for equal rights in Texas by women, African Americans, Latinos, and gay men and lesbians.

1–5 Evaluate the social and cultural changes that are likely to define Texas's political future.

Remember to visit page 22 for additional Study Tools

CONFLICT

Should Texas Become Five States?

Imagine if the *Mayflower* had landed on the Texas coast. If so, Texas might very well be made up of a number of small states, just like New England today. Even though Texas schoolchildren pledge, "Texas, one and indivisible," Texas is divisible. A provision in the 1845 resolution annexing the Republic of Texas to the United States allows for the creation of "New States, of convenient size, not exceeding four in number, in addition to said State of Texas." Presumably, Texas could be broken up into as many as five separate states. "Texas divisionism" was indeed a historical movement that resulted in dozens of proposals. For example, a bill introduced in the state legislature in 1915 sought to create the state of Jefferson out of the Texas Panhandle. John Nance Garner, vice president under President Franklin D. Roosevelt, made a five-way division proposal in the 1930s. So, should Texas be divided into five states?

Let's Face It—The State of Texas Is Too Big

Texans who are in favor of creating four additional states point out that Texas has more than 25 million residents. With a land area of almost 270,000 square miles, it is 10 percent larger than France and twice as big as Germany or Japan. If it were a country, its population would be greater than Australia's.

Texas is too big, too diverse, and too divided by competing interests to be managed by a single state government. What do citizens of El Paso really have in common with citizens of Dallas? Voters in these regions are not going to want the same kind of state government, nor should they be forced to have it.

Moreover, splitting Texas into five states would give its current citizens more U.S. senators and therefore more federal power. Texans would have more impact on presidential elections, because the electoral college gives each state two electoral votes for its senators, in addition to an electoral vote for each representative.

Leave My State Alone

Texas divisionism is not for modern times. That is why modern Texans are not interested in it. Carving up the state offends the strong state patriotism felt by millions of Texans. Even though critics say that Texas is ungovernable, one could say the same thing about the United States as a whole, which has more than twelve times the population of Texas.

Just because governing Texas is difficult does not mean the state should be broken up. True, in the long run, the Republican Party might benefit if highly Democratic South and Southwest Texas were split off—if that happened, the rest of the state might vote Republican forever. Likewise, removing ultra-Republican West Texas and the Panhandle would benefit Democrats in the rest of Texas. But no politician thinks that far ahead.

Another issue: If there were several new states, which ones would have the Dallas Cowboys and the Alamo? Let's keep one state, two senators, and one governor.

Where do you stand?

1. If Texas were divided into five states, where would you draw the new boundaries? (Hint: See the section on Texas cultural regions—Learning Outcome 1–3.)
2. If Texas remains united, does that unity give the state more influence than it loses by having only two senators? Why or why not?

Explore this issue online

- *The Handbook of Texas Online* provides a vast collection of articles on Texas and its history. For an article on divisionism, enter "handbook texas division proposals" into your favorite Internet search engine.
- Snopes.com, the Internet's leading site for verifying alleged fables, urban legends, and rumors, has a fine article on Texas divisionism. Search on "snopes texas division."

Introduction

A **political culture** reflects the political values and beliefs of a people. It explains how those people feel about their government—their expectations of what powers it should have and what services it should provide. A political culture is largely developed through *agents of socialization,* such as the family, religious institutions, peer groups, and schools. Political cultures are characterized by varying levels of ethnic and religious diversity and political tolerance. Participation in a political system depends on how people, shaped by culture, view their place within it.

We begin by exploring Texas's dominant political ideology and examining how it influences public policy. Then we look at the state's political subcultures and note the subtle variations in these subcultures from one region to another. Finally, we discuss the struggle for equal rights of various groups of Texans and consider cultural diversity in Texas today.

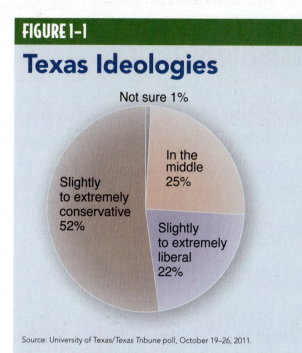

FIGURE 1–1

Texas Ideologies

Not sure 1%

In the middle 25%

Slightly to extremely conservative 52%

Slightly to extremely liberal 22%

Source: University of Texas/*Texas Tribune* poll, October 19–26, 2011.

1–1 Political Culture, Public Opinion, and Public Policy

Texas's political culture supports **conservatism.** This statement is reflected in Figure 1–1 above, which shows different **ideologies** held by Texans. In a recent public opinion survey, 52 percent of Texas registered voters rated themselves as "slightly to extremely conservative," while only 22 percent considered themselves to be "slightly to extremely liberal."

⭐ **Learning**Outcome **1–1**

Analyze the relationships among political culture, public opinion, and public policy in Texas.

1–1a Ideology

The Texas brand of conservatism is skeptical of state and national government involvement in the economy. Most Texans favor low taxes, modest state services, and few business regulations. Because they support economic individualism and free-market capitalism, Texans generally value profit as a healthy incentive to promote individual effort and economic development.

Inequality is seen as the inevitable result of free-market capitalism. Most Texans believe that an individual's quality of life is largely a matter of personal responsibility rather than an issue of public policy.

Business-Oriented Conservatism Some conservatives accept an active role for the government in promoting business. They are willing to support direct government subsidies and special tax breaks for businesses to encourage economic growth. They may also support state spending for infrastructure, such as transportation and education, that sustains commercial manufacturing activity. These conservatives often advocate vigorous state restrictions on labor unions.

Social Conservatism Social conservatives support energetic government activity to enforce what they view as moral behavior and traditional cultural values. For example, they usually champion strong law enforcement, drug control, and immigration controls. Social conservatives, many of whom are Christian fundamentalists, typically advocate the use of state power to restrict gambling, pornography, abortion, and same-sex relationships.

political culture A patterned set of ideas, values, and ways of thinking about government and politics.

conservatism A set of beliefs that includes a limited role for government in helping individuals and in economic affairs, and support for traditional values and lifestyles.

ideology A pattern of political beliefs about how society and the economy operate, including policy orientations consistent with that pattern; a set of beliefs consistent with a particular political perspective.

Texas Liberalism. A minority viewpoint in Texas is **liberalism.** Liberals believe that state government can be used as a positive tool to benefit the population as a whole. Most Texas liberals accept private enterprise as the state's basic economic system but believe excesses of unregulated capitalism compromise the common good. They endorse state policies to abate pollution, to enforce the rights of workers and consumers, and to guard against discrimination based on race, ethnicity, gender, and sexual orientation.

Liberals often believe that much social inequality results from the institutional and economic forces that are beyond a single individual's control. As a result, they support the use of government power to counterbalance these forces and to promote a better quality of life for middle- and lower-income people. For example, liberals argue that it is fair to tax those with the greatest ability to pay and to provide social services for the community as a whole.

A significant number of Texans have mixed views. On some issues, they take a liberal position, but on others they have a conservative perspective or no opinion at all. Others have moderate views—Figure 1–1 on the previous page shows that 25 percent of Texans say that they are "in the middle." That is, their beliefs lie between the conservative and liberal viewpoints.

1–1b Partisanship

Texans' conservative political views are reflected in their political party affiliation. Figure 1–2 above shows that 49 percent of Texas's registered voters self-identify as either Republicans or as independents who lean Republican. Only 37 percent of registered voters call themselves either Democrats or independents who lean Democratic. In practice, polling research confirms that independents who lean toward one or the other of the two parties usually behave as partisans, and the only true swing voters are independents who refuse to admit a leaning toward either party. These independents make up 13 percent of Texans who are registered to vote. Polling

liberalism A set of political beliefs that includes the advocacy of active government, including government intervention to improve the welfare of individuals and to protect civil rights.

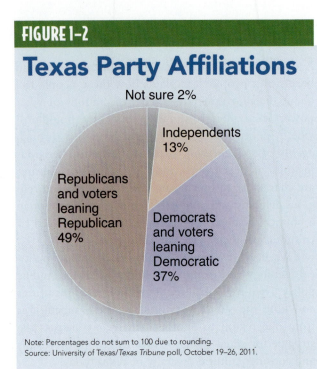

FIGURE 1–2

Texas Party Affiliations

Not sure 2%

Independents 13%

Republicans and voters leaning Republican 49%

Democrats and voters leaning Democratic 37%

Note: Percentages do not sum to 100 due to rounding.
Source: University of Texas/*Texas Tribune* poll, October 19–26, 2011.

and actual election results demonstrate the dominance of the Republican Party—the more conservative party—in Texas. We examine the ideological and policy differences between the two parties in greater depth in Chapter 5.

1–1c Public Opinion

When Texans are asked about their specific opinions on state taxes and social policies, a majority do indeed have conservative views, as shown in Table 1–1 on the facing page. The pattern is not as clear when it comes to state spending, however. During the state budget crisis of 2011, when voters were asked whether they supported spending cuts in various state services to balance the budget, a large majority of Texas voters refused to support cuts in any major state programs. In fact, 53 percent of those polled believe Texas spends too little on elementary and secondary education.

Political scientists were not surprised by these survey results. Many national and state surveys conducted over several decades indicate that many voters adopt the conservative label and voice general support for cutting the size of government, but when they are asked about cuts to specific programs, they balk. This is a paradox in public opinion—many voters identify themselves as conservatives and favor spending cuts in the abstract, but they support spending for most government programs in practice. The paradox creates the potential for decision-making gridlock, and it presents an enormous dilemma for policymakers. Texas officials have attempted to resolve this conflict by a pattern of modest public spending.

1–1d Public Policy

In Texas, conservative opinions have translated into conservative public policies. Compared to those in other states, taxes in Texas are very low, and despite the public's ambiguous attitudes about spending, the state has committed far fewer financial resources to public services than have most other states. Texas takes in less per capita revenue than all but four states, and it spends less per capita than forty-six other states. You'll find additional comparisons between Texas and the other forty-nine states in the *How Texas Compares* feature on the following page.

Texas, however, has not been reluctant to use the power of the state to enforce certain traditional values—to restrict abortions, to limit same sex-relationships, and to impose relatively severe penalties on lawbreakers. We will analyze Texas public policy in considerable depth in Chapter 11.

In the following sections, we examine other approaches to the political culture of Texas. We begin with a classic model for classifying state political subcultures, which was developed by political scientist Daniel J. Elazar. We then discuss regional cultural differences within the state, consider the struggle for equality by minorities in Texas, and conclude with a sketch of Texas's rich ethnic and demographic diversity.

FOR CRITICAL THINKING

Why, in your opinion, are Texans more conservative than Americans as a whole?

TABLE 1–1

Public Opinion and Public Policy in Texas

Although public opinion surveys indicate that the majority of Texans have conservative opinions on taxation and social issues, most Texans also support major state spending programs.

Public Policy Option	Percent Supporting	Percent Opposed
Tax Policies		
Implement a state income tax on individuals.	6%	94%
Increase the state sales tax rate.	12%	88%
Increase the state tax on business.	18%	82%
Spending Policies		
Cut funding for children's health program.	10%	90%
Cut funding for elementary and secondary education.	15%	85%
Cut funding for higher education.	27%	73%
Cut funding for new highways.	28%	72%
Close one or more adult prisons.	30%	70%
Social Policies		
Legalize marijuana.	33%	65%
Always allow abortion as a matter of personal choice.	36%	59%
Provide a pathway to citizenship for illegal aliens.	39%	51%
Require a sonogram (ultrasound) as a condition for abortion.	62%	37%
Use the death penalty for those convicted of violent crime.	74%	21%

Note: Some results do not sum to 100 percent because "no opinion" responses were not reported.

Sources: University of Texas/*Texas Tribune* polls, May 11–18, 2011 and October 19–26, 2011; Texas Lyceum Poll, May 24–31, 2011.

HOW **TEXAS** COMPARES

How Texas Ranks among the Fifty States

In 2011, the Texas Legislative Study Group compiled a list of rankings that compares Texas with the other forty-nine states in terms of public policy and quality of life. (See Table 1–2 below—first is highest and fiftieth is lowest.)

Texas's various rankings are often used to make a political point or further a political agenda. Many of the rankings in the table would be useful to liberals. For example, liberals could point with concern to Texas's low levels of spending on Medicaid and mental

health. Conservatives might look with pride at some of the other rankings, such as low tax rates and the vigorous enforcement of public safety. By and large, the public policy rankings show that Texas policies are conservative in comparison to other states.

TABLE 1–2

How Texas Ranks

Public Policy	Ranking	Quality of Life	Ranking
Public Safety		Percent of persons over age 25 with a high school diploma	50
Rate of incarceration	9	Average SAT scores	45
Number of executions	1	Home ownership rate	44
Public Education		Mortgage foreclosure rates	10
Average salary of public school teachers	33	Income inequality between rich and poor	9
High school graduation rate	43	Teenage birth rate	7
State and local spending per student	44	Percent of population living below federal poverty level	4
Tax Revenue and Spending		Percent of children living in poverty	4
Tax revenue per capita	46	Percent of population without health insurance	1
Tax expenditure per capita	47	Amount of atmospheric carbon dioxide emissions	1
Health-Care Spending		Amount of toxins released into water	1
Per capita spending on Medicaid	49		
Per capita spending on mental health	50		

FOR CRITICAL ANALYSIS Looking at the quality-of-life issues, explain how liberals might see these rankings as a call to government action. Discuss how conservatives, with their limited-government philosophy of self-reliance, would see these quality-of-life issues as a matter of personal responsibility and not within the proper purview of state government action.

1–2 Moralistic, Individualistic, and Traditionalistic Subcultures

Political scientists have used a number of approaches to study diversity in nations, regions, states, and

communities. One popular approach is that of Daniel J. Elazar, who depicted American political culture as a mix of three distinct subcultures—moralistic, individualistic, and traditionalistic—each prevalent in at least one area of the United States.[1]

1–2a Moralistic Subculture

Elazar used the term *moralistic* to describe a political subculture whose adherents are concerned with "right and wrong" in politics. The **moralistic subculture** believes government can be a positive force, one that values the individual but functions for the benefit of the general public. Voting and the discussion of public issues are not merely rights enjoyed by citizens. They are also opportunities to better the individual and society alike. Furthermore, politicians should not profit from their public service.

The moralistic subculture is strongest in New England and the northernmost parts of the Midwest and far West. Although historically a product of Puritan religious values, the moralistic subculture today is often associated with secular (nonreligious) attitudes.

1–2b Individualistic Subculture

LearningOutcome 1–2

Distinguish among moralistic, traditionalistic, and individualistic political subcultures.

The **individualistic subculture** embodies a practical view of government. The prime objective of government should be to further private enterprise, while its intervention into people's lives should be limited. Blurring the distinction between economic and political life, individualistic subculture sees both business and politics as appropriate avenues by which an individual can advance her or his interests. It is appropriate for business interests to play a strong role in politics. Conflicts of interest are a commonplace result of this subculture, and a degree of political corruption may be seen as largely inevitable.

The individualistic subculture predominates in the Middle Atlantic states and areas to the west, including the central and southern parts of the Midwest. Unlike New England, the Middle Atlantic states were not founded initially as religious colonies. Rather, these settlers were primarily interested in the economic potential of the New World.

1–2c Traditionalistic Subculture

Although the **traditionalistic subculture** is widespread in America, it is predominant in the southern states. In Texas, this subculture derives primarily from the plantation society of the Old South and the patrón system of northern Mexico and South Texas. Government is seen to have an active role, but it primarily serves to maintain dominant social and religious values. Government is also expected to support traditional class distinctions and to encourage the beliefs of the dominant religion.

The traditionalistic subculture holds politics to be the special preserve of the social and economic elite. Politics is a process of maintaining the existing order, and political participation is a privilege. Social pressure and restrictive election laws that limit participation are legitimate. The subculture supports personal rather than public solutions to problems.

The predominance of the traditionalistic subculture in the South is clearly tied to the biracial nature of early settlements and to the slave system. Maintenance of traditional hierarchical relationships obviously benefits the white race, the superior group under traditional arrangements. Lower-class whites have supported this system because it confirms their status as superior to that of African Americans (and in Texas, Latinos). Needless to say, African Americans and Latinos do not have the same attitudes toward the traditionalistic subculture as the white Texans.

1–2d Political Culture and Political Participation

Elazar considered Texas to have a mix of traditionalistic and individualistic subcultures. The traditionalistic overrides the individualistic subculture in East Texas, which was initially settled from the upper Old South and from the Mexican border areas, where the patrón system dominated early Texas. The individualistic supersedes the traditionalistic subculture throughout the rest of the state. As a result, in Texas, participation in politics is not as highly regarded as it is in states with a moralistic culture. Voter turnout in Texas is, in fact, well below the national average. Many Texans see politics largely as the domain of business interests.

Texans who might best be represented by other interests tend to ignore the significance of their role in the political process and how it might benefit them.[2]

moralistic subculture A political subculture that believes government can be a positive force—one that values the individual but functions to benefit the general public.

individualistic subculture A political subculture that views government as a practical institution that should further private enterprise but intervene minimally in people's lives.

traditionalistic subculture A political subculture that views government as an institution to maintain the dominant social and religious values.

1–3 Texas Cultural Regions

Geographer Donald W. Meinig has argued that the cultural diversity of Texas is more apparent than its homogeneity and that no unified culture has emerged from the various ethnic and cultural groups that settled the state. He believes that the "typical Texan," like the "average American," does not exist but is an oversimplification of the diverse social, economic, and political characteristics of the state's inhabitants.[3]

Both Meinig and Elazar saw modern regional political culture as largely determined by migration patterns—that is, people bring their culture with them as they move geographically. Meinig believed that Texas evolved into nine fairly distinct cultural regions (see Figure 1–3 on the facing page). While political boundaries are distinct, however, cultural divisions are often blurred and transitional. For example, the East Texas region shares political culture with much of the Upper South, whereas West Texas has cultural similarities with eastern New Mexico.

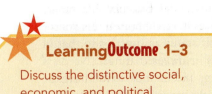

Learning Outcome 1–3

Discuss the distinctive social, economic, and political characteristics of major Texas regions.

The effects of the mass media, the mobility of modern Texans statewide and beyond, and immigration from Mexico also blur the cultural boundaries within Texas, between Texas and neighboring states, and between Texas and Mexico. The explanations of both Meinig and Elazar are limited because they do not take into account these modern-day realities. Still, they are useful guides to a general understanding of contemporary Texas regional cultures, attitudes, and beliefs.

1–3a East Texas

East Texas is a social and cultural extension of the Old South. It is basically rural and biracial. Despite the changes brought about by civil rights legislation, African American "towns" still exist alongside white "towns." Many social and economic institutions, such as churches, fraternal lodges, and chambers of commerce, remain segregated.

East Texas counties and towns are often dominated by old families, whose wealth is usually based on real estate, banking, construction, or retail merchandising. Cotton—once "king" of agriculture in the region—has been replaced by beef cattle, poultry, and timber. As the result of a general lack of economic opportunity, many young East Texans migrate to metropolitan areas, primarily Dallas–Fort Worth and Houston. At the same time, retiring urbanites who seek tranquility have begun to revitalize some small towns and rural communities that had previously lost population to the metropolitan areas. Fundamentalist Protestantism dominates the region spiritually and permeates its political, social, and cultural activities.

1–3b The Gulf Coast

Before 1900, Texas was an economic colony. It sold raw materials to the industrialized North and bought northern manufactured products. In 1901, however, the state's economy began to change. Spindletop, an oil well drilled near Beaumont, ushered in the age of Texas oil. Following the discovery of oil, the Gulf Coast experienced almost continuous growth, especially during World War II, the Cold War defense buildup, and the various energy booms of the late-twentieth and early-twenty-first centuries.

Out-of-state investors, largely from the northeastern states, backed Spindletop, and its success stimulated increased out-of-state investment. Local wealth was also generated and largely reinvested in Texas to promote long-range development. The Gulf Coast not only became an industrial and petrochemical center, but also one of the most important shipping centers in the nation and home to some of the country's largest ports. Nevertheless, much of the economy in this region is still supported by the sale of raw materials.

A Boom Based in Houston The petrochemical industry, which is concentrated on the Gulf Coast, has experienced unprecedented growth, creating a boomtown psychology. Rapid growth fed real estate development and speculation throughout the

FIGURE 1-3

Texas Cultural and Political Regions

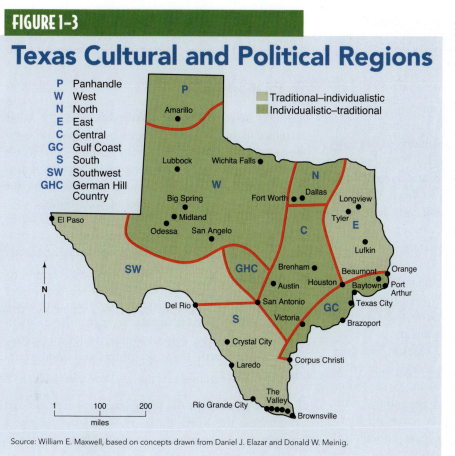

P	Panhandle
W	West
N	North
E	East
C	Central
GC	Gulf Coast
S	South
SW	Southwest
GHC	German Hill Country

Traditional–individualistic
Individualistic–traditional

Source: William E. Maxwell, based on concepts drawn from Daniel J. Elazar and Donald W. Meinig.

region. The Houston area especially flourished, and Houston's Harris County grew to become the third-most-populous county in the United States.

The Gulf Coast's growth after World War II was fueled by an influx of job seekers from East Texas and other rural areas of the state. This migration gave Houston the flavor of rural Texas in an urban setting. Houston's social and economic elite today is generally composed of second- and third-generation families whose wealth comes from oil, insurance, construction, land development, and banking.

Houston's rural flavor has diminished over the years. The growth of the service sector in the national and Texas economies was accompanied by migration to Texas from the "Frost Belt" (the states of the Northeast and the upper Midwest). This migration included both skilled and unskilled workers and added large numbers of well-educated young businesspeople and professionals to the Houston elite.

The Gulf Coast economy also attracts many people from Latin America, Africa, Europe, and Asia, giving modern Houston an international feel comparable to that of Los Angeles or New York. In fact, modern Houston has street signs in Vietnamese or Chinese, as well as English, in areas with large Vietnamese or Chinese populations.

Busts and Turmoil. In the 1980s and 1990s, the oil boom collapsed with drastic declines in the price of oil and other petroleum products. This collapse struck the Gulf Coast economy especially hard because of its heavy reliance on the petrochemical industry. Conversely, rising prices in the twenty-first century resulted in another oil-based boom for the region.

The implosion of Houston-based Enron Corporation early in the first decade of the 2000s affected financial markets nationwide, but it was especially damaging to Houston's economy, labor force, and national image. Enron was intertwined with the fabric of Houston's political, social, cultural, and financial life to an extent rarely seen in corporate America. A dynamic corporate citizen, Enron made significant contributions in almost every area.

Its collapse left many Houstonians with dramatically decreased retirement incomes and investments. Still, the Gulf Coast continues to be a remarkably vibrant and energetic region. Houston, the worldwide capital of oil and gas, boasts many corporate headquarters.

Texas initially weathered the 2008 economic and financial meltdown better than many other states, although by 2010 the unemployment rate had risen above 8 percent. Texas real estate also suffered fewer home foreclosures, primarily because the state had not experienced a housing boom comparable to those in many other states, such as Arizona, Florida, and Nevada. Under Texas law, mortgages are somewhat more difficult to obtain than in most states, and these restrictions provided some stability to the market. Nevertheless, during the worst of the recession, as many as one Texas home in ten was at risk of foreclosure.

1–3c West Texas and the Panhandle

The defeat of the Comanche Indian tribe in the 1870s opened West Texas to Anglo American settlement.

Migrating primarily from the southern United States, these settlers passed their social and political attitudes and southern Protestant fundamentalism on to their descendants.

West Texas Relatively few African Americans live in modern West Texas, but Latinos migrated into the region in significant numbers, primarily to the cities and the intensively farmed areas. West Texas is socially and politically conservative, and its religion is largely Baptist fundamentalism. West Texas voters in the past supported conservative Democrats, but today favor the Republican Party. Indeed, this is true of most conservative Texans throughout the state.

Sheep, goat, and cattle production are widespread in the southern portion of the area. In fact, San Angelo advertises itself as the "Sheep and Wool Capital of the World." Southern West Texas, below the Caprock Escarpment, is the major oil-producing area of Texas. The cities of Snyder, Midland, and Odessa owe their existence almost entirely to oil and related industries.

Northern West Texas is part of the Great Plains and the High Plains and is primarily agricultural, with cotton, grain, and feedlot cattle production predominating. In this semiarid part of West Texas, agricultural production is dependent on irrigation using water drawn from the Ogallala Aquifer. The large amounts of water drawn from the aquifer are gradually depleting it. This not only affects the present economy of the region through higher costs to farmers, but it also poses a threat to the region's economic future.

The Panhandle Railroads advancing from Kansas City through the Panhandle brought midwestern farmers into this region, and wheat production was developed largely by migrants from Kansas. Because the commercial and cultural focus of the region was Kansas City, the early Panhandle was basically midwestern in both character and institutions.

The modern Texas Panhandle, however, shares few cultural attributes with the Midwest. Its religious, cultural, and social institutions today have few discernible differences from those of northern West Texas. Feedlots for livestock and livestock production are major economic enterprises that were established because of the proximity of the region's grain production. The Panhandle economy is also supported by production of cotton and grains, the cultivation of which depends on extensive irrigation from

Metroplex The greater Dallas–Fort Worth metropolitan area.

the Ogallala Aquifer. Effective conservation of the Ogallala Aquifer is critical to the economic future of both northern West Texas and the Panhandle.

1–3d North Texas

Located between East and West Texas, North Texas exhibits many characteristics of both regions. North Texas today is dominated by the Dallas–Fort Worth **Metroplex.** Dallas is a banking and commercial center of national importance, and Fort Worth is the financial and commercial center of West Texas.

The La Réunion Colony Early North Texas benefited from the failure of the French socialist colony La Réunion, which included many highly trained professionals in medicine, education, music, and science. (La Réunion was located on the south bank of the Trinity River, across from modern downtown Dallas.) The colonists and their descendants helped give North Texas a cultural and commercial distinctiveness.

Initial Development When railroads first entered Texas from the North in the 1870s, Dallas became a rail center, and migration and capital from the northern states stimulated its growth. Fort Worth became a regional capital that looked primarily to West Texas. The Swift and Armour meatpacking companies, which moved plants to Fort Worth in 1901, were among the first national firms to establish facilities close to Texas's natural resources. More businesses followed, and North Texas began its evolution from an economic colony to an industrially developed area.

Explosive Growth North Texas experienced extraordinary population growth after World War II, with extensive migration from the rural areas of East, West, and Central Texas. The descendants of these migrants are now third- and fourth-generation urbanites and tend to have urban attitudes and behaviors. Recent migration from other states, especially from the North, has been significant. Many international corporations have established headquarters in North Texas. Their executive and support staffs contribute to the region's diversity and cosmopolitan environment.

Although North Texas is more economically diverse than most other Texas regions, it relies heavily on the banking, insurance, and defense and aerospace industries. Electronic equipment, computer products, plastics, and food products are also produced in the region.

1–3e Central Texas and the Hill Country

Central Texas and the German Hill Country both lie in the middle part of the state. Although geographically quite close to one another, they have distinct political cultures.

Central Texas The Central Texas region is often called the "core area" of Texas. It is roughly triangular in shape, with its three corners being Houston, Dallas–Fort Worth, and San Antonio. The centerpiece of the region is Austin, one of the fastest-growing metropolitan areas in the nation. Already a center of government and education, the Austin metropolitan area has become the high-tech "Silicon Valley" of Texas. Although the worldwide downturn in the high-tech sector after 2000 dealt a serious blow to the area's economy, high-tech industries still make a major economic contribution.

Austin's rapid growth is a result of significant migration from the northeastern United States and the West Coast, as well as from other regions in Texas. The influx of well-educated persons from outside Texas has added to the already substantial pool of accomplished Austinites, making it the intellectual and political capital of the state, as well as the economic center of Central Texas. The cultural and economic traits of all the other Texas regions intermingle in Central Texas, with no single trait dominant. Although the Central Texas region is a microcosm of Texas culture, the city of Austin stands out as an island of liberalism in a predominantly conservative state.

The German Hill Country The Hill Country north and west of San Antonio was settled primarily by immigrants from Germany but also by Czech, Polish, and Norwegian immigrants. Although the immigrants mixed with Anglo Americans, well into the twentieth century Central European culture and architecture were dominant. Skilled artisans were common in the towns. Farms were usually moderate in size, self-sufficient, and family owned and operated. Most settlers were Lutheran or Roman Catholic, and these remain the most common religious affiliations for modern residents.

> **"I am forced to conclude that God made** Texas on his day off, for pure entertainment, just to prove that all that diversity could be crammed into one section of earth by a really top hand."
>
> ~ MARY LASSWELL ~
> AMERICAN AUTHOR
> 1905–1994

The German Hill Country is still a distinct cultural region and remains a farming and ranching area. Although its inhabitants have become Americanized, they still cling to many Central European cultural traditions. The Hill Country is socially and politically conservative and has long been a stronghold of the Texas Republican Party.

Migration into the region, primarily by Anglo Americans and Latinos, is increasing. The most significant encroachment into the Hill Country is residential growth from rapidly expanding urban areas, especially San Antonio and Austin. Resorts, country homes, and retirement villages for well-to-do urbanites from the Gulf Coast and Dallas–Fort Worth area are beginning to erode the cultural distinctiveness of the German Hill Country.

1–3f South and Southwest Texas

South and Southwest Texas comprise an area known as the "Texas Border." The corresponding "Mexico Border" includes parts of the Mexican states of Chihuahua, Coahuila, Nuevo León, and Tamaulipas. It can be argued that the Texas Border and the Mexico Border are two parts of an economic, social, and cultural region with a substantial degree of similarity that sets it off from the rest of the United States and Mexico. The Border regions, which are expanding in size both to the north and to the south, have a **binational,** bicultural, and bilingual subculture in which **internationality** is commonplace and the people, economies, and societies on both sides constantly interact.[4]

South and Southwest Texas are "mingling pots" for the Latino and Anglo American cultures. Catholic Latinos often retain strong links with Mexico through extended family and friends in Mexico and through Spanish-language newspapers. Many Latinos continue to speak Spanish—in fact, Spanish is also the commercial and social language of choice for many of the region's Anglo Americans.

binational Belonging to two nations.

internationality Having family or business interests in two or more nations.

South Texas The earliest area settled by Europeans, South Texas developed a **ranchero culture** on the basis of livestock production that was similar to the feudal institutions in faraway Spain. **Creoles,** descended from Spanish (or, in some regions, French) immigrants, were the economic, social, and political elite, whereas the first Texas cowboys, the **Mestizos** and the Native Americans, did the ranch work. Anglo Americans first became culturally important in South Texas when they gained title to much of the real estate in the region following the Texas Revolution of 1835–1836. Modern South Texas however, still retains elements of the ranchero culture, including some of its feudal aspects. Large ranches, often owned by one family for several generations, are prevalent.

Still, wealthy and corporate ranchers and farmers from outside the area are becoming common.

Because of the semitropical South Texas climate, **The Valley** (of the Rio Grande) and the Winter Garden around Crystal City became major producers of vegetable and citrus products. These areas were developed by migrants from the northern United States in the 1920s and continue to be important multi-use agricultural assets. The development of citrus and vegetable enterprises required intensive manual labor, which brought about increased "re-migration" from Mexico. (Modern South Texas Latinos usually trace their U.S. roots to the 1920s or later because much of the Latino population was driven south of the Rio Grande after the Texas Revolution.)

The Border Economy
The Texas Border cities are closely tied to the Mexican economy, on which their prosperity depends. Although improving economically, these regions remain among the poorest in the United States.

The economy of the Texas Border benefits from **maquiladoras.** These are Mexican factories where U.S. corporations employ inexpensive Mexican labor for assembly and piecework. Unfortunately, lax environmental and safety standards have resulted in high levels of air, ground, and water pollution in industrialized areas. In fact, the Rio Grande is now one of America's most ecologically endangered rivers.

The **North American Free Trade Agreement (NAFTA),** which has helped remove barriers to trade among Canada, Mexico, and the United States, is an economic stimulus for the Texas Border region because it is a conduit for much of the commerce with Mexico.

Southwest Texas Southwest Texas exhibits many of the same **bicultural** characteristics as South Texas. Its large Mexican American population often maintains strong ties with relatives and friends in Mexico. The Roman Catholic Church is a significant influence on social and cultural attitudes on both sides of the border.

Southwest Texas is a major commercial and social passageway between Mexico and the United States. El Paso, the "capital city" of Southwest Texas and the sixth-largest city in Texas, is a military, manufacturing, and commercial center. El Paso's primary commercial partners are Mexico and New Mexico. The economy of the border cities of Southwest Texas, like that of South Texas, is closely linked to Mexico and has also benefited from the economic opportunities brought about by NAFTA. The agricultural economy of much of the region depends on sheep, goat, and cattle production, although some irrigated row-crop agriculture is present. Most of the labor on ranches, as well as in manufacturing and commerce, is Latino.

Immigration and National Security Poverty, military conflicts, crime, political disorder, and the suppression of civil liberties in Central America and Mexico have driven hundreds of thousands of immigrants into and across the border regions of the United States. This flow of immigrants continues but has begun to level off because of the recent economic turndown, tightened security measures, and fence construction. The problem of unauthorized immigration is a major issue in Texas, just as it is in the rest of the country. We look at some of the economic effects of illegal immigration in the *Join the Debate* feature on the facing page.

---

ranchero culture
A quasi-feudal system whereby a property's owner, or *patrón*, gives workers protection and employment in return for their loyalty and service. The rancher, or *ranchero*, and workers all live on the *rancho*, or ranch.

Creole A descendant of Spanish (or in some regions, French) immigrants to the Americas.

Mestizo A person of both Spanish and Native American lineage.

The Valley An area along the Texas side of the Rio Grande known for its production of citrus fruits.

maquiladora A factory in the Mexican border region that assembles goods imported duty-free into Mexico for export. A literal translation of the word is "twin plant."

North American Free Trade Agreement (NAFTA) A 1994 treaty calling for the gradual removal of tariffs and other trade restrictions among Canada, Mexico, and the United States.

bicultural Encompassing two cultures.

Do Unauthorized Immigrants Cost the Texas Taxpayer?

Every action has costs and benefits, and that includes illegal immigration. Currently, the United States has about 11 million *unauthorized immigrants* (the term used by the U.S. Department of Homeland Security). Texas itself has about 1.5 million illegal immigrants. While most such individuals come to the United States to work, others come to be with their families.

The Cost of Illegal Immigration Is Too High

Those who consider illegal immigration to be a major issue cite the high costs of allowing such people to stay in Texas. They argue that undocumented workers displace legal residents in the job market. Other expenses associated with illegal immigrants include the cost of educating young people, criminal justice expenses, and the cost of medical care. But even those who believe that illegal immigrants are a drag on the taxpayer admit that immigrants pay taxes, too. These taxes include Social Security, Medicare, sales, and property taxes.

A study of the costs and benefits of illegal immigrants by the Federation for American Immigration Reform (FAIR), an anti-immigration group, estimated that they cost Texas taxpayers more than $4.7 billion annually for education, incarceration, and medical care. According to this study, illegal immigrants also pay about $1 billion in taxes a year. Still, the end result is a net loss to Texas taxpayers.

Unauthorized Immigrants Pay More Than They Receive

Many argue that the supposed loss of jobs by Texans due to competition from illegal workers is a fiction. Most of the jobs that unauthorized immigrants undertake would be left vacant if not filled by them. Indeed, one study has shown that low-income Americans actually benefit from the increased economic activity that results from unauthorized immigration. The people who really suffer by competition from these immigrants are, ironically, other immigrants. In addition, the FAIR study just cited seemed to ignore the benefit to the nation of unauthorized immigrants who pay into Social Security and Medicare. Often, undocumented workers do so by obtaining falsified Social Security numbers. They will never be able to benefit from such payments, so the taxes collected are a net gain to the U.S. Treasury.

Further, another study, undertaken by Carole Strayhorn when she was state comptroller, finds a net benefit to Texas taxpayers from the presence of illegal immigrants. Strayhorn estimated that they generate $1.58 billion in state revenues but use only $1.16 billion in state services.

FOR CRITICAL ANALYSIS What government services are illegal immigrants ineligible to receive?

The Texas Border region is a major staging ground for the migration of both legal and illegal immigrants as well as human traffickers into the interior of Texas and the rest of the United States. The U.S. government's immigration control expenditures economically benefit the area. Military expenditures by the government are also important to the economy of South and Southwest Texas. Six U.S. military bases are located in the Texas Border region.

The Drug Trade The American craving for illegal, mind-altering substances provides a steady flow of American capital through the Texas Border into Mexico and South America. Most experts on the drug traffic contend that it cannot be eliminated as long as the U.S. market exists, but the struggle against the drug trade continues unabated.

This "invisible trade," because of its illegal status, inevitably results in violence. In that, it is similar to the failed American attempt to prohibit the sale and consumption of alcoholic beverages from 1920 to 1933. The collateral damage of the drug trade is readily visible. Stories of death and destruction lead the evening news and provide villains and endless plots for movies and television detective programs. The worst of the violence is confined to the border areas of Mexico, but the trade poses a threat on the Texas side as well.

Accompanying the drug traffic is a reverse cash flow from Mexico to the United States for weapons purchases. Weapons, ammunition, and even explosives are easily obtained in Texas and other states. They are then shipped illegally to Mexico and South America.

The Economic Effects of Illegal Activity

Smuggling provides a significant but unwholesome economic infusion to both sides of the border. It is not just a matter of the expenses, wages, and bribe money spent by drug, weapon, and human traffickers. Consider also the expenditures by the Mexico, Texas, and U.S. governments for narcotics and immigration agents, related military operations, additional police, prison construction and operation, and equipment purchases. The result is increased employment. Border security and the smuggling of humans, drugs, and weapons will continue to be major political issues in the foreseeable future.

FOR CRITICAL THINKING

Should San Antonio be considered part of Central Texas—or part of South or Southwest Texas?

1–4 The Struggle for Equal Rights

The politics of some cultural regions have begun to lose their distinctive identities as Texas has become more metropolitan in outlook and more economically and ethnically diverse. With these changes, a number of groups have begun to aspire toward greater cultural, political, social, and economic equality.

Anglo men traditionally monopolized status, wealth, and rights in organized Texas society. They wrote the rules of the game and used those rules to protect their position against attempts by women, African Americans, and Latinos to share in the fruits of full citizenship. Only after the disenfranchised groups organized and exerted political pressure did the doors of freedom and equality begin to open. Table 1–3 on the facing page summarizes key court cases that established equal rights for all citizens of Texas—and America.

1–4a Women in Texas

suffrage The right to vote.

Women in the Republic of Texas could neither serve on juries nor enjoy **suffrage,** the right to vote. Still, unmarried women retained many of the rights that they had enjoyed under Spanish law, which included control over their property. Married women retained some Spanish law benefits because, contrary to English common law, Texas marriage did not join the married couple into one legal person with the husband as the head. A married woman in Texas could own inherited property, share ownership of community property with her husband, and make a legal will. Her husband had control of all the property, though, both separate and community. An employer could not hire a wife without her husband's consent.[5]

Divorce laws were restrictive on both parties, but a husband could win a divorce for his wife's "amorous or lascivious conduct with other men, even short of adultery," or if she had committed adultery only once. In contrast, a wife could gain a divorce only if "the husband had lived in adultery with another woman." Physical violence was not grounds for divorce unless the wife could prove a "serious danger" that it might happen again. In practice, physical abuse was tolerated.[6]

Gaining the Right to Vote Led by Minnie Fisher Cunningham, Texas suffragists organized, spoke out, marched, and lobbied for the right to vote in the World War I period. They were opposed by Governor James E. Ferguson. When Ferguson became embroiled in political controversy, suffragists effectively joined the movement advocating Ferguson's impeachment. In 1917, Ferguson was removed from office.[7]

Texas women continued to actively participate in the political arena, although they lacked the right to vote. They supported William P. Hobby for governor—Hobby was considered receptive to women's suffrage. The tactic was ultimately successful, and women, with some delays, gained the right to vote in the 1918 Texas primary.[8]

Suffrage momentum at the national level resulted in a proposed constitutional amendment establishing the right of women to vote throughout the United States. Following more than five years of "heavy artillery" from Cunningham and the Texas Equal Suffrage Association, opposition in the legislature crumbled. Texas became one of the first southern states to ratify the Nineteenth Amendment, which granted women full voting rights in 1920.[9]

LearningOutcome 1–4

Trace the struggle for equal rights in Texas by women, African Americans, Latinos, and gay men and lesbians.

TABLE 1-3

Key United States Supreme Court Decisions Protecting Rights to Equality and Privacy

These important United States Supreme Court decisions expanded minority rights in Texas and nationwide.

Landmark Supreme Court Case	Unconstitutional Texas Practice	U.S. Constitutional Violation
Smith v. Allwright (1944)	Permitting the Democratic Party to conduct white primaries. Other southern states also allowed this practice.	No state shall deny any person the right to vote because of his or her race—the Fifteenth Amendment.
Sweatt v. Painter (1950)	Requiring racially segregated law schools. Professional schools were segregated throughout the South.	No state shall deny any person the equal protection of the law—the Fourteenth endment.
Hernández v. State of Texas (1954)	Denying Latinos the right to serve on juries.	No state shall deny any person the equal protection of the law—the Fourteenth Amendment.
Brown v. Board of Education of Topeka (1954)	Mandating statewide segregation of public schools and most facilities open to the public. Texas was among seventeen mostly southern states with statewide laws requiring segregation at the time of the decision.	No state shall deny any person the equal protection of the law—the Fourteenth Amendment.
Roe v. Wade (1973)	Making abortion illegal. Thirty states outlawed abortions for any reason in 1973.	No state shall deny liberty without due process of law—the Fourteenth Amendment.
Lawrence v. Texas (2003)	Making homosexual conduct a crime. Fourteen mostly southern states made homosexual conduct a crime at the time of the decision.	No state shall deny liberty without due process of law—the Fourteenth Amendment.

Gaining Equal Rights Women were given the right to serve on juries in 1954. In 1972, Texas voters ratified the Equal Rights Amendment to the Texas Constitution. This step, together with passage of the Marital Property Act in 1967, significantly advanced women's equality and heralded the beginning of a more enlightened era in Texas. The Marital Property Act granted married women equal rights in insurance, banking, real estate, contracts, divorce, child custody, and property rights. It was the first such comprehensive family law in the United States.[10]

Abortion Rights Until 1973, abortion in Texas, as in many states, was illegal. In that year, Texas lawyers Sarah Weddington and Linda Coffee argued a case before the United States Supreme Court that still stands at the center of national debate—*Roe v. Wade*. The Court's *Roe* decision overturned statutes throughout the nation that criminalized abortions and, in doing so, established a limited, national right of privacy for women to terminate a pregnancy.[11]

Abortion rights have never been popular in Texas, however. In 2011, the Texas legislature passed a law that a woman must undergo a sonogram (ultrasound) and have the fetal image described by the physician prior

LIBRARY OF CONGRESS

Minnie Fisher Cunningham (1882–1964), an early advocate of giving women the vote in Texas, was president of the Texas Equal Suffrage Association.

to terminating a pregnancy. The law also requires a 24-hour waiting period before the actual procedure can be performed.

1–4b African Americans in Texas

Africans from other parts of the United States were brought to Texas as slaves and served in that capacity until the end of the Civil War. They first learned of their freedom on June 19, 1865, a day now celebrated as "Juneteenth." During Reconstruction (1865–1877), African Americans in Texas voted and served in numerous political positions, but the end of Reconstruction and white opposition eventually ended their effective political participation.

Civil rights were regularly denied following Reconstruction. African Texans were legally denied the right to vote in the Democratic Party's **white primary.** Schools and public facilities such as theaters, restaurants, beaches, and hospitals were legally segregated by race. Segregation laws were enforced by law enforcement officers as well as by white Texan cultural norms and by unofficial organizations using terror tactics. Although segregation laws were not usually written to cover Latinos, who were legally white, in practice such laws were enforced against them as well. The **Ku Klux Klan (KKK),** local sheriffs and police, and the Texas Rangers actively participated in violence and intimidation of both Latinos and African Texans. Lynching—extra-legal execution—was also used against members of both groups, often after torture.

The Power of the Ku Klux Klan The KKK was first organized in the late 1860s to intimidate freed African slaves. The group was reborn in the 1920s with a somewhat altered mission. The new Klan saw itself as a patriotic, Christian, fraternal organization for native-born white Protestants. Its members perceived a general moral decline in society, precipitated by "modern" young people. The Klan also believed that the "white Christian race" and its values were endangered not only by African Americans, but also by Jews, Catholics, Latinos, Germans, and other "foreigners."

white primary The practice of excluding African Americans from Democratic Party primary elections in Texas. First enforced by law and later by party rules, this practice was found unconstitutional in *Smith v. Allwright* (1944).

Ku Klux Klan (KKK) A white supremacist organization. The first Klan was founded during the Reconstruction era following the Civil War.

Acting on its paranoia, in the 1920s the Klan set out to impose its version of Christian morality on society using intimidation, violence, and torture. As many as eighty thousand Texans may have joined this "invisible empire" in an effort to make the world more to their liking. Many elected officials—U.S. and state legislators as well as county and city officials— were either avowed Klansmen or friendly neutrals. The Klan's influence on Texas was a major political issue from 1921 through 1925.[12]

Making the Right to Vote Effective In this racially charged atmosphere, a number of organizations committed to civil rights were founded or grew in size during the 1920s. These included the National Association for the Advancement of Colored People (NAACP), established in 1909, and the League of United Latin American Citizens (LULAC), which was formed in Corpus Christi in 1929.

When Dr. Lawrence A. Nixon, an African American living in El Paso, was denied the right to vote in the Democratic primary, the NAACP instituted legal action. In 1927, in *Nixon v. Herndon,* the United States Supreme Court found the Texas white primary law to be unconstitutional. In response, the Texas legislature transferred control of the primary from the state government to the Democratic State Executive Committee, and the discrimination continued. Dr. Nixon sued again, and in 1931 the Supreme Court ruled the new scheme unconstitutional as well. Texas Democrats then banned African American Texans from party membership altogether. In 1935, in *Grovey v. Townsend* the Court upheld this ploy, and the Texas Democratic primary remained an all-white organization.[13]

Although it had suffered a temporary setback in the episode, the NAACP had proved its potential as a viable instrument for African American Texans to achieve justice. African Americans throughout the nation finally won the right to participate in state Democratic primaries in 1944, when the United States Supreme Court ruled in *Smith v. Allwright* that all methods used to establish a white primary were unconstitutional.[14] Not until 1967, however, did any African Americans serve in the Texas legislature. These pioneers included Joe Lockridge of Dallas and Curtis Graves of Houston, who were elected to the state House of Representatives, and Barbara Jordan of Houston, who won a seat in the state Senate.

Chipping Away at Segregation Until 1954, when the United States Supreme Court issued its

Texas Representative Barbara Jordan.

Desegregation The political and social fallout from the *Brown v. Board of Education* public school desegregation decision did not bypass Texas.[17] When the Mansfield school district, just southeast of Fort Worth, was ordered by a federal court to integrate in 1956, angry whites surrounded the school and prevented the enrollment of three African American children. Governor Allan Shivers declared the anti-integration demonstration an "orderly protest" and sent the Texas Rangers to support the protesters. Because the federal government took no action to enforce the court ruling, the school remained segregated. Only in 1965, when it faced a loss of federal funding, did the Mansfield schools desegregate.[18]

In 1970, Federal District judge William Wayne Justice in *United States v. Texas* ordered the complete desegregation of all Texas public schools. The decision was one of the most extensive desegregation orders in history and included a process for executing the order in detail. The U.S. Court of Appeals for the Fifth Circuit largely affirmed the decision but refused to extend its provisions to Latino children.[19]

Latino A person whose ancestors originated in a Spanish-speaking country.

Hispanic An alternate word for *Latino* used officially by the U.S. government.

1-4c Latinos in Texas

In much of the United States, a large portion of the **Latino** population has its origins in Puerto Rico, in Cuba, and in other Spanish-speaking countries. In Texas, however, the great majority of Latinos are Mexican American. (The feminine form of Latino is *Latina*.) While the term *Latino* is widely used, **Hispanic** also has some circulation and is, in fact, the standard term used by the federal government. Often, Latinos of Mexican origin prefer *Mexican American* as a more precise description. Some Mexican Americans, especially political activists, describe themselves as *Chicano* or *Chicana* (the feminine form of the noun).

The Raymondville Peonage Cases Like most African Americans, Latinos were relegated to the lowest-paid jobs in Texas, as either service workers or farm workers. The low status of Latinos was demonstrated by the practice of peonage, which existed in some Texas counties. A Latino man might be charged as a vagrant. His fine would be paid by a farmer, and he would be required to repay the farmer by forced labor. The practice violated federal antislavery statutes.

revolutionary ruling in *Brown v. Board of Education*, segregation of the races was legal. Segregation was grounded in *Plessy v. Ferguson*, an 1896 Supreme Court ruling that established the doctrine of "separate but equal."[15] Even before *Brown*, the Court had begun to chip away at the "separate-but-equal" doctrine. One of the major cases in which it did so was *Sweatt v. Painter*, a 1950 case based in Texas.

In 1946, Heman Sweatt, an African American postal worker, was denied admission to the University of Texas Law School, which by Texas law was segregated. With help from the NAACP, Sweatt sued. Because Texas had no law school for African American Texans, the legislature hurriedly sought to establish one. The new law school unfortunately lacked both faculty and a library, and as a result the NAACP again sued the state. After much litigation, the United States Supreme Court ruled that the new African American law school was not equal to the University of Texas Law School and ordered Sweatt admitted to that institution.

This ruling did not actually overturn the "separate-but-equal" doctrine, but it did challenge the universal practice of providing African Americans with "equal" facilities that were absurdly unequal.[16]

AP PHOTO/PAT SULLIVAN, FILE

Julián Castro has been mayor of San Antonio since 2009.

In 1926, local officials in Willacy County made a serious blunder when they forced two individuals into servitude—one was a former page in the U.S. House of Representatives, and the other also was a resident of Washington, D.C. The resulting Raymondville peonage cases resulted in the conviction of several public officials and farmers. The outcome of the trials was unpopular in the agricultural areas, and the lives of farm workers changed little.[20]

The American G.I. Forum Latino Texan veterans of World War II returned from fighting to find that discrimination still existed in their home state. A decorated veteran and medical doctor, Major Hector Garcia, found farm laborers enduring inhumane living conditions, deplorable medical conditions in slums, and disabled veterans ignored by the Veterans Administration. With other World War II veterans, Dr. Garcia organized the American G.I. Forum in a Corpus Christi elementary school classroom in 1948. This organization spread throughout the United States and played a major role in winning Latino Americans full citizenship and civil respect.[21]

One incident that propelled the Forum to prominence was the funeral of Private Felix Longoria, a decorated soldier killed in the war. His body was returned to Three Rivers, Texas, for burial in the Mexican section of the cemetery, which was separated from the white section by barbed wire. The funeral home director refused to let the Longoria family use the chapel because "whites would not like it." Longoria's widow asked Dr. Hector Garcia for support. In the end, Senator Lyndon B. Johnson arranged for Longoria to be buried at Arlington National Cemetery.[22]

Equality under the Law Segregated schools for Latino Texan children were commonplace, even though no Texas law provided for them. In 1948, LULAC and the American G.I. Forum successfully challenged these inequities in *Delgado vs. Bastrop ISD*. A federal district court agreed that segregation without a specific state law requiring the separation was not permitted. The Latino desegregation battle continued into the 1960s, with repeated lawsuits to force desegregation.[23]

One of the most important civil rights cases of the 1950s was based in Texas—*Hernández v. State of Texas*, decided by the United States Supreme Court in 1954 just days before its *Brown v. Board of Education* ruling. Pete Hernández, a Latino, was convicted of murder by an all-Anglo jury. Latino attorneys challenged the conviction, arguing that the systematic exclusion of Latinos from jury duty in Texas violated Hernández's rights to equal protection of the law under the Fourteenth Amendment of the U.S. Constitution. Texas courts had historically ruled that Latinos were white, so excluding them from all-Anglo (white) juries could not be legal discrimination.

Attorney Gustavo (Gus) Garcia argued before the Supreme Court that Latinos, although white, were "a class apart" and suffered discrimination on the basis of their "class." The Court agreed and ruled that Latinos were protected by the Constitution from discrimination by other whites. The *Hernández* decision was a forerunner of future decisions prohibiting discrimination by gender, disability, or sexual preference.[24]

Farm Workers' Struggles The fight of farm workers to organize into labor unions was the primary focus for much of the Latino civil activism in the 1960s and 1970s. In rural areas, large landowners controlled the political as well as the economic system and were united in opposition to labor unions. The United Farm Workers Organizing Committee (UFWOC) led a strike against melon growers and packers in Starr County

Texas Political SOCIAL MEDIA

The League of United Latin American Citizens (LULAC) has Texas and U.S. pages on Facebook, but the national page is much busier. Find it by searching on "lulac national."

in 1966, demanding a $1.25 minimum wage and resolution of other grievances. Starr County police officers and the Texas Rangers were accused of brutality as they arrested and prosecuted strikers for minor offenses.

In July 1967, strikers and their supporters began a march to Austin to demand redress of their grievances. Press coverage intensified as politicians, members of other labor unions, and the Texas Council of Churches accompanied the protesters. Governor John Connally traveled to intercept the march and inform strikers that their efforts would have no effect. Ignoring the governor, the protesters continued on to Austin and held a rally at the state capitol. The rally was broken up by Texas Rangers and other law enforcement officers. The Texas Farm Workers Union (TFWU) sued the Rangers for their actions during the strike and at the capitol. Although the strikers won a number of legal victories, in the end the organizing effort was crushed.[25]

© BRIAN MCGLOIN/DEMOTIX/CORBIS

The Pride Bigger than Texas Festival and Parade celebrates gay pride and diversity in downtown San Antonio, Texas.

1–4d Gay and Lesbian Texans

Discrimination against gay, lesbian, and transgendered Texans has long been considered a God-given right by some Texans. Furthermore, a state *antisodomy law* formerly criminalized intimate sexual conduct by persons of the same gender.

Lawrence v. Texas In 2003, a Harris County sheriff's deputy discovered two men engaging in sexual activity in a private residence. The men were arrested and convicted under the antisodomy statute. Their case reached the United States Supreme Court as *Lawrence v. Texas*. By a six-to-three majority, the Court held that intimate consensual sexual conduct was part of the liberty protected by substantive due process under the Fourteenth Amendment to the U.S. Constitution. The decision also invalidated sodomy laws in thirteen other states, thereby protecting same-sex behavior in every state and territory in the United States.[26]

Limiting the Rights of Same-Sex Couples

Nationally, the right to marry is the current frontline of the gay, lesbian, and transgendered battle for equal rights. The federal Defense of Marriage Act (DOMA) complicates the battle. Enacted on September 21, 1996, DOMA defines marriage as a legal union between a man and a woman and further stipulates that states do not have to recognize same-sex marriages conducted in other states. The definition of *marriage* is at the center of the conflict. Is marriage a religious ceremony, or is it a secular contract? If religious, there would be no role for the state. If secular, one might argue that religious beliefs should not restrict the union. One problem is that governments have loaded the marriage concept with much baggage, including Social Security benefits, preferential tax rates, family insurance benefits, and community property laws.

In 2005, by the overwhelming majority of 76 percent, Texans amended the state constitution to ban both gay and lesbian marriages and civil unions. The amendment also denies hospital visitation rights, community property rights, and survivors' benefits for gay and lesbian couples. The authority to make medical decisions for an incapacitated loved one is also prohibited. Lesbians and gay men in Texas continue to face discrimination in employment, housing, and public accommodations, and gay or lesbian children often lack protection in the state's schools.

FOR CRITICAL THINKING

What rights, if any, should same-sex couples enjoy in Texas? Regardless of what rights you consider appropriate, is it possible that Texas citizens might support a deliberately limited set of rights in a future vote? Why or why not?

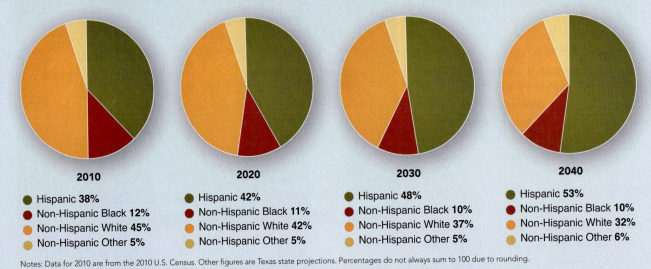

Projections for 2020, 2030, and 2040 are based on a low-immigration scenario—half of the 1990–2000 migration rate.

2010
- Hispanic **38%**
- Non-Hispanic Black **12%**
- Non-Hispanic White **45%**
- Non-Hispanic Other **5%**

2020
- Hispanic **42%**
- Non-Hispanic Black **11%**
- Non-Hispanic White **42%**
- Non-Hispanic Other **5%**

2030
- Hispanic **48%**
- Non-Hispanic Black **10%**
- Non-Hispanic White **37%**
- Non-Hispanic Other **5%**

2040
- Hispanic **53%**
- Non-Hispanic Black **10%**
- Non-Hispanic White **32%**
- Non-Hispanic Other **6%**

Notes: Data for 2010 are from the 2010 U.S. Census. Other figures are Texas state projections. Percentages do not always sum to 100 due to rounding.

Hispanics may be of any race. "Non-Hispanic Other" consists of the following non-Hispanic groups: Asian, American Indian, Native Alaskan, Native Hawaiian, Other Pacific Islander, and two or more races.

Sources: U.S. Census, Texas State Data Center, and author's calculations.

demographics
Population characteristics, such as age, gender, ethnicity, employment, and income, that social scientists use to describe groups in society.

1–5 Cultural Diversity Today

Texas is one of the fastest-growing states in the nation. No longer predominantly rural and agrarian, Texas is becoming more culturally diverse as immigrants from other nations and migrants from other states continue to find it a desirable place to live. The 2010 census showed a significant trend toward greater ethnic diversity. Figure 1–4 above shows that the growing diversity of Texas's population is projected to continue. Increased diversity could have a significant impact on Texas's politics and culture.

Voter participation in Texas is historically low—the state ranks forty-fifth among the states in voter turnout. Social scientists argue that this is attributable to political conditioning as well as social and economic realities. Latino participation is low even by Texas standards. Because Latinos are predicted to outnumber non-Hispanic whites in Texas by 2020 or even 2015, however, there could be significant political impact if this sleeping political giant arises.

Equally important, changes in the ethnic makeup of the state's population will present decision makers with enormous challenges. Figure 1–5 and Figure 1–6 on the facing page show that income inequality parallels ethnic divisions in Texas. Poverty rates are higher and overall incomes are lower among African American and Latino Texans. Lower incomes are associated with limited educational opportunity, lack of health insurance, and lower rates of participation in the state's civic life. Poverty is a factor that contributes to crime, family breakups, and illegitimate births, even as it drives up the cost of state social services. How Texas deals with changes in its **demographics** is likely to be the focus of political controversy for years to come. In time, the Democrats could become competitive again, or even dominant. Conservatives might lose their grip on public policy in Texas.

★ **LearningOutcome 1–5**

Evaluate the social and cultural changes that are likely to define Texas's political future.

FOR CRITICAL THINKING

What specific effects could the growing number of Latinos in Texas have on the future politics of the state?

FIGURE 1–5

Net Family Income
in Texas

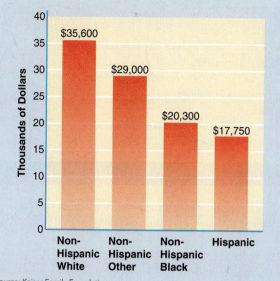

Source: Kaiser Family Foundation.

FIGURE 1–6

Percentage of Persons
Living in Poverty in Texas

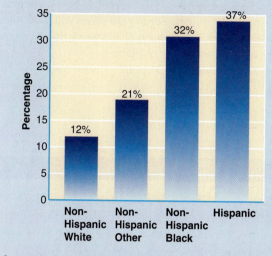

Source: Kaiser Family Foundation.

TEXANS IN

CONFLICT Culture and Diversity

Cultural and ethnic differences among Texans guarantee that political conflict will always be with us. The dominance of conservative political ideology in the state does not eliminate conflict. Even among conservatives, the question remains: How conservative should we be? The problem is illustrated by the recent state budget crisis in Texas. If taxes are not to be raised, what should be cut? Public opinion polls show that a strong majority of Texans oppose both new taxes and significant cuts to major state programs. If simple arithmetic makes it impossible for both of these objectives to be met, then something will have to give. Texans face questions such as these:

- Should Texas conservatives compromise their antitax principles—or should the state make major cuts to education and other programs?

- Do the regions of Texas really have different political cultures—or is it simply that they contain different proportions of various types of people?

- Should Texas save unborn lives by making abortions more difficult to obtain—or does such a step interfere unacceptably with the rights of women?

- If the Latino share of Texas's population rises in the future, will that eventually trigger a political transformation of the state—or are Latino Texans conservative enough to perpetuate the state's current ideological preferences?

TAKE ACTION

Get involved and learn about your own culture. Talk to grandparents, parents, uncles, and aunts to learn what they know about your culture and family history. Record as much oral history as you can about their personal lives, experiences, and political recollections as well as family myths and traditions. You may find this information priceless as you talk to your own children and grandchildren about their culture. You may be able to find resources on the Internet to help you research the background and richness of your family's culture. Consider investigating the life of a hero who shares your culture.

STUDY TOOLS

Ready to study?

- Review what you've read with the quiz below. Check your answers on the Chapter in Review card at the back of the book. For any questions you miss, read the corresponding Learning Outcome section again to prepare for class and your exam.
- Rip out and study the Chapter in Review card.

. . . Or you can go online to CourseMate

at www.cengagebrain.com for these additional review materials:

- Practice Quizzes
- Key Term Flashcards or Crossword Puzzles
- Audio Summaries
- Simulations, Animated Learning Modules, and Interactive Timelines
- Videos
- American Government NewsWatch

Quiz

1. A patterned set of ideas, values, and ways of thinking about government and politics is:
   a. partisanship.   b. political culture.   c. political behavior.

2. What is the set of political beliefs, a minority view in Texas, that includes the advocacy of active government, including government intervention to improve the welfare of individuals and to protect civil rights?
   a. conservatism   b. liberalism   c. libertarianism

3. Which of the following is an outcome of social conservatism's heavy influence on public policy in Texas?
   a. high levels of public spending relative to other states
   b. low levels of taxation relative to other states
   c. opposition to abortion rights

4. What characteristics best describe the traditionalistic political subculture?
   a. It is more dominant in west Texas than in the east.
   b. It supports public, rather than personal, solutions to problems.
   c. It expects government to uphold dominant social and religious values.

5. Of the policies below, choose the one that best fits Texas's individualistic subculture:
   a. high levels of public spending
   b. low taxes
   c. universal health insurance for children

6. Which two American political subcultures characterize Texas political culture?
   a. traditionalistic and individualistic
   b. individualistic and moralistic
   c. moralistic and traditionalistic

7. What is the 1994 economic agreement that has greatly expanded economic ties between Mexico and Texas and deepened trade and cultural ties along the border region?
   a. The Maquiladora Program
   b. The North American Free Trade Agreement
   c. La Reunion

8. Which area of Texas is distinctive for its extensive settlement by German immigrants.
   a. East Texas   b. North Texas   c. The Hill Country

9. What region of Texas is the major oil-producing area and heavily reliant on agriculture and livestock?
   a. East Texas   b. West Texas   c. the Gulf Coast

10. What was the significant outcome of the U.S. Supreme Court decision *Smith v. Allright* (1944) for African Americans in Texas politics?
    a. It ended racial segregation in public schools.
    b. It ended the Democratic Party's "white primary."
    c. It identified lynching as a violation of the 14th Amendment's Equal Protection Clause.

11. Which organization is a longstanding advocacy organization for a wide variety of Latino political, legal, and social interests?
    a. The League of United Latin American Citizens
    b. The National Association for the Advancement of Colored People
    c. The League of Justice

12. What was the outcome of the U.S. Supreme Court decision in *Lawrence v. Texas* (2003)?
    a. It outlawed racial profiling by police.
    b. It recognized the right of migrant Latino farm workers to organize.
    c. It recognized a constitutional right to privacy for gays and lesbians.

13. Of the following, which group has seen the least progress towards achievement of its civil rights goals in Texas?
    a. African Americans   b. Women   c. Gays and Lesbians

14. Present demographic trends predict that what ethnic group will constitute a new majority in Texas by 2040, with potentially dramatic political consequences?
    a. African Americans   b. Anglos   c. Hispanics

15. Income inequality falls heavily along ethnic/racial lines in Texas. According to recent data, what group experiences the highest poverty rate?
    a. Hispanics   b. Asian Americans   c. African Americans

Texas in the Federal System

J RAEDLE/GETTY IMAGES

★ Learning Outcomes

The **Learning Outcomes** labeled 1 through 4 are designed to help improve your understanding of the chapter. After reading this chapter, you should be able to:

2–1 Differentiate among federal, unitary, and confederal forms of government, and identify three types of powers found in the U.S. federal system.

2–2 Explain the constitutional bases and the development of dual federalism and cooperative federalism.

2–3 Describe how federalism has affected the development of our civil liberties and civil rights, particularly through the rise of the incorporation doctrine and the fall of the separate-but-equal doctrine.

2–4 Evaluate recent federalism controversies involving Texas, including those surrounding coercive federalism, unfunded mandates, health-care reform, and same-sex marriage.

Remember to visit page 44 for additional Study Tools

CONFLICT

Should States Have Their Own Illegal-Immigration Laws?

About 11 million illegal immigrants—called *unauthorized immigrants* by the national Department of Homeland Security—live in the United States. In Chapter 1, we discussed whether illegal immigrants are a burden on the Texas taxpayer. Controlling illegal immigration also raises questions about states' rights and those of the national government—that is, questions concerning how our *federal form* of government should work.

The U.S. Constitution clearly grants the national government the right to establish uniform laws concerning *naturalization*, the granting of citizenship to immigrants. But what about laws directed against illegal immigration? Should the states be able to pass state laws that are stricter than national laws? Should the power to control illegal immigration be shared by state and national governments? Or are the states barred from exercising authority over immigration?

Alabama, Arizona, Georgia, Indiana, South Carolina, and Utah have passed their own stringent laws to stem illegal immigration. The United States Supreme Court has found several provisions of the Arizona law to be unconstitutional, but it did agree that local and state police can demand proof of legal status from people who are arrested.[1] Has the Supreme Court gone too far in reining in the states, and if so, should Texas establish its own immigration laws?

Defend State Sovereignty—and Texas Should Crack Down

We have two questions here: should the states have concurrent powers over immigration policy, and if they do, should this power be exercised? Most Texans are very supportive of state sovereignty, even if they question the need to crack down on illegal immigrants. Leaders such as Governor Rick Perry have defended Arizona's right to pass its own immigration laws, even if those laws are "not the right direction for Texas."

Others believe that Arizona has charted a course that Texas should follow. When it comes to immigration, federal law enforcement has failed. Texas should at least follow Arizona and other states in creating a law that encourages state and local police to demand that arrested suspects show their papers. As in Arizona, border-related violence and crime due to illegal immigration would be reduced in Texas. There is nothing in the Constitution that explicitly prohibits the states from having their own immigration-enforcement policies. If a future Supreme Court does a better job of defending states' rights, Texas and other states could go further in protecting their own citizens.

Texas Doesn't Need a New Immigration Policy

Plenty of Texans are willing to defend national authority, in immigration and other areas. These Texans include minority group members who remember how states' rights were used in the past to deny civil rights to African American and Latino citizens. As noted, many states' rights advocates, such as Governor Perry, also oppose Arizona-style immigration laws. Many, if not most, Texans have long seen their state as culturally binational. Texas business interests have always strongly supported guest-worker programs. Warm relations with Mexico have traditionally been one key to Texas's prosperity.

Provisions thrown out by the Supreme Court—such as the requirement that police stop potential illegal immigrants who are suspected of no crime—would result in endless harassment of brown-skinned citizens. How many middle-class whites are going to be asked for their papers? Arizona-style immigration laws create distrust of the police and undermine law enforcement. Texas is better off leaving immigration policy to Washington, D.C.

Where do you stand?

1. If Texas adopted an Arizona-type immigration law, who would benefit, and who would lose?
2. Is it possible to more vigorously enforce immigration laws without negatively affecting police efforts to reduce what we normally think of as crime? Why or why not?

Explore this issue online

- For videos, recordings, and articles on United States Supreme Court decisions such as *Arizona v. United States*, see the site of the Oyez Project of the Illinois Institute of Technology, Chicago-Kent College of Law. To find it, enter "oyez" into your favorite Internet search engine.
- Searching on "immigration texas" will yield a wide variety of opinion pieces about immigration in the Lone Star State.

Introduction

The relationship between the state of Texas and the federal government has been tense in recent years. Texas policymakers have increasingly viewed the federal government as encroaching on the state's sovereignty, as the federal government has attempted to enforce new laws, rules, and regulations in the state.

From health-care reform to immigration and environmental policy, the government of Texas and that of the nation disagree on the proper role of each in creating, enacting, and enforcing public policy. Tension between the national government and the states, however, is not new and has continually redefined our concepts of federalism.

2-1 What Is Federalism?

Government systems are often classified based on the degree of centralization (see Figure 2–1 below). The three primary types of systems are unitary, confederal, and federal. Most nations in the world are governed by a **unitary system,** in which the national government has ultimate authority. Unitary governments may be democratic, like Japan or Denmark, or they may be undemocratic, like North Korea or Saudi Arabia. All of these nations have unitary governments because one government has authority over the entire nation.

Unitary governments may choose to create local or regional governments for administrative purposes, but the local governments are creations of the national government and have only the powers that the national government chooses to give them.

It is interesting to note that all American states have unitary governments. Counties, cities, and other units of local government are established by the state and have only those powers that the state has granted to them.

Britain had a centralized, unitary system at the time of the American Revolution, and what the colonists regarded as excessive centralization helped spark our independence movement. After independence, Americans reacted to their experiences with an excessive centralization by creating a national government that was so decentralized as to be unworkable.

Under the Articles of Confederation, all power was retained by the state governments, and the central government had only the power that states chose to give it. Such a system, in which regional governments have all authority, with central institutions subordinate to the state or regional governments, is called a confederacy, or **confederal system.** Because this form is unstable, there are no real examples of confederal forms in the modern world, though some might argue

unitary system A system of government in which one central government has ultimate authority, and any regional or local governments are subordinate to the central government.

confederal system A system of government in which member state or regional governments have all authority and any central institutions have only the powers that state or regional governments choose to give them.

FIGURE 2-1

In a unitary system, power flows from the central government to the local and state governments. In a confederal system, power flows in the opposite direction—from the state governments to the central government. In a federal system, the flow of power, in principle, goes both ways.

The Flow of Power
in Three Systems of Government

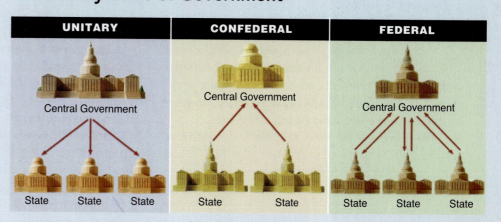

that the European Union has many characteristics of a confederacy.

2–1a The Federal System

In reaction to the impractical Articles of Confederation, at the U.S. Constitutional Convention in 1787 Americans invented an entirely new form of government—a federal system. Federalism represents an attempt to combine the advantages of a unitary government (national unity and uniformity where they are necessary) with the advantages of a confederacy (local control and political diversity from state to state where they are possible).

The concept of federalism has flourished and has been widely adopted, especially in nations with large areas and diverse populations. Today, Australia, Brazil, Canada, Germany, India, and Mexico are among the major nations that use a federal system.

What Is a Federal System? A **federal system** of government is one in which governmental power is divided and shared between a national "or central" government and state or regional governments. In the United States, governmental power is shared by the national and state governments.

The framers of the U.S. Constitution opted to give more authority to the central government than it had possessed under the Articles of Confederation. One of their critical challenges was the creation of a representative government for a large nation with a diverse population. The framers of the Constitution wanted

to achieve a balance between parochial interests and broader national concerns. The federal system was the solution to this challenge. James Madison wrote in *Federalist Paper* No. 10:

> By enlarging too much the number of electors [voters], you render the [elected] representative too little acquainted with all their local circumstances and lesser interests; as by reducing it too much, you render him unduly attached to these, and too little fit to comprehend and pursue great and national objects. The federal Constitution forms a happy combination in this respect; the great and aggregate interests being referred to the national, the local and particular to the State legislatures.[2]

The federal system, therefore, would help to create a balance between local concerns and national issues.

The National–State Balance of Power In the nation's history, power has tended to migrate from the states to the national government. In recent years, however, there has been substantial push-back against this centralization. Will the states succeed in regaining power from the national government? At this point, the answer is not entirely clear. It is certain, however, that political figures in Texas have been pushing for a shift in power away from the federal government.

2–1b Types of Powers in Our Federal System

There are three types of powers in the U.S federal system—delegated, reserved, and concurrent (see Figure 2–2 on the facing page). Examples of these powers are listed in Table 2–1 on the facing page.

Delegated Powers The powers that the Constitution gives to the national government are **delegated powers.** These include the enumerated powers found in Article I, Section 8, of the U.S. Constitution, as well as other powers that have evolved over time. There are three types of delegated powers—expressed, implied, and inherent.

Expressed powers are those found in Article I, Section 8, and are explicitly listed in the U.S. Constitution. **Implied powers** are powers that are assumed to exist so that the government can perform those functions that are expressly delegated.

Inherent powers are powers of the national government that, although not always expressly granted by the Constitution, are necessary to ensure the country's integrity and survival as a political unit in a world of competing nations. The Constitution does speak of such inherent powers as the ability to wage war and

FIGURE 2-2

The Constitutional Division of Powers
in Our Federal Government

As illustrated here, the Constitution grants certain powers to the national government (delegated powers) and reserves other powers exclusively for state governments. Some powers, called concurrent powers, can be exercised at either the national or the state level, but generally the states can exercise these powers only within their own borders.

DELEGATED
(National government)
★ To coin money
★ To conduct foreign relations
★ To regulate interstate commerce
★ To declare war
★ To raise and support the military
★ To establish post offices
★ To admit new states
★ Powers implied by the necessary and proper clause

CONCURRENT
(Shared powers)
★ To levy and collect taxes
★ To borrow money
★ To make and enforce laws
★ To establish courts
★ To provide for the general welfare
★ To charter banks and corporations

RESERVED
(State governments)
★ To regulate intrastate commerce
★ To conduct elections
★ To provide for public health, safety, welfare, and morals
★ To establish local governments
★ To ratify amendments to the federal Constitution
★ To establish a state militia

make treaties. Other inherent powers, however, are not discussed. An example of an inherent power not mentioned in the Constitution is the power to annex territory.

Reserved Powers The second group of powers in the federal system are **reserved powers.** These are the powers that are reserved to the states. The existence of these powers is implicit in the main body of the Constitution. Their legitimacy is also confirmed by the Tenth Amendment, part of the Bill of Rights.

Concurrent Powers Lastly, there are **concurrent powers,** which are those powers shared by both the national government and the states. They include the power to levy taxes and the power to make and enforce laws.

FOR CRITICAL THINKING

Are there any activities currently undertaken by the national government that you would rather see performed by the state of Texas? Does Texas do anything that could be done better by the national government? Explain your reasoning.

2–2 The U.S. Constitution and Federalism

The U.S. Constitution addresses the sharing of power between the states and the federal government in various sections. Article I, Section 8, for instance, lists the

TABLE 2-1

Examples of Major State and Federal Powers

Delegated Powers (Held by the Federal Government)	Reserved Powers (Exclusive to State Governments)	Concurrent Powers (Shared by Federal and State Governments)
To declare war.	To conduct elections.	To borrow money.
To raise armies.	To provide for the public health, welfare, morals, and safety.	To levy taxes.
To enter into treaties.	To ratify constitutional amendments.	To make and enforce laws.
To coin money.	To establish and provide for local governments.	To establish courts.
To regulate international and interstate commerce.		To charter banks.

reserved powers
In relation to the U.S. Constitution, the powers that belong to the states. The legitimacy of these powers comes in part from the Tenth Amendment.

concurrent powers
Powers that are shared by both the national and state governments.

LearningOutcome 2–2

Explain the constitutional bases and the development of dual federalism and cooperative federalism.

enumerated powers "expressly" granted to Congress by the Constitution. Article VI, Section 2, provides the **supremacy clause,** which reads:

This Constitution, and the Laws of the United States which shall be made in Pursuance thereof; and all Treaties made, or which shall be made, under the Authority of the United States, shall be the supreme Law of the Land; and the Judges in every State shall be bound thereby, any Thing in the Constitution or Laws of any State to the Contrary notwithstanding.

In the event that a conflict should arise between federal and state law, the supremacy clause states that federal law must be followed. The **Tenth Amendment** to the U.S. Constitution also helps to define the balance of power in the federal system. According to the Tenth Amendment, "The powers not delegated to the United States by the Constitution, nor prohibited by it to the States, are reserved to the States respectively, or to the people." As you will learn later in this chapter, the Fourteenth Amendment also affects the balance of power in the federal system, in part by binding the states to the rights set forth in the national Bill of Rights.

2–2a The Expressed Powers of the Federal Government

Conflicts between the national government and states have arisen on a number of occasions, in part because of different understandings of two sections of the U.S. Constitution—Article I, Section 8 (see Table 2–2 on the facing page), and the Tenth Amendment.

supremacy clause Article VI, Section 2, of the U.S. Constitution, which states that the U.S. Constitution, as well as laws and treaties created in accordance with the U.S. Constitution, supersede state and local laws.

Tenth Amendment The section of the U.S. Constitution that reserves powers to the states. It reads as follows: "The powers not delegated to the United States by the Constitution, nor prohibited by it to the States, are reserved to the States respectively, or to the people."

commerce clause An enumerated power in Article I, Section 8, of the U.S. Constitution that gives Congress the power to regulate interstate commerce.

necessary and proper clause The last clause in Article I, Section 8, of the U.S. Constitution, which gives Congress implied powers; also known as the *elastic clause*.

Article I, Section 8, enumerates the powers granted to Congress, including the power to regulate interstate commerce. It is this **commerce clause** that was used by its supporters to justify the Patient Protection and Affordable Care Act (Obamacare), as well as other broad national government actions.

More important for a discussion on federalism, however, is the last clause in Article 1, Section 8: "To make all Laws which shall be necessary and proper for carrying into Execution the foregoing Powers, and all other Powers vested by this Constitution in the Government of the United States, or in any Department or Officer thereof." This is known as the **necessary and proper clause,** or the *elastic clause*, of the U.S. Constitution. It was given a very expansive meaning early in the nation's founding.

2–2b McCulloch v. Maryland

In 1819, in *McCulloch v. Maryland*, the United States Supreme Court issued a ruling that took a broad view of the powers of the U.S. Congress. The state of Maryland sought to limit competition with banks chartered by the state. It attempted to tax the Bank of the United States, which had been created by the federal government. The head of the Baltimore branch of the Bank of the United States refused to pay the tax. The Supreme Court had to decide two issues: (1) whether a state could tax an arm of the national government, and (2) whether the creation of the Bank of the United States was constitutional.

The Court ruled that because of the supremacy clause and because "the power to tax is the power to destroy," state governments could not tax the national government. Chief Justice John Marshall wrote, "The Government of the Union, though limited in its powers, is supreme within its sphere of action, and its laws, when made in pursuance of the Constitution, form the supreme law of the land."[3] Chief Justice Marshall also argued that, while the creation of a bank was not an enumerated power, the necessary and proper clause gave Congress authority to create the bank.

The Court concluded that if the end, or goal, is legitimate, then the means are constitutional. If Congress has the power to regulate commerce, for instance, then Congress can enact legislation that will help it carry out that end.

2–2c Dual Federalism and the Tenth Amendment

Even with the broad powers granted to the federal government by *McCulloch v. Maryland*, the distinctions between the two levels of government were far from

TABLE 2-2

Powers Granted to Congress under Article I, Section 8

The Congress shall have power to:

- Lay and collect taxes, duties, imposts, and excises.
- Pay the debts and provide for the common defense and general welfare of the United States; but all duties, imposts, and excises shall be uniform throughout the United States.
- Borrow money on the credit of the United States.
- Regulate commerce with foreign nations, among the several states, and with the Indian tribes.
- Establish a uniform rule of naturalization and uniform laws on the subject of bankruptcies throughout the United States.
- Coin money, regulate the value thereof and of foreign coin, and fix the standard of weights and measures.
- Provide for the punishment of counterfeiting the securities and current coin of the United States.
- Establish post offices and post roads.
- Promote the progress of science and useful arts by securing for limited times to authors and inventors the exclusive right to their respective writings and discoveries.
- Constitute tribunals inferior to the Supreme Court.
- Define and punish piracies and felonies committed on the high seas and offenses against the law of nations.
- Declare war, grant letters of marque and reprisal, and make rules concerning captures on land and water.
- Raise and support armies, but no appropriation of money to that use shall be for a longer term than two years.
- Provide and maintain a navy.
- Make rules for the government and regulation of the land and naval forces.
- Provide for calling forth the militia to execute the laws of the Union, suppress insurrections, and repel invasions.
- Provide for organizing, arming, and disciplining the militia and for governing such part of it as may be employed in the service of the United States, reserving to the states respectively, the appointment of the officers and the authority of training the militia according to the discipline prescribed by Congress.
- Exercise exclusive legislation in all cases whatsoever over such district (not exceeding ten miles square) as may, by cession of particular states and the acceptance of Congress, become the seat of the government of the United States.
- Exercise like authority over all places purchased by the consent of the legislature of the state in which the same shall be, for the erection of forts, magazines, arsenals, dockyards, and other needful buildings.
- Make all laws which shall be necessary and proper for carrying into execution the foregoing powers, and all other powers vested by this Constitution in the government of the United States or in any department or officer thereof.

---

clear. Scholars have dubbed the type of federalism that existed through the nineteenth century and the early part of the twentieth century as **dual federalism.**

Corwin's Analysis of Dual Federalism The dominant concept of federalism until the 1930s, dual federalism can be characterized by four features:

1. The national government possesses enumerated powers only.
2. The purposes that the national government may constitutionally promote are few.
3. Within their respective spheres, the two levels of government—federal and state—are "sovereign" and "equal."
4. The relation of the two levels with each other is one of tension rather than collaboration.

These four characteristics were postulated by Edward S. Corwin in his 1950 eulogy to dual federalism. Corwin argued, "What was once vaunted as a

Constitution of Rights, both State and private, has been replaced by a Constitution of Powers."[4] While this claim may be debated, it was clear that from the 1930s on a new understanding of the relationship between federal and state governments was in effect.

The Tenth Amendment A strong reading of the Tenth Amendment was the bulwark for dual federalism. Such a reading ensured that states such as Texas retained, to the greatest degree possible, those powers that were not given to the federal government. Many people believed that the Tenth Amendment limited the powers of the national government to those stipulated in Article I, Section 8.

Other interpretations were possible, however. In the process of writing the Tenth Amendment,

> **dual federalism** The understanding that the federal government and state governments are both sovereign within their respective spheres of influence.

Thomas Tudor Tucker, a member of the new U.S. House of Representatives, proposed adding the word *expressly* so that the amendment would read, "The powers not *expressly* delegated to the United States." He believed that the addition would limit the powers of the federal government to those explicitly listed in the Constitution. James Madison and others argued against the proposal, and it was rejected.[5]

As a result, the Tenth Amendment could be interpreted as limiting national powers either considerably or hardly at all. Chief Justice Roger Taney, who followed Chief Justice Marshall, sought to rein in the powers of the central government. When faced with a case that pitted the federal government's power to regulate commerce against the states' internal *police power,* the Court would typically side with the states.[6] (**Police power** does not refer to the police, but to a government's authority to legislate for the protection of the health, morals, safety, and welfare of its people.) Taney's interpretation of the Constitution provided a basis for the doctrine of dual federalism.

2–2d The Development and Rise of Cooperative Federalism

The exclusion of the word *expressly* from the Tenth Amendment made it much easier for the national government to expand its powers when a new set of national and global challenges triggered a shift in power from state governments to the federal government. Two world wars, the Great Depression, advances in technology, the civil rights movement, and the Cold War with the Soviet Union seemed to justify centralized power. According to Edward Corwin, "The

> **"The powers not delegated to the United States** by the Constitution, nor prohibited by it to the States, are reserved to the States respectively, or to the people."
>
> ~ THE TENTH AMENDMENT TO THE U.S. CONSTITUTION ~

Federal System has shifted base in the direction of a consolidated national power, while within the National Government itself an increased flow of power in the direction of the President has ensued."[7]

The Rise of Cooperative Federalism Dual federalism was replaced by **cooperative federalism,** a relationship in which "the National Government and the States are mutually complementary parts of a *single* government mechanism, all of whose powers are intended to realize the current purposes of government according to their applicability to the problem in hand."[8] Under cooperative federalism, the national government has used its power to encourage the states to pursue certain public-policy goals. When the states cooperate, they receive matching funds or additional assistance from the national government. When the states do not cooperate, these funds can be withheld.

The development of cooperative federalism was made possible by a vast expansion of federal grant-in-aid programs. Federal grants to state and local governments have a long and controversial history. Although some grants from the national government to the states began as early as 1785, the adoption of the income tax in 1913 drastically altered the financial relationship between the national and state governments. The new revenues enjoyed by the national government made extensive aid to state and local governments more possible.

The Great Depression of the 1930s had a brutal impact on state and local government finances. Increased demand for state and local services, even as revenues were rapidly declining, stimulated a long series of New Deal grant-in-aid programs, ranging from welfare to public health and unemployment insurance.

Categorical Grants Most of these early grant-in-aid programs were **categorical grants.** Under such aid programs, Congress appropriates funds for a specific purpose and sets up a formula for their distribution. The receiving government agrees to match the federal money with its own, and it actually administers the program. For example, federal funds are made available for Medicaid, but it is the state that actually

police power A government's authority to legislate for the protection of the health, morals, safety, and welfare of the people. The term does not refer to law enforcement officers.

cooperative federalism A relationship in which the national government and the states are mutually complementary parts of a single government mechanism.

categorical grants Federal aid to state or local governments for specific purposes, granted under restrictive conditions and often requiring matching funds from the receiving government.

pays client benefits. The receiving government also must meet minimum federal standards. For example, states are forbidden to spend federal money in any way that promotes racial discrimination.

Block Grants Today, much federal aid takes the form of **block grants.** These grants specify general purposes such as job training or community development but allow the state or local government to determine precisely how the money should be spent.

Conditions may also be established for the receipt of block grants, but state and local governments have greater administrative flexibility than they do with categorical grants. Federal transportation, welfare, and many other grants have been reformed to allow for significant **devolution** of power to the states through block grants.

2–2e Federal Grants-in-Aid to Texas

The federal government is one of the largest sources of revenue for the Texas state government. Table 2–3 below shows the 2012–2013 sources of estimated state revenue, the amount, the percentage of the total, and the percentage change from 2010– 2011. Of the $183.1 billion in state revenue, $71.2 billion comes from the federal government—38.9 percent of the total state revenue.

Federal Aid and the Economic Crisis The latest expansion of federal grants was a temporary response to the economic crisis that struck in September 2008. In an attempt to stem the effects of the "Great Recession," Congress passed a series

of massive economic stimulus and bailout bills. Among them was the American Recovery and Reinvestment Act of 2009, which pumped $12.1 billion of mostly temporary federal funds into Texas's treasury during fiscal year 2010–2011. More than one-half of these stimulus funds were spent on education, with much of the remainder going to joint federal–state programs, such as transportation, Medicaid, and unemployment benefits.

The infusion of these funds allowed the Texas legislature to balance the state's budget temporarily, despite plummeting state tax revenues. Still, the stimulus grants were extremely controversial. Governor Perry took a high-profile stance against several grants that he believed placed too many restrictions on the state. For example, Texas refused approximately $500 million in unemployment aid because the funds were conditioned on the state expanding eligibility for the program. We show where the state ranks in federal aid in Table 2–4 in the *How Texas Compares* feature on page 33.

The Growth in Federal Aid The percentage of Texas's revenue coming from the federal government has grown. In 1978, about a quarter of the state's revenue was provided by the federal government. During the worst years of the Great Recession, the

> **block grants** Federal grants to state or local governments for more general purposes and with fewer restrictions than categorical grants.
>
> **devolution** The surrender of powers to local authorities by a central government.

TABLE 2–3

Estimated Texas Revenue by Source for Fiscal Year 2012–2013

This table shows the sources of all types of Texas state revenue. Notice that federal funds account for almost as large a share of those revenues as state taxes do.

Revenue Source	Amount (in millions)	Percentage of Total Net Revenue	Percentage Change from 2010–2011
Tax collections	$80,576	44%	+8.6%
Federal income	$71,248	39%	−5.4%
Fees, fines, licenses, and penalties	$14,987	8%	+1.7%
Interest and investment income	$1,799	1%	−14.1%
Lottery income	$3,391	2%	+2.5%
Land income	$1,409	1%	−36.6%
Other revenue sources	$9,682	5%	−0.1%
Total net revenue	$183,092	100%	+0.8%

Source: Comptroller of Public Accounts 2012–2013, Certification Revenue Estimate, December 2011.

percentage of federal funds exceeded 40 percent. Figure 2–3 below shows the percentage of revenue that Texas received from the federal government from 1977 to 2013. This development can be explained by the formulas the federal government uses to calculate need. The state's growing population, combined with a large number of low-income families and an increase in its elderly population, has contributed to this growth in revenue from the federal government.

FOR CRITICAL THINKING

Is it appropriate for the national government to "bribe" Texas and other states to undertake various actions by offering grants? Why or why not?

2–3 Federalism, Civil Liberties, and Civil Rights

Some Americans confuse *civil liberties* with *civil rights* and use the terms interchangeably. Scholars, however, make a distinction between the two. They point out that whereas civil liberties are limitations on government action, setting forth what the government cannot do, civil rights specify what the government *must* do—to ensure equal protection under the law for all Americans, for example.

The growth in power of the national government relative to state governments has had a decisive impact on the development of our civil liberties and civil rights throughout the course of the twentieth century. During this period, the United States Supreme Court, step by step, came to require that state governments respect the liberties guaranteed in the national Bill of Rights. The Court also curbed the ability of the states to violate the civil rights of African Americans, members of other minority groups, and women.

2–3a The Fourteenth Amendment and the Bill of Rights

The Reconstruction Era was a period in which the "Radical Republicans" in Congress took control of public policy. They enfranchised the recently freed African American male population and limited the political and voting rights of those who fought against the Union. During this period in

FIGURE 2–3

This figure shows that Texas, like most states, has become increasingly reliant on federal funding to finance state programs like health services, highways, and education.

Source: Texas Legislative Budget Board.

Percentage of Texas Revenue
Coming from the Federal Government (1977–2013)

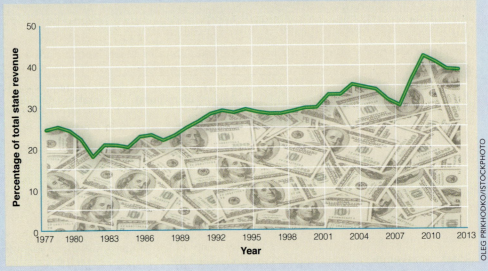

HOW TEXAS COMPARES

Texas's Rank among the Fifty States for Federal Grants

From 2000 to 2009, the state of Texas and its local governments received $240 billion in federal aid, making it the third-largest recipient of federal dollars in that decade—but Texas has a large population.

While Texas may have been the third-largest recipient of federal dollars for the past decade, it ranks forty-fourth in the dollars it received per capita over that period. In 2009, Texas received $1,426 per person, while the national average was $1,798.

TABLE 2-4

Ranking Federal Grants to Texas

Federal Grants-in-Aid to Texas	Texas's Rank (1 = highest; 50 = lowest)	Comment
Total federal aid to Texas state and local governments, 2000–2009.	3	Texas has 8 percent of the U.S. population, but it received 6 percent of federal dollars in 2000–2009.
Federal aid to Texas state and local governments, per capita for 2009.	43	
Federal aid to Texas state and local governments, per capita for 2006.	37	Former Texas governor George W. Bush was in the White House that year.
Return on every dollar paid in federal taxes.	37	In fiscal year 2008, Texas received 89 cents for every dollar paid in federal taxes.

Sources: U.S. Census Bureau; Texas Legislative Budget Board.

 **FOR CRITICAL ANALYSIS** Texas has a large poor population with real needs for government services, but it also has a political culture that tends to reject big government. Should Texas lawmakers fight for a greater slice of the federal pie?

Texas history, Republicans—the party of Abraham Lincoln—controlled the Texas state government. Governor Edmund Davis and other Republican politicians proved to be very unpopular, however. The allegedly corrupt—and certainly pro–African American—practices of Governor Davis proved to be too much for white Texans. It was in this period that a number of African Americans were elected to the Texas legislature. The Reconstruction Era was also a period in which the federal government encroached heavily on state governments in the former Confederate states.

The Incorporation Doctrine One outcome of the Civil War was the enactment of the Fourteenth Amendment, which made a variety of significant contributions to the American system of government. One of its more important contributions is the **incorporation doctrine.**

WHAT IS THE INCORPORATION DOCTRINE? This doctrine holds that state governments are bound to uphold most of the rights found in the Bill of Rights in the U.S. Constitution. Before the development of the incorporation doctrine, the protections found in the Bill of Rights were protections from federal intervention—not state action.

> **incorporation doctrine**
> The doctrine that under the Fourteenth Amendment to the Constitution, most rights found in the Bill of Rights cannot be encroached upon by the states.

The relevant section of the Fourteenth Amendment reads as follows:

> No State shall make or enforce any law which shall abridge the privileges or immunities of citizens of the United States; nor shall any State deprive any person of life, liberty, or property, without due process of law; nor deny to any person within its jurisdiction the equal protection of the laws.

THE DEVELOPMENT OF THE DOCTRINE. Over the course of the twentieth century, the United States Supreme Court came to interpret this clause to mean that the protections found in the Bill of Rights could not be denied by the states. While a few rights found in the Bill of Rights have not been incorporated by the Supreme Court, most have been, as we shall see in Chapter 3. Texas has been part of several Supreme Court cases that have expanded our protections against state government actions.

Aguilar v. Texas, for instance, helped to clarify the incorporation of the Fourth Amendment, which provides protections against unreasonable searches and seizures.[9] *Pointer v. Texas* helped to incorporate the Sixth Amendment, which grants the accused the right to confront witnesses testifying against him or her.[10]

Who Is a Citizen? The Fourteenth Amendment also defined, for the first time, who was an American citizen. This provision has given rise to a current controversy. In recent years, Texas lawmakers have challenged the definition of citizenship currently accepted by the U.S. judicial system. The Fourteenth Amendment defines U.S. citizens with the following language: "All persons born or naturalized in the United States and subject to the jurisdiction thereof, are citizens of the United States and of the State wherein they reside." Therefore, according to standard interpretations, anyone born in the United States is a citizen.

Furthermore, Article I, Section 8, of the original U.S. Constitution gives Congress the power to establish a uniform "rule of naturalization." That is, it gives the U.S. Congress the authority to create rules for immigration and naturalization. As a result, the courts have held that immigration law is a responsibility of the federal government, not state governments. We discussed this issue in the chapter-opening *Texans in Conflict* feature.

separate-but-equal doctrine The doctrine resulting from the United States Supreme Court ruling in *Plessy v. Ferguson*, which legalized segregation.

Opposition to Birth-Right Citizenship In the last several years, Texas lawmakers, frustrated that the federal government has failed to take on the issue of unauthorized immigration, have attempted to address the issue at the state level. In recent legislative sessions, lawmakers have attempted to circumvent the Fourteenth Amendment by sponsoring legislation that would deny the rights of citizenship to babies born in the United States to undocumented parents. They have argued that because the parents of these infants have broken the law, the infants should not receive the benefits of citizenship.[11]

If such a bill were to become law in Texas, the United States Supreme Court would have to settle the conflict between the state and federal governments. State representative Leo Berman, who introduced such a bill in the Texas House of Representatives, said, "We want to be sued into federal court where our attorney general can take this all the way to the U.S. Supreme Court."[12]

2–3b Civil Rights versus States' Rights

Heated civil rights battles developed during the period of cooperative federalism. As the federal government became increasingly active in promoting the rights of African Americans and other minority group members, states, especially southern states, claimed that the national government was encroaching on states' rights.

The Separate-but-Equal Doctrine In 1896, during the period of dual federalism, the United States Supreme Court established the **separate-but-equal doctrine** in *Plessy v. Ferguson*.[13] The Court interpreted the Fourteenth Amendment in ways that provided maximum protection for states' rights. Under *Plessy*, segregation did not violate the constitutional requirement that no state shall deny any person the equal protection of the laws. The Court held that state and local governments could pass laws requiring racial segregation as long as physical facilities were equal for both races.

FLAWS OF SEPARATE-BUT-EQUAL. The separate-but-equal doctrine ignored the intent in passing segregation laws to communicate a sense of social inferiority to African Americans by making it a crime for them to associate with whites. The Court also ignored the fact that facilities for African Americans were either clearly inferior or nonexistent. Following the *Plessy* decision, southern states

Herman Sweatt was denied entrance to a Texas law school. He sued the state. The Supreme Court ruled in his favor.

JOSEPH SCHERSCHEL/TIME & LIFE PICTURES/GETTY IMAGES

enacted **Jim Crow laws** that required segregation in almost every aspect of life.

CHIPPING AWAY AT THE DOCTRINE. After World War II, the separate-but-equal doctrine was slowly weakened. As described in Chapter 1, on page 17, Texas was the setting for one of the first attacks on the doctrine in *Sweatt v. Painter*.[14] Heman Marion Sweatt, an African American, hoped to attend law school in Texas, but the law school at the University of Texas did not admit African Americans. Black students in Texas who wanted to attend law school were told to go out of state for their education. The United States Supreme Court ruled that Texas was not providing the separate accommodations required under the separate-but-equal doctrine.

Sweatt v. Painter led to the creation of what is now the Thurgood Marshall School of Law at Texas Southern University. Graduates of this school comprise the largest number of African American attorneys admitted to practice law in Texas. Perhaps more significantly, *Sweatt v. Painter* helped pave the way for *Brown v. Board of Education of Topeka*, which eventually reversed *Plessy*.[15]

The End of Separate-but-Equal *Brown v. Board of Education* would lead to the desegregation of schools (see Chapter 1, page 17). The Twenty-fourth Amendment (which outlawed the poll tax), the Civil Rights Act of 1964, the Voting Rights Act of 1965, and many other laws that promoted equality would follow. Southern states saw such legislation as an encroachment on their sovereignty, their rights as states.

To this day, Texans debate issues of states' rights. When *American Idol* pop singer Kelly Clarkson tweeted that she loved Texan Ron Paul, a member of Congress and a Republican presidential candidate, because "he believes in states having their rights," she was harshly criticized by those for whom *states' rights* is a coded endorsement of racism.

Republican commentator David Azerrad has recommended that Republicans "speak of federalism, not states' rights."[16] For many, the language of states' rights continues to harken back to a time when segregation was enforced by the states. Minority group members see states' rights expressed in laws that can hinder minority political participation, reduce access to public services, and lead to law enforcement strategies that result higher incarceration rates among African Americans and Latinos.

FOR CRITICAL THINKING

Why do you think that the civil rights movement took off in the 1950s and 1960s rather than earlier or later?

2–4 Federalism Controversies in Texas

While some Texans may see support for states' rights as a way to thwart civil rights for racial and gender minorities, other—more conservative—Texans believe that advocacy of states' rights reflects a genuine concern with liberty issues. They believe that the federal government simply has become too powerful. It not only performs functions better handled by the states, but it also wields excessive power over both state governments and individuals.

Previously, we examined the U.S. Constitution and how the national political and legal climate has affected the relative powers of the

Jim Crow laws State and local laws that promulgated racial segregation.

LearningOutcome 2–4

Evaluate recent federalism controversies involving Texas, including those surrounding coercive federalism, unfunded mandates, health-care reform, and same-sex marriage.

national and state governments. Now we look at issues of federalism from a Texas perspective. How have the national government's powers affected the state? How have political leaders coped with the changing nature of federalism? Not all of the interactions between Texas and the rest of the Union have been negative, as we show in the *Texas Politics and Federalism* feature on the facing page.

2–4a Coercive Federalism and Texas

Many Texans would agree that a shift away from cooperative federalism has been under way since the late 1970s. This new form of federalism, foreshadowed by the civil rights laws, has been called **coercive federalism.** In this version of federalism, the national government directs the policies that the states must adopt. Power is centralized in the federal government, which, in the opinion of many, increasingly obstructs the states (the national government "preempts" the state governments). As evidence of this shift, the U.S. Advisory Commission on Intergovernmental Relations has reported that more than half of all preemption laws—going back to the nation's founding—were enacted in the 1970s and 1980s.[17]

This encroachment on states' rights was not due to any single ideology. John Kinkaid, a scholar of federalism, wrote, "Liberals, lacking revenue for major increases in equity programs, and conservatives, lacking public support for major reductions in equity programs, switched from fiscal to regulatory tools."[18] Because neither liberals nor conservatives had the political support to expand or contract programs that promoted equity, lawmakers in Congress and the White House opted to enact new rules.

coercive federalism A relationship between the national government and states in which the former directs the policies that the states must adopt.

Texans' Response to Coercive Federalism During his 2011–2012 presidential bid, Texas governor Rick Perry invoked the Tenth Amendment frequently. The governor's Web site describes his governing principles in this way:

> States are best positioned to deal with state issues, a fact the founding fathers had in mind when they included the 10th Amendment in the Bill of Rights. Over the years, that right has been clouded by ongoing federal encroachments that are reflected in a recent series of attempts by Washington to seize even more control over numerous Texas programs, including some of the most successful initiatives of their kinds in the country.[19]

Governor Perry sees the health-care reform legislation, Environmental Protection Agency regulations, and attempts to limit the emission of carbon dioxide into the atmosphere as recent examples of the national government placing undue burdens on Texas.

The Texas Legislature has followed Governor Perry's lead. In 2011, Texas House Speaker Joe Straus created the Select Committee on State Sovereignty to consider bills that try to limit the federal government's activities in health-care reform, the manufacture of ammunitions and firearms, and water resources. One bill also urged the president to support the Defense of Marriage Act, while others called for constitutional changes that would allow states to reject federal laws. The committee gave Texas lawmakers an opportunity to express their objection to national government policies. Of the twenty-eight bills referred to the committee, only one concurrent resolution, which called for a balanced budget amendment, was signed by the governor.

Support for Federal Action Supporters of federal efforts, in contrast, see the national government

Texas created the AMBER Alert system to help find missing children. It's now nationwide.

REUTERS/FRED PROUSER FSP/SV

States as Policy Laboratories—the AMBER Alert System

One of the advantages of a federal system is that states are able to experiment with public policy. With fifty different states, the nation has fifty laboratories that can produce a variety of possible solutions to common problems. If a state solution fails, at least the whole nation is not committed to the policy. If these solutions work, however, they can then be expanded to other jurisdictions. The AMBER Alert System is a good example of a successful policy solution in Texas that was expanded nationwide. AMBER stands for "America's Missing: Broadcast Emergency Response."

The Origins of the System

In 1997, Dallas area child advocates asked the local police department and broadcasters to implement the AMBER Alert System—a law enforcement tool that would encourage local communities to help in the search for missing children. The request followed an incident in which a nine-year-old child named Amber Hagerman was abducted and murdered in Arlington, Texas. AMBER Alerts are shared with the community through a variety of broadcasting tools. One common method has been the use of electronic signs on major thoroughfares to announce the most serious cases involving missing children and missing persons, in the hope that someone in the broader community might be able to help locate these individuals.

Going National

The AMBER Alert System was very effective in helping to find missing children in Texas, so the federal government considered implementing it nationwide. In 2003, the AMBER Alert Act was passed, creating a nationwide system for finding abducted children. The federal government gives participating states funds as well as assistance in establishing voluntary standards. The program has now expanded to all fifty states and allows for communication among law enforcement authorities across state lines. Because child abductors often try to flee from the states where they committed the abduction, national coordination ensures that an alert is shared across state borders. In 2010, 25 percent of the cases nationwide "had recoveries out of the state/territory of the original activation."[20] Interestingly, Texas was second only to Michigan in the number of alerts issued in 2010.[21]

FOR CRITICAL ANALYSIS What kinds of projects would all states be happy to adopt if they are successful—and what kinds of projects might be successful in some states but resisted in others? (Hint: What kinds of projects are tied to ideological positions?)

as requiring the states to assume necessary responsibilities that they have tended to shirk. As an example, they point to the high proportion of Texans without health-care insurance. Currently, Texas has one of the largest percentages of uninsured residents of any state.[22]

Supporters of federal involvement also point to the way in which the Texas Commission on Environmental Quality (TCEQ) has attempted to enforce air and water quality standards. The Alliance for a Clean Texas reported that TCEQ "seems incapable of meeting many challenges in a straightforward and efficient enough manner to effectively protect the health of our citizens and the environmental integrity of our state's natural resources." If the state does not meet the air quality standards called for by the federal government, then the state could lose federal funds for transportation projects. We look at environmental issues in the *How Texas Compares* feature on the following page.

2–4b Unfunded Mandates

An **unfunded mandate** is an obligation that the federal government imposes on state governments without providing adequate national funding to

> **unfunded mandates**
> Obligations that the federal government imposes on state governments without providing adequate funding to support the programs.

Texas's Environmental Rankings among the Fifty States

Texas has taken the lead in several environmental areas, but it has major weaknesses as well.

TABLE 2-5

Ranking the Texas Environment

Environmental Quality Measure	Texas's Rank (1 = highest; 50 = lowest)	Did You Know?
Wind power.[23]	1	In 2010, Texas produced enough wind energy to power 2.7 million homes.
Clean water.[24]	38	The cities of Arlington, Fort Worth, and Austin have top-rated water utilities, while Houston has one of the lowest-rated water utilities.
The number of days when monitored concentrations of a criteria pollutant exceed a National Ambient Air Quality Standard multiplied by the total number of people living in the affected area.[25]	2	The total number of people-days is 1,135,690,880.
Pollution in areas where cancer risk exceeds one in one thousand, considering all sources of pollution.[26]	6	The GoodGuide Scorecard (search on "goodguide") has information on pollution in specific locations.
The number of people exposed to levels of hazardous air pollutants that exceed the Clean Air Act's noncancer risk goal.[27]	1	The number of people exposed is 3,489,874.

Texas has led the nation in developing alternative sources of energy that produce clean energy. From El Paso to the Texas Panhandle, thousands of wind turbines have been installed and are generating enough energy to power more than 2 million homes. Wind energy diminishes our reliance on other sources of energy that pollute the environment, namely coal-fired power plants. Texas has taken some positive steps to address air quality while at the same time addressing energy efficiency.

Texas is also headquarters to the world's petrochemical industry, which produces many jobs for Texans. Unfortunately, it also produces a significant amount of pollution. For Texans living near polluting industries, federal antipollution initiatives may be welcome news.

Texas ranks at or near the top of the list of states producing hazardous air pollutants. Some of these come from dry cleaners, gas stations, and auto body paint shops. Pollution is also produced by automobiles, airplanes, ships, tractors, and other such machines, as well as chemical plants, petroleum refineries, power plants, and other major industries. This last group would be most affected by recent attempts to limit carbon dioxide emissions. These industries also face increasing levels of regulation by the federal Environmental Protection Agency.

Because Texas has so many of these industries, there is widespread fear that federal regulations could do excessive harm to the state's economy. The possible loss of jobs and profits is a major concern for Texans. While pollution is a major health threat for Texans, policymakers will seek to balance environmental concerns and economic security.

FOR CRITICAL ANALYSIS Should regulating air quality be a national responsibility, or should it be the job of the states? Should the federal government move in to regulate air quality if a state fails to meet deadlines for reducing emissions?

JIM WEST/REPORT DIGITAL–REA/REDUX

Texas leads the nation in wind power.

mandates on lower levels of government. The state of Texas has also enacted a fair number of unfunded mandates that require local governments to take certain actions without adequate funds to implement the requirements.

The Texas Association of Counties, which works on behalf of the state's 254 counties, has been critical of the state's unfunded mandates. It reports, "Unfunded mandates impose costs on Texas counties and their taxpayers into the millions of dollars statewide and force counties to increase local property tax rates to pay for edicts from above."[29] The state has required county governments to provide legal services, health services, and children's protective services as well as the funding to pay for them.

In 2011, the Texas Legislature attempted to address this issue but was unable to pass a bill. Governor Perry entered the fray by creating the Task Force on Unfunded Mandates, which was charged with identifying unfunded mandates that the state passes on to local governments. The Task Force also offers recommendations on how to limit those mandates. It remains to be seen whether the number and cost of unfunded mandates imposed on Texas and on local governments will decline in the future.

2–4c Health-Care Reform: A Challenging Case in Federalism

Probably no controversy better illustrates the competing visions of our federal system than the recent saga of national health-care reform. Shortly after the passage of the Patient Protection and Affordable Care Act in 2010, Texas attorney general Greg Abbott joined twenty-five other states' attorneys general in opposing the new health-care law. At issue was the law's requirement that individuals purchase health insurance. (The Patient Protection

support the program. Even with the passage of the Unfunded Mandates Reform Act of 1995, signed by President Bill Clinton, the federal government has continued to impose unfunded mandates on the states. Loopholes and exemptions have made it possible for Congress to obligate Texas and other states to implement certain policies or risk losing federal funds.

Criticism of Unfunded Mandates

Governor Rick Perry has been critical of unfunded mandates, whether developed by Democrats or Republicans. For example, he has criticized President George W. Bush's No Child Left Behind Act for obligating states to make changes to their educational systems without providing sufficient federal funds to implement the programs.[28] Unfunded mandates may allow national lawmakers the opportunity to take credit for addressing problems without also taking political heat for increased federal spending.

State Mandates Affecting Local Governments The federal government is not the only government that imposes unfunded

Many Texans reacted negatively to the passage of Obamacare, including this protester whose shirt reads "Don't Mess with Texas Women."

JEFF MALET/NEWSCOM

and Affordable Care Act is also called the Affordable Care Act and has been nicknamed "Obamacare.")

The *individual mandate,* as it has come to be known, would require individuals who can afford health-care insurance, but are uninsured, to purchase it. Failure to do so would result in a penalty fee added to an individual's federal income tax. States such as Texas have frequently required individuals to purchase other types of insurance, such as automobile liability insurance. Attorney General Abbott, however, claimed that the national government has never mandated that individuals "buy any good or service as a condition of lawful residence in the United States."[30]

The Health-Care Problem The $2.5 trillion health-care industry accounts for 17 percent of the United States economy, as measured by the gross domestic product (GDP). Millions of Americans have no health insurance, but doctors and hospitals are required to treat those seeking emergency medical treatment. Critically ill patients cannot be turned away because they are not insured or cannot afford treatment. The costs of covering the uninsured, therefore, are shared by those who can afford coverage. It is estimated that the uninsured cost the average American family and employer $1,017 in health-care premiums. This added cost paid by the insured has been called a "hidden tax" on the American people.[31]

In Texas, 25 percent of residents (6.2 million Texans) do not have health insurance coverage. Nationally, 16 percent of Americans are uninsured. Children account for 1.3 million of the uninsured in Texas.[32] According to Families USA, the new health-care reform law will lead to 4.2 million newly insured. This would reduce the number of uninsured by roughly two-thirds. Families USA also estimates that 31,700 lives will be saved and 222,500 businesses will be helped by health-care reform.[33] The need to improve coverage in Texas is evident, but the new Affordable Care Act has raised some interesting questions about the power of the federal government.

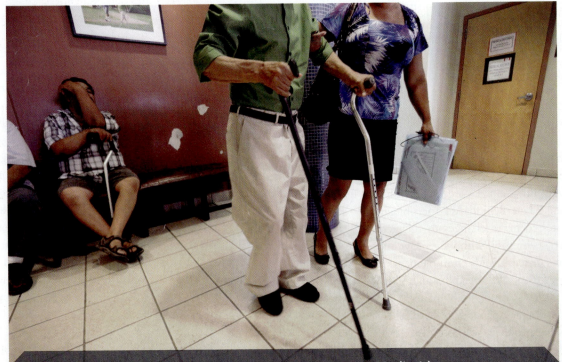

AP PHOTO/ERIC GAY

Texas already has one of the nation's most restrictive Medicaid programs, offering coverage only to the disabled, children, and parents who earn less than $2,256 a year for a family of three. Without a Medicaid expansion, the state's working poor will continue relying on emergency rooms—the most costly treatment option—instead of primary care doctors.

The Constitutional Questions The limits on what Congress can do are stipulated in Article 1, Section 8, of the U.S. Constitution. Congress has the power to regulate interstate commerce, and it is this power that Congress used to justify the Affordable Care Act. Congress argued that because it has the power to regulate interstate commerce—and the buying of health insurance is a commercial activity—it has the power to regulate health-care coverage.

Some disagreed that the act regulated commerce and concluded that it infringed on states' rights. While it is the case that some powers are shared between the states and the federal government, others are exclusive to either one or the other. For example, the power to regulate interstate commerce is granted to Congress. The power to provide for the public health and safety—a part of a government's police power—is more commonly exercised by state governments. Indeed, during much of the nineteenth and part of the twentieth centuries, the United States Supreme Court reserved police power to the states almost completely. Since the 1930s, however, the Court has often tended to see police power as a concurrent power.

Attorney General Greg Abbott has argued that the act does not regulate commerce, but rather that it infringes on the police power of the states: "Because Congress does not have the authority to impose the individual mandate, it violates the Tenth Amendment by straying into a sphere of state sovereignty. This falls into the area of the police power, or the general health and safety of the people."[34]

The Supreme Court Decision Given that different federal appeals courts arrived at different conclusions in assessing the constitutionality of the individual mandate, the Supreme Court had no choice but to take up the issue. In June 2012, the Court's majority endorsed most of the act, but with constitutional cautions. Four justices voted to uphold the act in its entirety. Four wanted to strike it down completely. As a result, the opinion of Chief Justice John Roberts, who joined neither bloc, was decisive. Roberts concluded that the commerce clause did not allow Congress to require a commercial action, such as buying insurance. It could only regulate actions, not require them. The individual mandate, however, is still constitutional because Congress has the right to place incentives in the tax code, and the mandate is just such an incentive.

A second part of Roberts's ruling was more encouraging to states' rights advocates. In a surprising move, Roberts struck down a provision of the Affordable Care Act that required the states to drastically expand eligibility for the Medicaid program or lose all of their national Medicaid funding. Roberts argued that this provision gave the states no option but to agree because the loss of funds would be too great. For the first time, the Supreme Court placed a limit on the federal government's ability to engage in coercive federalism. The restriction was not very severe, however, because Congress presumably still has the power to coerce the states if it limits itself to smaller penalties.[35]

2–4d Same-Sex Marriage and the Full Faith and Credit Clause

In 1996, when the issue of same-sex marriage first materialized in a serious way, the federal government enacted the Defense of Marriage Act (DOMA). This national law allowed individual states to reject marriages between members of the same sex that were performed or recognized in other states. DOMA also prevents the national government from extending federal benefits based on marriage to same-sex couples, even if their union is recognized by their home state.

Today, several states allow same-sex marriages, and the number of states that recognize such marriages is growing. In Texas, however, same-sex marriages are outlawed. Texans amended the state constitution in 2005 to define *marriage* exclusively as a union between a man and a woman.

The Full Faith and Credit Clause As it happens, the U.S. Constitution is not silent on this issue. Article IV, Section 1, requires states to recognize "the public acts, records, and judicial proceedings of every other state." This provision is known as the full faith and credit clause. This clause requires that Texas and all other states recognize the official documents and court rulings of other states. But does that mean that same-sex marriages celebrated in New York must be recognized in Texas? Currently, the answer is "no." Given the rapid rise in acceptance of same-sex marriage in the United States, however, the answer might not remain "no" forever.[36]

The Courts Will Decide A number of DOMA cases are working their way up through the courts. One case, based in Massachusetts, could lead to federal recognition of same-sex marriages when they are recognized by the states. Another case, originating in California, could potentially result in nationwide recognition of such marriages based on the full faith and

Dozens of proponents attended a rally at the Capitol in Austin, Texas, on Wednesday, February 14, 2001, in support of Texas House Bill 496, the Defense of Marriage Act, which limited marriages to heterosexual unions.

credit clause. Both cases are likely to be heard by the United States Supreme Court. Some expert observers believe that the Court may require federal benefits for same-sex couples in states that recognize same-sex marriages, but it is not likely to favor nationwide legalization. Such a result would maximize states' rights, even though one ruling would be seen as politically conservative and the other as politically liberal.

FOR CRITICAL THINKING

In your opinion, what kinds of incentives are legitimate when the national government wants to encourage the states to undertake a particular course of action? At what point do incentives become excessive?

CONFLICT Federalism

As you have learned in this chapter, differing views on the relative power of the state and national governments cut to the heart of the issues that divide Texans. Among these disputes are the following:

- Do national environmental regulations threaten jobs in Texas—or are they essential to protect the health of Texas's citizens?

- Is the Affordable Care Act a reasonable attempt to address a serious problem—or does it represent drastic overreach by the national government?

- Is national action to protect minority g bers still important—or should such act curtailed as no longer necessary?

- Is it legitimate for the federal government to grants to pressure state governments to adop national policies—or do such actions amount to a coercive federalism that violates states' rights?

TAKE ACTION

Are you interested in learning more about the debates on federalism? Consider joining the Federalist Society or the American Constitution Society for Law and Policy. You could attend meetings of these organizations and even present student research papers at them. Joining such organizations may give your résumé a little more cachet. Be aware that the American Constitution Society is a progressive organization, and the Federalist Society is conservative and libertarian.

You can also watch YouTube videos sponsored by the two organizations. The videos will provide you with information about the issues that continue to be part of the political debate. To learn more, use your favorite search engine to visit the Web sites of the American Constitution Society and the Federalist Society by searching on "acslaw" and "fed-soc," respectively.

AP PHOTO/CONROE COURIER/ERIC S. SWIST

Texas Governor Rick Perry holds a copy of the United States Constitution as he speaks to supporters during a campaign stop in The Woodlands.

STUDY TOOL

Ready to stu ...d with the quiz below.
- ...on the Chapter in Review card at ...ok. For any questions you miss, read
  - Review ...ng Learning Outcome section again to Che ...ss and your exam.
  - ...t study the Chapter in Review card.

... Or you can go online to CourseMate

at www.cengagebrain.com for these additional review materials:

- Practice Quizzes
- Key Term Flashcards or Crossword Puzzles
- Audio Summaries
- Simulations, Animated Learning Modules, and Interactive Timelines
- Videos
- American Government NewsWatch

Quiz

1. The United States has a _____ form of government while all fifty states have a _____ form of government.
   a. unitary; federal b. federal; unitary c. federal; confederal

2. A federal form of government is one in which:
   a. all powers are concentrated in the national government.
   b. all powers are concentrated in the state governments.
   c. powers are divided and shared between the national and state governments.

3. What term is used to refer to delegated powers of the federal government that, although not always expressly granted by the Constitution, are necessary to ensure the nation's integrity and survival as a political unit? An example is the power to annex territory.
   a. reserved powers b. implied powers c. inherent powers

4. An example of a concurrent power in the American political system would be is the power to:
   a. conduct foreign relations.
   b. coin money.
   c. establish courts.

5. Which of the following is NOT a constitutional basis for the expansion of the national government's power versus the states?
   a. Tenth Amendment
   b. supremacy clause
   c. necessary and proper clause

6. Which of the following best describes the period of dual federalism?
   a. the period we are under today.
   b. It was the period when the national government exercised the most power over the states.
   c. It was the period when the national government and state governments were both sovereign within their spheres of influence.

7. Which major event launched the period of cooperative federalism?
   a. Civil War b. Great Depression c. World War II

8. Which of the following, refers to federal aid given to state or local governments for specific purposes, granted under restrictive conditions and often requiring matching funds from the receiving government?
   a. mandates b. block grants c. categorical grants

9. The incorporation doctrine applied to the states most of the:
   a. Bill of Rights
   b. Fourteenth Amendment's equal protection clause
   c. commerce clause

10. The United States Supreme Court's decision _____ established the doctrine of separate-but-equal and the Court's decision in _____ abolished it.
    a. *Aquilar v. Texas; Plessy v. Ferguson*
    b. *Brown v. Board of Education; McCulloch v. Maryland*
    c. *Plessy v. Ferguson; Brown v. Board of Education*

11. The Supreme Court recently ruled that states have coequal power as federal government to regulate illegal immigration."
    a. true b. false

12. What aspect of the Fourteenth Amendment have Texas lawmakers recently attempted to circumvent through legislation due to federal inaction?
    a. abortion b. birth-right citizenship c. limits on gun rights

13. A relationship between the national government and states in which the former directs the policies that the states must adopt is called:
    a. devolution. b. dual federalism. c. coercive federalism.

14. Which of the following is an argument in favor of the Affordable Care Act ("Obamacare") in regard to Texas?
    a. It would lower Texas's comparatively high rate of uninsured individuals.
    b. It expands the state's power to act on its own in health care.
    c. It would provide greater freedom for individual Texans to decide whether to purchase health insurance or not.

15. The full faith and credit clause of the U.S. Constitution is most controversial in Texas (as well as other states) when it is applied to the issue of:
    a. illegal immigration.
    b. same-sex marriage.
    c. environmental protection.

The Texas Constitution in Perspective

© BETTMANN/CORBIS

★ Learning Outcomes

The **Learning Outcomes** labeled 1 through 4 are designed to help improve your understanding of the chapter. After reading this chapter, you should be able to:

3–1 Identify Texas's historic constitutions and the cultural and political forces that shaped their distinctive features.

3–2 Identify the rights protected by the Texas Bill of Rights and those also protected by the U.S. Constitution, and describe restrictions on Texas voters.

3–3 Describe separation of powers, checks and balances, the three branches of state government, and the three types of local government in Texas.

3–4 Explain the process of amending and revising the Texas Constitution and the reasons that amendments are frequently necessary.

Remember to visit page 63 for additional Study Tools

★ SECEDE

CONFLICT

Does Texas Have the Right to Secede from the Union?

The U.S. Constitution contains no language on the topic of states leaving the United States, that is, seceding from the Union. The national government does have the power to put down insurrections, but does a vote to secede by a state legislature or convention count as an insurrection? Before the American Civil War (1861–1865), most Southerners believed that states had a right to secede. By 1865, however, after 750,000 deaths, southern secession was over.[1]

Some people believe that Texas faces different circumstances. The Republic of Texas existed until 1845. Does that mean that there could be another Republic of Texas someday? Not too many years ago, Texas governor Rick Perry said, "Texas is a unique place. When we came into the Union in 1845, one of the issues was that we would be able to leave if we decided to do that." Unilateral secession, however, was ruled unconstitutional by the United States Supreme Court in 1869.[2] Still, as late as 1997, Texas Rangers confronted a "Republic of Texas" group in an armed mountain fortress in West Texas. This group believes that Texas is an independent nation because it was not legally annexed to the United States.

Yes, Texas Can Secede If It Wants To

There are certainly enough "Texas Secede" bumper stickers around the state to remind Texans that secession sentiment has not died out. More than 30 percent of Texas voters, when questioned, believe that the state has the right to secede. One in five of those polled would actually vote to leave the Union. Finally, two-thirds of Texans believe that the state would be better off as an independent country.

As pointed out in Chapter 1, the annexation documents that allowed Texas to join the Union in 1845 do contain a provision allowing Texas to split itself into a total of five states. So it would follow that Texas can, in fact, do whatever it wants, even if this means seceding from the Union.

Pure Fantasy and Forklore

The argument that Texas has the right to secede is not based on law. Contrary to what some Texans believe, the documents under which Texas was brought into the Union contain no language allowing Texas to leave. Even the provision concerning dividing the state into five smaller states may be a dead letter—any division would probably require the approval of the U.S. Congress. As noted, the Supreme Court has ruled that no state can secede unilaterally (although the Court did suggest that a state could secede if it had the national government's permission). Governor Perry's statements to the contrary, the secession issue was settled once and for all in 1865. The union between Texas and the other states is complete, perpetual, and indissoluble.

Where do you stand?

1. Many secessionists believe that the national government has become too powerful. Is it, in fact, true that the power of the national government has grown faster than the powers of the state governments?
2. What difficulties might Texas face if it did become an independent nation again?

Explore this issue online

- Entering "texas secede" into your favorite Internet search engine will yield the Web sites of several organizations that advocate the secession of Texas, as well as news stories and encyclopedia articles on the topic.
- Searching on "rot terrorism" will bring up stories about illegal activity by members of the Republic of Texas (RoT) group.

Introduction

The real character of a government is determined less by the provisions of its constitution than by the minds and hearts of its citizens. State government is a process of decision making conditioned by a state's history, its people, and the pressures exerted by interest groups and political parties.

Still, our national and state governments would be vastly different were it not for their constitutions. The exact meaning of constitutional provisions may be disputed, as can be seen in the chapter-opening *Texans in Conflict* feature. There is general agreement, however, that a constitution should be respected as the legal basis for the fundamentals of government decision making. Constitutions serve as rationalizations for the actions of courts, legislatures, executives, and the people themselves. Indeed, the very idea of having a written constitution has become part of the political culture—the basic system of political beliefs in the United States.

Constitutions establish major governing institutions, assign them power, and place both implicit and explicit limits on the power that has been assigned. And, because Americans respect constitutions, they promote **legitimacy,** the general public acceptance of a government's right to govern.

3-1 Texas Constitutions in History

Like all constitutions, early Texas constitutions reflected the interests and concerns of the people who wrote and amended them. Many of their elements paralleled those of other state constitutions, but others are unique to Texas.

> ### Learning Outcome 3–1
> Identify Texas's historic constitutions and the cultural and political forces that shaped their distinctive features.

3–1a Early Texas Constitutions

The constitutions of the Texas Republic and the first state constitutions of Texas were products of the plantation culture of Anglo-Protestant slaveholders. These early constitutions adopted some institutions from Texans' experiences during Mexican rule and forthrightly rejected others.

The Constitution of the Republic of Texas The first Texas constitution after independence from

CORBIS

Sam Houston was elected president of the Republic of Texas in 1843. He represented the state as a senator when Texas joined the United States in 1845, became governor in 1859, and was deposed for opposing Texas's secession to the Confederacy. The city of Houston is named for him.

Mexico was written in 1836 for the Republic of Texas. In reaction to the influence of the Catholic Church during Mexican rule, the largely Protestant Texans wrote a constitution that carefully separated church and state. Clergy of any faith were forbidden from holding office. The document altered the antislavery policies of the old Mexican government—owners could not free their own slaves without the consent of the Republic's congress. Descendants of Africans and Indians were denied citizenship. Texans, remembering the abuses of Mexican president Santa Anna, limited the terms of the Republic's presidents to three years and prohibited them from reelection to consecutive terms.

The Constitution of the Republic did adopt some provisions of Spanish-Mexican law, including

legitimacy The general acceptance of a government's right to govern. Also, the legality of a government's existence as established by a constitution.

homestead protections, protection for a wife's property rights, and the concept of **community property,** meaning that property acquired during marriage would be owned equally by husband and wife. These elements of Mexican law would later be absorbed into American political culture, as other states adopted similar provisions.

Still, the Republic's constitution was mostly a product of the political culture of the Anglo-American southern planters. It incorporated English **common law.** It also lifted many provisions almost word for word from the U.S. Constitution and from the constitutions of southern states such as Tennessee, from which many Texas settlers had come.

Acting in haste because of the fear of attack by Mexican cavalry, the Republic's constitutional convention wrote a concise document establishing a *unitary* form of government (see Chapter 2), free of many of the detailed restrictions that would later limit Texas's government.

The Constitution of 1845 A new constitution was written in 1845 in preparation for Texas's admission to the United States. It is interesting to note that it required a two-thirds vote in the Texas House to establish any corporation and made bank corporations illegal altogether.

Although the Constitution of 1845 contained many provisions similar to those of the Republic's constitution, it also introduced features recognizable in today's state constitution. For example, it was almost twice as long as the Republic of Texas's constitution and included restrictive language on the legislature, which was allowed to meet only once every two years. The statehood constitution limited state debt to $100,000, except in cases of war, insurrection, or invasion, and it established a Permanent School Fund.

Only one amendment to the 1845 Constitution was ever adopted. It limited the governor's power by providing for the election of some of the officers that governors previously were allowed to appoint. In this way, it marked the beginnings of the **long ballot** with which Texans are familiar today.

The Constitution of 1861 The Constitution of 1861 was almost identical to the Constitution of 1845. It did reflect that Texas had become one of the Confederate states at war with the Union. This constitution increased the debt ceiling and prohibited the emancipation of slaves.

3–1b Reconstruction Constitutions and Their Aftermath

While earlier constitutions contained a number of elements still found today in the Texas Constitution, it was the aftermath of the Civil War—Reconstruction and the reaction to that process—that affirmed Texans' distrust of government and set the stage for today's state constitution.

The Constitution of 1866 After the Civil War, Texans wrote a document that they thought would satisfy the federal government and permit the readmission of Texas under President Andrew Johnson's mild Reconstruction program. The Constitution of 1866 nullified secession, abolished slavery, and renounced Confederate war debts. Still, it did not fully satisfy the requirements set down by President Johnson. Texans, however, were correct in assuming that Johnson would accept it. Under its terms, a civilian government was elected and operated for several months, despite some interference from the national Freedmen's Bureau, which had been set up to protect the former slaves.

Johnson's lenient policies were unacceptable to the Republican-controlled U.S. Congress, which took control of Reconstruction in 1867. Under the authority of the Reconstruction Act, the U.S. military purged the civilian-elected authorities and restored military rule. Texas would be under military occupation until the entire Reconstruction process was complete.

The Constitution of 1869 Under congressional Reconstruction, top former Confederates and persons

homestead An owner-occupied property, protected in Texas from forced sale under most circumstances.

community property Property acquired during marriage and owned equally by both spouses.

common law Law based on precedents (previous court rulings). The common law has been in continuous development in English-speaking countries since medieval times.

long ballot A ballot that permits the election of a large number of independent executive and judicial officers. If a chief executive has the power to appoint most executive and judicial officers, the result is a *short ballot.*

who refused to swear an "ironclad oath" of loyalty to the Union were temporarily barred from participation in politics. While those barred made up only about 10 percent of the population, they included almost the entire former leadership of Texas politics and society. The remaining voters, including newly enfranchised African Americans, elected eighty-one whites and nine blacks to the Texas constitutional convention in 1868.

The convention produced a document that centralized state power in the hands of the governor, lengthened the chief executive's term to four years, and allowed the governor to appoint all major state officers, including judges. It provided for annual legislative sessions, weakened local government controlled by traditional elites, and centralized the public school system. The 1868 convention demonstrated little of the fear of centralized government power that was later to become a major characteristic of Texas politics. The proposed constitution was ratified in 1869.

Reconstruction under the Constitution of 1869
The Constitution of 1869 served as the instrument of government for an era that white Texans would regard as the most abusive in the state's history. An enabling act allowed Republican governor E. J. Davis to fill about 8,500 jobs in state government that had been left vacant by enforcement of the ironclad oath. The legislature authorized a state police force that had the authority to operate anywhere in the state, overruling local law enforcement officials.

THE USE OF THE STATE POLICE. The state police were hated by the white majority because blacks made up a sizable portion of the force and because the force was used to put down violent opposition to Reconstruction. In four counties where law and order broke down, Governor Davis declared martial law and sent in the state police to regain state control. Davis also took control of voter registration, intimidated unsupportive newspapers, and arrested several political opponents.

ECONOMIC POLICIES. The economic policies of the Davis administration were also unlike anything that had ever been seen in Texas. Both taxes and spending increased dramatically, in part to fund road building and the public school system. High taxes led to widespread tax evasion, and lavish government spending led to a large state debt. The government also subsidized the construction of railroads in the state. These subsidies, along with other legislation that financially benefited Republican-oriented interests, helped inspire

the widespread view that the Davis administration was the most corrupt in Texas history.

ASSESSMENTS OF DAVIS. For most white Texans, Reconstruction left a bitter memory of a humiliating, corrupt, extravagant, and even tyrannical government. Some recent historians, however, writing in the wake of the modern civil rights movement, have argued that Davis was not personally corrupt and that, during Reconstruction, his activist government attempted to play a positive role in people's lives while protecting the civil and political rights of former slaves. We take an additional look at this argument in the *Join the Debate* feature on the following page.

Whichever historical view is more accurate, it is clear that the period that followed was a conservative white reaction to the policies of the Davis administration. In 1874, Democrat Richard Coke was elected governor in a landslide victory.

The Constitutional Convention of 1875
Most Texans were determined to strip power from state government by writing a new constitution. The Texas Grange, whose members were called Grangers, organized in 1873. Campaigning on a platform of "retrenchment and reform," it managed to elect at least forty of its members to the constitutional convention of 1875. Like most of the ninety delegates, they were Democrats who were determined to strike at the heart of big government. To save money, the convention did not publish a journal, reflecting the frugal tone of the final constitution.

RESTRAINING THE EXECUTIVE BRANCH. The convention cut salaries for governing officials, placed strict limits on property taxes, and restricted state borrowing. It was also miserly with the power it granted government officials. It stripped most of the governor's powers, reduced the term of office from four to two years, and required that the attorney general and state judges be elected rather than appointed by the governor.

CURBING THE LEGISLATURE. Nor did the legislature escape pruning by the convention. Regular legislative sessions were to be held only once every two years, and legislators were encouraged to limit the length of the sessions. Legislative procedure was detailed in the constitution, with severe restrictions placed on the kinds of policies the legislature might enact. In fact, a number of public policies were written into the constitution itself.

Was Reconstruction Truly a Disaster for Texas?

Texas and southern legend has it that Reconstruction (1865–1877) was a time when the victorious North took savage vengeance on the defeated Confederacy. The North, according to legend, raised taxes, ruined the economy, and used armed forces to perpetuate regimes that were radical, unjust, and corrupt. In Texas, the administration of Governor E. J. Davis (1870–1874) was the last chapter in Reconstruction and was followed by the return of those who, in southern tradition, were called "Redeemers." The victory of the Redeemers was symbolized in Texas by the adoption of the Constitution of 1876. Does it really follow, though, that the Reconstruction government was terrible for Texas?

The Davis Regime Was Indeed a Disaster

Traditional Texas historians regard the Davis regime as the most corrupt and abusive in the history of the state. Large gifts of public funds were made to special interests, such as railroads. Tax rates skyrocketed to pay for allegedly wasteful public programs. In spite of high taxes, the government accumulated an ever-growing public debt. Law and order seemed to disappear, and much of the state fell prey to desperadoes. Using the state police and militia to maintain his powerful political machine, Davis was a true tyrant.

Davis's actions provoked a backlash that was led by the Redeemers. Even some modern commentators who oppose the frankly reactionary policies of the Redeemers blame Davis for provoking a backlash. Without the centralizing policies of the Davis administration, Texas might not be saddled today with a constitution that cripples any attempt at progressive government action.

Davis Was Simply Ahead of His Time

Other historians encourage reconsideration of Davis's record. Almost all of the measures he sponsored are now generally accepted public policy. Texas taxpayers pay for education and road building. Taxes today are higher than they ever were under Davis. State subsidies to businesses are now widespread. Racial discrimination is illegal. Nothing that Davis did upset white Texans more than the recruitment of African Americans into the state police. Yet African American law enforcement officers are so commonplace today as to attract no notice at all.

Finally, Davis cannot be blamed for the breakdown in law and order that accompanied Reconstruction. Precisely through the hated state police, Davis took robust and unprecedented action to reestablish the rule of law. The Redeemers, in contrast, suppressed African American political participation by using violent acts that would be called terrorism today.

FOR CRITICAL **ANALYSIS** Do you think that the Davis administration really harmed Texas, and if so how? If the Davis administration had spent less and imposed fewer taxes, would Davis be viewed in such a negative light today? Why or why not?

STRENGTHENING LOCAL GOVERNMENT. Local government was strengthened, and counties were given many of the administrative and judicial functions of the state. Although the Grangers had opposed the idea of public education, they were persuaded to allow it if segregated schools were established by local governments.

RATIFYING THE CONSTITUTION. The convention largely reacted to the perceived abuse of state power by attempting to abolish it. Despite opposition from African Americans, Republicans, most cities, and railroad interests, voters ratified the constitution in 1876, and it remains in effect today.

The events leading up to the Constitution of 1876 were not favorable for developing a constitution that would adapt easily to the pressures and changes in the

century that followed. The decade of the 1870s was an era of fear and reaction. It produced a constitution directed more toward solving the problems arising from Reconstruction than meeting the challenges of generations to follow—it was literally a reactionary document.

FOR CRITICAL THINKING

Would Texas history have been much different if the national government had been more strongly committed to defending the rights of the former slaves? Why or why not?

3-2 The Texas Constitution Today: Rights and Liberties

Many students begin their examination of state constitutions with some kind of ideal or model constitution in mind. In truth, there is no ideal constitution that would serve well in each of the fifty diverse states, nor is it possible to write a state constitution that would permanently meet the changing needs and concerns of citizens.

Further, government is much more than a constitution. Constitutions cannot guarantee good government—honest and effective government must grow out of the political environment fostered by leaders, citizens, parties, and interest groups. Scoundrels will be corrupt and unconcerned citizens will be apathetic under even the best of constitutions.

State constitutions are not unrelated to good government, however. A workable constitution is necessary for effective government, even if it is not sufficient to guarantee it. Low salaries may discourage independent, high-caliber leaders from seeking office. Constitutional restrictions may make it almost impossible for state government to meet the changing needs of its citizens. Institutions may be set up in such a way that they will operate inefficiently and irresponsibly.

★ **LearningOutcome 3–2**

Identify the rights protected by the Texas Bill of Rights and those also protected by the U.S. Constitution, and describe restrictions on Texas voters.

3-2a Fundamental Liberties

Although the Texas Constitution has been the target of much criticism, it contains a bill of rights (Article 1) that is often held in high regard because it reflects basic American political culture and contains provisions that are similar to those found in other state charters and the U.S. Constitution.

The Fourteenth Amendment to the U.S. Constitution provides that no state shall deny any person life, liberty, or property without the due process of law. As the United States Supreme Court has interpreted this amendment, the states must respect most of the provisions of the U.S. Bill of Rights because they are essential to due process. As a result, many individual rights are protected by both the state and federal courts. If state courts fail to protect an individual's rights, that person can also then seek a remedy in the federal courts. Table 3–1 below shows important basic rights protected by both the U.S. and the Texas Constitutions.

TABLE 3–1

Basic Rights in the Texas and U.S. Constitutions

Basic Right	Texas Constitution	U.S. Constitution
Right to religious liberty.	Article 1, Sections 4–7	First and Fourteenth Amendments
Right to freedom of expression.	Article 1, Sections 8 and 27	First and Fourteenth Amendments
Right to keep and bear arms.	Article 1, Section 23	Second and Fourteenth Amendments
Protection against having to quarter troops.	Article 1, Section 25	Third Amendment
Protection against unreasonable search and seizure.	Article 1, Section 9	Fourth and Fourteenth Amendments
Right to grand jury indictment for felonies.	Article 1, Section 10	Fifth Amendment
Right to just compensation for taking property for public use.	Article 1, Section 17	Fifth and Fourteenth Amendments
Right to due process of law.	Article 1, Section 19	Fifth and Fourteenth Amendments
Protection against double jeopardy.	Article 1, Section 14	Fifth and Fourteenth Amendments
Protection against forced self-incrimination.	Article 1, Section 10	Fifth and Fourteenth Amendments
Right to fair trial by jury.	Article 1, Section 10	Sixth and Fourteenth Amendments
Protection against excessive bail or cruel and unusual punishment.	Article 1, Sections 11 and 13	Eighth and Fourteenth Amendments

3–2b The Rights of Texans

State constitutional guarantees are not redundant because the U.S. Constitution establishes only *minimum* standards for the states. Texas's courts have interpreted some state constitutional provisions in ways that broaden basic rights beyond these minimums.

Rights Gained by Judicial Interpretation For example, although the United States Supreme Court refused to interpret the Fourteenth Amendment as guaranteeing equal public school funding,[3] Texas's Supreme Court interpreted the efficiency clause of the Texas Constitution (Article 7, Section 1) as requiring greater equity in public schools.[4]

By using Texas's constitutional and **statutory law** (law passed by the legislature), Texas courts have struck down polygraph tests for public employees, required workers' compensation for farm workers, expanded free speech rights of private employees, and affirmed free speech rights at privately owned shopping malls.

Additional Listed Rights The Texas Bill of Rights guarantees additional rights not specifically mentioned by the U.S. Constitution. Notably, Texas has adopted an amendment to prohibit discrimination based on sex. A similar guarantee was proposed as the Equal Rights Amendment to the U.S. Constitution, but it was not ratified by the states. The Texas Constitution also guarantees victims' rights and access to public beaches.

It forbids imprisonment for debt or committing the mentally ill for an extended period without a jury trial. It also prohibits monopolies and the suspension of the **writ of habeas corpus** under any circumstances. Article 16 protects homesteads and prohibits garnishment of wages, except for court-ordered child support.

Although the state constitution forbids same-sex marriages, the Texas Bill of Rights and other provisions guarantee the average citizen a greater variety of protections than do most other state constitutions. We provide additional discussion of the rights of Texans in Chapter 10.

3–2c The Right to Vote

A major way that state governments determine the character of democracy in America is by setting the requirements for **suffrage** (the right to vote). The administration of elections is also key. Article 6 of the Texas Constitution deals with suffrage requirements. It denies the right to vote to persons under age eighteen, certain convicted felons, and individuals found mentally incompetent by a court of law. (We discuss the development of Texans' suffrage rights in Chapter 4.)

Although constitutional restrictions in Texas on who can vote are now as modest as in any other state, Texas voters still lack opportunities to participate in the initiative, referendum, and recall. In an **initiative,** voters place statutory or constitutional changes on the ballot by petition. A **referendum** results when the legislature places a measure on the ballot for popular approval or disapproval. In a **recall,** citizens petition for a special election to remove an official before his or her term expires. These procedures are available in many states and even in some Texas cities, but not for statewide issues in Texas.

Texas permits voters to decide directly on only three matters: constitutional amendments, the state income tax, and legislative salaries. Texas's political parties sometimes place referenda on their primary ballots, but the results are not legally binding.

FOR CRITICAL THINKING

Consider some of the rights enjoyed by Texans that are not necessarily guaranteed to Americans in general. *Why might the state have established these particular rights?*

3–3 The Texas Constitution Today: Institutions

To prevent the concentration of power in the hands of any single institution, the national government

---

statutory law Law passed by legislatures.

writ of *habeas corpus* A court order requiring that an individual be presented in person and that legal cause be shown for confinement. The writ may result in release from unlawful detention.

suffrage The right to vote.

initiative A citizen-initiated ballot proposal that becomes law if passed. The initiative is permitted in some Texas cities but not at the state level.

referendum A vote on a ballot proposal initiated by the state legislature.

recall A special election to remove an official before the end of his or her term, initiated by citizen petition. Permitted in some Texas cities but not at the state level.

and all state governments have established a **separation of powers** among three branches: the legislative, executive, and judicial. The function of the legislative branch is to make laws. It is by law that governments define crime, establish the basis of civil suits, determine who will pay how much in taxes, and set up government programs and the agencies that administer them. The function of the executive branch is to carry out the law, to arrest criminals, to collect taxes, to provide public services, and to hire government employees and supervise their day-to-day conduct. The function of the judicial branch is to interpret the law as it applies to individuals and institutions.

Despite the separation of powers, there is still the potential for any of the branches to abuse the powers they have been given. Therefore, the Texas Constitution also follows American tradition in setting up a system of **checks and balances.** Table 3–2 below illustrates that, under certain circumstances, one branch of government can be restrained or balanced by another. For example, the veto power that deals with lawmaking (a legislative function) is given to the governor (an executive). The powers of impeachment and conviction, which deal with determining guilt (a judicial function), are given to the legislature. The state senate (a house of the legislature) confirms appointments the governor makes in the executive branch.

Although there is a separation of powers, the checks-and-balances system requires that each branch must have the opportunity to influence the others. The three branches specialize in separate functions, but there is some sharing of powers as well. In Chapters 7 through 9, you will see how extensively these three branches of government interact.

> **"It is possible to read the history of this country** as one long struggle to extend the liberties established in our Constitution to everyone in America."
>
> ~ MOLLY IVINS ~
> AMERICAN NEWSPAPER COLUMNIST
> 1944–2007

⭐ **Learning Outcome 3–3**

Describe separation of powers, checks and balances, the three branches of state government, and the three types of local government in Texas.

---

separation of powers The principle of dividing governmental powers among the legislative, executive, and judicial branches.

checks and balances A principle of American government in which each of the three branches is given powers that enable it to check (restrain or balance) the other branches.

TABLE 3–2

Texas's Constitutional Checks and Balances

Checks on the Legislative Branch	Checks on the Executive Branch	Checks on the Judicial Branch
• The governor may veto bills passed by the legislature, subject to a two-thirds vote to override.	• The Texas House of Representatives may impeach an executive by a majority vote.	• The governor appoints judges to fill vacancies in district and higher courts until the next election.
• The governor may use the line-item veto on appropriations bills.	• Texas's Senate may convict and remove an executive by a two-thirds vote.	• The Texas House may impeach and the Senate may remove state judges.
• The governor may call special legislative sessions and set their agendas.	• The Senate confirms official appointments of the governor by a two-thirds vote.	• The legislature sets judicial salaries.
• The governor may address the legislature and designate emergency legislation to be considered in the first thirty days of the session.	• The legislature creates nonconstitutional executive agencies, assigns them powers, and appropriates their funds.	• The legislature establishes many lower courts by statute.
• The courts may use *judicial review* to declare legislative acts unconstitutional.	• The courts may declare actions of the governor or state agencies unconstitutional or illegal.	• The legislature may pass new laws if it disagrees with court interpretation of existing ones.
		• Two-thirds of the legislature may propose constitutional amendments to overturn court decisions.

3–3a The Legislative Branch

The legislative article (Article 3) is by far the longest in the Texas Constitution. It assigns legislative power to a **bicameral** (two-house) legislative body consisting of the 31-member Texas Senate and the 150-member House of Representatives. Each senator is elected for a four-year term from a single-member district. Senators must be at least twenty-six years old, must be citizens, and must have resided in the state for five years and in the district for one year. A representative serves only two years and must be at least twenty-one years old, a citizen, and a resident of the state for two years and of the district for one year.

Terms Like thirty-four other states, Texas does not limit the number of terms legislators may serve. Voters are left to decide whether to retain experienced incumbents or replace them with fresh legislators.

Salaries The Texas Constitution sets annual salaries at $7,200, unless the Texas Ethics Commission recommends an increase and voters approve it. The Ethics Commission has made no such recommendation but has exercised its power to increase the per diem (daily) allowance while the legislature is in session.

Although New Hampshire pays its legislators only $200, no other populous state sets legislative pay so low as Texas. Note that most large states have full-time legislatures with unlimited annual sessions and yearly salaries over $40,000.

Short and Infrequent Sessions Texas restricts the legislature to **biennial regular sessions** (convened once every two years). Because sessions are also limited to 140 days, important legislation may receive inadequate consideration, and many bills are ignored altogether. Still, the 2011 Texas legislature introduced an incredible 10,889 bills and resolutions and passed 5,974 (55 percent) of them, while spending about $1 billion for every day in session.

Most states provide annual regular legislative sessions, and fourteen states place no limit on their length. Texas is among only five states with biennial legislative sessions. Low salaries and limited sessions make it difficult for the Texas legislature to function as a professional institution and may make members more dependent on interest groups for income and research on public policy. Recent research indicates that more professional legislatures—those with higher salaries, longer sessions, and better staffs—are significantly more responsive to public opinion and enact policies that are more congruent with public preferences.[5]

Special Sessions The governor may convene a **special session** to consider specific legislative matters. These sessions may last no more than thirty days. Except to deal with rare matters of impeachment, Texas's legislature may not call itself into a special session or determine the issues to be decided in such a session. Special sessions are more restricted in Texas than in any other state.

Detailed Constitutional Requirements The Texas Constitution establishes more specific procedural requirements than most other state constitutions. Although the provision is often suspended, the constitution requires that a bill must be read on three separate days unless four-fifths of the legislature sets aside the requirement. The constitution stipulates when bills may be introduced and how they will be reported out of committee, signed, and entered in the journal once enacted. It even specifies how the enacting clause will read.

Although most state constitutions require a balanced budget, Texas's constitutional restriction seems more effective than most. Article 3, Section 49, strictly limits the legislature in authorizing state debt except under rare conditions. The comptroller of public accounts is required to certify that funds are available for each appropriations measure adopted. Although specific constitutional amendments have authorized the sale of bonds for veterans' real estate programs, student loans, parks and water development, and prison construction, Texas's per capita state debt remains among the lowest in the nation.

STATUTE-LIKE DETAILS. Constitutional detail further confines the legislature by establishing policies on topics that in most states would be handled by legislative statute. Much of the length of Article 3 results from its in-depth description of state policies such as the Veterans' Land Program, Texas park and water

bicameral Consisting of two houses or chambers. Refers to a legislative body with two parts, such as a senate and a house of representatives (or state assembly).

biennial regular sessions Regular legislative sessions scheduled by the constitution and held once every two years.

special session A legislative session called by the Texas governor, who also sets its agenda.

development funds, student loans, welfare programs, a grain warehouse self-insurance fund, and the municipal donation of outdated firefighting equipment.

The constitution establishes the design of the great seal of Texas, authorizes the legislature to pass fence laws, and even explains how the state must purchase stationery. Article 16 authorizes the legislature to regulate cattle brands; Article 11 permits the building of seawalls. By including such **statute-like details** in the Texas Constitution, its framers guaranteed that even relatively unimportant decisions that could easily be handled by the legislature can be changed only by constitutional amendment.

DEADWOOD. Events may outstrip detailed constitutional provisions, leaving **deadwood** (inoperable provisions) that voters must constantly approve amendments to remove. For example, Article 9, Section 14, provides for the establishment of county poorhouses. The distrust of the legislature, however much it may have been deserved in 1876, has put a straitjacket on the state's ability to cope with the challenges of the twenty-first century.

3–3b The Executive Branch

Article 4 establishes the executive branch, with the governor as its head. The governor must be a citizen, at least thirty years of age, and a resident of the state for five years immediately preceding his or her election to a four-year term. The constitution no longer limits the governor's salary. According to statute, it is now $150,000.

The Governor's Term of Office Texas does not impose term limits on its chief executive. Many states limit the governor to a maximum of two consecutive terms. In most states, Governor Rick Perry would not have been allowed to run for reelection in 2010. It is precisely his long tenure in office that has allowed Perry to become an extremely powerful governor despite limitations in Texas's constitution and statutes. Governor Perry has been able to put political allies on all state boards, even though members serve six-year overlapping terms. During this same period, he also has been able to put his brand on the judiciary by filling frequent vacancies on the bench resulting from early retirements.

> ### "Texas is a state of mind. Texas is an obsession.
> Above all, Texas is a nation in every sense of the word."
>
> ~ JOHN STEINBECK ~
> AMERICAN AUTHOR
> 1902–1968

The Plural Executive The provisions for gubernatorial terms, qualifications, and salary are somewhat less restrictive in Texas than in most states. Yet the power of the office has severe constitutional restrictions. Although the constitution states that the governor shall be the chief executive, the document, in fact, establishes a **plural executive** by dividing executive powers among a number of independently elected officers—the governor, lieutenant governor, attorney general, comptroller of public accounts, commissioner of the general land office, and three railroad commissioners.

There are also provisions for a state board of education to be either elected or appointed. The constitution stipulates that the governor appoint the secretary of state.

To become effective, Texas's governor must maximize influences within the majority party, access to publicity, appointive powers, the veto, and the power to call special sessions. Otherwise, the governor can become hemmed in by constitutional and statutory restraints.

HIERARCHICAL VERSUS PLURAL EXECUTIVES. Like the national government, Alaska, Hawaii, and Maine have hierarchical executive systems, in which the chief executive appoints important executive officers as subordinates. Most other states have a plural executive system, in which several major executives are independently elected and are not answerable to the governor.

Few states, however, elect as many executive officers as Texas. Seven states have abolished the office of lieutenant governor as an executive elected statewide, and some have made offices as important as the attorney general appointed rather than elected. Rarely are comptrollers or land, educational, or agricultural officers elected as they are in Texas.

statute-like detail Detailed state constitutional policies of narrow scope. Often handled in other states by statutes passed by legislative bodies.

deadwood State constitutional provisions voided by conflicting U.S. constitutional or statutory law. Also, provisions made irrelevant by changing circumstances.

plural executive An executive branch with power divided among several independent officers and a weak chief executive.

CRITICISMS OF THE PLURAL EXECUTIVE SYSTEM.

Critics charge that electing so many executives confuses voters about lines of administrative responsibility and about whom they should hold accountable for problems in state government. Advocates of a hierarchical executive system argue that it allows for streamlining, coordination, and efficiency by a highly visible chief executive's office that the public can easily hold accountable. Advocates of a plural executive, however, believe that a hierarchical system concentrates too much power in the hands of the governor and allows the chief executive to appoint officers that the public should be allowed to elect.

Additional Boards and Agencies

In the tradition of the constitutional plural executive, the legislature by statute has also established an elected commissioner of agriculture and has exercised its option to have the state board of education elected independently of the governor. The result of electing so many state executive officers is a long, confusing ballot. Voters find it difficult to assign responsibility in a system of diffused power.

Most of the remaining agencies that the legislature establishes to administer state programs are headed by appointed multimember boards with substantial independence from the governor.

Powers of the Governor

Generally, the governor appoints only supervisory boards to six-year staggered terms with the approval of two-thirds of the state senate. Each agency's board then appoints its director. In other words, the governor usually does not appoint agency administrators directly—the agencies' boards do. These powers of the governor are referred to as **indirect appointive powers.**

The governor has limited **removal powers** to supplement these indirect appointive powers. The governor may fire his or her own staff and advisors at will, but removing state officers is more difficult. The governor may fire appointed officers only if two-thirds of the Senate agrees that there is just cause for removal. Firing, therefore, is almost as difficult as impeachment and conviction.

Furthermore, the governor may not remove anyone appointed by a preceding governor. The governor's **directive authority** (the power to issue binding orders to executive-branch agencies) is quite restricted, and **budgetary power** (the power to recommend to the legislature how much it should appropriate for various executive agencies) is limited by the competing influence of the Legislative Budget Board.

The Veto Power

Statutes and the constitution alike combine to make the governor a relatively weak executive, but the veto gives the governor effective influence over legislation. Texas's legislature has not mustered the necessary two-thirds vote to override a governor's veto in more than forty years. The Texas legislature often lacks the opportunity to override a veto because major legislation may be adopted during the last days of the session. The Texas Constitution allows the governor ten days to act during the session and twenty days after it adjourns. During the final ten days, the governor may avoid the threat of an override by simply waiting until the legislature adjourns before vetoing the bill.

Texas is among forty-three states that give the governor the **line-item veto**—the power to strike out particular sections of an appropriations bill without vetoing the entire legislation. Several states also allow their governors to item-veto matters other than appropriations, but Texas does not. The governor of Texas lacks both the **reduction veto** (to reduce the dollar amount of appropriations without deleting the clause in question altogether) and the **pocket veto** (the power to kill bills simply by failing to sign them after the end of the session).

3–3c The Courts

Just as the constitution limits the power of the chief executive, Article 5 fragments the court system. Texas

---

indirect appointive powers The authority to appoint supervisory boards but not operational directors for most state agencies.

removal powers The authority to fire appointed officials. The Texas governor has limited removal powers, which extend only to officials the governor has appointed and are subject to the consent of two-thirds of the state senators.

directive authority The power to issue binding orders to executive-branch agencies—severely limited in Texas.

budgetary power The authority to propose a spending plan to the legislative body. A limited power of the Texas governor because of the competing influence of the Legislative Budget Board.

line-item veto Executive authority to strike out sections of a bill and allow the remainder to become law. Limited in Texas to appropriations bills.

reduction veto The power to reduce dollar amounts in an appropriations bill without deleting the clauses in question altogether. Texas's governor does not have this power.

pocket veto The power to kill legislation by failing to sign it following the end of the legislative session. This power is not available to Texas's governor.

is the only state other than Oklahoma that has two courts of final appeal. The highest court for civil matters is the nine-member Texas Supreme Court. The top court for criminal matters is the nine-member Texas Court of Criminal Appeals.

Lower Courts The constitution also creates courts of appeals, as well as district, county, and justice of the peace courts. In doing so, it grants the legislature some flexibility as to number and jurisdiction of these lesser courts. Article 5 also describes the selection of grand and trial juries and such administrative officers as sheriff, county clerk, and county and district attorneys.

The number and variety of courts are confusing to the average citizen, and coordination and supervision among the courts are minimal. State courts have also come under attack because of the lack of qualified judges. The constitution specifies only general qualifications for county judges and justices of the peace, who need not be lawyers. There may have been good reasons for laypeople to serve as judges in a simple, rural setting, but today many Texans regard such judges as an anachronism.

Choosing Judges The manner of selecting judges is another factor in how qualified these judges are. Texas judges are chosen in **partisan elections,** in which they run as Democrats or Republicans.

Trial judges are elected to serve for four years and appeals court judges for six, but judges traditionally leave office before the end of their last term. The governor has the power to fill most vacancies until the next election. This power gives the governor enormous influence over the makeup of the courts because, once in office, judges are usually returned to office without serious challengers in the next election.

A majority of the states do not use partisan elections to select judges but employ other systems such as nonpartisan elections, appointment by the governor, or combined systems. We examine one such method in the *How Texas Compares* feature on the following page.

3–3d Local Government

The Texas Constitution subordinates local governments to the state, but it also decentralizes government power by assigning many state responsibilities to local governments, especially counties. In Articles 9 and 16, the constitution provides a rigid organizational structure for counties. Voters of the entire state were once required to approve amendments to let individual counties abolish unneeded offices such as treasurer, weigher, and surveyor. The constitution now authorizes county voters to abolish certain offices, but there is no provision for county home rule. As it does in state government, the constitution divides and diffuses county powers through a plural executive system.

Municipal Charters

The legislature has the power to set up structures for city governments and offers several standard alternative **general-law charters** to municipalities with a population below five thousand. Cities with populations of more than five thousand may adopt **home-rule charters** that establish any organizational structure or program that does not conflict with state law or the constitution.

Special Districts

Generally, the legislature has the power to provide for the establishment of limited-purpose local governments known as **special districts.** Numerous special districts are also established by the constitution itself, and eliminating any of these requires an amendment. Many districts have been created to perform functions that general-purpose local governments, such as counties and cities, cannot afford to undertake because of constitutional tax and debt limits. Special districts have multiplied because of these constitutional restrictions. As a result, the number of taxing and spending authorities has grown. Except for school districts, these bodies operate largely outside the public's view.

partisan elections Elections in which candidates are nominated by political parties.

general-law charter A document authorizing the establishment of a city with a population below five thousand. The city's structure and organization are prescribed and limited by state law.

home-rule charter A document organizing a municipality with a population greater than five thousand that allows it to use any organizational structure or institute any program that complies with state law.

special district A limited-purpose local government that provides a narrow range of services not provided by general-purpose local governments, such as cities or counties. Examples include municipal utility districts, hospital authorities, and transit authorities.

FOR CRITICAL THINKING

Should Texas limit the number of terms legislators serve? Or would term limits also restrict legislators' experience and therefore make them more vulnerable to the influence of lobbyists?

HOW TEXAS COMPARES

Selecting Judges

Although citizens of most states elect their judges, some critics regard this effort at popular control as undesirable. A judge may become too much the politician and too little the independent magistrate to apply the law uniformly. Several states have attempted to solve these problems by providing for nonpartisan election of judges. Other states give their governors or legislators the power to appoint and reappoint high court judges without direct voter input.

Appointive-Elective Plans

Many states have attempted to combine the advantages of appointment with the benefits of election. In some states, the governor appoints a judge for the first term, after which the judge must run for reelection against candidates who may file for the office.

merit plan A method of selecting judges based on the candidate's qualifications rather than politics. Also known as the *Missouri Plan*.

Different states use some variation of the **merit plan** (also known as the *Missouri Plan*), in which the governor must make an appointment from a list nominated by a judicial qualifying commission for an initial term. Following the initial term, voters decide whether to retain the appointed judge based on his or her record. Figure 3–1 below shows the methods used to select supreme court judges in various states.

FIGURE 3–1

State-by-State
Selection of Supreme Court Judges

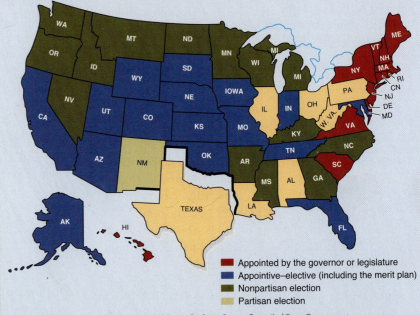

- ■ Appointed by the governor or legislature
- ■ Appointive–elective (including the merit plan)
- ■ Nonpartisan election
- ■ Partisan election

Sources: Bureau of Justice Statistics; National Center for State Courts; Council of State Governments.

FOR CRITICAL ANALYSIS Should Texas consider adopting a merit plan in an effort to focus the judicial selection process on qualifications and reduce the effects of special interest campaign contributions? Or should voters be allowed to elect judges in partisan elections just as they elect other officials?

3–4 Amending and Revising the Texas Constitution

Given the level of detail in the Texas Constitution, it is frequently necessary to amend it to reflect changing realities. The number of amendments that have passed indicates that Texans understand the need to amend the constitution, even though they have steadfastly resisted any attempts to systematically revise it.

3–4a Amendment Procedures

Article 17 of the Texas Constitution provides that the *proposal of constitutional amendments* must be by two-thirds of the total membership of each house of the legislature (at least twenty-one senators and one hundred representatives). **Ratification** of constitutional amendments requires approval by a majority of those persons voting on the amendment in either a general or a special election. Because constitutional amendments must be supported by a super-majority of legislators, many of them are relatively uncontroversial. Historically, voters have approved more than 70 percent of proposed constitutional amendments.

3–4b Criticisms of the Texas Constitution

The Texas Constitution is one of the longest, most detailed, and most frequently amended state constitutions in the nation. With ninety thousand words, it is the second longest constitution after Alabama's. With 474 amendments, it is the fourth-most-amended state constitution because Texans have often responded to emerging challenges by further amending their constitution.

> **LearningOutcome 3–4**
>
> Explain the process of amending and revising the Texas Constitution and the reasons that amendments are frequently necessary.

A Confusing Document Critics argue that the state must resort to the amendment process often because the Texas Constitution is badly written, poorly organized, and confusing. One sentence rambles on for 765 words, and several approach 300 words in length. The content is ambiguous and overlapping. For example, provisions dealing with local government are scattered throughout Articles 3, 5, 8, 9, 11, and 16. This poor draftsmanship has led to a restrictive interpretation of its provisions, public ignorance of its contents, and uncertainty as to its intentions. Although only two state constitutions (along with the U.S. Constitution) contain fewer than ten thousand words, few are as restrictive as the Texas Constitution.

Frequent Elections The continuing need to amend detailed and restrictive state constitutions means that citizens are frequently called on to pass judgment on proposed amendments. Although some of the Texas Constitution's defenders maintain that giving voters the opportunity to express themselves on amendments reaffirms popular control of government, voters display little interest in constitutional amendment elections. Faced with trivial, confusing, or technical amendments, often only 10 to 15 percent of the voting-age population votes on constitutional amendments. Lately, voter turnout has often dropped into the single digits.

3–4c Attempts to Revise the Texas Constitution

Attempts to revise the constitution have met with successive failures. Generally, opponents of change have argued that revision would grant too much power to the state government.

The Proposed Revision of 1972 In 1972, Texas voters amended the constitution to provide for its revision. Under the provisions of that amendment, the legislature established a constitutional revision commission of thirty-seven members appointed by the governor, lieutenant governor, speaker of the house, attorney general, chief justice of the supreme court, and presiding judge of the court of criminal appeals.

The commission made several proposals. Meeting in 1974, the legislature acted as a constitutional convention and agreed to many of these recommendations. The convention was divided over the issue of a right-to-work provision to restrict organized labor, however, and the final document could not muster the two-thirds vote needed to submit the proposal to the electorate.

The Proposed 1975 Amendments In the 1975 regular session, the legislature proposed eight constitutional amendments to the voters. Together, the proposed amendments were substantially the same as proposals the legislature had previously defeated. If they had been adopted, the amendments would have shortened the constitution by 75 percent through reorganization and by eliminating statute-like details and deadwood.

The legislature would have been strengthened by annual sessions, and a salary commission would have set the legislators' salary. Although limited to two terms, the governor would have been designated as the chief planning officer and given removal powers and certain powers of fiscal control. The court system would have been unified and its administrative procedure simplified. Local governments would have operated under broader home-rule provisions, and

> **ratification** The approval of a constitutional amendment by a majority of voters.

Constitutions' Length, Detail, and Their Need for Amendments

As of 2013, the U.S. Constitution had been in effect for 224 years but had been amended only twenty-seven times. It has endured mammoth and fundamental changes in government and society largely because it does not lock government into a rigid framework. Because the U.S. Constitution addresses only the most basic elements of government and leaves much to Congress, the president, and the courts, few formal amendments have been necessary.

Most state constitutions, in contrast, are poorly written and arranged. Some provisions are so badly drafted that they are interpreted to be even more restrictive than the framers intended, and as a result, new amendments must be added to authorize states to perform vital functions in a modern society.

Although the process of amending the Texas Constitution can be as difficult as it is in other states, Texans have amended their constitution 474 times since 1876. This has resulted in the Texas Constitution's having more than three times as many amendments as the average state constitution. Only three state constitutions—those of South Carolina (497), California (525), and Alabama (854)—have more amendments than that of Texas. We compare some major features of the constitutions of Texas, the nation, and the average state in Table 3–3 below.

TABLE 3–3
Constitutions Compared

	Texas Constitution	U.S. Constitution	Fifty-State Average
Length (in words)	90,000	7,575	38,427
Amendments	474	27	147
Age (years)	136	224	111
Frequency of amendments	3.5 per year	1 every eight years	1.3 per year

 **FOR CRITICAL ANALYSIS** Does the frequent need to amend a state's constitution empower the people?

counties would have been authorized to pass general ordinances and to abolish unneeded offices.

Opponents' chief arguments were against more power for the legislature, greater government costs, and the possibility of an income tax—all of which are serious issues for many Texans. Because the legislature had written the proposals, it was easy for the Texas voter to see such things as annual sessions and flexibility concerning salaries as a "grab for power" that would substantially increase government expenditures. Despite an emotional campaign, only 23 percent of registered voters cast ballots in the election, and they overwhelmingly rejected the proposed amendments.

3–4d Why Are State Constitutions So Long?

Although there is considerable variation among state constitutions, most are much longer than the national constitution, and they frequently deal with details of both structure and policy. Consequently, as changing political and social conditions require changes in government structure and policy, formal constitutional amendments are necessary. We compare state and national constitutions and their amendments in the *How Texas Compares* feature above. The details of and the frequent amendments to state constitutions occur for several reasons.

Using Excessive Detail Public officials, interest groups, and voters seem to view their state constitutions as more than the basic law of the state. They fail to make a clear distinction between *what ought to be* and *what ought to be in the constitution.* Thus, all sorts of inappropriate details are included in the documents.

A constitution is fundamental law. It deals with the basic principles of government and is organic law—superior law that establishes governing institutions and organizes their formal power relationship. Accordingly, constitutions ideally should describe how decisions will be made but not actually establish policies, which must change with political and social conditions.

Reversing Court Decisions States have added detailed amendments to overturn the effects of controversial court interpretations of general constitutional provisions. For example, supreme courts in Hawaii, Iowa, Massachusetts, New Jersey, and Vermont found that denying the benefits of marriage to same-sex couples was a violation of state constitutions. As a result, Hawaii added a constitutional amendment to overturn the court decision that had allowed same-sex marriage, and a majority of other states (including Texas) have now added amendments that identify marriage as an exclusively heterosexual right.

Protecting Interest Groups Institutions and interest groups frequently feel safer when their interests are protected in a constitution, which is more difficult to change than ordinary law. This has caused many state constitutions to become long lists of protections for vested interests.

Curbing the Power of the States State governments have a peculiar position in the federal system. They are presumed to have all the powers that have not been explicitly prohibited to them. Thus, citizens who are wary of strong government have felt the need to impose detailed constitutional restrictions on the states.

When state governments misuse their powers, the response from citizens is usually to place additional constitutional limitations and restrictions on those governments. The result is a longer constitution but probably not a more responsible government. A government bound by a rigid constitution cannot respond effectively to changing needs. Excessive restrictions may actually guarantee unresponsive, and hence irresponsible, government.

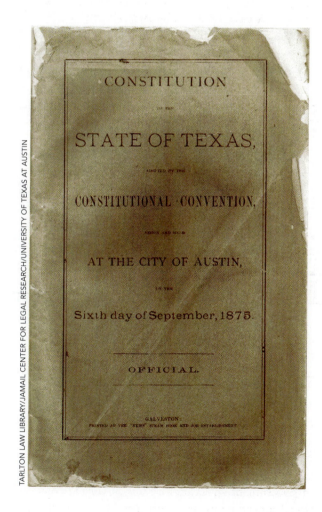

CONSTITUTION

STATE OF TEXAS,

CONSTITUTIONAL CONVENTION,

AT THE CITY OF AUSTIN,

Sixth day of September, 1875.

OFFICIAL.

GALVESTON.

TARLTON LAW LIBRARY/JAMAIL CENTER FOR LEGAL RESEARCH/UNIVERSITY OF TEXAS AT AUSTIN

FOR CRITICAL THINKING *Critics argue that the Texas Constitution should be written in general language, details should be omitted, and day-to-day decisions should be left to the legislature, the governor, and the courts. But would shortening the constitution give too much power to the state government?*

TEXANS IN

CONFLICT The Constitution

Given that the Texas Constitution controls the actions of the state government in such minute detail, understanding the constitution is essential to understanding how the government of Texas functions. All of the many ways in which the state government affects your life—through educational policies, law enforcement, and taxation, for example—are shaped by the constitution of the state. The Texas Constitution, therefore, is more than just a historical artifact. It is one of the forces that shape the character of Texas today. It follows that Texans will be at odds about their constitution. Texans face questions such as the following:

- Did the Reconstruction Era demonstrate the need to limit the power of state government—or did such attitudes simply follow from a desire to limit the rights of African Americans?

- Were Texans right to ban same-sex marriage through a constitutional amendment—or was such a step a violation of human dignity?

- Would Texas be better served by a professional legislature with longer sessions—or does the current system of "citizen legislators" do an effective job of protecting people's freedoms?

- Does electing judges in partisan elections lead to corrupt practices—or are such elections an important way of empowering the Texas voter?

TAKE ACTION

One way of getting active is to connect with groups that support your view of constitutional rights. You can locate these groups by doing an Internet search on their names.

If you consider yourself a conservative, you might be interested in one or more of the following organizations:

- The National Rifle Association, which supports broad rights to keep and bear arms.
- Students for Concealed Carry, which fights to repeal restrictions on campus firearms.
- The Texas Alliance for Life, a pro-life, anti-abortion group.
- The Texas Eagle Forum, which advocates conservative views of personal liberty.
- The Federalist Society, which has similar views.

If you lean in a liberal direction, consider these organizations:

- The Texas Freedom Network, which focuses on religious liberty.
- The Anti-Defamation League, which also supports religious freedom from a Jewish perspective.
- NARAL Pro-Choice America, which supports abortion rights.
- The Brady Campaign, which advocates gun control.
- The Texas Coalition to Abolish the Death Penalty, which opposes capital punishment.

STUDY TOOLS

Ready to study?

- Review what you've read with the quiz below. Check your answers on the Chapter in Review card at the back of the book. For any questions you miss, read the corresponding Learning Outcome section again to prepare for class and your exam.
- Rip out and study the Chapter in Review card.

. . . Or you can go online to CourseMate

at **www.cengagebrain.com** for these additional review materials:

- Practice Quizzes
- Key Term Flashcards or Crossword Puzzles
- Audio Summaries
- Simulations, Animated Learning Modules, and Interactive Timelines
- Videos
- American Government NewsWatch

Quiz

1. Which of the following was NOT a feature of early Texas constitutional culture?
   a. recognition of community property
   b. reliance on common law in the legal system
   c. establishment of Catholicism as the state religion

2. How did the Reconstruction Constitution of 1869 influence the present Texas Constitution (written in 1876)?
   a. It embodied strong principles of white supremacy from the Confederacy.
   b. Its strong centralization of government power led to a backlash in favor of limited government.
   c. Its weakness led to a widespread recognition of the need for a more powerful government.

3. What powerful and reactionary political group was particularly influential in shaping the new constitution at the constitutional convention of 1875?
   a. Grangers
   b. Radical Reconstructionists
   c. Populists

4. Which of the following statements is true of the Texas Bill of Rights?
   a. It is much less protective of civil liberties than the U.S. Constitution is.
   b. It extends greater protection to civil liberties than the U.S. Constitution does.
   c. Unlike the U.S. Constitution, the Texas Constitution has no bill of rights.

5. Which of the following civil liberties or rights is NOT guaranteed by the Texas Constitution?
   a. right to a fair trial by jury
   b. right to vote for those 18 and older
   c. same-sex marriage rights

6. A writ of *habeas corpus* refers to:
   a. a court order requiring that an individual be presented and that legal cause be shown why he or she is confined.
   b. the right to be free from unreasonable searches and seizures.
   c. the right of citizens to vote on a ballot proposal initiated by the state legislature.

7. Which of the following statements about the Texas Constitution of 1876 is FALSE?
   a. It provided for separation of powers.
   b. It provided for a unicameral legislature.
   c. It provided for a plural executive.

8. In what ways does the separation of powers in the Texas government differ from that in the U.S government?
   a. There is a House of Representatives.
   b. There is a Senate.
   c. There are two "supreme courts."

9. What phrase is used to describe the type of executive created by the Texas Constitution, in which executive power is fragmented and the governor shares power with other, separately elected individuals?
   a. hierarchical executive
   b. plural executive
   c. cabinet-form executive

10. Passage of an amendment to the Texas Constitution includes all of the following steps EXCEPT:
    a. the proposed amendment must be approved by a majority of the voters in a statewide election.
    b. the proposed amendment must be signed by the governor.
    c. the proposed amendment must be approved by a two-thirds vote in the Texas House.

11. Compared to the U.S. Constitution, the Texas Constitution is _____ and has _____ amendments.
    a. longer; fewer   b. longer; more   c. shorter; more

12. According to the text and most constitutional scholars, good constitutions should:
    a. be brief and include a basic framework for government rather than specific provisions and policies.
    b. be detailed with a lot of statutory language.
    c. require continual modifications to meet changing needs.

TX.GOV
4

Voting and Elections

★ LearningOutcomes

The **Learning Outcomes** labeled 1 through 5 are designed to help improve your understanding of the chapter. After reading this chapter, you should be able to:

4–1 Explain the participation paradox in electoral politics.

4–2 Describe the leading predictors of whether a person votes, some of the ways that the right to vote has been restricted in Texas, and why voter turnout is low in Texas.

4–3 Discuss the differences among primary, general, and special elections, as well as between open and closed primaries.

4–4 Examine how elections are conducted in Texas.

4–5 Identify factors that provide the greatest advantages to candidates in Texas state elections, and discuss the difficulty of controlling spending in Texas campaigns.

Remember to visit page 91 for additional Study Tools

BOB DAEMMRICH/IMAGE WORKS

TEXANS IN
CONFLICT

Should Texas Require Voter Identification?

A number of states now require citizens to produce some form of photo identification before they are allowed to vote. In 2007, the Texas Senate narrowly rejected a bill that would have required every voter to present official photo identification in addition to her or his voter-registration card. At the time, Texas was following in the footsteps of Florida, Georgia, and Indiana. In 2011, a similar bill was passed into law. At that time, a total of eight states had voter ID laws on their books, adopted in an attempt to reduce alleged voter fraud.

According to the Voting Rights Act of 1965, states with a history of racial discrimination—including

WWW.TXDPS.STATE.TX.US

Texas—have to demonstrate to the U.S. Department of Justice that changes to the voting laws do not harm the voting power of racial or ethnic minorities. According to the Justice Department, Texas has failed to meet that standard. In August 2012, a U.S. appeals court ruled that the new law violated the 1965 act. The law makes it unacceptably difficult to obtain a photo ID, and it is not possible in all cases to obtain such ID free of charge. Requiring a payment to vote violates the Twenty-fourth Amendment to the U.S. Constitution, which bans poll taxes.[1]

Yes, Texas Should Require Voter ID

Supporters of an official photo ID requirement argue that voter fraud is much more likely without such a law. Without a photo ID requirement, ineligible persons (including noncitizens) can go to the polls and pass themselves off as eligible voters. Requiring voters to present official photo identification, such as a driver's license or a passport, reduces the possibility of such fraud.

Public confidence in our democratic system suffers when voter fraud occurs. Texas has investigated one hundred cases of election fraud in the past decade and has secured fifty convictions. A Texas voter ID law has nothing to do with discrimination against anyone—it is race neutral, gender neutral, and just neutral all around.

Such a Law Would Disenfranchise Eligible Voters

Opponents of the photo ID law claim that it is a solution to a problem that does not exist. Of those fifty election fraud convictions, precisely one was for impersonating a voter. So, a voter ID law would not solve a real problem, but it would keep legitimate voters who do not have acceptable photo IDs from voting. In Texas, these voters are found among those with low levels of education and income, minorities, and younger voters. Between 200,000 and 300,000 Hispanic citizens in Texas do not have a driver's license or a state-issued ID. These numbers tell it all—photo ID laws are a new kind of racial discrimination. The law is simply an attempt to disenfranchise voters who tend to vote for Democrats, which is why the "reform" was put through by the Republicans on a party-line vote.

Where do you stand?

1. If you are in favor of photo ID laws, what benefits do you think they provide to society?
2. If you believe that a photo ID law is discriminatory, explain why certain ethnic and minority groups may find it harder to obtain driver's licenses or other state-issued identification cards.

Explore this issue online

- Entering "voter id" into an Internet search engine will bring up a variety of pages on recent controversies about the subject in different parts of the country.
- Search on "voting rights 1965" to learn more about the Voting Rights Act of 1965, including the reasons it was adopted and its consequences.

Introduction

Democracy makes demands on its citizens, in both time and money. A sacrifice of time is required if voters are to inform themselves of the qualifications of the many candidates who compete in the spring for nomination in party primary elections. Then, in the general election in November, roughly 4,200 of these party nominees ask voters to elect them to numerous local, state, and national offices.

4–1 Political Participation

Voting in an election is the most basic and common form of political participation. Many people take part in other ways, such as discussing political issues with friends and co-workers, writing letters to local representatives or to newspaper editors, distributing campaign literature or contributing to a campaign, and placing bumper stickers on cars. Some people are members of interest groups, ranging from neighborhood groups to trade associations. Others serve on political party committees or act as delegates to conventions. Still others participate in demonstrations or sit-ins—for example those sponsored by the Tea Party movement in recent years.

Still, elections are the defining characteristic of a representative democracy. It is through our votes that we hold elected officials accountable. After all, votes are what matter to politicians, at least to those who are interested in winning and holding office. If we vote—and use our votes to reward and punish elected officials for what they do while in office—politicians have an incentive to do what we want. If we do not vote, elected officials are largely free to do what they will.

One problem is that a single individual's vote is rarely decisive because few elections are decided by a single vote. So, why do people vote? Among political scientists, the fact that people continue to vote is known as the **participation paradox**. The point of the paradox is not to suggest that people should not vote, but rather to highlight that

participation paradox
The fact that individuals continue to vote even though their votes rarely influence the result of an election.

they vote for reasons other than the hope of deciding an election outcome.

In one sense, choosing to vote is much like deciding to attend a sporting event. For example, people do not go to a professional baseball game to affect the outcome. They go for other reasons, such as they like the game of baseball or care about a particular team. The same is true for voting. Education, income, age, interest, and party identification are important indicators of a person's desire to participate.

Texas Political SOCIAL MEDIA

If you search on Facebook for "texas young voters," you'll find the page of the League of Young Voters Education Fund–Texas. This group trains and educates young people to participate in the democratic process.

FOR CRITICAL THINKING

Why do voters continue to cast ballots when a single vote is very unlikely to determine the outcome of an election?

4–2 Who Votes?

Over the years, political scientists have learned quite a lot about why people go to the polls. A relatively small number of demographic and political variables are especially important.[2] The most important demographic variables are education, income, and age. The more education a person has, the more likely the person is to vote. The same is true for income, even controlling for education. Age also matters. As people grow older, they are more likely to vote, at least until they become very old.

Why do these factors matter? The answer is straightforward: people who are educated, have high incomes, and are older are more likely to care about and pay attention to politics. Thus, they are more likely to vote.

In addition to demographic factors, certain political variables influence the likelihood of voting. Notably, these factors include a person's level of interest in politics and intensity of identification with political parties. The more interested a person is in politics, the more likely that person is to vote. The effect is

LearningOutcome 4–2

Describe the leading predictors of whether a person votes, some of the ways that the right to vote has been restricted in Texas, and why voter turnout is low in Texas.

fairly obvious but nevertheless quite important. People who do not have much education or income are still likely to vote if they have a strong interest in politics.

Identification with either of the major political parties also makes a person more likely to vote. Strong partisan identifiers, on average, care a lot more about who wins than do people who do not identify with the parties. Political parties also seek to mobilize strong identifiers, who are most likely to be contacted by the party and its candidates during election campaigns.

Of course, other factors can also help to explain electoral participation, but the small set of demographic and political variables just discussed tells us quite a lot. With this information, we can determine the chances of whether a person will or will not vote in a particular election. We also can account for most of the differences in turnout among different groups, such as African Americans, Asian Americans, Latinos, and whites.

4–2a Qualifications for Voting in Texas

The legal qualifications for voting in Texas are surprisingly few and simple. Anyone who is (1) a citizen of the United States, (2) at least eighteen years of age, and (3) a resident of the state is eligible to register and vote in Texas. The only citizens prohibited from voting are those who have been declared "mentally incompetent" in formal court proceedings and those currently serving a sentence for a felony conviction or who are on parole or probation for such an offense.

Residence Requirements Establishing residence for voting is no longer a matter of living at a place for a specified time. Residence is defined primarily in terms of intent—that is, people's homes are where they intend them to be. No delay in qualifying to vote is permitted under United States Supreme Court rulings, except for the short period of time in which the application is processed and the registrant's name is entered on the rolls. In accordance with the Court's ruling, that delay in Texas is fixed at thirty days.

Registering to Vote Meeting these qualifications does not mean that a person can simply walk into the voting booth on Election Day. To vote, a person must be registered. As a result of the Voting Rights Acts of 1965 and 1970, a number of United States Supreme Court rulings, and congressional action, the registration procedure is almost as simple as voting itself. This was not always true, as you will see when you read about legal constraints later in this chapter.

A person may register in person or by mail at any time of the year up to thirty days before an election. Since the passage of federal "motor voter" legislation, a person can also register when obtaining or renewing a driver's license. Indeed, every person renewing a driver's license is asked whether he or she wants to register to vote. The secretary of state makes postage-free registration applications available at any county clerk's office and at various other public offices. Spouses, parents, or offspring also can register the applicant, provided that they are qualified voters.

The present Texas registration system is as open and modern as that of any other state that requires advanced registration. A number of states, including Maine, Minnesota, and Wisconsin, permit Election-Day registration, and North Dakota has no registration at all. There, a person just walks in, shows identification, and votes.[3]

Purging the Voter Rolls Once they register, voters are automatically sent renewals at their address of record by January 1 in even-numbered years, but these renewals cannot be forwarded to new addresses. Thus, voters are permanently registered unless their nonforwardable certificate is returned by mail to the voter registrar.

Names on returned certificates are stricken from the eligible voters list and placed on a strike list. The strike list is attached to the list of voters for each precinct. For three months, previously registered voters whose names are on the strike list can vote in their old precincts if they have filled out a new voter-registration card for their new residence. Note that they can vote only for those offices that both residences have in common. Thus, a person who has moved can vote on at least a part of both the first and the runoff primary ballots. Coroners' reports, lists of felony convictions, and adjudications of mental incompetence are also used to purge the list of eligible voters.

Making It Easier to Vote Once registered, voting in Texas is fairly easy. Consider that in counties with a 5 percent or greater language minority, Texas requires that all ballots and election materials be printed in other languages, in addition to English. Texas also was one of the first states to institute early voting, which allows people to vote at a number of different sites before Election Day. Indeed, many people who are unable to vote on Election Day can vote in advance by mail.

Recent decisions have halted the trend of making voting easier in Texas. Most notably, the voter identification (ID) requirement enacted in 2011 requires voters to show one of five forms of identification when they go to vote: a driver's license, a military ID, a passport, a concealed handgun license, or a voter ID card that the state provides for free. Student photo IDs issued by colleges and universities are not acceptable. If the United States Supreme Court eventually allows the law to go into effect, most observers expect it to dampen turnout, particularly among minorities. We discussed this law in greater detail in the chapter-opening *Texans in Conflict* feature.

4–2b Voter Turnout in the United States and in Texas

Making registration and voting easier was expected to result in increased **voter turnout**—the proportion of eligible Americans who actually vote. In fact, the percentage of U.S. citizens who cast a ballot has remained relatively constant for many years. Some presidential elections attract a higher turnout than others. *Midterm elections*—in which candidates for Congress are on the ballot, but presidential candidates are not—always experience a lower turnout. National turnout did fall somewhat beginning in 1972. In recent years, however, nationwide voter turnout has experienced a modest recovery.

The Consequences of Lowering the Voting Age

The reason for the decrease in voter turnout in the United States after 1972 is straightforward: 1972 was the first election year following the adoption of the Twenty-sixth Amendment to the U.S. Constitution, which lowered the minimum voting age from twenty-one to eighteen.

The amendment was passed at the height of the Vietnam War, with proponents arguing that a person who could be drafted and sent off to war should be able to vote. By extending the vote to younger citizens, the amendment expanded the eligible voting population. As we have already seen, however, young people are less likely to vote than are older persons. Since they were given the right to vote, citizens in the eighteen- to twenty-year-old age group have rarely posted turnout rates as high as 40 percent, even in presidential election years. Thus, adding this age group to the pool of eligible voters in 1972 reduced the overall turnout rate.

Historical Turnout Trends If we go further back in time, variations in voter turnout become more dramatic. Figure 4–1 on the facing page shows voter turnout dating back to 1872 for both the United States and Texas. Turnout is given as a percentage of the **voting-age population (VAP),** those residents eighteen and older, regardless of citizenship or felony status. The graph line for the United States indicates the turnout drop from 1972 on, which we just discussed. A temporary dip in the 1940s was caused by World War II and its aftermath.

THE TURNOUT CONSEQUENCES OF WOMEN'S SUFFRAGE. A drop in national voting rates in 1920 resulted from a cause similar to the one experienced in 1972. In 1920, women received the right to vote nationwide as a result of the Nineteenth Amendment to the U.S. Constitution. For many years after 1920, women were much less likely to vote than men, and so expanding the electorate had the effect of reducing turnout by the voting-age population.

THE TEXAS EXPERIENCE. The line representing Texas turnout swings more dramatically than the national one. In the 1880s, turnout rose as former confederates regained the right to vote. Texas turnout reached an all-time high in 1896, at the height of the Populist movement. Thereafter, concerted efforts by the Texas establishment to keep African Americans—and low-income whites—from voting seriously depressed the turnout figures. In December 1902, Texas instituted a poll tax, which required voters to pay for the privilege of casting their ballot. With the poll tax in place, voter turnout dropped to the low 30 percent range. Following the enfranchisement of Texas women in 1920, turnout hit its all-time low of 20 percent.

Turnout in Texas finally began to recover following World War II. The poll tax was revoked for national elections in 1964, and for Texas state elections in 1966. The Voting Rights Act of 1965 also made it much easier for African Americans to vote across the South. Somewhat surprisingly, these developments had little effect on voter turnout in Texas.

voter turnout The percentage of those eligible to vote who actually vote.

voting-age population (VAP) The total number of resident persons who are eighteen years of age or older, regardless of citizenship or felony status.

FIGURE 4-1

The graph shows voter turnout as a percentage of the voting-age population (VAP), except for the years 1924 to 1956 in Texas when the percentages reflect the vote-eligible population (VEP).

Sources: U.S. Bureau of the Census; *Texas Almanac.*

Voter Turnout in
Presidential Election Years, United States and Texas

Even the enfranchisement of eighteen- to twenty-year-olds in 1972 fails to show up in the Texas figures.

VAP versus VEP The voting-age population is actually an imperfect tool for measuring voter turnout. A more accurate way to measure turnout is to give it as a percentage of the **vote-eligible population (VEP),** that is, those persons who actually have the right to vote. From the 1930s until the 1970s, the voting-age population was a reasonable proxy for the vote-eligible population. Thereafter, the two figures began to diverge, growing further apart with every passing year. To understand why, consider what VEP represents. VEP does not include noncitizens, who cannot vote. It does not include felons who have temporarily lost the right to vote. It does, however, include soldiers and other Americans currently located overseas, because such persons have a right to cast absentee ballots.

Nationally, the number of Americans abroad approximately matches the number of felons ineligible to vote. The real difference between VAP and VEP results from new immigrants, both legal and illegal. The number of such persons in the United States has grown considerably since the 1970s. It has grown even faster in Texas. Figure 4–2 on the following page shows voter turnout in the United States and Texas as a percentage of the vote-eligible population since 1980. Unlike Figure 4–1, this chart shows both midterm and presidential elections. You can see that midterm turnout is reliably lower than in presidential years. Also,

national turnout appears to be rising slightly, more so than in Texas.[4]

International Comparisons Turnout in American general elections is significantly lower than that in most other democracies around the world. Table 4–1 on the following page shows turnout in recent elections for the world's wealthiest democracies. (Elections in some nations are distinctly imperfect, so we have removed the least-democratic nations from the list.) Turnout in the United States is much lower than in other industrialized nations, such as France, Germany, and Japan. Turnout, however, is also low in other English-speaking nations, such as Canada and the United Kingdom (Britain). These countries have some cultural similarities to the United States. (High-ranking Australia is also English speaking, but voting is required by law in that country.)

Low voter turnout in the United States appears to have institutional causes. One cause is the two-party system—a large number of political parties appears to improve turnout. Another is the fact that we require voters to register. In many nations, citizens are automatically registered to vote when they meet age requirements.[5]

> **vote-eligible population (VEP)**
> The total number of persons who are eligible to vote. Excludes noncitizens and felons whose eligibility to vote has not yet been restored. Includes citizens living abroad who can cast absentee ballots.

FIGURE 4-2

Voter Turnout
in the United States and Texas since 1980

The graph shows voter turnout as a percentage of the vote-eligible population (VEP).

Source: United States Elections Project, George Mason University.

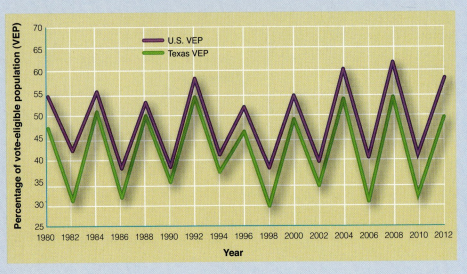

TABLE 4–1
Voter Turnout around the World

This list excludes nations that do not have free elections, based on ratings from Freedom House, an international organization.

Nations with GDP Greater than $750 Billion	Voter Turnout (most recent election)
Turkey*	86.5%
Australia*	81.0%
Brazil*	80.6%
Italy	79.1%
Indonesia	74.8%
France	71.2%
Netherlands	71.1%
Japan	69.3%
Germany	64.6%
Mexico	64.6%
Korea, South	64.2%
Spain	63.3%
United Kingdom (Britain)	61.1%
United States	57.9%
India	56.5%
Canada	53.8%

*In these countries, those who do not vote are required to pay a fine.
Source: International Institute for Democracy and Electoral Assistance.

4–2c Low Voter Turnout in Texas

Not only is turnout in the United States low by international standards, Figure 4–1 on page 69 and Figure 4–2 above show that it is lower still in Texas. Turnout in most of the South also has remained fairly stable at levels well below the national average. In the presidential elections of 2012, for example, Texas VEP voter turnout was 49.6 percent, or 8.3 percentage points below the nation as a whole.

Many Texans think that Texas is in the mainstream of American society. Why, then, is there such a difference in political behavior between Texas and other urbanized and industrialized states? Why does Texas more closely resemble the states of the Deep South in voter turnout? The answer may lie in the state's laws, socioeconomic characteristics, political structure, and political culture.

Legal Constraints Traditionally, scholars interested in the variation in turnout across the American states have focused on laws regulating registration and voting. Clearly, the most important of these laws restricted who may vote. They include the poll tax, property ownership requirements, and the outright exclusion of African Americans and women.

Although these restrictions disappeared some time ago, other barriers to registration and voting persisted, and some remain in effect today.[6] Does a state promote political participation by setting the minimum necessary limitations and making it as convenient as possible for the citizen to vote? Or does a state repeatedly place barriers on the way to the polls, making the act of voting physically, financially, and psychologically as difficult as the local sense of propriety will allow? There is no doubt into which category Texas once fell—the application has been uneven, but historically Texas was among the most restrictive states in its voting laws.

Nearly all of these restrictions, however, have been changed by amendments to the U.S. Constitution, state and national laws, rulings by the U.S. Department of Justice, and judicial decisions. Even a cursory examination of these restrictions and the conditions under which they were removed makes one appreciate the extent to which Texas's elections were at one time closed. Consider the following changes in Texas voting policies.

- *The Poll Tax* The payment of a poll tax as a prerequisite for voting was adopted in 1902. The cost was $1.75 ($1.50 plus an optional $0.25 for the county) and represented more than a typical day's wages for some time. As a result, many poor Texans were kept from voting. When the Twenty-fourth Amendment was ratified in 1964, it voided the poll tax in national elections. Texas was one of only two states to keep the tax for state elections until it was held unconstitutional in 1966.[7]
- *Women's Suffrage* An attempt was made to extend suffrage to women in 1917, but the effort failed by four votes in the Texas legislature. Women were allowed to vote in the primaries of 1918, but not until ratification of the Nineteenth Amendment in 1920 did full suffrage come to women in Texas.
- *The White Primary* African Americans were barred from participating when the first Democratic Party primary was held in 1906. When movement toward increased participation seemed likely, Texas made several legal changes to avoid United States Supreme Court rulings allowing African Americans to vote. Not until 1944 were the legislature's efforts to deny African Americans access to the Democratic primaries finally overturned.[8]
- *The Military Vote* Until 1931, members of the National Guard were not permitted to vote. Members of the military began to enjoy the full rights of suffrage in Texas in 1965, when the United States Supreme Court voided the Texas constitutional exclusion.[9]
- *Long Residence Requirements* The Texas residence requirement of one year in the state and six months in the county was modified slightly by the legislature to allow new residents to vote in the presidential part of the ballot. Not until a 1972 ruling of the United States Supreme Court, however, were such requirements abolished altogether.[10]
- *Property Ownership* Texas required voters in bond elections to be property owners until the United States Supreme Court made property ownership unnecessary for revenue bond elections in 1969 and for tax elections in 1969 and in 1975.[11]
- *Annual Registration* Even after the poll tax was abolished, Texas continued to require voters to register every year until annual registration was prohibited by the federal courts in 1971.[12]
- *Early Registration* Texas voters were required to meet registration requirements by January 31, earlier than the cutoff date for candidates' filings and more than nine months before the general election. This restriction was voided in 1971.[13]
- *Jury Duty* Texas law provided that the names of prospective jurors must be drawn from the voting rolls. Some Texans did not like to serve on juries, and not registering to vote ensured that they would not receive a jury summons. Counties now use driver's licenses for jury lists.

Texas used almost every technique available except the literacy test and the grandfather clause to deny the right to vote or to make it expensive in terms of time, money, and aggravation.[14] These restrictions are not in place today. Most legal barriers to voting in Texas have been removed. As mentioned previously, the Texas legislature has taken a number of steps to make voting easier than in many other states. Thus, examining Texas laws may help us understand why turnout was low in the past. The current laws do not help us understand why turnout in Texas remains low today. For this, we need to look elsewhere.

Socioeconomic Factors Texas is known as the land of the "big rich"—cattle barons and oil tycoons. What is not so well known is that Texas is also the land of the "big poor" and that more than 4 million persons—more than in any other state—live in poverty here. Although nationally the proportion of people living below the poverty level in 2008 was 13.2 percent, in Texas the proportion was 15.8 percent. Almost 25 percent of African American and Latino Texans have incomes below the poverty level.

Of the more than 4 million individuals in Texas living in poverty, more than one-third are children. Understandably, formal educational achievement is also low. Of Texans older than twenty-five years of age, one in four has not graduated from high school. Among African Americans, the ratio is about one in three, and among Latinos, it is almost one in two.[15]

Given that income and education are such important determinants of electoral participation, low voter turnout is exactly what we should expect in Texas. Because income and education levels are particularly low for African Americans and, especially, Latinos, voter turnout is particularly low for these groups. Voting by Texas minorities is on the rise, however, and this has led to much greater representation of both groups in elected offices. These trends should continue as income and education levels among minorities improve.

Political Structures Another deterrent to voting in Texas is the length of the ballot and the number of elections. Texas uses a *long ballot* that provides for the popular election of numerous public officers (whom some people believe should be appointed). In an urban county, the ballot may call for the voter to choose from as many as two hundred candidates vying for fifty or more offices. The frequency of votes on constitutional amendments contributes to the length of the ballot in Texas.

Voters are also asked to go to the polls for various municipal, school board, bond, and special district elections. Government is far more fragmented in Texas than in other states, and this makes any single election less meaningful and perhaps more frustrating for voters.

Political Culture Rates of voter participation may vary due to political culture. As defined in Chapter 1, political culture is the set of political values and beliefs that are dominant in a society. Borrowed from social anthropologists, the concept has been useful in describing all political systems, from those of developing countries to modern industrial democracies. It has been especially useful in the study of American politics, where federalism has emphasized the diversity among regions, states, and communities.

THE THREE SUBCULTURES. As discussed in Chapter 1, the American political culture is actually a mix of three subcultures, each prevalent in at least one area of the United States.[16] The *moralistic subculture* is a product of the Puritan era and is strongest in New England.

> ## "Good thing we've still got politics in Texas—finest
> form of free entertainment ever invented."
>
> ~ MOLLY IVINS ~
> POLITICAL COMMENTATOR
> 1944–2007

The *traditionalistic subculture* derives from the plantation society of the Deep South. The *individualistic subculture* was born in the commercial centers of the Middle Atlantic states and moved west and south along the Ohio River and its tributaries. The varying mixtures of these cultures give American politics its flavor.

THE IMPACT ON TURNOUT. Students of electoral politics should note that "the degree of political participation (i.e., voter turnout and suffrage regulations) is the most consistent indicator of political culture."[17] The moralistic subculture holds that people not only have the right to discuss public issues and vote, but that such activities are also beneficial to citizens and society alike.

In contrast, the traditionalistic subculture views politics as the special preserve of the social and economic elite, and as a process of maintaining the existing order. Political participation is seen as a personal privilege. Social pressure as well as restrictive election laws may be used to limit voting.

The individualistic subculture blurs the distinction between economic and political life. Business and politics are both appropriate avenues by which an individual can advance his or her interests. As a result, conflicts of interest are fairly common and not seen as a serious problem. In this subculture, business interests can play strong role, and running for office is difficult without business support.

In Texas, low voter turnout may be due in part to its mix of the traditionalistic and the individualistic political subcultures. As a result, participation in politics is not as highly regarded as it is in other states, particularly those with a moralistic culture, and politics in Texas is largely the domain of business interests. People may be less likely to vote in Texas because they do not value political participation itself and because they tend to think that they play only a small role in politics.

FOR CRITICAL THINKING

Why does Texas have some of the lowest voter turnout statistics in the nation? Should Texas adopt additional reforms to make voting easier?

4–3 Primary, General, and Special Elections in Texas

Winning office is typically a two-stage process. First, a candidate must win the Democratic or Republican Party nomination in a primary election. Second, the candidate must win in the general election, running against the other party's nominee. It is possible for a candidate to get on the general-election ballot without winning a primary election (as will be discussed shortly), but this is rare. As in most other states, elections in Texas are dominated by the Republican and Democratic parties.

4–3a Primary Elections

Three successive methods for selecting political party nominees have been used in American history: the caucus, the party convention, and the direct primary. Each was perceived as a cure for the ills of a previously corrupt, inefficient, or inadequate system. The first, established in 1800, was the *caucus*, which consisted of those members of a particular political party serving in the legislature. (The caucus system of the early nineteenth century should not be confused with the modern-day caucuses used to elect delegates to party conventions.)

> ⭐ **Learning Outcome 4–3**
>
> Discuss the differences among primary, general, and special elections, as well as between open and closed primaries.

Party Conventions The "insider" politics of the caucus room motivated the reformers of the Jacksonian era to throw out "King Caucus" and to institute the *party convention* system by 1832. In this system, local party organizations select delegates to a party convention, and these delegates then nominate the party's candidates for office and write a party platform. The convention system was hailed as a surefire method of ending party nominations by the legislative bosses. Legislative bosses, however, were replaced by local bosses and municipal "machines."

The Direct Primary By 1890, the backroom politics of the convention halls again moved reformers to action, and the result was the **direct primary,** adopted by many states between 1890 and 1920. Texas's first direct primary was held in 1906, under the Terrell Election Law passed in 1903. It enables party members to participate directly in their party's selection of a candidate to represent them in the general election.

The White Primary Traditionally regarded as private activities, primaries were at one time largely beyond the concern of legislatures and courts. Costs of party activities, including primaries, were covered by donations and by assessing each candidate who sought a party's nomination. Judges attempted to avoid suits between warring factions of the parties as much as they did those involving church squabbles over the division of church property. This was the background to a 1935 decision by the United States Supreme Court. The Court upheld the right of the Texas Democratic Party to bar African Americans from participating in the party primary.[18]

Political party activities were increasingly circumscribed by law, however. The Court reversed itself in 1944 and recognized the primary as an integral part of the election process. African Americans could no longer be banned from participation in party primaries.[19]

In a one-party state, which Texas was at the time, the party primary may be the only election in which meaningful choice is possible. Because the Democratic Party seldom had any real opposition in the general election, winning the nomination was, for all practical purposes, winning the office. The party balance in Texas has changed quite a lot in recent years, however. The Republicans have overtaken the Democrats and now hold every statewide elected office.

Who Must Hold a Primary? In Texas, any party receiving 20 percent of the gubernatorial vote must hold a primary, and all other parties must use the convention system.[20] New parties must meet additional requirements if their nominees are to be on the general-election ballot. In addition to holding a convention, these parties must file with the secretary of state a list of supporters equal in number to 1 percent of the total vote for governor in the last general election. The list may consist of the names of those who participated in the party's convention, those signing a nominating petition, or a combination of the two. Persons named as supporters must be registered voters who have not participated in the activities (primaries or conventions) of either of the two major parties.

Each page (although not each name) on the

> **direct primary** An election in which voters directly select the nominees from a political party who will run in the general election. The primary is "direct" because voters vote directly for candidates, and not for delegates who later choose the nominee.

nominating petition must be notarized. Such a requirement is, as intended, difficult to meet and therefore inhibits the creation of new political parties.[21]

Financing Primaries Party primaries are funded partly by modest candidate filing fees, but most of the primaries' costs come from the state treasury. The parties' state and county executive committees initially make the expenditures, but the secretary of state reimburses each committee for the difference between the filing fees collected and the actual cost of the primary. To get on the party primary ballot, a candidate needs only to file an application with the state or county party chair and pay the prescribed fee. The categories of fees, applicable also for special elections, are summarized in Table 4–2 at the right.

So that no person is forced to bear an unreasonable expense when running for political office, the legislature (prodded by the federal courts) provided an alternative to the filing fee. The alternative for candidates seeking nomination to statewide office is a petition bearing the names of five thousand voters. For district and lesser offices, the petition must bear the signatures of a number of voters equal to 2 percent of the vote for the party's candidate for governor in the last election, up to a maximum of five hundred required signatures.

The Majority Rule In Texas, as in other southern states (except for Tennessee and Virginia) that were once predominantly Democratic, nominations are by an absolute majority (50 percent plus 1) of the popular vote. If no candidate receives a majority of votes cast for a particular office in the first primary, a **runoff primary** is required in which the two candidates receiving the greatest number of votes run against each other. Beyond the southern states, where the balance between the two major parties has traditionally been more equal, only a plurality of the votes (more votes than for anyone else) is typically required, so no runoff is necessary.

Scheduling Primaries Primary elections in Texas are held on the first Tuesday in March of even-numbered years. The runoff primary is scheduled for the fourth Tuesday in May, or more than two months after the initial party primary election. Although there are earlier presidential primaries, no other state schedules primaries to nominate candidates for state offices so far in advance of the general election in November.

Primary Turnout Voter turnout in Texas primaries is much lower than in general elections. Consider 2010, for example. Despite competitive contests for governor in 2010, particularly in the Republican primary, only 2.1 million Texans voted, approximately 12 percent of the 18 million people who were eighteen years of age or older. The people who do vote in primary elections are hardly representative of the population—they tend to be better educated, more affluent, and more ideologically committed.

Open and Closed Primaries Party primaries are defined as either *open* or *closed*. These terms refer to whether or not participation is limited to party members.

THE OPEN PRIMARY. Because the purpose of a primary is to choose the party's nominee, it may seem logical to exclude anyone who is not a party member. Not every state accepts that argument, however. Texas and fifteen other states have an **open primary,** in which voters decide at the polls (on Election Day) in which primary they will participate. Voters may not cast a ballot in more than one primary on Election Day, and once a voter has voted in the first primary, that voter cannot switch parties and participate in the runoff election or convention of any other party.

TABLE 4–2

Fees for Listing on the Party Primary Ballot in Texas, Selected Offices

Office	Fee
U.S. Senator	$5,000
U.S. Representative	$3,125
Texas Statewide Officer	$3,750
State Senator	$1,250
State Representative	$750
County Commissioner	$750–$1,250
District Judge	$1,500–$2,500
Justice of the Peace, Constable	$375–$1,000
County Surveyor	$75

runoff primary A second primary election that pits the two top vote-getters from the first primary against each other when the winner in the first primary did not receive a majority. The runoff primary is used in states such as Texas that have a majority election rule in party primaries.

open primary A type of primary in which a voter can choose on Election Day in which party's primary the voter will participate.

THE CLOSED PRIMARY. In contrast, the typical **closed primary** requires that a person specify a party preference when registering to vote. The party's name may then be stamped on the registration card at the time of issuance. Each voter may change a party affiliation at any time up to a set deadline before participating in a primary or a convention. Voters are limited, however, to the activities of the party they have formally declared as their preference. If an individual registers as an independent (no party preference), that person is excluded from the primaries and conventions of *all* parties. Twenty states have closed primaries.

MIXED PRIMARY. Some states have a *semiclosed* (or *semiopen*) system, in which independents are allowed to vote in either primary. Five other states have a mixed system, in which one party has an open (or semiopen) and the other a closed (or semiclosed) primary. Another three states use a *top-two primary,* in which candidates from different parties compete in a single primary and the top two vote-getters proceed to the general election.

Primary elections clearly differ considerably from state to state, but those differences have little bearing on the general election. Whether voters participate in a party primary or not, they are completely free to vote for any party candidate—Democrat, Republican, or the candidate of another party—in the general election in November.

Crossover Voting

The opportunity always exists in Texas for members of one political party to invade the other party's primary. This is called **crossover voting.** Often, such voting is meant to increase the chances that the nominee from the other party will be someone whose philosophy is like that of the invader's own party.

For example, Democrats might cross over to vote for the more moderate candidate in the Republican primary, or Republicans might cross over into the Democratic primary to support the candidate who is least objectionable from their viewpoint. An alternative goal might be sabotage—to help nominate a candidate with little chance of prevailing in the general election.

4–3b General Elections

The purpose of party primaries is to nominate the party's candidates. General elections, in contrast, allow voters to choose from among competing party nominees and write-in candidates.

General elections differ from primaries in at least two important ways. First, general elections are the official public elections to determine the individuals who will actually serve in national, state, and county offices. Therefore, they are administered completely by public (as opposed to party) officials of state and county governments. Second, unlike Texas's primaries, in which an absolute majority of the vote is required, the general election is decided by a **plurality vote,** whereby the winning candidate needs to receive only the largest number of the votes cast for all the candidates for that office.

The Timing of General Elections

General elections in Texas are held every other year on the same day as national elections—the first Tuesday after the first Monday in November of even-numbered years. In years divisible by four, we elect the president, vice president, all U.S. representatives, and one-third of the U.S. senators. In Texas, all 150 members of the state house are elected during these years and roughly half (15 or 16) of the 31 senators. A number of board and court positions at the state level, as well as about half of the county positions, are also filled.

Most major state executive positions, however (governor, lieutenant governor, attorney general, and so forth), are not filled until the midterm national election, when the U.S. representatives and one-third of U.S. senators (but not the president) again face the voters. All state representatives and half of the senators are also elected in these years. Some board members, judges, and county officers are elected as well.

The Relationship between State and National Elections

Holding simultaneous national and state elections has important political ramifications. During the administration of Andrew Jackson, parties first began to tie the state and national governments together politically. A strong presidential candidate and an effective candidate for state office can benefit significantly by cooperating and campaigning under the party label. This usually works best, of course, if the candidates are in substantial agreement with each other in political philosophy and on the issues.

In Texas, which is more politically conservative than the average American state,

---

closed primary A type of primary in which a voter can participate only by voting for candidates of the party of which the voter is a member.

crossover voting Voting by members of one political party in the other party's primary to influence the result.

plurality vote An election rule that the candidate with the most votes wins, regardless of whether that candidate has an absolute majority.

fundamental agreement between the national and state parties has often been lacking. This has been especially true for the Democratic Party. Popular Democrats in the state often disassociate themselves from the more liberal presidential nominees of the party. As a Democratic candidate for governor in 2010, Bill White played down his connections to the presidential candidates of his party, including Bill Clinton and Barack Obama.

Midterm State Elections

When the Texas Constitution was amended in 1972 to extend the terms of the governor and other major administrative officials from two years to four years, elections to fill these offices were set for midterm election years. This change had two main effects.

INSULATION BETWEEN STATE AND NATIONAL RACES. First, separation of the presidential and state executive campaigns insulates state candidates from the ebb and flow of presidential politics and allows them to disassociate themselves from the national political parties. Elections for statewide office now largely reflect Texas issues and interests.

REDUCED TURNOUT. Second, the separation reduces turnout in statewide elections and makes the outcomes more predictable. As discussed earlier, turnout in midterm elections is much lower than in presidential election years, when many people are drawn to the polls by the importance of the presidency and the visibility of presidential campaigns. Independent and marginal voters are more likely to participate, and election results for congressional and state-level offices are less predictable. In midterm election years, however, the less-informed and the less-predictable voters are more likely to stay home, and the contest is largely confined to political party regulars. Most incumbent state politicians prefer to cast their lot with this more limited and predictable midterm electorate.

There is a partisan dimension to this preference. Currently, statewide incumbents are Republican. Lower turnout in the midterm elections tends to favor candidates of that party, because the demographic groups that vote Republican are more likely to vote.

4–3c Special Elections

As the name implies, special elections are designed to meet special or emergency needs, such as ratifying constitutional amendments or filling vacant offices. Special elections are held to fill vacancies only in legislative bodies that have general (rather than limited) lawmaking power. Typical legislative bodies with general power are the U.S. Senate and U.S. House of Representatives, state legislatures, and city councils in home-rule cities. (All other vacancies, including judgeships and county commissioners, are filled by appointment.) Runoffs are held when necessary. Special elections provide for the filling of a vacancy only until the end of the regular term or until the next general election, whichever comes first.

Nonpartisan Special Elections

Because special elections are not partisan, the process of getting on the ballot is relatively easy and does not involve a primary.[22] All that is required is the filing of the application form in a timely and appropriate manner and the payment of the designated filing fee. Unlike general elections, the winner of a special election must receive a majority of the votes. Thus, a runoff special election may be necessary when no candidate wins outright the first time around.

The runoff requirements have been enacted in piecemeal fashion, illustrating how public policy is often enacted for political advantage. Those in control of the legislature can and do change the rules of the game to benefit those who share their political views.

The Example of Senator Yarborough

Before 1957, all special elections required only a plurality vote. During a special election in 1957 to fill a vacant U.S. Senate seat, a liberal candidate, Ralph Yarborough, appeared likely to win. The Texas House (then controlled by conservative Democrats) quickly passed a bill requiring a runoff in any election to fill a vacated U.S. Senate seat.

A few liberal legislators were able to delay the bill in the Texas Senate until after the election, in which Yarborough led the field of twenty-three candidates. Because he received only 38 percent of the popular vote, it is possible that Yarborough would have lost in a runoff. Sixteen days later, the senate passed the bill, and it was signed into law by the governor—too late to affect Yarborough's election. Once in office, Senator Yarborough was able to capitalize on his incumbency and served for thirteen years.

FOR CRITICAL THINKING

How much do filing fees limit candidates' access to the Texas ballot? Should election laws attempt to discourage frivolous candidates?

4–4 The Administration of Elections

Texas's secretary of state is the state's chief elections officer, and he or she therefore interprets legislation and issues guidelines. The secretary of state has the responsibility of disbursing funds to the state and county executive committees to pay for primary elections and is the keeper of election records, both party and governmental. The secretary of state also receives certificates of nomination from parties that have conducted primaries and conventions and uses these certificates to prepare the ballot for statewide offices. Along with the governor and a gubernatorial appointee, the secretary of state sits on the three-member board that canvasses election returns for state and district offices.

Esperana "Hope" Andrade was appointed by Governor Perry as Texas Secretary of State in 2008.

AP PHOTO/HARRY CABLUCK

4–4a County-Level Administration

Except for the preparation of the statewide portion of the ballot, county-level officials actually conduct general elections.

The Traditional System Counties may choose from three options for the administration of general elections. The first option is to maintain the decentralized system that the counties have used for decades. Under this system, the major portion of responsibility rests with the county clerk. By the time the clerk receives the state portion of the ballot from the secretary of state, he or she will have constructed the county- and precinct-level portion after having already received applications and certifying the candidates' names. The board of elections, consisting of the county judge, sheriff, clerk, and chair of the two major party executive committees, arranges for polling places and for printing ballots.

The county tax assessor–collector processes all voter applications and updates the voting rolls. The county commissioners' court draws precinct voting lines, appoints election judges, selects voting devices, canvasses votes, and authorizes payment of all election expenses from the county treasury.

Alternative County Options The two other options available are designed to promote efficiency.

One option is for the county commissioners' court to transfer the voter-registration function from the tax assessor–collector's office to that of the county clerk, thus removing the assessor-collector from the electoral process.

The other option represents more extensive reform. It calls for all election-related duties of both the assessor-collector and the county clerk to be transferred to a county election administrator. This officer is appointed for a term of two years by the County Election Commission. In counties that choose this option, the election commission replaces the board of elections. (The membership of the commission is the same as that of the board, except that the county clerk serves instead of the sheriff.)

4–4b Ballot Construction

Like so many other features of an election system, ballot construction reflects both practical and political considerations. Two basic types of general-election ballots are available—the party-column ballot and the office-block ballot.

The Party-Column Ballot The names of all the candidates of each party are listed in parallel columns on the **party-column ballot.** This type of ballot traditionally has been used

party-column ballot
A type of ballot used in a general election on which all of the candidates from each party are listed in parallel columns.

A typical paper ballot in Texas.

in Texas. It itemizes the offices as prescribed by law in descending order of importance, and the candidates are listed in each row. Beside each name is a box (on paper ballots) or a lever (on voting machines) that the voter must mark or pull if the voter wishes to vote a split ticket. At the top of each column is the party's name and a box or lever. To vote a straight-party ticket, the voter need only mark the box or pull the lever for the party of his or her choice.

The Office-Block Ballot The names of the candidates are listed in rows beneath each office on the **office-block ballot** (see Figure 4–3 on the facing page). To vote a straight-party ticket, the voter must pick that party's candidates in each of the columns. A majority of the states now use the office-block ballot, also called the *Massachusetts ballot* because it originated in that state. Minor parties in Texas and independent voters advocate the use of this type of ballot because it makes straight-ticket voting for the major parties more difficult.

The Politics of Ballot Construction Understandably, supporters of the major Texas political parties strongly favor the use of the party-column ballot. It enables lesser-known candidates to ride on the coattails of the party label or of a popular candidate running for major office. There may also be an extra payoff in the use of this type of ballot when a party is listed in the first column. The parties are slated from left to right on the ballot according to the proportion of votes that each party's candidate for governor received in the most recent gubernatorial election.

office-block ballot

A type of ballot used in a general election where the offices are listed across the top, in separate columns, and the candidates' names are listed in rows beneath each office.

Thus, the majority party—today, the Republicans—benefits by occupying the coveted first column on the ballot. Democrats come second, followed by third-party candidates and candidates of parties that were not on the ballot in the last election. Independents come last.

Most Texas counties have moved away from a strict party-column ballot. Partly because of the adoption of electronic voting systems (discussed later in this chapter), ballots in these counties combine features of both the office-block and the party-column designs, as shown in Figure 4–4 on page 80. (To be absolutely clear, *electronic* refers to computerized ballots, not Internet-based voting.) As with the office-block ballot, candidates are listed beneath each office. As with the party-column ballot, however, one can vote a straight-party ticket with a single mark. Above the lists of specific offices, voters are first given the option to vote a straight ticket.

4–4c Getting on the Ballot

For a name to be placed on the general-election ballot, the candidate must be either a party nominee or an independent. For any party that received at least 5 percent of the vote for any statewide office in the previous general election, the full slate of candidates is placed on the ballot automatically. Thus, the Republican and Democratic parties have no problem submitting candidate names, and certification by the appropriate party officials for primary or convention winners is routine.

Making Life Hard for Third Parties and Independents Minor parties have a more difficult time. The two largest minor parties, however, have broken the 5 percent barrier from time to time. These are the Green Party and the Libertarian Party. Both received more than 5 percent in 2010 and earned a place on the 2012 ballot. Any other minor parties must petition for a ballot position.

Independent candidates for president and candidates of parties that do not break the 5 percent barrier have the most difficult challenge because they must present a petition with signatures exceeding 1 percent of the total state vote for president in the last election. In 1992, Ross Perot's supporters presented 54,275 signatures, which qualified him to appear on the ballot.

For all other offices except president, the total vote for governor is the basis for determining the required number of signatures for both independents and third-party candidates. For statewide office, signatures equaling 1 percent of the total gubernatorial vote are needed; for multicounty district offices, 3 percent; and for all other district and local offices, 5 percent. Although the

FIGURE 4-3

In contrast to the party-column ballot, which lists candidates of each party in parallel columns, the office-block ballot lists candidates in rows beneath each office. Notice also that voters cannot easily vote a straight-party ticket.

Example of a
Typical Office-Block Ballot

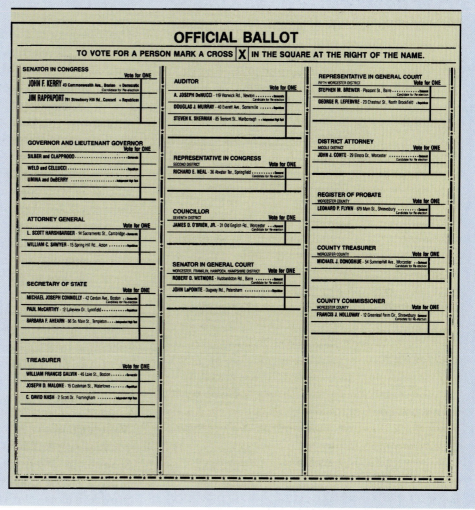

The names of write-in candidates must be posted at the election site, possibly in the election booth. A candidate not properly registered cannot win, regardless of the votes he or she receives. Even when registered, write-in candidates are seldom successful.

required number of signatures is relatively small for some offices (a maximum of five hundred at the local level), the process of gaining access to the ballot by petition can be difficult.[23] As a general rule, candidates using the petition route seek twice the required number to ensure the petition's certification.

Write-In Candidates Write-in candidates are not listed on the ballot—voters must write them on the ballot. These candidates often are individuals who have entered and lost in a party primary. Write-in candidates have had a somewhat easier time as a result of a law subsequently passed by the legislature. A candidate must file a declaration of candidacy with the secretary of state seventy days before Election Day. With the declaration, the candidate must include either the filing fee or a nominating petition with the required number of signatures.

4-4d The Secret Ballot and the Integrity of Elections

The essence of the right to vote is generally viewed as the right to cast a ballot in secret, have the election conducted fairly, and have the ballots counted correctly. The **Australian ballot,** adopted by Texas in 1892, includes names of the candidates of all

> **Australian ballot**
> A ballot printed by the government (not by political parties) that allows people to vote in secret.

FIGURE 4-4

A Typical Ballot Used
in Bexar County, Texas

Republican candidates were listed first in 2012 because their candidate (Rick Perry) received the most votes in the previous gubernatorial election. Note that voters are able to vote for all of the candidates of a single party—that is, to vote a *straight ticket*—by making a single mark on the ballot.

Straight Party
(Partido Completo)
- ○ Republican Party (REP)
  (Partido Republicano)
- ○ Democratic Party (DEM)
  (Partido Democratico)
- ○ Libertarian Party (LIB)
  (Partido Libertario)
- ○ Green Party (GRN)
  (Partido Verde)

FEDERAL
(FEDERAL)

United States Representative, District 20
(Representante de los Estados Unidos, Distrito Núm. 20)
- ○ Clayton Trotter (REP)
- ○ Charles A. Gonzalez (DEM)
- ○ Michael "Commander" Idrogo (LIB)

United States Representative, District 21
(Representante de los Estados Unidos, Distrito Núm. 21)
- ○ Lamar Smith (REP)
- ○ Lainey Melnick (DEM)
- ○ James Arthur Strohm (LIB)

United States Representative, District 23
(Representante de los Estados Unidos, Distrito Núm. 23)
- ○ Francisco "Quico" Canseco (REP)
- ○ Ciro D. Rodriguez (DEM)
- ○ Martin Nitschke (LIB)
- ○ Ed Scharf (GRN)
- ○ Craig T. Stephens (IND)

United States Representative, District 28
(Representante de los Estados Unidos, Distrito Núm. 28)
- ○ Bryan Underwood (REP)
- ○ Henry Cuellar (DEM)
- ○ Stephen Kaat (LIB)

STATE
(ESTADO)

Governor
(Gobernador)
- ○ Rick Perry (REP)
- ○ Bill White (DEM)
- ○ Kathie Glass (LIB)
- ○ Deb Shafto (GRN)
- ○ Write-(Voto Escrito)

Lieutenant Governor
(Gobernador Teniente)
- ○ David Dewhurst (REP)
- ○ Linda Chavez-Thompson (DEM)
- ○ Scott Jameson (LIB)
- ○ Herb Gonzales, Jr. (GRN)

Attorney General
(Procurador General)
- ○ Greg Abbott (REP)
- ○ Barbara Ann Radnofsky (DEM)
- ○ Jon Roland (LIB)

Comptroller of Public Accounts
(Contralor de Cuentas Públicas)
- ○ Susan Combs (REP)
- ○ Mary J. Ruwart (LIB)
- ○ Edward Lindsay (GRN)

Commissioner of the General Land Office
(Comisionado de la Oficina General de Tierras)
- ○ Jerry Patterson (REP)
- ○ Hector Uribe (DEM)
- ○ James L. Holdar (LIB)

Commissioner of Agriculture
(Comisionado de Agricultura)
- ○ Todd Staples (REP)
- ○ Hank Gilbert (DEM)
- ○ Rick Donaldson (LIB)

Railroad Commissioner
(Comisionado de Ferrocarriles)
- ○ David Porter (REP)
- ○ Jeff Weems (DEM)
- ○ Roger Gary (LIB)
- ○ Art Browning (GRN)

Justice, Supreme Court, Place 3
(Juez, Corte Suprema, Lugar Núm. 3)
- ○ Debra Lehrmann (REP)
- ○ Jim Sharp (DEM)
- ○ William Bryan Strange, III (LIB)

Justice, Supreme Court, Place 5
(Juez, Corte Suprema, Lugar Núm. 5)
- ○ Paul Green (REP)
- ○ Bill Moody (DEM)
- ○ Tom Oxford (LIB)

Justice, Supreme Court, Place 9
(Juez, Corte Suprema, Lugar Núm. 9)
- ○ Eva Guzman (REP)
- ○ Blake Bailey (DEM)
- ○ Jack Armstrong (LIB)

Judge, Court of Criminal Appeals, Place 2
(Juez, Corte de Apelaciones Criminales, Lugar Núm. 2)
- ○ Lawrence "Larry" Meyers (REP)
- ○ J. Randell Stevens (LIB)

Judge, Court of Criminal Appeals, Place 5
(Juez, Corte de Apelaciones Criminales, Lugar Núm. 5)
- ○ Cheryl Johnson (REP)
- ○ Dave Howard (LIB)

Judge, Court of Criminal Appeals, Place 6
(Juez, Corte de Apelaciones Criminales, Lugar Núm. 6)
- ○ Michael E. Keasler (REP)
- ○ Keith Hampton (DEM)
- ○ Robert Ravee Virasin (LIB)

Member, State Board of Education, District 3
(Miembro de la Junta Estatal de Educación Pública, Distrito Núm. 3)
- ○ Tony Cunningham (REP)
- ○ Michael Soto (DEM)
- ○ Dean Kareem Higley (LIB)
- ○ Write-in(Voto Escrito)

Member, State Board of Education, District 5
(Miembro de la Junta Estatal de Educación Pública, Distrito Núm. 5)
- ○ Ken Mercer (REP)
- ○ Rebecca Bell-Metereau (DEM)
- ○ Mark Loewe (LIB)

State Senator, District 19
(Senador Estatal, Distrito Núm. 19)
- ○ Dick Bowen (REP)
- ○ Carlos Uresti (DEM)
- ○ Mette A. Baker (LIB)

State Senator, District 25
(Senador Estatal, Distrito Núm. 25)
- ○ Jeff Wentworth (REP)
- ○ Arthur Maxwell Thomas, IV (LIB)
- ○ Write-in (Voto Escrito)

State Representative, District 116
(Representante Estatal, Distrito Núm. 116)
- ○ Trey Martinez Fischer (DEM)

State Representative, District 117
(Representante Estatal, Distrito Núm. 117)
- ○ John V. Garza (REP)
- ○ David McQuade Leibowitz (DEM)

State Representative, District 118
(Representante Estatal, Distrito Núm. 118)
- ○ Joe Farias (DEM)

State Representative, District 119
(Representante Estatal, Distrito Núm. 119)
- ○ Michael E. Holdman (REP)
- ○ Rolando Gutierrez (DEM)

State Representative, District 120
(Representante Estatal, Distrito Núm. 120)
- ○ Ruth Jones McClendon (DEM)

State Representative, District 121
(Representante Estatal, Distrito Núm. 121)
- ○ Joe Straus (REP)

State Representative, District 122
(Representante Estatal, Distrito Núm. 122)
- ○ Lyle Larson (REP)
- ○ Masarrat Ali (DEM)

State Representative, District 123
(Representante Estatal, Distrito Núm. 123)
- ○ Mike Villarreal (DEM)

State Representative, District 124
(Representante Estatal, Distrito Núm. 124)
- ○ José Menéndez (DEM)
- ○ Douglas P. Hanson (LIB)

State Representative, District 125
(Representante Estatal, Distrito Núm. 125)
- ○ Joaquin Castro (DEM)
- ○ Jeffrey C. Blunt (LIB)

Justice, 4th Court of Appeals District, Place 2 Unexpired Term
(Juez, Corte de Apelaciones, Distrito Núm. 4, Lugar Núm. 2, Duración Restante del cargo)
- ○ Marialyn Barnard (REP)
- ○ Rebeca C. Martinez (DEM)

Justice, 4th Court of Appeals District, Place 6
(Juez, Corte de Apelaciones, Distrito Núm. 4, Lugar Núm. 6)
- ○ Sandee Bryan Marion (REP)

District Judge, 45th Judicial District
(Juez del Distrito, Distrito Judicial Núm. 45)
- ○ Barbara Hanson Nellermoe (DEM)

---

political parties on a single ballot printed at the public's expense and available only at the voting place.[24] Given a reasonably private area in which to mark the ballot, the voter was offered a secret ballot for the first time.

The Integrity of the Elections Process

Although there are legal remedies such as the issuance of injunctions and the threat of criminal penalties, Texas has looked primarily to "political" remedies in its effort to protect the integrity of the electoral process. Minor parties have reason to be concerned that irregularities in elections administered by members of the major parties may not be observed or, if observed, not reported. Even in the absence of wrongdoing, the testimony by individuals with opposing interests that an election has been conducted properly helps ensure public faith in the process.

Traditional practice has been that in general and special elections, the county board of elections routinely appoints as election judges the precinct chair of the political party whose members constitute a majority on the elections board. Each election judge is required to select at least one election clerk from a list submitted by the county chair of each political party. Moreover, the law now recognizes the status of poll watchers, and both primary candidates and county chairs are authorized to appoint them.

Multilingualism

In more than a hundred Texas counties, the ballot is printed in both English and Spanish. In 2002, the U.S. Department of Justice ordered Harris County, which includes Houston, to provide ballots (and voting material) in Vietnamese as well (see Figure 4–5 on the facing page). It is the only county in Texas to be included in the order and the only county outside California to face this requirement. In some parts of the country, other languages are required, including Chinese, Eskimo, Filipino, Japanese, and Korean. In Los Angeles County alone, ballots are printed in seven different languages.

THE VOTING RIGHTS ACT OF 1965. The accommodation of the multilingual ballot is a result of the Voting Rights Act of 1965 and its subsequent amendment in 1992. According to Section 203 of the act, a political subdivision (typically, a county) must provide language assistance to voters if significant numbers of voting-age citizens are members of a single-language minority group and do not speak or understand English "well enough to participate in the electoral process." Specifically, the legal requirement is triggered when more than 5 percent or ten thousand of voting-age citizens meet the criteria.

FIGURE 4–5

This ballot lists a special election before offering the straight party option and then lists the candidates for the separate offices.

Source: Harris County Clerk's Office, Houston, Texas, November 6, 2012.

An English-Vietnamese Ballot Used in Harris County for the 2012 General Election

SAMPLE BALLOT   LÁ PHIẾU MẪU
Harris County – November 6, 2012 – General and Special Elections
Quận Harris – 6 tháng Mười Một, 2012 – Các Cuộc Tổng Tuyển Cử và Bầu Cử Đặc Biệt

Straight Party
Bỏ phiếu cho các ứng cử viên của cùng một đảng

☐ Republican Party
 Đảng Cộng Hòa

☐ Democratic Party
 Đảng Dân Chủ

☐ Libertarian Party
 Đảng Tự Do

☐ Green Party
 Đảng Xanh

President and Vice President
Tổng Thống và Phó Tổng Thống

☐ Mitt Romney / Paul Ryan
 Republican Party *Đảng Cộng Hòa*

☐ Barack Obama / Joe Biden
 Democratic Party *Đảng Dân Chủ*

☐ Gary Johnson / Jim Gray
 Libertarian Party *Đảng Tự Do*

☐ Jill Stein / Cheri Honkala
 Green Party *Đảng Xanh*

☐ Write-in
 Bầu chọn ứng cử viên không có tên trong lá phiếu

United States Senator
Thượng Nghị Sĩ Hoa Kỳ

☐ Ted Cruz
 Republican Party *Đảng Cộng Hòa*

☐ Paul Sadler
 Democratic Party *Đảng Dân Chủ*

☐ John Jay Myers
 Libertarian Party *Đảng Tự Do*

☐ David B. Collins
 Green Party *Đảng Xanh*

United States Representative, District 2
Dân Biểu Hoa Kỳ Khu vực số 2

☐ Ted Poe
 Republican Party *Đảng Cộng Hòa*

☐ Jim Dougherty
 Democratic Party *Đảng Dân Chủ*

☐ Kenneth Duncan
 Libertarian Party *Đảng Tự Do*

☐ Mark A. Roberts
 Green Party *Đảng Xanh*

United States Representative, District 7
Dân Biểu Hoa Kỳ Khu vực số 7

☐ John Culberson
 Republican Party *Đảng Cộng Hòa*

☐ James Cargas
 Democratic Party *Đảng Dân Chủ*

☐ Drew Parks
 Libertarian Party *Đảng Tự Do*

☐ Lance Findley
 Green Party *Đảng Xanh*

United States Representative, District 8
Dân Biểu Hoa Kỳ Khu vực số 8

☐ Kevin Brady
 Republican Party *Đảng Cộng Hòa*

☐ Neil Burns
 Democratic Party *Đảng Dân Chủ*

☐ Roy Hall
 Libertarian Party *Đảng Tự Do*

United States Representative, District 9
Dân Biểu Hoa Kỳ, Khu vực số 9

☐ Steve Mueller
 Republican Party *Đảng Cộng Hòa*

☐ Al Green
 Democratic Party *Đảng Dân Chủ*

☐ John Wieder
 Libertarian Party *Đảng Tự Do*

☐ Vanessa Foster
 Green Party *Đảng Xanh*

United States Representative, District 10
Dân Biểu Hoa Kỳ, Khu vực số 10

☐ Michael McCaul
 Republican Party *Đảng Cộng Hòa*

☐ Tawana W. Cadien
 Democratic Party *Đảng Dân Chủ*

☐ Richard Priest
 Libertarian Party *Đảng Tự Do*

United States Representative, District 18
Dân Biểu Hoa Kỳ Khu vực số 18

☐ Sean Seibert
 Republican Party *Đảng Cộng Hòa*

☐ Sheila Jackson Lee
 Democratic Party *Đảng Dân Chủ*

☐ Christopher Barber
 Libertarian Party *Đảng Tự Do*

United States Representative, District 22
Dân Biểu Hoa Kỳ Khu vực số 22

☐ Pete Olson
 Republican Party *Đảng Cộng Hòa*

☐ Kesha Rogers
 Democratic Party *Đảng Dân Chủ*

☐ Steve Susman
 Libertarian Party *Đảng Tự Do*

☐ Don Cook
 Green Party *Đảng Xanh*

United States Representative, District 29
Dân Biểu Hoa Kỳ, Khu vực số 29

☐ Gene Green
 Democratic Party *Đảng Dân Chủ*

☐ James Stanczak
 Libertarian Party *Đảng Tự Do*

☐ Maria Selva
 Green Party *Đảng Xanh*

United States Representative, District 36
Dân Biểu Hoa Kỳ, Khu vực số 36

☐ Steve Stockman
 Republican Party *Đảng Cộng Hòa*

☐ Max Martin
 Democratic Party *Đảng Dân Chủ*

☐ Michael K. Cole
 Libertarian Party *Đảng Tự Do*

Railroad Commissioner
Ủy Viên Ngành Hỏa Xa

☐ Christi Craddick
 Republican Party *Đảng Cộng Hòa*

☐ Dale Henry
 Democratic Party *Đảng Dân Chủ*

☐ Vivekananda (Vik) Wall
 Libertarian Party *Đảng Tự Do*

☐ Chris Kennedy
 Green Party *Đảng Xanh*

Railroad Commissioner, Unexpired Term
Ủy Viên Ngành Hỏa Xa, Nhiệm Kỳ Vô Thời Hạn

☐ Barry Smitherman
 Republican Party *Đảng Cộng Hòa*

☐ Jaime O. Perez
 Libertarian Party *Đảng Tự Do*

☐ Josh Wendel
 Green Party *Đảng Xanh*

Justice, Supreme Court, Place 2
Chánh Án, Tối Cao Pháp Viện, Vị Trí số 2

☐ Don Willett
 Republican Party *Đảng Cộng Hòa*

☐ RS Roberto Koelsch
 Libertarian Party *Đảng Tự Do*

Justice, Supreme Court, Place 4
Chánh Án, Tối Cao Pháp Viện, Vị Trí số 4

☐ John Devine
 Republican Party *Đảng Cộng Hòa*

☐ Tom Oxford
 Libertarian Party *Đảng Tự Do*

☐ Charles E. Waterbury
 Green Party *Đảng Xanh*

Justice, Supreme Court, Place 6
Chánh Án, Tối Cao Pháp Viện, Vị Trí số 6

☐ Nathan Hecht
 Republican Party *Đảng Cộng Hòa*

☐ Michele Petty
 Democratic Party *Đảng Dân Chủ*

☐ Mark Ash
 Libertarian Party *Đảng Tự Do*

☐ Jim Chisholm
 Green Party *Đảng Xanh*

Presiding Judge, Court of Criminal Appeals
Chánh Án Chủ Tọa, Tòa Kháng Án Hình Sự

☐ Sharon Keller
 Republican Party *Đảng Cộng Hòa*

☐ Keith Hampton
 Democratic Party *Đảng Dân Chủ*

☐ Lance Stott
 Libertarian Party *Đảng Tự Do*

Judge, Court of Criminal Appeals, Place 7
Chánh Án, Tòa Kháng Án Hình Sự, Vị Trí số 7

☐ Barbara Parker Hervey
 Republican Party *Đảng Cộng Hòa*

☐ Mark W. Bennett
 Libertarian Party *Đảng Tự Do*

Judge, Court of Criminal Appeals, Place 8
Chánh Án, Tòa Kháng Án Hình Sự, Vị Trí số 8

☐ Elsa Alcala
 Republican Party *Đảng Cộng Hòa*

☐ William Bryan Strange, III
 Libertarian Party *Đảng Tự Do*

Member, State Board of Education, District 4
Hội Viên, Hội Đồng Quản Trị Giáo Dục Tiểu Bang, Khu Vực số 4

☐ Dorothy Olmos
 Republican Party *Đảng Cộng Hòa*

☐ Lawrence Allen, Jr.
 Democratic Party *Đảng Dân Chủ*

TRIGGERING THE CLAUSE. The 2010 Census shows that more than eighty thousand people living in Harris County identify themselves as Vietnamese. The U.S. Department of Justice determined that at least ten thousand of them are old enough to vote but are not sufficiently proficient in English, thereby triggering the requirement. Given the levels of U.S. immigration, the number of ballot languages is almost certain to increase.

Early Voting All Texas voters can now vote before Election Day.[25] Some voters can vote by mail, specifically those who plan to be away from the county on Election Day, those who are sick or disabled, anyone who is sixty-five years or older, and people who are in jail but are otherwise eligible to vote. The rest of us can vote early only in person.

Generally, **early voting** begins the seventeenth day before Election Day and ends the fourth day before Election Day. In addition to traditional Election-Day voting sites, such as schools and fire stations, early voting also takes place at grocery and convenience stores. This innovation has clearly made voting easier in Texas, and people are taking advantage. In the 2010 midterm election, more than 53 percent of the votes were cast before Election Day, and in 2012, early votes were 63 percent of the total. Although people are voting earlier, they are not voting in greater numbers, as noted earlier in the chapter.

The growing tendency toward early voting may still have important implications for when and how politicians campaign. At least 30 percent of all votes nationwide in 2008 were cast before Election Day. More than 50 percent were cast early in eleven states: Arizona, Colorado, Florida, Georgia, Nevada, New Mexico, North Carolina, Oregon, Tennessee, Texas, and Washington.[26]

Counting and Recounting Ballots We take for granted that when we vote, our votes count. As we learned in Florida in the 2000 presidential elections, this is not always true. The first machine count of ballots in Florida showed George W. Bush with a 1,725-vote lead. In a mandatory machine recount of the same ballots, the same machines cut his lead to 327. We were also told that some 2 to 3 percent of the ballots were not counted at all. How could this happen? The answer is simple: Machines make mistakes. Some ballots are not counted. Some may even be counted for the wrong candidate. This shocked many Americans.

early voting The practice of voting before Election Day by mail, at more traditional voting locations such as schools, and at grocery and convenience stores.

chads The small pieces of paper produced in punching data cards, such as punch-card ballots.

PROBLEMS WITH CHADS. Experts have known for a long time that vote counting contains a fair amount of error. By most accounts, the error rate averages 1 to 2 percent, although it can be higher, depending on the ballot and the machines themselves. The error rate is largest for punch-card ballots, which have been commonly used in big cities in Texas and other states.

To vote with a punch card, you insert the ballot into a slot in the voting booth and then use a stylus to punch holes corresponding to candidates' names. There are two sources of error associated with these ballots. First, some voters do not fully punch out the pieces of paper from the perforated holes. That is, these pieces of paper, which are called **chads,** remain attached to the ballot. Second, even when the chads are completely detached, machines do not read each and every ballot.

These problems are of importance to voters. They are typically of little consequence for election outcomes, however. Counting errors tend to cancel out, meaning that no candidate gains a much greater number of votes. Errors are important only when elections are very close, within a half percentage point, which is not very common. When it does happen, the losing candidate can request a recount.

RECOUNT PROCEDURES. Texas has fairly specific laws about recounts. A candidate can request a recount if he or she loses by less than 10 percent. This is a fairly generous rule compared to other states. Most candidates do not request a recount unless the margin is much closer, say, one percentage point or less.

The candidate who requests a recount must put up a deposit—$60 per precinct where paper ballots were used and $100 per precinct using electronic voting—and is liable for the entire cost unless he or she wins or ties in the recount. In a large county, a recount can be quite costly. Consider Dallas County, which has almost seven hundred precincts. Despite this drawback, the current practice marks a real improvement over the days when often ineffective judicial remedies were the only recourse.

The Texas Election Code states that "only one method may be used in the recount" and "a manual recount shall be conducted in preference to an electronic recount." The procedures are fairly detailed. What may be most interesting is the set of rules for how the partial removal of a chad should be interpreted. Indeed, canvassing authorities are allowed to determine whether "an indentation on the chad from the stylus or other object is present" and whether "the chad reflects by other means a clearly ascertainable intent of the voter to vote."[27] This leaves much room for discretion on the part of canvassing authorities in the various Texas counties.

Electronic Voting Partly in response to the events in Florida—and the seeming potential for similar problems in Texas—a number of counties introduced **electronic voting** in the 2002 midterm elections. Instead of punching holes in ballots or filling in bubbles on scannable sheets, most voters today cast ballots by touching computer screens. The technology is similar to what is used in automated teller machines (ATMs) and promises an exact count of votes. It is now used for voting throughout much of Texas and the United States. As with the introduction of any new technology, however, problems have occurred.[28]

FOR CRITICAL THINKING

What are the arguments for and against bilingual ballots?

4–5 Election Campaigns in Texas

The ultimate aim of party activity is to nominate candidates in the party primary or convention and get them elected in the general election. The campaign for the parties' nomination is often more critical in one-party areas of the state—Democrats in South Texas and in some large urban areas and Republicans in many rural and suburban areas. This is true because the dominant parties' nominee is almost certain to win the general election. In statewide elections, the crucial electoral decision is often made in the Republican primary. The Republican candidate then has a relatively clear path to winning office.

Candidates seeking their parties' nomination pursue a different campaign strategy during the primary than they do in the general election. The primary electorate is usually much smaller and made up of more-committed partisans. As a result, primary candidates are likely to adopt a more ideological or even strident tone that appeals to activists. Once they have won their primaries, candidates will often moderate their views to win over swing voters and independents in the general election.

For little-known candidates, money and the endorsement of party elites are more crucial in the primary than in the general election. Little-known candidates can frequently count on the party label to sweep them into office in general elections.

⭐
Learning Outcome 4–5

Identify factors that provide the greatest advantages to candidates in Texas state elections, and discuss the difficulty of controlling spending in Texas campaigns.

4–5a The General-Election Campaign

To a large extent, election outcomes are predictable. Despite all the media attention paid to the conventions, the debates, the advertising, and everything else involved in election campaigns, certain factors powerfully structure the vote in national and state elections.[29] In state elections, two factors predominate: party identification and incumbency.

The Stronger Party's Advantage When one political party has more support in a state than the other, the candidates of the preferred party have an advantage in general elections. When most Texans identified with the Democratic

electronic voting Voting using touch screens similar to those in automated teller machines (ATMs).

AP PHOTO/PAT SULLIVAN

Former Texas Solicitor General Ted Cruz became the official Republican candidate for the U.S. Senate after the July 2012 primary runoff.

Party, Democratic candidates dominated elected offices throughout the state. As Texans have become more Republican in their identification, Republican candidates have done very well. Indeed, as was mentioned earlier, Republicans now hold every statewide elected office.

Party identification varies considerably within Texas, however, and this has implications for state legislative elections. For example, in some parts of the state (particularly in the big cities), more people identify with the Democratic Party than the Republican Party. Democratic candidates typically represent those areas in the state house and senate.

The Advantage of Incumbency

Incumbent candidates—those already in office—are more likely to win in general elections. This is particularly true in state legislative elections, where the districts are fairly homogeneous and the campaigns are not very visible. Incumbency, however, is also important in elections for statewide office. To become an incumbent, a candidate has to beat an incumbent or else win in an open-seat election, which usually involves a contest among a number of strong candidates. By definition, therefore, incumbents are good candidates with the advantage of office. They are in a position to help their constituents and thus increase their support from voters.

Party identification and incumbency are important, but they are not the whole story. These factors do grant candidates an advantage or disadvantage as they embark on their campaigns. Other elements—such as the mobilizing of supporters and choosing which issues to address—also matter on Election Day.[30]

Mobilizing Groups of Supporters

In elections for any office, groups play an important role. A fundamental part of any campaign is getting out the vote among groups that support the candidate. Candidates often focus on groups with known political allegiances.[31] For example, at the state level, Republican candidates tend to focus their efforts on businesspersons, while Democratic candidates look for support among teachers.

Other groups that candidates seek to mobilize include African Americans and Latinos. Traditionally, Democratic candidates concentrated on these minority groups, though Republican governor George W. Bush devoted substantial attention to the Latino community in Texas. Mobilizing groups does not necessarily involve taking strong public stands on their behalf. Indeed, the mobilization of controversial groups may be conducted quietly, often through targeted mailings and phone calls.

Choosing Issues

The issues are important in any campaign. At the state level in Texas, taxes, education, immigration, and religious issues are salient, and abortion matters considerably. The issues candidates select tend to reflect their party affiliations, but some issues are favored by all politicians. Few candidates, after all, are in favor of higher taxes and fewer funds for education and law enforcement. Where candidates differ is in their emphasis on particular issues and policy proposals.

Issue choices depend heavily on public opinion polls. Through polls, candidates attempt to identify the issues that the public considers to be important. Candidates can then craft policy positions to address those issues. The process is ongoing, and candidates pay close attention to changes in opinion and to the public's response to the candidates' own positions. Polling is fundamental to modern election campaigns in America, and campaign messages are often presented in advance to focus groups—test groups of selected citizens. Focus groups help campaign strategists tailor their messages to appeal to particular audiences.

The Campaign Trail

Deciding where and how to campaign is critical to a campaign strategy. Candidates spend countless hours "on the stump," traveling about the state or district to speak before diverse groups. In a state as large as Texas, candidates for statewide office must pick and choose areas so as to maximize their exposure. Unfortunately for rural voters, this means that candidates spend most of their time in urban and

Congresswoman Eddie Bernice Johnson from Texas's thirtieth district was first elected to that office in 1992, defeating the Republican nominee by a wide margin.

suburban areas where they can get the attention of a large audience through the local media.

THE IMPORTANCE OF THE MEDIA. Nowadays, no candidate gets elected merely by stumping. The most direct route to the voters is through the media. There are twenty media markets in Texas. These include approximately two hundred television and cable stations and more than five hundred radio stations. In addition, seventy-nine daily newspapers and many more weekly newspapers are dispersed throughout the state's 254 counties.[32] Candidates hire public relations firms and media consultants, and advertising plays a big role. The new media—the Internet and other sources—also play a growing role in Texas politics, as we explain in the *Texas Politics and Elections* feature below.

NEGATIVE CAMPAIGNING. These days, a successful campaign often relies on **negative campaigning,** in

negative campaigning
A strategy used in election campaigns in which candidates attack opponents' issue positions or character.

Texas Politics and ... ELECTIONS

The New Media

Getting one's political message out in Texas has come a long way since the 1800s. Then, politicians campaigned through letter writing and newspaper articles. In the early 1900s, Texan politicians went on train tours and reached thousands of potential voters. In the early 2000s, the new media of virtual politics and social networking now reach millions of Texans.

Some of the Quaint Old Ways

In 1911, radio broadcasting began at the University of Texas and Texas A&M campuses. By the 1920s, radio stations were broadcasting across Texas. Radio news was often political news. Television entered the process in 1948 when a Fort Worth TV station broadcast a speech by President Harry Truman. Spanish TV made its debut in 1954.

It used to be a big deal for a politician or a government agency to have a Web site. Today, of course, every political candidate must have one. Incumbents, such as governors, can use state-provided Web sites to promote their agenda and to enhance their images. Young people, however, rarely go to a stand-alone Web site. Instead, they use social media to find out what they need to know about politics and other subjects. Nonetheless, for older Texans, Web sites are still a source of political information.

Although it may seem like a part of the old media, cable television definitely changed the political landscape. Texans have access to an increasingly large number of specialized channels, including news channels. One result has been the growth of partisan news reporting. But even cable news is starting to seem quaint. With young people increasingly obtaining political information from YouTube and other Web sites, Texas Tech University has even created its own channel on YouTube. Politicians, if they haven't already, will soon follow with their own channels.

From Talk Radio to the Future—Universal Social Media

From traditional radio channels to Internet radio sources, Texans can listen to and participate in talk radio in both English and Spanish. Many talk radio stations provide partisan political news. As more politicians see the benefit of online talk radio programs, more will be created. Many such outlets can be used for podcasts.

Even Web logs (blogs) now seem a bit passé and are on a downward trajectory. Following a blog is time consuming. Younger Texans, in particular, are looking for the "quick and dirty" small bits and pieces of information that are offered through Facebook, Twitter, Google+, and other social media. In the future, expect to see interconnections among social media sites, including Delicious, Digg, Flicker, YouTube, Facebook, LinkedIn, and many more.

 **FOR CRITICAL ANALYSIS** How might smartphone apps change the political landscape?

which candidates attack opponents' issue positions or character. As one campaign consultant said, "Campaigns are about definition. Either you define yourself and your opponent or [the other candidates do]. . . . Victory goes to the aggressor."[33] Although often considered an unfortunate development in American politics, negative campaigning can serve to provide voters with information about the candidates and their issue positions.

Timing The timing of the campaign effort can be very important. Unlike presidential elections, campaigns for state offices, including the governorship, begin fairly late in the election cycle. Indeed, it is common to hear little from gubernatorial candidates until after Labor Day. We often do not hear from candidates for the legislature until a month before the election.

Candidates often reserve a large proportion of their campaign advertising budget for a last-minute media "blitz." Early voting, however, may affect this strategy. In 2012, about 63 percent of the votes in Texas were cast early, during the weeks leading up to the election, which means that the final campaign blitz may come too late to have an effect on many voters. Consequently, candidates in the future may be less likely to concentrate so much on the final days of the campaign.

4–5b Campaign Finance

Election campaigns are expensive, which means that candidates need to raise plenty of money to be competitive. Indeed, the amount of money a candidate raises can be the deciding factor in the campaign. Just how much a candidate needs depends on the level of the campaign and the competitiveness of the race. High-level campaigns for statewide office are usually multimillion-dollar affairs.

The Cost of Campaigns In recent years, the race for governor has become especially expensive. In 2002, Tony Sanchez spent nearly $70 million, a striking sum that consisted mostly of his own funds. He still lost handily to incumbent Governor Rick Perry, who spent just

> "Politics has become so expensive that **it takes a lot of money even to be defeated."**
>
> ~ WILL ROGERS ~
> AMERICAN HUMORIST
> 1879–1935

under $30 million. In 2006, the four candidates who were vying spent a much smaller amount, about $46 million in total, with Perry leading the way at $23 million. In 2010, Perry spent $40 million to Bill White's $25 million and won yet again.

Although lower-level races in Texas usually do not cost millions of dollars, they can be expensive. This is certainly true if a contested office is an open seat, where the incumbent is not running for reelection, or if an incumbent is from a marginal district, in which the incumbent won office with less than 55 percent of the vote. It is not unusual for a candidate in a competitive race for the state house to spend between $100,000 and $200,000.

Where does this money come from? Candidates often try to solicit small individual contributions through direct-mail or e-mail campaigns. To raise the millions required for a high-level state race, however, they must solicit "big money" from wealthy friends or business and professional interests that have a stake in the outcome of the campaign. Another source of big money is loans—candidates often borrow heavily from banks, wealthy friends, or even themselves.[34]

Political Action Committees (PACs) Banks, corporations, law firms, and professional associations, among others, may organize and register their **political action committees (PACs)** with the secretary of state's office. PACs serve as a vehicle through which interest groups collect money and then contribute it to political candidates. During the 2009–2010 election cycle in Texas, more than 1,300 PACs were active, and they spent more than $130 million.

Where Does the Money Go? In today's election campaigns, there are many ways to spend money. Newspaper ads, billboards, radio messages, bumper stickers, yard signs, and phone banks are all staples in traditional campaigns. Candidates for statewide and urban races must rely on media advertising, particularly television, to get the maximum exposure they need in the three- to four-month campaign period. Campaigns are becoming professionalized. Candidates now often hire consulting firms to manage their campaigns. The consultants may contract with public opinion pollsters, arrange advertising, and organize direct-mail or e-mail campaigns that can target certain areas of the state.

political action committee (PAC)
An organization that raises and then contributes money to political candidates.

EXAMPLES FROM HARRIS COUNTY, TEXAS. We can get some idea about spending in campaigns from what candidates pay for advertising and political consultants in Harris County, which includes Houston:

- A thirty-second TV spot costs about $1,500 for a daytime ad, $2,000 to $5,000 for an ad during the evening news, and $5,000 to $20,000 during prime time (8:00 P.M. to 11:00 P.M.), depending on the show's popularity rating. For some popular programs such as *CSI* (Crime Scene Investigation), the cost can be as much as $25,000.
- Prime time for most radio broadcasting is "drive time" (5:00 A.M. to 10:00 A.M. and 3:00 P.M. to 8:00 P.M.), when most people are driving to or from work. Drive-time rates range from $250 to $2,000 per sixty-second spot.
- Billboards can run from $600 to $15,000 a month, depending on the location. Of course, billboards on busy highways are the most expensive.
- Newspaper ads cost around $250 per column inch—$300 to $500 on Sunday. In 2008, a half-page ad in the *Houston Chronicle* that ran on the day before the election cost about $15,000. Advertising rates for election campaigns are actually higher than standard rates because political advertisers do not qualify for the discounts that regular advertisers receive.
- Hiring a professional polling organization to conduct a poll in Harris County costs $15,000 to $30,000.
- Hiring a political consulting firm to manage a campaign in Harris County runs up to $50,000 plus a percentage of media buys. (Typically, the percentage is paid by the television and radio stations.) Most firms also get a bonus ranging from $5,000 to $25,000 if the candidate wins.[35]

STAYING COMPETITIVE. Clearly, money is important in election campaigns. Although the candidate who spends the most money does not always win, a certain amount of money is necessary for a candidate to be competitive. With regard to high-level statewide races in Texas, one prominent politician wryly noted that even if "you don't have to raise $10 million, you have to raise $8 million."[36]

Attempts to Control Campaign Finance

Prompted by the increasing use of television in campaigns and the increasingly large sums needed to buy television time, the federal government and most state governments passed laws regulating campaign finance in the early 1970s. The Federal Elections Campaign Act of 1972 established regulations that apply only to federal elections, those for president, vice president, and members of Congress. It provided for public financing of presidential campaigns with tax dollars, limited the amount of money that individuals and PACs could contribute to campaigns, and required disclosure of campaign donations.

In 1976, the Supreme Court declared that it was unconstitutional to set spending limits for campaigns that were not publicly funded. As a result, there are no spending limits for congressional races.[37]

soft money Money spent by political parties on behalf of political candidates, especially for the purposes of increasing voter registration and turnout.

independent expenditures Funds that individuals and organizations spend to promote a candidate without working or communicating directly with the candidate's campaign organization.

Rising Costs

Not surprisingly, expenditures in election campaigns continue to increase. The Federal Election Commission (FEC) reported that $211.8 million was spent in the 1976 election of the president and members of Congress, with $122.8 million spent in the presidential race alone. Of the $60.9 million spent in the elections of the 435 House members, more money was spent on behalf of the candidates in Texas ($4.5 million) than on those of any other state except California.[38] Such expenditure levels (averaging only $140,000 per seat) appear modest by today's standards.

By 2010, the average was nearly $1.7 million per U.S. House of Representatives seat and substantially larger for U.S. Senate elections—$27 million in most recent contests in 2008. The level of campaign spending is likely to continue to rise.

Soft Money and Independent Expenditures

Later amendments to the Federal Elections Campaign Act made it legal for national political parties to raise and spend unlimited amounts of **soft money** on behalf of political candidates. Party funds could be used to help candidates in a variety of ways, especially through voter-registration and get-out-the-vote drives.

The United States Supreme Court further opened up spending in 1985 by deciding that **independent expenditures** could not be limited. As a result, individuals and organizations could spend as much as they wanted to promote a candidate as long as they were not working or communicating directly with the candidate's campaign organization.

The Campaign Reform Act and *Citizens United*

The 2002 Campaign Reform Act limited independent expenditures by corporations and labor unions, but this was overturned by the Supreme Court in its 2010 decision in *Citizens United v. Federal Election Commission*.[39] This may have implications for state and local bans on corporate spending, including those in Texas. The 2002 act also deprived the parties of their soft money resources, but activists simply set up nonparty organizations to collect and disperse such funds. Understandably, it has been difficult to effectively control money in election campaigns.

State Regulations FEC regulations apply only to candidates for national office. For candidates running for state offices in Texas, the most important provisions of Texas law regarding money in campaigns are as follows:

- Candidates may not raise or spend money until an official campaign treasurer is appointed.
- Candidates and PACs may not accept cash contributions for more than an aggregate of $100, but checks in unlimited amounts are permitted.
- Direct contributions from corporations and labor unions are prohibited, although this may change in the wake of the recent Supreme Court decision *Citizens United v. Federal Elections Commission*.
- Candidates and treasurers of campaign committees are required to file sworn statements listing all contributions and expenditures for a designated reporting period to the Texas secretary of state's office.
- Both criminal and civil penalties are imposed on anyone who violates the law's provisions.
- Primary enforcement of campaign regulations is the responsibility of the Texas Ethics Commission.

Although these provisions may sound imposing, the fact is that raising and spending money on Texas campaigns is still relatively wide open. For example, corporations and labor unions may not give directly to a candidate, but they may give through their PACs. Note also that there are no limits on the amount a candidate may spend. Probably the most important effect of the campaign-finance laws in Texas is the requirement of disclosure. How much money a candidate raises, who makes contributions, and how campaign funds are spent are matters of public record. This information may be newsworthy to reporters, bloggers, or others who wish to inform the public.

BOB E. DAEMMRICH/SYGMA/CORBIS

Ann Richards became the forty-fifth Texas governor from 1991 to 1995.

4–5c Who Is Elected

It is useful to think of elected offices in Texas as a pyramid. At the bottom of the pyramid are the most local of offices. At the top is the governor. Moving from bottom to top, the importance of the office increases and the number of officeholders decreases. It thus becomes more and more difficult for politicians to ascend the pyramid, and only the most effective politicians rise to the top. This tells us a lot about candidates and elections in Texas and elsewhere.

In local elections, the pool of candidates is diverse in many ways, including by educational background, income, and profession. Moving up the pyramid, however, we see that candidates become much more homogeneous. For statewide office, the typical candidate is middle or upper class, from an urban area, and has strong ties to business and professional interests in the state.

Most elected state officers in Texas, including the governor, lieutenant governor, and attorney general, need to be acceptable to the state's major financial and corporate interests and to its top law firms. These interests help statewide candidates raise the large amounts of money that are critical to a successful race.

Electing Minorities and Women Successful candidates for statewide office in Texas have traditionally been white Protestant males. Before 1986, when Raul Gonzalez was elected to the Texas Supreme Court, no Latino or African American had been elected to statewide office, though these two ethnic groups combined represent one-half of the state's population. The only female governor until that time was Miriam A. "Ma" Ferguson, who served as surrogate for her husband, Jim, in the 1920s. Ann Richards was elected state treasurer in 1982, becoming the second woman ever to be elected to statewide office in Texas.

> **"I THOUGHT I KNEW TEXAS** pretty well, but I had no notion of its size until I campaigned it."
>
> ~ ANN RICHARDS ~
> AMERICAN POLITICIAN AND
> GOVERNOR OF TEXAS
> 1990–1994

Since that time, women and minorities have made substantial gains in statewide offices. Ann Richards became the first woman elected Texas governor in her own right. Kay Bailey Hutchison captured the state treasurer's office and in 1993 won a special election to become the first woman from Texas elected to the U.S. Senate. Dan Morales was the first Latino to win a state executive office when he captured the attorney general's office. More history was made when Morris Overstreet of Amarillo won a seat on the Texas Court of Criminal Appeals and became the first African American elected to statewide office.

Recent Advances Women and ethnic groups are starting to make inroads in other elected offices in Texas. In the eighty-third legislature (2013–2014), 31 women were elected to the 150-member House and 6 to the 31-member Senate. Women have also held the post of mayor in five of the state's largest cities: Houston, Dallas, San Antonio, El Paso, and Austin. Latinos hold 40 seats in the state legislature, and African Americans occupy 20 seats. Among the state's 36 U.S. congressional representatives, there are 3 women, 6 Latinos, and 4 African Americans. Clearly, Texas politics has changed considerably over a short period of time.

FOR CRITICAL THINKING Consider that in 2002, Democrat Tony Sanchez spent $70 million in a race for governor, but lost to Republican incumbent Rick Perry, who spent $30 million. *What do these facts tell us about the influence of money in election campaigns?*

CONFLICT Voting and Elections

Some people believe that if the nation's founders could see how elections are conducted today, they would be shocked at the degree to which candidates "pander to the masses." It is less likely, however, that the founders would be shocked at the influence of money in election campaigns. After all, the founders themselves were an elite group who believed that the upper classes should dominate politics. Today, most Americans in general and Texans in particular reject that reasoning. Yet there are many issues related to elections that divide Texans. They include the following:

- Are voter photo IDs essential to prevent voter fraud—or do they chiefly serve to discriminate against poor and minority voters?

- In general, do current Texas laws make it easy enough to vote—or should the legislature take further steps to make voting convenient?

- Is the open primary, used in Texas, best because voters can choose their party on Election Day—or would a closed primary be better because it allows party members more control over who represents them?

- Should campaign contributions be seen as a constitutionally protected form of speech—or are they too often a source of corruption within the political system?

TAKE ACTION

One of the distinguishing features of Texas politics is the number and variety of elections held in the state. Texas elects a large number of officials to do different things at different levels of government. See for yourself: find a Texas county's Web site by entering the name of the county into an Internet search engine as "[NAME] county texas." Then locate a sample ballot. Ballots are usually stored on the county clerk's section of the site.

If one county's Web site does not have a sample ballot, try the site of another county, such as Bexar, Dallas, Denton, El Paso, Harris, Jefferson, or Travis, all of which include a full sample ballot before primary and general elections. Examine the ballot from top to bottom, keeping in mind that it may take some time. Indeed, in some areas people may be asked to vote for more than one hundred different offices, from governor to railroad commissioner, from state representative to city council members, from state judges to county judges, justices of the peace, and constables. There are other offices as well, and often a constitutional amendment or two is included.

RON T. ENNIS/FORT WORTH STAR-TELEGRAM/MCT/GETTY IMAGES

A variety of signage meets voters outside the Handley-Meadowbrook Community Center in Fort Worth, Texas, on Election day, Tuesday November 4, 2008.

STUDY TOOLS

Ready to study?

- Review what you've read with the quiz below. Check your answers on the Chapter in Review card at the back of the book. For any questions you miss, read the corresponding Learning Outcome section again to prepare for class and your exam.
- Rip out and study the Chapter in Review card.

. . . Or you can go online to CourseMate

at **www.cengagebrain.com** for these additional review materials:

- Practice Quizzes
- Key Term Flashcards or Crossword Puzzles
- Audio Summaries
- Simulations, Animated Learning Modules, and Interactive Timelines
- Videos
- American Government NewsWatch

Quiz

1. What is meant by the *participation paradox* in electoral politics?
   a. Voter turnout is so low even though each individual's vote makes a difference.
   b. Most voters know little about the candidates or policies for which they are voting.
   c. Individuals continue to vote even though their votes rarely influence the result of an election.

2. Which of the following are three of the most accurate predictors of voter turnout?
   a. age, education, and income
   b. gender, region, and age
   c. religion, education, and race

3. All of the following predict that a person will be *less likely* to vote EXCEPT:
   a. being poor
   b. having a low level of education
   c. having strong partisan identification

4. Which of the following is defined as "the total number of persons who are eligible to vote, excluding noncitizens and felons whose eligibility to vote has not yet been restored."
   a. voting-age population (VAP)
   b. vote-eligible population (VEP)
   c. registered voters

5. Which of the following socioeconomic factors help explain why voter turnout in Texas is lower than the national average?
   a. Texas is a rich state and its residents are generally more satisfied with existing conditions.
   b. Texas's political culture is heavily influenced by the moralistic subculture.
   c. Texas has a population with a higher poverty rate and lower education rates than the national average.

6. A primary election in which a voter can vote only for candidates of the party of which the voter is a member is a:
   a. direct primary   b. closed primary   c. runoff primary

7. What is a key difference between primary elections and general elections?
   a. Primary elections are nonpartisan while general elections are partisan.
   b. Primary elections are partisan while general elections are nonpartisan.
   c. Candidates in primary elections must win by a majority vote while candidates in general elections must only win by a plurality vote.

8. The Texas primary election system can be described as:
   a. direct and closed
   b. direct and open, with runoff elections
   c. indirect and open, with runoff elections

9. Who actually administers elections in Texas?
   a. county officials
   b. state government officials
   c. political parties

10. As hoped, the introduction of early voting in Texas has increased voter turnout.
    a. true   b. false

11. Factors giving an advantage to some candidates over others in general elections include:
    a. being a new candidate to the office.
    b. ability to mobilize supporting groups.
    c. coming from the minority party.

12. Which of the following is true of campaign-finance law in Texas?
    a. It places fewer restrictions on campaign contributions than federal campaign-finance laws.
    b. It places more restrictions on campaign contributions than federal campaign finance laws.
    c. It is identical to federal campaign-finance laws.

13. Not only does negative campaigning discourage prospective voters, but it usually doesn't work as a campaign tactic.
    a. true   b. false

 TX.GOV
5

Political Parties

ANDREW HARRER/BLOOMBERG/GETTY IMAGES

★ Learning Outcomes

The **Learning Outcomes** labeled 1 through 4 are designed to help improve your understanding of the chapter. After reading this chapter, you should be able to:

5–1 Describe the functions and chief characteristics of American political parties.

5–2 Distinguish between liberals and conservatives and between likely supporters of Texas Republicans and Democrats. Explain how the Republican Party became the dominant party in the state.

5–3 Explain the differences between temporary and permanent party organizations in Texas.

5–4 Define *realignment*. Describe why a majority of Texas voters now identify with the Republican Party, and explain why more Texas voters may identify with the Democratic Party in the future.

Remember to visit page 112 for additional Study Tools

CONFLICT

Should Texas Use Caucuses When Nominating Presidential Candidates?

Every four years, presidential primaries and caucuses pick the delegates who attend the Democratic and Republican national conventions. At those conventions, the delegates nominate each party's candidate.

Texas uses a primary system—with one quirk that we will get to shortly. On the day of the primary, voters are asked to go to their respective precincts and to cast their vote for a Republican or Democratic presidential candidate. The primaries are *open*—that is, a voter can choose to participate in either the Republican or the Democratic Party primary at the polls.

In the caucus system for choosing delegates to the national conventions, voters are asked to participate in open meetings to endorse candidates. In smaller states that use caucuses, many caucus participants have met the candidates in person and spoken with

them directly about issues.

In Texas, the Democratic Party —but not the Republican Party—uses a caucus system to choose about one-third of the delegates to its national convention. This process led to controversy in 2008, when Hillary Clinton came out slightly ahead in the primary vote. After the caucuses were over, however, Barack Obama had more delegates. Essentially, the results were a tie—Clinton went from leading by 4 out of 126 delegates to trailing by 5 out of 193—but there were hard feelings.

Many have argued that Texas should use a single method for choosing all delegates to prevent such a result. Would Texans be better off if the two parties switched to a caucus system exclusively?

Let's Motivate Voters—Use a Caucus System

Those who want to switch to a caucus system argue that it leads to much more direct participation by voters. While the system is informally called a caucus system, it is in reality a convention system, with the bottom-level precinct convention open to every party supporter. The discussions are open and often intense, allowing participants to be more involved and informed.

A caucus system is considerably more flexible than a primary system. Participants effectively register for the party of their choice simply by attending the precinct convention. It is easy to change the date of a caucus, if necessary. Caucuses are also less expensive because there is no need for early voting and there are no paid poll workers. As mentioned, caucus participants often meet the candidates in person.

The Texas Primary System Works—So Don't Change It

Many Texans support the primary method and wish that the Democrats would abolish their two-stage system. Many more people as a percentage of eligible voters participate in primary elections, which are much more private than caucuses since they use a secret ballot. The caucus system doesn't support early voting or voting by mail. A caucus requires voters who are sick, can't get a babysitter, or are elderly and infirm to make it to the caucus on the one night it occurs.

Most Texans would not be comfortable arguing with other participants about the pros and cons of the candidates. Our democracy has long been based on secret ballots. Now is not the time for change.

Where do you stand?

1. Would you be comfortable speaking publicly about your favorite candidate in front of a group of people?
2. If you are in favor of the primary system, why does it seem better for you personally?

Explore this issue online

- To see what happened in the 2012 Texas primaries, enter "texas primary 2012" into an Internet search engine. Observe that the important primary race in 2012 was for the Republican nomination for the U.S. Senate—the presidential contests were already decided.
- To bring up a page with debates on the merits of primaries and caucuses, type in "caucus primary pro con."

Introduction

The founders created our complicated system of federal government and provided for the election of a president and members of Congress. The U.S. Constitution, however, makes no mention of political parties. Indeed, these early leaders held negative attitudes about parties. George Washington warned of the "baneful (harmful) effects of the spirit of party" in his farewell address. James Madison, in *Federalist Paper No. 10*, criticized parties or "factions" as divisive but admitted that they were inevitable. Madison and others thought that parties would encourage conflict and undermine consensus on public policy. Yet, despite their condemnation of parties, these early American politicians engaged in partisan politics and initiated a competitive two-party system.

Parties, then, are apparently something we should live neither with nor without. They have been with us from the start of this country and will be with us for the foreseeable future, influencing our government and public policy. It is important, therefore, to gain an understanding of what they are all about.

5–1 Functions and Characteristics of Political Parties

What is a political party? The term conjures up various stereotypes. We may imagine smoke-filled rooms, where party leaders or bosses make important behind-the-scenes decisions. Alternatively, we may think of activists or regulars who give time, money, and enthusiastic support to their candidates. Finally, we may consider the voters who proudly identify themselves as Democrats or Republicans.

Essentially, a political party is a broad-based coalition of individuals whose primary goal is to win elections. Gaining control of government through popular elections is the key goal for political parties, and most of the activities that parties pursue are directed toward this end. Parties recruit and nominate candidates for public office. They encourage coalitions of groups and interests—in an attempt to build majorities that can elect their candidates. Political parties are vital to democracy in that they provide a link between the people and the government. Parties make it possible for the ordinary citizen to participate in the political system.

5–1a Functions of Political Parties

Political parties developed and survived because they perform important functions. These functions include nominating and electing members to public office, educating and mobilizing voters, and running the government.

Nominating and Electing Party Members The first function of parties is to nominate and elect their members to public office. Except for most Texas local elections, which are *nonpartisan* by law, candidates are nominated by political parties, and parties run the election process.

Educating Voters The second function of political parties is to simplify the issues so that voters understand the alternative positions on questions of public policy. In other words, parties educate the public. They help make sense of the issues and provide voters with cues on how to vote.

Mobilizing Voters The third function of parties is to encourage participation in the electoral process. Citizens are persuaded to become active in support of party candidates, for example, by contributing money to campaigns, telephoning other voters to get their support, and canvassing door to door. The more organized the party, the more effective it becomes in getting out the vote for its candidates.

Running the Government Finally, the fourth function of parties is to run the government. The president, members of Congress, governors, state representatives, and Texas state judges are all elected to public office under a party label. Once elected, these officials try to advance the positions of their party. In our political system, however, it is often difficult for parties to fully manage government because the separate branches of government may not be under the control of the same party.

5–1b Characteristics of American Political Parties

The American political party system has exhibited three distinct characteristics not always found elsewhere in the world: (1) pragmatism, (2) decentralization, and

(3) the two-party system. In the current political environment, however, several of these traditional characteristics—especially pragmatism—have come under pressure.

Pragmatism In politics, **pragmatism** means that measures should be judged on the basis of their practical results rather than on the basis of principles.[1] In other words, a pragmatist is interested in what works on a practical basis. Traditionally, American parties have been willing to compromise principles to appeal successfully to a majority of voters and gain public office. Taking a stand that appeals to a large number of interests helps to build a winning coalition.

A campaign strategy designed to attract all groups and to repel none will not bring the party's ideology into sharp focus, however. Because taking clear stands on controversial issues may alienate potential members of the party's electoral coalition, pragmatic parties and candidates prefer to de-emphasize issues and instead attempt to project a generalized positive image. Broad, fuzzy campaign themes that stress leadership, statesmanship, family life, and personality often take precedence over issues.

THE ORIGINS OF PARTY PRAGMATISM. In the past, party pragmatism was enhanced because both major parties contained a broad spectrum of political ideologies. As late as the 1960s, a number of Republicans considered themselves to be liberals. For their part, in those days many Democrats were well to the political right of the average Republican. In some ways, the parties were as much cultural bodies as ideological ones. For many citizens, membership in a party often had less to do with modern-day political beliefs than with which side their ancestors supported during the Civil War.

THE DECLINE OF PRAGMATISM. Most observers agree that American political parties have become more ideological and more polarized in recent years. To a considerable extent, the parties have sorted themselves out ideologically. Liberal Republicans are extinct, and conservative Democrats are a dwindling breed. Studies have demonstrated that the most conservative Democrat in the U.S. House of Representatives is now slightly to the left of the most moderate Republican.

A consequence is that many party activists now consider it unacceptable to compromise with the other party. This inflexible spirit has been building for many years, both nationally and in Texas. At the national level, it reached new heights in 2010 and thereafter with the election of a new group of Republicans to the U.S. House who were backed by the Tea Party movement. The 2010 elections also dramatically thinned the ranks of the remaining Democratic conservatives. For almost a century political commentators were accustomed to contrasting the pragmatic American party coalitions with the more ideological Conservatives, Christian Democrats, Social Democrats, and Socialists of Europe. Today, the contrast no longer holds.

Decentralization At first glance, American party organizations may appear to be neatly ordered and hierarchical, with power flowing from the national to state to local parties. In reality, however, American parties reflect the American federal system, with its **decentralization** of power. Political party organizations operate at the precinct—or **grassroots**—level, the local government (city, county, or district) level, the state level (especially in elections for governor), and the national level (especially in elections for president).

LOCAL INDEPENDENCE. Figure 5–1 on the following page illustrates the nature of power in American political parties. State and local party organizations are semi-independent actors who exercise considerable discretion on most party matters. Local and state political cultures, leaders, traditions, and interests influence the practices that state and local parties follow, the candidates they recruit, and the campaign money they raise. Local and state factors likewise affect the innovations that parties introduce, the nature of the interests to which they respond, and the campaign strategies they create. Most importantly, local factors determine the policy orientations of the candidates who run under the party label.[2]

THE GROWTH OF NATIONAL PARTY POWER. Compared with party systems in other countries, the American party system is quite decentralized. Figure 5–1, however, also suggests how power has shifted to the national party organizations in recent years.

> **pragmatism** The philosophy that measures should be judged on the basis of their practical results rather than on an ideological basis.
>
> **decentralization** Exercise of power in political parties by state and local party organizations rather than by national party institutions.
>
> **grassroots** The lowest level of party organization. In Texas, the grassroots level is the precinct level of organization.

FIGURE 5-1

The Decentralized
Nature of American Political Parties and the Importance of the National Party's Service Function

The diagram shows the semi-independent relationship that exists among national, state, and local party organizations and the increasingly important services and funds provided by the national party organization.

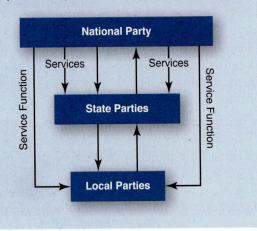

Both the Democratic and the Republican national parties have become stronger and more involved in state and local party activities through various service functions.

By using new campaign technologies—computer-based mailing lists, direct-mail solicitations, and the Internet—the national parties have raised millions of dollars. As a result, they have assumed a greater role by providing unprecedented levels of assistance to state parties and candidates. This assistance includes candidate recruitment, research, public opinion polling, computer networking, and production of radio and television commercials. It also includes direct mailings, consultations on redistricting issues, and millions of dollars' worth of campaign funding.

Not surprisingly, as national parties provide more money and services to state and local parties, they exercise more influence over state and local organizations, issues, and candidates.[3]

single-member district system A system in which one candidate is elected to a legislative body in each election district.

THE ROLE OF IDEOLOGICAL UNITY. The growing ideological coherence within the parties is also a force for centralization, although *nationalization*

might be the better term. The party organizations are not the enforcers of ideological orthodoxy. Consider the Republicans. Most of their impetus toward ideological unity comes from elected leaders, national ideological interest groups such as the Club for Growth, and conservative media such as Fox News. The various forces that make up the conservative movement impose ideas on the party organization, not the other way around. This is true both nationally and in Texas.

The Two-Party System In a majority of states, political competition is primarily competition between the Democratic and Republican parties. Third parties have tried to gain office but with little success, in part because the two major parties have adopted their issues. (For example, many issues advocated by the People's Party of the 1890s—the Populists—were adopted by the Democrats.)

THE EFFECT OF SINGLE-MEMBER DISTRICTS. Voters, potential campaign contributors, and political activists also tend to avoid supporting a losing cause. Our electoral system, the **single-member district system,** encourages this pragmatic behavior. If only one representative can be elected in a district, voters will cast their ballots for the major-party candidates who have the best chance of winning.

DIFFICULTIES IN GETTING ON THE BALLOT. In Texas, third parties such as the Libertarian Party and the Green Party must receive at least 5 percent of the vote in the previous election to gain automatic ballot status. Failure to gain this 5 percent means that third parties can get on the ballot only by launching petition drives that gather the signatures of registered voters who did not vote in either major party's primary. Independent candidates must also meet this standard. For example, in the 2006 gubernatorial election, independent candidates Carole Keeton Strayhorn and Kinky Friedman were forced to collect 45,000 signatures from eligible voters who had not voted in the March 7 primary to compete against incumbent governor Rick Perry in the November election.

Texas Political SOCIAL MEDIA

For a nonpartisan look at Texas politics, find the Austin bureau of the *Houston Chronicle* on Facebook by searching on "texas politics." It is also worth following the *Texas Tribune* on Twitter.

5–2 The Development of the Texas Party System

LearningOutcome 5–2

Distinguish between liberals and conservatives and between likely supporters of Texas Republicans and Democrats. Explain how the Republican Party became the dominant party in the state.

Although the United States has had a **two-party system** for most of its existence, many states and localities—including Texas—have been dominated by just one party at various times in history. Texas was formerly a one-party Democratic state, but in recent years the state parties have become competitive in congressional and state-level races. To understand political parties in Texas, it is necessary to examine the historical dominance of the Democratic Party, the emergence of two-party competition in the state, and the current preeminence of the Republican Party.

5–2a The One-Party Tradition in Texas

Under the Republic of Texas, there was little party activity. Political divisions were usually oriented around support of, or opposition to, Sam Houston, a leading founder of the Republic. After Texas became a state, though, the Democratic Party dominated Texas politics until the 1990s.

This legacy of dominance was firmly established by the Civil War and the era of Reconstruction, when Yankee troops, under the direction of a Republican Congress, occupied the South. Democratic control resumed after Republican governor Edmund J. Davis (a former Union soldier) was voted out in 1873. The Democrats exercised almost complete control over Texas politics until the surprising victory of Republican gubernatorial candidate Bill Clements in 1978.

The Populist Challenge The Democratic Party was at times challenged by more liberal third parties. The most serious of these challenges came in the late nineteenth century with the Populist revolt. The People's Party grew out of the dissatisfaction of small farmers who demanded government regulation of rates charged by banks and railroads. These farmers—joined by sharecroppers, laborers, and African Americans—mounted a serious election bid in 1896 by taking 44.3 percent of the vote for governor.

Eventually, however, the Democratic Party defused the threat of the Populists by co-opting many of the issues of the new party. The Democrats also effectively disenfranchised African Americans and poor whites in 1902 with the passage of the poll tax.

The Democratic Primary Two events in the early twentieth century solidified the position of the Democrats in Texas politics. The first was the institution of party primary "reforms" in 1906. For the first time, voters could choose the party's nominees by a direct vote in the party primary. Hence, the Democratic primary became a substitute for the two-party contest in the general election. In the absence of Republican competition, the Democratic primary was the only game in town, and it provided a competitive arena for political differences within the state.

The Great Depression The second event to help the Democrats was the Great Depression of the 1930s. Although the Republican presidential candidate, Herbert Hoover, carried Texas in 1928, Republicans were closely associated with the Depression. The effect of this association, plus memories of the Civil War and Reconstruction, ensured Democratic dominance in state government until the early 1990s.

5–2b Conservatives versus Liberals

It is necessary to define the terms *conservative* and *liberal* to understand the ideological basis for factionalism in political parties in Texas. This can be a difficult task because the meanings change with time and the terms may mean different things to different people.

Conservatives Conservatives believe that individuals should be left alone to compete in a free market unfettered by government control—they argue that

two-party system
A political system characterized by two dominant parties competing for political offices, in which third parties have little chance of winning.

government regulation of the economy should be kept to a minimum. Conservatives extol the virtues of individualism, independence, and personal initiative.

CONSERVATIVES AND GOVERNMENT. Despite small-government rhetoric, conservatives often support government involvement and funding to promote business. That may include construction of highways, tax incentives for investment, and other government aids to business. The theory is that these aids will encourage economic development and hence prosperity for the whole society. At the same time, conservatives are likely to oppose or advocate the trimming of government programs that involve redistribution of wealth, such as welfare, health-care assistance, and unemployment compensation.

CONSERVATIVES AND MORALITY. Many conservatives emphasize traditional values associated with the family and the church and favor government action to preserve what they see as the proper moral values of society. Because conservatives hold a more skeptical view of human nature than liberals do, they are more likely to be tougher on perceived threats to personal safety and the public order as well as to traditional and religious values. For example, conservatives are more likely to favor stiffer penalties for criminals, including capital punishment. While conservatives usually combine support for the free market with support for traditional values, they may stress only one of these views.

Libertarians One particular viewpoint often associated with conservatism is libertarianism. In recent years, the Libertarian Party has become an active, if not always influential, force in Texas politics. The Libertarian Party has a hands-off philosophy of government that appeals to many Texas conservatives. Libertarians differ from other conservatives, however, in their support for social as well as economic liberty.

Applying their doctrine to the issues, Libertarians oppose Social Security, campaign-finance reform, gun control, and many foreign policies. They consider programs such as Social Security to be "state-provided welfare." The party supports civil liberties and even the legalization of marijuana. It is against a hard line on illegal immigrants. It also opposes U.S. intervention in world affairs.

The Libertarian Party faces the same hurdles as other third parties do: poor financing, a lack of media coverage, and, in some states, access to the ballot. Further, many of its positions have been co-opted by a libertarian faction of the Republican Party, whose leading member is Texas congressman Ron Paul.

Liberals Liberals believe that it is often necessary for government to regulate the economy and to promote greater social equality. They point to great concentrations of wealth and power that have threatened to control government, destroy economic competition, and weaken individual freedoms. Government power, they believe, should be used to protect the disadvantaged and to promote equality.

LIBERALS AND SOCIAL BENEFITS. Consequently, liberals are generally supportive of the social-welfare programs that conservatives oppose or would restrict. They champion wage and hour laws, the right to form unions, federal unemployment and health-care insurance, subsidized housing, and improved educational opportunities. They are also more likely to favor progressive taxes—taxes with rates that increase as incomes rise. The individual income tax is an example of a progressive tax.

LIBERALS AND CIVIL LIBERTIES. Liberals possess a more optimistic view of human nature than conservatives do. They believe that individuals are essentially rational and therefore that social change will ultimately bring improvement in the human condition. Liberals want government to protect the civil rights and liberties of individuals. They are frequently critical of interference with any exercise of the constitutional rights of free speech, press, religion, assembly, association, and privacy. They often reject conservatives' attempts to "legislate morality" because of the potential for interference with individual rights.

5–2c Conservatives and Liberals in the Texas Democratic Party

For many years, factions within the Texas Democratic Party provided voters with choices similar to those in a two-party system. The election that selects the Democratic Party's nominees—the Democratic primary—was the most important election in Texas.

Until the 1990s, conservative Democrats were much more successful than their liberal counterparts in these primaries. In part, this was because Republican voters, facing no significant primary race of their own, regularly crossed over and supported conservative Democratic candidates. Voters in the general elections, facing a choice between a conservative Democrat and a conservative Republican, usually went with the

Steve Maxwell, the chairman of the Tarrant County Democratic Party, introduces Kenneth Sanders, a candidate for the U.S. Congress, in the summer of 2012.

traditional party—the Democrats. These Republican crossover votes enabled conservative Democrats, with few exceptions, to control the party and state government until the late 1970s.

Conservative Democrats

The conservative Democrats in Texas provide a very good example of the independent relationship of national, state, and local party organizations shown in Figure 5–1 on page 96. Texas conservatives traditionally voted Democratic in state and local races but often refused to support the national Democratic candidates for president. Indeed, the development of the conservative Democratic faction in Texas was an outgrowth of conservative dissatisfaction with many New Deal programs of Franklin D. Roosevelt in the 1930s and Fair Deal programs of Harry Truman in the 1940s.

Thereafter, conservative Democrats in Texas continued to have cool relationship with the national party. Many of them supported Republican presidential candidates: Dwight Eisenhower in 1952 and 1956, Richard Nixon in 1968 and 1972, and Ronald Reagan in 1980 and 1984.

The Success of the Conservative Democrats

Several factors accounted for the historical success of conservative Democrats, but the most important were the power and resources of the conservative constituency. The state's power elite, including the oil, gas, and sulfur industries, has always been strongly conservative. Other large corporations, larger farms and ranches (agribusiness), owners and publishers of many of the state's major daily newspapers, and veterans have contributed to conservative clout.

The most affluent people in the state have been willing and able to contribute their considerable resources to the campaigns of like-minded politicians. These segments of the population are also the most likely to vote in elections. This was a significant advantage to conservative Democrats competing in their party's primary, in which turnout in the past has been particularly low.

Liberal Democrats

Liberals in the Texas Democratic Party consist of groups that have supported the national party ticket and its presidents (Roosevelt, Truman, Kennedy, Johnson, Carter, Clinton, and Obama). These groups include the following:

- *Organized labor,* in particular the American Federation of Labor–Congress of Industrial Organizations (AFL-CIO).
- *African American groups,* including the National Association for the Advancement of Colored People (NAACP).
- *Latino groups,* such as the American G.I. Forum, League of United Latin American Citizens (LULAC), Mexican American Democrats (MAD), and Mexican American Legal Defense and Educational Fund (MALDEF).
- *Various professionals, teachers, and intellectuals.*
- *Small farmers and ranchers,* especially supporters of the Texas Farmers Union.
- *Environmental groups,* such as the Sierra Club.
- *Abortion rights groups,* such as the Texas Abortion Rights Action League (TARAL).
- *Trial lawyers* (lawyers who represent plaintiffs in civil suits and defendants in criminal cases).

In the past, liberal Democratic politicians in Texas were rarely successful, and when they did enjoy success, it rarely lasted for more than a few years. Recently, however, liberal Texas Democrats have had more success in capturing their party's nomination, largely because conservatives are voting in the Republican primary. In the last few years, liberal or moderate Democrats have been routinely nominated for all statewide races. This last point illustrates the irony for liberal Democrats. Although they have gained strength within their party

Democratic st...
the state's gr...
particularl...
Dem...
ur...

...with the quiz below.
...e Chapter in Review card at
... r any questions you miss, read
...ning Outcome section again to
...our exam.
• Rip ...Chapter in Review card.

... Or you can go online to CourseMate

at www.cengagebrain.com for these additional review materials:

- Practice Quizzes
- Key Term Flashcards or Crossword Puzzles
- Audio Summaries
- Simulations, Animated Learning Modules, and Interactive Timelines
- Videos
- American Government NewsWatch

Quiz

1. A broad-based coalition of individuals whose primary goal is to win elections is called a(n):
   a. focus group.   b. interest group.   c. political party.

2. Which of the following is a recent trend affecting political parties?
   a. increasing ideological polarization
   b. a movement of power away from the national political parties
   c. a strong increase in the influence of third parties

3. The American political party system, which includes Texas's system, exhibits three characteristics that are not common in party systems in other parts of the world. Which of the following is NOT one of these characteristics?
   a. decentralization of party organization
   b. pragmatism in policy positions
   c. narrow focus on specific issues versus images

4. What is significant about the single-member district system?
   a. It encourages multiple parties.
   b. It strongly encourages a two-party system.
   c. It makes American political parties highly centralized.

5. What third party most seriously challenged the dominance of the Texas Democratic Party in the late nineteenth century?
   a. Libertarian Party
   b. Greenback Party
   c. People's Party

6. From the end of Reconstruction in 1874 until the 1960s Texas was a one-party state dominated by:
   a. Republicans.   b. Democrats.   c. Populists.

7. A conservative is more likely than a liberal to believe:
   a. the government should promote greater social equality.
   b. the government should stay out of individuals' moral and religious affairs.
   c. the government should promote free market and pro-business policies.

8. The party of liberalism in Texas is the:
   a. Republican Party.
   b. Democratic Party.
   c. Libertarian Party.

9. What explains the rapid rise of the Republican Party in the late 1990s and early 2000s?
   a. Conservatives have defected from the Democratic Party to the Republican Party.
   b. The number of liberal voters in Texas has dramatically declined over the past few decades.
   c. Libertarians have stolen large numbers of liberal voters away from the Democratic Party.

10. A gathering of party members who voted in the party's primary for the purpose of electing delegates to the county or district convention is a:
    a. precinct convention.   b. primary.   c. caucus.

11. Which of the following is NOT a level of organization in the permanent party organization in Texas?
    a. precinct   b. county   c. district

12. The presidential preference primary:
    a. allows voters in the party primary to vote on the party's presidential nominee.
    b. allows only registered members of a party to vote on the party's presidential nominee.
    c. allows designated party leaders to vote on the party's presidential nominee.

13. The 2002 election was critical in Texas politics because it marked the first time in the state's history that all statewide offices were filled by members of the:
    a. Libertarian Party.
    b. Republican Party.
    c. Democratic Party.

14. Most political experts believe the Republican and Democratic parties in Texas will be challenged or energized in the future by:
    a. the increasing size of government in Texas.
    b. the growing population of Hispanics in Texas.
    c. the shift in population from urban to rural communities in Texas.

15. What is concrete evidence of "dealignment" in Texas politics?
    a. the increasing vote for Republican candidates
    b. the increasing incidence of split-ticket voting
    c. the increasing ideological intensity of the voting population

Interest Groups

BOB DAEMMRICH, THE IMAGE WORKS

★ LearningOutcomes

The **Learning Outcomes** labeled 1 through 5 are designed to help improve your understanding of the chapter. After reading this chapter, you should be able to:

6–1 Define *interest groups,* and explain what they do.

6–2 Describe the different types of interest groups.

6–3 Distinguish between direct and indirect forms of influencing government, and identify the different actors that lobbyists attempt to influence.

6–4 Describe the work of lobbyists, and explain what they do and do not have to report.

6–5 Identify some of the factors that affect the power of interest groups, and define *revolving door, iron triangles,* and *issue networks.*

Remember to visit page 138 for additional Study Tools

CONFLICT

Should We Let the University of Texas Raise Its Tuition?

Everybody likes a deal. By some measures, in-state tuition and required fees for undergraduates at the University of Texas at Austin are a deal indeed. The university's in-state tuition and fees for academic year 2011–2012 were $9,792. In comparison, the University of California at Berkeley costs $14,461, and the University of Michigan at Ann Arbor runs $13,437. Of course, private schools are far more expensive. Currently, there is a national debate over the rising cost of a college degree. Naturally, there is a debate in Texas as well.

Times are tough for just about every state government. It was no surprise, therefore, when the Texas Senate suggested in 2011 that the University of Texas budget be reduced by $65 million. The ultimate result would be reduced faculty, reduced administrative staff, and higher tuition rates. By mid-2012, the regents of the University of Texas agreed to raise out-of-state tuition by 2 percent, to more than $33,000 per year. For now, they have decided not to raise in-state tuition. Future tuition rates are uncertain, and Texans are in conflict about how much young residents should pay for a college degree.

Students Should Pay What It Really Costs

Many observers with libertarian leanings believe that students everywhere, including Texas, should pay the full cost of higher education, or at least the full cost over and above private-sector donations. After all, if students don't pay these costs, state taxpayers in general will have to. Why should all Texans, including poor ones, have to subsidize—through their taxes—the lucky few who get to go to the University of Texas?

Other advocates of a tuition hike would not go that far. They point out, however, that if tuition is frozen while state funding declines, the university will have to raid its other budget lines to support its students. It will become harder to recruit, retain, and properly reward top faculty. In the end, "doing more with less" boils down to doing less. A recent ranking of world universities placed UT–Austin thirty-fifth among its global peers. That ranking will fall if tuition isn't raised, and Texas will be the poorer for it.

Increase Efficiency Instead

Opponents of a tuition increase point out that in the last three decades, the cost of a four-year degree nationwide has risen 300 percent (corrected for inflation). This huge increase shows that universities have done little to increase efficiency. No one can really believe that the quality of higher education has increased 300 percent. By 2012, tuition at UT–Austin had increased by more than 80 percent in less than a decade. It's time to stop the gravy train.

What the University of Texas needs to do is harness technology to increase productivity. And technology today costs less and less. Instead of raising tuition, the university administration should find ways to develop effective online courses and to increase the use of online activities in regular courses. These steps would lower the cost of teaching per student. Increased tuition simply allows faculty members to demand and obtain higher salaries—and universities to add more administrative staff. But higher salaries and more bureaucrats don't necessarily mean better education.

Where do you stand?

1. If you were running the University of Texas, would you freeze tuition? Why or why not?
2. What arguments might the head of the faculty council use in favor of raising tuition?

Explore this issue online

- The *Texas Tribune* has extensive online coverage of college and university issues in Texas. Enter "texas tribune higher education" into an Internet search engine.
- The *Daily Texan* is the school newspaper of the University of Texas. Find it by searching on "daily texan."

Introduction

When Texas billionaire Harold Simmons was told by the Texas Commission on Environmental Quality (TCEQ) that he could not import radioactive waste from other states, he did it anyway. His company, Waste Control Specialists, planned to bury the waste at its waste dump near Andrews, Texas. This site sits in close proximity to two water tables, including sections of the Ogallala Aquifer—an important source of water for the High Plains region of the United States. The TCEQ warned that "groundwater is likely to intrude into the proposed disposal units and contact the waste from either or both of two water tables near the proposed facility."[1]

After permission to bring in the waste was initially rejected, the company put its lobbyists to work. The team included a former executive director of the TCEQ, Jeff Saitas. The company lobbied the TCEQ's current executive director, Glenn Shankle, who overruled the technical team. Shortly thereafter, Waste Control Specialists was given permission. A few months later, Shankle followed Saitas, leaving the TCEQ to become a lobbyist for Waste Control Specialists. The revolving-door problem, in which policymakers and regulators leave government positions only to return as lobbyists for the industries they once regulated, is a challenge in a pro-business, antiregulation state like Texas.

6–1 Interest Groups and the Policymaking Process

⭐ **LearningOutcome 6–1**

Define *interest groups*, and explain what they do.

The introductory anecdote illustrates what is at stake in the political process. The state of Texas regulates one of the most productive economies in the world. It has an annual gross state product of $1.3 trillion.[2] The state government's total spending is $173.5 billion.[3] Special interest groups often depend on government spending and lobby policymakers for a share of the government largess. Road construction companies can ask the governor to help increase spending on infrastructure projects. Schoolteachers can lobby the legislature against cuts to public education. Advocates for the infirm can ask lawmakers to maintain spending for health care.

Because the state spends so much money on the many public goods, interest groups want a piece of government spending. Many interest groups lobby the government either to spend more or, if under threat from cutbacks, to maintain current spending levels.

6–1a Lobbying

Although agriculture and energy make up a large sector of the Texas economy, the state has diversified its economy significantly since the mid-1980s. The state's population is almost 26 million people and is growing fast. The racial and ethnic makeup of the state is one of the most diverse in the country. Texas attracts people from a variety of religious backgrounds, has a highly dispersed age demographic, and is becoming more tolerant of gay and lesbian individuals. The state has both large poor and middle-income populations.

Interest Groups and the Size of the State Texas's diversity brings with it a greater variety of special interest groups. Citizens with special interests organize around their concerns, **lobbying** the government for fair and equal treatment, for protection from more powerful groups, and for protection of liberties.

Some states have such huge markets that they are in a position to enact legislation that determines what entire industries produce and how they produce it. Texas is such a state. Manufacturers wanting to sell in Texas modify their products to meet the specifications set by state regulations. They also lobby Texas officials to set standards that are favorable to their industries.

The Many Points of Access to Government Citizens organize into interest groups to protect themselves, their interests, and their values. The structure of state government provides groups with many different avenues to influence state policy. Not only can special interest groups lobby the 150 members of the Texas House and 31 members of the Texas Senate, but they can also petition officers in the Texas executive-branch—the thousands of executive branch appointees and bureaucrats. These groups can bring lawsuits before the courts, and they can also rally the public's support.

6–1b What Are Interest Groups?

Citizens may act alone to influence government, and millions do. When citizens join with others

> **lobbying** Direct contact between an interest group representative and an officer of government.

in an organization designed to influence government, however, they form an **interest group.** The media frequently speak of the interests of women, minorities, employers, and others, but these special interests must unite in a cooperative effort to promote policy objectives before they may be thought of as interest groups.

Interest groups are organizations that pursue public-policy goals on behalf of their members. These groups have a narrower base than political parties. Unlike the parties, they do not nominate candidates for office and may work with officials of both parties to secure their goals. Although many interest groups endorse and support candidates for office, their primary purpose is to influence government decision makers.

Interest groups are also called *pressure groups*. This name derives from the fact that interest groups try to apply pressure on decision makers to select one particular course of action from among several choices. Officeholders are sensitive to interest group pressure because of the groups' potential impact on elections. These groups can provide voting power, endorsements, campaign contributions, and volunteers in election campaigns. They also employ **lobbyists** to express their policy positions to public officials.

6-1c Why People Join Interest Groups

People join interest groups for many reasons. Most individuals lack the status, knowledge, political skills, and money to succeed in influencing government on their own. Joining with others creates a network of like-minded people who can pool their talents and other resources to pursue their political ends. Furthermore, work and family obligations leave little time for most people to become experts on the complexities of policy issues.

The solution is to create or hire an **advocacy** organization to protect one's economic, recreational, social, or political interests. The organization can monitor government activities and alert its members to the need to call or write public officials as needed. A group with many members who are contacting officials at the same time is more likely to achieve favorable results.

The Benefits of Joining Joining groups can also advance career and social goals. People who belong to an organization that meets periodically increase their circle of friends and business contacts. Getting to know others in your trade or profession can lead to job offers, the exchange of knowledge, and the enjoyment of socializing with others who share your interests. Active membership leads to networking with economic, social, and political benefits.

In addition, the culture of a profession may require membership—that is, it is regarded as unprofessional not to be a member. People are expected to stay current in their field. All organizations exist to disseminate information or knowledge, but an organization may also have other tangible benefits that make the dues a bargain. For example, malpractice insurance is available to teachers, attorneys, and medical providers through their professional organizations. A monthly or quarterly magazine or newsletter may be the factor that attracts members to a group. Publications of nature and conservation groups are usually so attractive that people might join simply to enjoy the magazine.

The Ultimate Goal Whatever the principal reason for joining, the ultimate goal is to influence government. After all, the government regulates occupations and professions. It decides who pays how much in taxes and who receives the benefits of those tax dollars through public spending programs. No aspect of life is untouched by the political system.

Those who do not pay attention to what is going on in Washington, D.C., and Austin and their local city hall will still feel the effects of what occurs there. Government is a process of determining who gets what and who pays—it is a process of determining whose values will prevail. As U.S. Representative Barbara Jordan famously said, "Government is too important to be a spectator sport."

Texas Political
SOCIAL MEDIA
Most interest groups have established a presence using social media. Two groups in Texas that are worth investigating are the Texas Association of Business and the Texas State Teachers Association. Both have active Facebook pages.

interest group An organization that expresses the policy desires of its members to officers and institutions of government. Also known as a pressure group.

lobbyist In state law, a person who directly contacts public officials to influence their decisions. Registered lobbyists are paid to represent the interests of their employers.

advocacy The promotion of a particular public-policy position.

6–2 Types of Interest Groups

Interest groups can be classified in a multitude of ways. The simplest is to categorize them as economic, noneconomic, or both.

6–2a Economic Interest Groups

The traditional categories of economic interests operating at the state level are business and the professions, education, local government, agriculture, and labor. Groups in each category seek financial advantages for their members. Business and agriculture are always interested in keeping their taxes low, securing subsidies, avoiding regulation, and receiving government contracts to increase profits.

Education and local government groups want greater state support for local governments and increased salaries and benefits for public employees.

Local government groups try to block unfunded state mandates and gain more control (or less state control) over local affairs. Labor unions seek legislation to make it easier to organize workers into unions and to obtain generous workers' compensation and workplace safety regulations.

> **LearningOutcome 6–2**
>
> Describe the different types of interest groups.

6–2b Noneconomic Interest Groups

Noneconomic groups seek the betterment of society as a whole—as defined by the group. Such organizations may advocate reform of political, social, or economic systems in ways that do not necessarily affect their members' pocketbooks.

The Free Rider Problem Such groups are difficult to form because the groups work for goods that supposedly benefit everyone. This creates an incentive for individuals who will benefit from the work of a noneconomic interest group to become what political scientist Mancur Olson called a *free rider*.[4]

A free rider is an individual who benefits from the work of an interest group, but who does not participate in the collective actions that made the benefits possible. For example, environmental reformers maintain that society as a whole benefits from their activism. Clean air and water promote the well-being of all.

Incentives to Join Many individuals who join noneconomic interest groups are motivated to participate by any of three factors: intense passion, selective incentives, and social pressure. Individuals who join the Texas Right to Life movement, for example, are motivated by strong beliefs about conception and when life begins. The intensity of passion that a citizen possesses motivates that person to join. Other organizations recruit members by

ERIC GAY/AP PHOTO

When public educational funding in Texas was threatened with cuts, even children were asked to take part in demonstrations.

offering selective incentives such as T-shirts, coffee mugs, and newsletters as a way to attract members.

Other noneconomic interest groups rely on social pressure to attract members to join. Neighborhood organizations can pressure neighbors to join a local civic association because those who fail to join are conspicuous by their absence from the life of the community. The threat of ostracism leads many to join such groups.

Noneconomic interest groups benefit when they have large memberships because that translates into greater political clout. Group members can write letters, call, and even vote for or against members of the legislature and other candidates for office. Some noneconomic interest groups that lack deep financial resources can make up for this lack in sheer size.

6–2c Mixed Interest Groups

Many groups do not fit neatly into the economic or noneconomic classification because they pursue social goals that have clear economic effects. Discrimination in any form—on the basis of age, disability, ethnicity, gender, or native language—is a social problem. It can result in a variety of negative consequences, such as lower wages or fewer promotions in the workplace. Groups pursuing both social equality and economic goals are classified as mixed or hybrid organizations.

Few, if any, demands on the political system affect all classes of citizens equally. Some benefit, some suffer inconvenience, and others experience economic loss from any policy adopted. Table 6–1 alongside gives some examples of Texas interest groups in the economic, noneconomic, and mixed categories.

6-2d Government Groups

Agencies of government also lobby each other. Governments are not generally recognized as interest groups, but they are affected by what various political institutions and jurisdictions decide. The governor's staff promotes political

> ## "Government is too important to be a spectator sport."
>
> ~ BARBARA JORDON ~
> U.S. REPRESENTATIVE FROM TEXAS
> 1973–1979

agendas in the legislature. Cities, school districts, and other local governments are seriously affected by legislative decisions on the finances and authority of local government bodies. They are also affected by rules set by state executive-branch agencies. Therefore, local governments often protect and promote their interests by employing lobbyists or assigning employees to function as lobbyists when needed.

In recent years, the hiring of lobbyists by government agencies has become controversial. Critics argue that the public elects legislative representatives, not lobbyists, to represent its interests. Hiring lobbyists is simply an added cost to taxpayers. But cities, universities, and other public agencies respond that they are at a tremendous disadvantage when they do not have the assistance of lobbyists.

When the Texas Department of Transportation hired lobbyist Robert Black, a spokesperson for Governor Rick Perry defended the action by saying,

TABLE 6–1

Interest Group Classifications and Selected Examples

Classification	Sector	Examples
Economic	Agriculture	Texas Farm Bureau
	Business	Texan Association of Business, Chambers of Commerce
	Labor	Texas AFL-CIO, American Federation of State, County and Municipal Employees
	Occupations and professions	Texas Association of Realtors, Texas Trial Lawyers Association
Noneconomic	Patriotic	American Legion
	Public interest	Common Cause Texas, Texans for Public Justice
	Religious	Texas Christian Life Commission
Mixed	Education	Texas State Teachers Association
	Environment and recreation	Texas Nature Conservancy, Citizens' Environmental Coalition
	Race and gender	League of United Latin American Citizens, NAACP, Women's Health and Family Planning Association of Texas
	Local government	Texas Municipal League, Texas County Judges and Commissioners Association

"The fact of the matter is the transportation bureaucracy in Washington, D.C., is incredibly extensive and to have people on the ground who can traverse that bureaucratic maze is highly valuable."[5] Cities and other local governments that do not hire lobbyists to represent their interests do indeed find themselves at a disadvantage.

FOR CRITICAL THINKING

Why might economic interest groups be more powerful than other types of groups?

6–3 What Interest Groups Do

The primary goal of an interest group is to influence all branches of government at all levels to produce policies favorable to its members and to block policies that might be harmful to their interests.

6–3a Negative and Positive Views of Interest Groups

LearningOutcome 6–3

Distinguish between direct and indirect forms of influencing government, and identify the different actors that lobbyists attempt to influence.

Interest groups are instrumental in drawing *selected* citizens into political participation to influence public policies, most often in a way that encourages the promotion of narrow, selfish interests. Indeed, critics focus on the harm that can result from powerful groups' demanding that public policy reflect their values. Critics of the system of influence also worry about corruption and intimidation of public officials by special interests. The need for campaign contributions, they believe, makes elected officials especially vulnerable to pressure. The bottom line for critics is their concern that special interests will prevail over the interests of the general public.

Advantages of Interest Groups Democracy, however, calls for politically attentive and active

citizens. From this perspective, interest groups educate their members about issues and mobilize them to participate in constitutionally approved ways. Simultaneously, interest groups inform and educate public officials.

Interest groups provide policymakers with valuable information as they lobby individual government officials and as they testify before legislative committees. Because state law makes it a crime to knowingly share false information with state lawmakers, most special interest groups are careful to provide truthful, if one-sided, information.[6] This information can be costly and time consuming to gather. Because interest groups provide the information free of cost, taxpayers are spared the expense.

Competing Interest Groups The number and variety of interest groups also help ensure that no one group will be dominant. A state such as Texas, which has a diverse and complex economic system, tends to produce a wide variety of interest groups. This diversity of interest groups in Texas makes it difficult for any one group to dominate the state's politics. As a result, the public may be protected from public policy that benefits one group at the expense of the many.

Agricultural, energy, legal, banking, medical, religious, racial, ethnic, and educational interest groups are just a few of the organized interests in Texas, and all compete with one another for favorable legislation. Table 6–2 below summarizes some of the positive and negative effects of interest group activity.

TABLE 6–2

Positive and Negative Effects of Interest Group Activity

Positive	Negative
Variety of groups ensures competition	Representation of only narrow interests
Political participation and mobilization	Secret communications with public officials
Education of members and public officials	Corruption or intimidation of public officials
Shared information that is free to taxpayers	Biased information for decision makers
Increased political representation, based on voluntary association and free speech	Unequal political representation, based on financial resources and organizational skills

6–3b Direct Means of Influencing Government

Interest groups employ several tactics to directly influence policymakers, including lobbying officeholders, filing lawsuits, getting their advocates appointed to state boards, testifying before legislative committees, and organizing public demonstrations.

Lobbying the Legislative and Executive Branches Lobbying is direct contact between an interest group representative and a legislative or executive-branch official or employee for the purpose of influencing a specific public-policy outcome. Legislatures create, finance, and change government programs, and many individuals and groups affected by these legislative decisions try to influence the process. The average voter may not be aware that enormous sums of money, privilege, and prestige are also at stake in the executive decision-making process.

The executive branch or administration is charged with the **implementation** (carrying out) of legislative policy. The legislature delegates a great deal of **discretion** to executive agencies, both directly and indirectly. The legislative branch **delegates** power to the executive branch to select the means to carry out laws. Administrative agencies complete the policymaking process by promulgating rules or regulations that specify how a law will be applied to actual situations. Organized interest groups have a real interest in shaping the regulations that will apply to them.

In short, because what government does is not simply the result of legislative decisions, lobbyists must actively monitor and seek to influence executive-branch rulemaking and enforcement as well.

Filing Suit in Court
Organized interests use the courts to further their causes for several reasons. One is that a lack of funds or public support dictates that their resources be

BOB DAEMMRICH/THE IMAGE WORKS

Here a lobbyist for the Consumers Union in Austin meets with congressional aides in the Texas Capitol. He works on bills for consumers' rights.

spent on litigation. Lawsuits are less expensive than trying to influence the legislature, and public opinion is supposed to be irrelevant to judicial outcomes.

A second reason for using the courts is that they may be a last resort when an interest group has not prevailed in the legislative or executive decision-making process. Courts can declare legislation unconstitutional or rule that executive decisions are illegal. Interest groups may find that the courts may apply an interpretation of the law that benefits their interests in ways that the rulings of an administrative agency did not.

A third purpose is to delay the implementation of a law or rule. Courts often stay (suspend) implementation of a rule while a case is pending. The members of the interest group can continue to operate as before. Filing a lawsuit, even when a group expects to lose, can delay the application of costly rules.

A fourth reason to file suit is to gain public attention. Media coverage of the lawsuit brings public attention to the case and may also bring pressure on decision makers to change their policies or to negotiate with the filer to settle on a more favorable public policy.

Advising and Serving on State Boards State laws in Texas generally require that a majority of the members of an appointed board come from the profession, occupation, business, or activity the state agency is regulating. The mere existence of such laws is testimony to the power of interest groups to institutionalize their influence on government. These board members and commissioners are part-time officials

implementation The carrying out by the executive branch of policies made by the legislature and rulings issued by the judiciary.

discretion The power to make decisions on the basis of personal judgment rather than specific legal requirements.

delegate To legally transfer authority from one official or institution to another.

and full-time practitioners of the occupation that they have the power to regulate. They personally exercise power as state officials even as they represent an interest group that lobbies the agency and provides it with information.

This blurring of the line between the state and a special interest is called **co-optation**. The **public interest** is endangered when state officials act as agents for a group that the agency regulates. A **conflict of interest** exists when the decision maker is personally affected by the decision being made.

Organizing Demonstrations

Groups periodically use marches and demonstrations to obtain publicity for a cause. Press coverage is all but guaranteed. This sort of "theater" is especially suited for television news. When the legislature is in session, demonstrations are plentiful. During the 82nd legislative session, public school teachers, immigrants' rights groups, Tea Party members, and countless others rallied in Austin to express support or opposition to a whole host of bills.

One challenge for interest groups using this kind of tactic is to enlist enough members to be impressive and at the same time keep control of the demonstration. Violating the law, blocking traffic, damaging property, and using obscenities do not win support from fellow citizens or public officials with the power to change the conditions the group is protesting.

Grassroots versus Astroturf Lobbying

Interest groups that can mobilize large numbers of supporters to contact officials have a clear advantage. Such groups are well organized at the grassroots level. Some economic interest groups, however, have developed the tactic of artificially fabricating what looks like grassroots support. Money can substitute for genuine enthusiasm. Organizers can be paid, and public support subsidized. This type of activity has been dubbed **astroturf lobbying,** after AstroTurf, a trademarked artificial grass used in some football stadiums. (The Houston Astrodome, used by the Houston Astros, was the first major facility to use the product.)

6–3c Indirect Means of Influencing Government

Besides trying to directly influence state policymakers, interest groups endeavor to shape the political environment in which policy decisions are made. They engage in political campaigns and other public relations efforts to create a favorable political climate in which to pursue their particular group's agenda.

Electioneering

Although interest groups do not nominate candidates for office, one candidate may be more supportive of a group's cause than another. The organization may decide to endorse and recommend that its members vote for the candidate more inclined to support their issue. The organization's newsletter or magazine will carry this message, as will mass e-mails and other communications.

A second means of helping candidates favorable to the group's goals is to sponsor a political action committee (PAC). As explained in Chapter 4, the sole purpose of a PAC, which is legally separate from the interest group, is funneling money to candidates.

Many interest groups are strong enough to influence the outcome of elections. They may be in a position to make significant campaign contributions. In some cases, interest groups are powerful enough to have their own employees selected for public office. Several of the state's major law firms, which also have powerful lobbying arms, boast members of the Texas legislature and executive branch as current or former partners. Similarly, executives from large corporations or sizable interest groups are often selected to serve on government boards and commissions.

Educating the Public

Interest groups frequently find it advisable to ply the general public with messages that build a positive image of the group's members. Well-funded interest groups employ the services of public relations firms to build reputations for honesty, desirable products and services, concern for the well-being of community members, and good citizenship.

GETTING THE WORD OUT. An interest group may use the organization's magazine, annual reports to stockholders, and press releases to newspapers as vehicles for building its reputation. Such materials, of course, will seek to educate the public about the wisdom of the policies supported by the organization. Groups may

co-optation The capturing of a state institution by members of an interest group. In effect, state power comes to be exercised by the members of a private interest.

public interest The good of the whole society, without bias for or against any particular segment of the society.

conflict of interest The situation that exists when a public official is in a position to make a decision that might result in personal economic benefit or advantage.

astroturf lobbying The fabrication of public support for issues supported by interest groups that gives the impression of widespread public support.

purchase print and broadcast advertisements to shape and mobilize public opinion on behalf of their members or to neutralize opposition to their cause.

FRAMING THE ISSUES. It is important for a group that wants government to take action to articulate the need or problem in exactly the right language. Framing the problem correctly allows the group to stay in control of the issue and evoke a positive official response.

Interest groups usually prefer to influence public officials before the issue becomes a public controversy. Once an issue becomes public, opponents will try to redefine it negatively. For example, people who want to promote school vouchers that may be used at religious schools must emphasize the responsibility of the state to assist all children to learn. Opponents will seek to convince the public that such aid is a violation of the "separation of church and state." Words are the weapons of political battle, and most political struggles are group-against-group contests.

Socializing Interest groups know that friendships can be formed at social functions. Informal occasions allow people to interact in comfortable settings. A lobbyist may invite a public official to lunch or to a party to establish a positive relationship. Formal occasions designed to honor a person can also serve to build positive relationships. Invitations to speak before a group are a way to cultivate friendships. The purpose of these social invitations is to establish a positive impression that pays off when public officials vote or make policy decisions on issues important to the interest group. Socializing is a good investment for a group, regardless of whether there is an immediate need for a public official's support.

Access to public officials is the prerequisite for influencing public decisions. Getting in the door to discuss a matter of concern in time to shape the public-policy outcome is the goal. Indirect means of influencing government often pave the way for direct lobbying. Groups that have established good reputations with public officials have a built-in advantage. Still, even the most successful groups can expect to lose sometimes.

FOR CRITICAL THINKING

Do you find any of the standard techniques for influencing government described here to be ethically dubious? Why or why not?

The Craft of Lobbying

Whether they work for a single client or have a massive client list, lobbyists use a variety of strategies to influence the branches of government. The techniques of persuasion and the resources employed vary with the policy at issue and the size and skill of the lobbyist's operation.

LearningOutcome 6–4

Describe the work of lobbyists, and explain what they do and do not have to report.

6–4a Lobbying the Legislature

Clearly, anyone who directly contacts public officials to influence their behavior should be extroverted and enjoy socializing. The lobbyist's first job is to become known and recognized by members of the legislature and any executive officials relevant to the interest he or she represents.

Lobbying before the Legislative Session Begins
Before a legislative session begins, a lobbyist must have successfully completed several tasks:

- Learn which members are predisposed to support the cause, who is on the other side, and who can be swayed.
- Memorize the names and faces of the members, their nonlegislative occupations, the counties they represent, and a little about their families.
- Establish rapport through contact with the members of the legislature.
- Get to know the staffs of legislators, because the member can be influenced through them.
- Know the legislative issues, including the arguments of opponents.

Approaching the Legislators How does a lobbyist approach a member of the legislature or the leadership? How do you get in the door, and what do you say when you get in? How important is the staff of a legislator to a lobbyist? Is it necessary to see all 181 members of the Texas legislature, the lieutenant governor, and the governor? Because a session has only 140 days, it should be clear that lobbying must precede the convening of the legislature.

The eighteen-month period between regular sessions leaves ample time to work on relationships, learn what proposals have a chance of receiving a favorable response, draft legislation, and line up sponsors to introduce bills in the house and senate at the beginning of the next session.

Honesty Is the Best Policy

To maintain a relationship, the lobbyist must provide the legislator with accurate information about the legislation that the lobbyist's group is supporting or opposing. This includes off-the-record admissions of the pluses and minuses of the legislation. Honesty is, in fact, the best policy for a lobbyist when dealing with a public official. No public official will appreciate being the victim of a "snow job." That said, an interest group can sometimes gain points by supplying arguments that an official can use to mislead others. In this circumstance, it can be said that "honesty serves dishonesty."

Wining and Dining Also Help

A lobbyist can befriend a legislator in several ways that may eventually pay off. Lobbyists have information that may be valuable to a legislator, and they may be able to help draft an important piece of legislation for the official. Providing an occasional free meal or acknowledging a helpful legislator at a banquet in the legislator's honor also has merit from the lobbying perspective. All these actions are necessary to create and maintain goodwill, without which nothing is possible.

Key Endorsements

Not all members of the legislature are equal. Establishing rapport and obtaining feedback from the powerful presiding officers—the speaker of the house and lieutenant governor—are especially useful. No endorsement is more important to an interest group than that of the presiding officers. If an endorsement for the group's legislative proposal is not forthcoming, the lobbyist must persuade the presiding officers to be neutral in the legislative struggle.

Securing the endorsement of the chair of each committee through which the legislation must pass before it can go to the floor for a vote is an advantage second only to that of securing the support of the presiding officers. Similarly, legislation sought by local governments must have the endorsement of community leaders, or it is doomed to fail.

6–4b Lobbying Administrative Agencies

Both administrators and interest group representatives seek each other out to provide and obtain information. For example, if the Texas Educational Diagnosticians Association (TEDA) and colleges of education want to know whether the examination for certification is scheduled for revision, they would contact the State Board for Educator Certification to find out. The issue is important to the TEDA because the content and difficulty of the examination affect the number of recruits to the profession. The faculties know that changes in the examination by the state mean changes in the curriculum. The inquiry about the examination also allows the interest groups to communicate their professional opinion about the current examination and make suggestions about any changes.

The Rulemaking Process

A lobbying agency's economic interest clients are especially interested in influencing the rules and guidelines that control how they do business because the rules of doing business directly affect profits. Agencies issue guidelines to govern the actions of their employees—bureaucrats—in applying the law.

The agency also issues formal rules that prescribe the standards of conduct followed by citizens subject to the law. The rulemaking process in Texas gives all interested parties an opportunity to influence the agency's decision. Notice of intent to make a rule must be published in the *Texas Register.* A timeline for written public comment on the proposed rule is established. At the close of the comment period, the agency analyzes the public's views. It then publishes a "final rule" that has the same force as law.

Although all citizens have the right to take part in the rulemaking process, only those aware of and interested in a proposed rule actually participate. Ordinary citizens do not subscribe to the *Texas Register,* but corporations, labor unions, law firms, and major interest groups do. They know when to mobilize their members to influence decision making. Interest groups contact members by mail, e-mail, Facebook and Twitter, or phone, and ask them to call or write the agency about the rule. Sometimes, preaddressed cards with the desired message are distributed to members to sign and mail to the agency.

Agency-Client Links

A natural linkage exists between an agency and its clientele. Most state agencies are headed by boards and commissions drawn from the industry, trade, profession, or activity the agency regulates. Those who govern and those who are governed know each other because they usually share the same occupations or business interests. State board or commission members are recruited from the businesses or occupations that they

Texas Register The official publication of the state that gives the public notice of proposed actions and adopted policies of executive-branch agencies.

held together by mutual self-interest. These relationships can become a subsystem in the legislative and administrative decision-making processes. Called **iron triangles,** these alliances operate largely outside public view because they dominate a narrow range of routine decisions that are of marginal interest to the general public but are of critical importance to the interest groups and bureaucrats involved.

For example, petroleum interests have formed a close association with the Texas Railroad Commission, whose members they help elect. Agricultural interests have established a similar symbiotic relationship with the commissioner of agriculture and agriculture committees in the state legislature. In addition, highway contractors have formed an alliance with the Texas Department of Transportation and interested legislators. We will illustrate these alliances more extensively in Chapter 8, as we discuss the state's bureaucracy.

Issue Networks.

Whereas iron triangles are more or less permanent alliances among legislators, bureaucrats, and interest groups dealing with a narrow set of issues, other broader public issues like health care, abortion, and environmental protection activate wider-ranging coalitions. These alliances can include interest groups, career bureaucrats, academic researchers, think tanks, political bloggers, newspaper editors, neighborhood leaders, radio talk-show hosts, and other community activists. We call these coalitions **issue networks.** Such alliances are dynamic—different activists and interest groups organize around different public issues.[33]

Iron triangles are most likely to control rather routine decisions. Economic concerns dominate their agenda as they seek subsidies, tax breaks, and regulations favorable to those interests. Issue networks have broader policy interests and hence have more participants, but these alliances are still relatively small and often temporary. Often, two issue networks face off against each other on opposite sides of an important issue.

Political Movements

Issue networks have the potential to blossom into a larger **political movement.** When issue networks tap into concerns that are important to masses of people, they may develop a large following with a fairly stable membership. One such political movement is the Tea Party.

Beginning with a relatively small network of activists opposing the federal bailouts of the financial industry, the Tea Party movement gained strength after the passage of President Barack Obama's stimulus bill (the American Recovery and Reinvestment Act of 2009). By the time health-care reform was passed (the Patient Protection and Affordable Care Act of 2010), the Tea Party had evolved into a full-fledged antigovernment movement. A small alliance of interested groups had transformed itself into a significant political movement.

In Texas, the Tea Party movement has had enormous success. Its support led to a strong Republican showing in the 2010 elections. A Republican supermajority in the Texas legislature, receptive to the conservative agenda, enacted several bills popular with Tea Party and pro-business groups. During the 82nd Texas legislative session, pro-life groups lobbied successfully for two major pieces of legislation that would restrict a woman's right to choose an abortion—a bill requiring a pre-abortion sonogram and one that abolished funding for Planned Parenthood. These laws serve as a testament to how interest group alliances can become powerful forces both in elections and in the policy-making process.

iron triangle A working coalition among administrative agencies, interest groups, and legislative committees that share a common interest in seeing either the implementation or the defeat of certain policies and proposals.

issue network Fluid alliances of individuals and organizations that are interested in a particular policy area and join together when policymaking topics affect their interests.

political movement A mass alliance of like-minded groups and individuals seeking broad changes in the direction of government policies.

FOR CRITICAL THINKING

In the subsection "Identifying the Most Powerful Groups," we identified five of the most influential interest groups in Texas. *Why do you think these particular groups are so powerful?*

TEXANS IN

CONFLICT Interest Groups

Despite their constitutional protection, interest groups are one of the most controversial features of our democratic system. Some of the controversies that interest groups inspire include the following:

- Can lobbying improve legislation—or does it almost always result in adding flaws and loopholes to the laws?

- When businesspersons or professionals are appointed to a state board that regulates their particular business or profession, does Texas benefit from the knowledge of these experts—or is it more likely that they will put the welfare of their industry above the welfare of the average citizen?

- How much of a problem is it if some individuals can benefit from the activities of an interest group without actually joining it?

- Finally, are there too many lobbyists—or is the real problem that ordinary people do not have anyone to lobby for them?

TAKE ACTION

- Go to the Texas Ethics Commission's Web site to discover which people, corporations, labor unions, and nonprofit organizations are lobbying Texas state government. Enter "texas ethics" into an Internet search engine.

- Learn how to lobby. Go to the Texas State Teachers Association Web site by searching on "tsta." Click on the "Issues & Action" tab, and then click on "Guide to Lobbying" under the "Take Action at the State Level!" menu.

- Identify a state or local interest group related to your career or professional ambitions. Research this group—start by typing the name of the group into an Internet search engine—and identify the officers, membership dues, size of membership, issues being promoted, and name and frequency of any publications. Continue your research by consulting the Texas Ethics Commission's reports on campaign contributions or lobbyists to see how active the group is in Texas.

- Using a search engine, enter the name of a major corporation, a labor union, a professional organization, a nonprofit organization, and a public interest group. See what public-policy issues each is promoting in Texas and in the nation.

- You can find out who spent the most money lobbying Texas's decision makers by searching on "austins oldest profession."

STUDY TOOLS

Ready to study?

- Review what you've read with the quiz below. Check your answers on the Chapter in Review card at the back of the book. For any questions you miss, read the corresponding Learning Outcome section again to prepare for class and your exam.
- Rip out and study the Chapter in Review card.

. . . Or you can go online to CourseMate

at **www.cengagebrain.com** for these additional review materials:

- Practice Quizzes
- Key Term Flashcards or Crossword Puzzles
- Audio Summaries
- Simulations, Animated Learning Modules, and Interactive Timelines
- Videos
- American Government NewsWatch

Quiz

1. How do interest groups differ from political parties?
   a. Interest groups primarily exist to contest and win elections.
   b. Interest groups primarily exist to influence public policy.
   c. Interest groups primarily exist to raise money for political candidates.

2. Direct contact between an interest group representative and an officer of government is called:
   a. advocacy.   b. co-opting.   c. lobbying.

3. Which of the following is the best example of a noneconomic interest group?
   a. Texas Farm Bureau
   b. Texas Association of Business
   c. Common Cause

4. Which of the following is the best example of an economic interest group?
   a. Texas Christian Life Commission
   b. Texas AFL-CIO
   c. American Legion

5. A major difficulty for noneconomic interest groups in mobilizing potential members is that an individual who will not participate will still benefit from the group's work. This is the:
   a. revolving door phenomenon
   b. free rider problem
   c. iron triangle

6. Which of the following is NOT an incentive for potential members to join noneconomic interest groups?
   a. government jobs
   b. selective incentives
   c. social pressure

7. Interest groups engage in all of these activities EXCEPT:
   a. lobbying.
   b. electioneering.
   c. agency administration.

8. Identify an allegedly negative effect of interest group activity.
   a. competition created by the variety of groups
   b. representation of narrow interests
   c. political participation and mobilization

9. All of the following are examples of indirect means that interest groups use to influence government EXCEPT:
   a. litigation.
   b. electioneering.
   c. educating the public.

10. In Texas, interest group lobbyists have increased opportunity to advocate within the judicial system compared to the federal judicial system.
    a. true   b. false

11. All of the following are methods that lobbyists use to gain access to and influence legislators EXCEPT:
    a. seeking key endorsements from important committee members and presiding officers.
    b. wining and dining legislators.
    c. exchanging cash donations for support on key pieces of legislation.

12. Lobbyists in Texas are required to register with which of the following?
    a. State Lobbying Committee
    b. Speaker of the House
    c. Texas Ethics Commission

13. Which of the following factors does NOT enhance the influence of interest groups?
    a. low voter turnout
    b. a part-time legislature
    c. a two-party system

14. The term that describes the working coalition among administrative agencies, interest groups, and legislative committees that share a common interest in seeing either the implementation or the defeat of certain policies and proposals is _____.
    a. the issue network
    b. the iron triangle
    c. the revolving door

15. What is the key concern about the revolving door phenomenon?
    a. the presence of bribery
    b. the fact that legislators don't have enough time in office to study issues themselves
    c. the conflicts of interest that may result from retiring legislators who lobby their peers

The Legislature

AP PHOTO/JACK PLUNKETT

★ Learning Outcomes

The **Learning Outcomes** labeled 1 through 5 are designed to help improve your understanding of the chapter. After reading this chapter, you should be able to:

7–1 Summarize the redistricting process, define *gerrymandering*, and describe the composition of the state legislature.

7–2 Evaluate the concept of a "citizen legislature" and the consequences of low compensation, short sessions, and small staffs.

7–3 Identify the presiding officers of the Texas House and Senate, and distinguish among the different types of legislative committees.

7–4 Explain the powers of the presiding officers and committee chairs, the ways in which legislators can delay or block bills, and how a bill becomes a law.

7–5 Identify and describe the various legislative boards and committees at the disposal of the legislative leadership.

Remember to visit page 168 for additional Study Tools

139

Should Texas Have a Full-Time Legislature?

AP PHOTO/HARRY CABLUCK

Texas is a big state with a big population and big problems. Still, its legislature is in session fewer days than the legislature in just about any other large state. Texas legislators meet in continuous session every two years for only 140 days. Of necessity, all elected legislators in Texas are part-timers. They are paid $7,200 per year plus a small amount each day that the legislature is in session, so unless they are independently wealthy, they must have other jobs. In addition, Texas legislators have relatively small legislative staffs. Members of the Texas House typically have three assistants, while state senators have about seven. As a result, there is not enough staff available to research all pending legislation.

The National Conference of State Legislatures recently found that even though Texas legislators meet for relatively few days over a two-year period, they still spend more than twenty-five hours a week on average each year working as legislators. That means that their $7,200 annual pay doesn't even come close to the minimum wage. Some Texans believe that the state constitution should be changed to provide for a full-time legislature, like those in California, Michigan, New York, and Pennsylvania.

Texas Needs Full-Time Legislators

Having a part-time legislature might have made sense in an era when Texas was sparsely populated and faced few complex issues, but today is a different story. A full-time, better-paid legislature would attract better people and a wider source of prospective legislators. We would certainly see improvements in the quality of representation.

Also, Texas would probably stop the "speed legislating" that is so popular today. In the 140 days of the 82nd Legislative Session in 2011, the Texas legislature passed more than three times as many bills as the 111th U.S. Congress did between January 2009 and January 2011.

Because of time constraints, lawmakers rely on interest groups such as the American Legislative Exchange Council (ALEC) to write the bills that they then claim as their own. Legislators cannot become familiar with all of the legislation on which they vote and instead depend on interest group sources for information and advice.

A Full-Time Legislature Would Do Too Much

If you think a lot of bills are passed in Texas today, you might see twice as many if the legislature met in a year-long session. After all, full-time legislators quite naturally will come up with more laws. What else do they have to do? Those additional laws will increase government intervention in the economy and in people's lives. Legislators in Texas and elsewhere govern best when they govern least. It is true that because of poor pay there is a lot of turnover in the legislature—but that's a good thing. No one benefits from career politicians, except the politicians themselves. Full-time legislators would be out of touch with reality. If they aren't in their home districts, where their constituents can complain to them about what goes on in Austin, then they won't have their feet on the ground.

Look at what has happened to states that do have full-time legislators. They are the ones with the biggest deficits and the most problems. Let's leave Texas politics as it has always been—different, but for a reason. Texas itself is different!

Where do you stand?

1. Why might current part-time Texas legislators want to keep the status quo?
2. Why might it be beneficial to have less turnover in the legislature?

Explore this issue online

- For information on state legislatures, locate the Web site of the National Conference of State Legislatures by entering "ncsl" into an Internet search engine. (Several other groups share the "ncsl" initials, but the legislative group should be at the top of the page.)
- Searching on "full part time legislatures" will bring up debates in states around the country on whether legislators should serve full time.

Introduction

The Texas legislature is bicameral. It consists of two chambers: the 31-member Texas Senate and the 150-member Texas House of Representatives. By establishing a bicameral legislature, the framers of the Texas Constitution followed the pattern set for the national Congress and used in every state other than Nebraska, which has a unicameral, or one-house, legislature.

On most matters, the two chambers share equal powers, and both of them must agree on a proposed bill for it to become law. The senate does have the special power to confirm or approve the governor's appointments of state officers.

The chief argument for the use of bicameral legislative bodies is that one chamber can serve as a check on the other so that legislation will not be passed hastily, without adequate reflection. Because it slows legislative action, bicameralism can also lead to gridlock, as one chamber passes policy changes and the other uses delaying tactics.

One wing of the capitol houses the 31-member Texas Senate, and the other wing houses the 150-member Texas House of Representatives.

JEREMY WOODHOUSE/SPACES IMAGES/CORBIS

7–1 Selecting Legislators

The 150 members of the Texas House are all elected for two-year terms when the state holds its general election in even-numbered years. At that time, only half of the state senators are elected because they serve four-year staggered terms. All legislators are elected from single-member districts. Several factors affect the selection of the members of the Texas legislature, including political considerations, the politics of districting, and their formal qualifications.

> **Learning Outcome 7–1**
>
> Summarize the redistricting process, define *gerrymandering*, and describe the composition of the state legislature.

7–1a Geographic Districts

In Texas, as in other states, the legislature used the 2010 census data to draw the geographic boundaries for electoral districts. Because Texas has experienced dramatic population growth, its many district lines had to be redrawn to reflect the change. The districts for the 83rd Legislative Session are shown in Figures 7–1 and 7–2 on the following page.

These districts are approximately equal in population size, as required by the United States Supreme Court decision in *Reynolds v. Sims*. In this case, the Supreme Court ruled, "Simply stated, an individual's right to vote for state legislators is unconstitutionally impaired when its weight is in a substantial fashion diluted when compared with votes of citizens living in other parts of the State."[1] The Court, in short, established the "one person, one vote" standard that requires each legislator to represent approximately the same number of people.

Redistricting Following each ten-year census, the number of U.S. representatives allotted to each state changes. This reallocation is known as **reapportionment**. Texas has added representatives following each census since 1940, so reapportionment always has an effect on how its district boundaries are redrawn. **Redistricting**, or redrawing district lines, is required because of reapportionment and also because of changes in the relative population of various parts of the state.

Should the Texas legislature fail to redistrict, the state constitution provides that the task be performed by the Legislative Redistricting Board. The board is **ex officio**, which

> **reapportionment** The reallocation of U.S. representatives by state following a ten-year census.
>
> **redistricting** The redrawing of the boundaries of districts that elect U.S. representatives and state legislators. It is mandatory following a census but can be done at other times as well.
>
> **ex officio** Holding a position automatically because one also holds some other office.

FIGURE 7-1

Texas House of Representatives Districts
83rd Legislature, 2013–2014

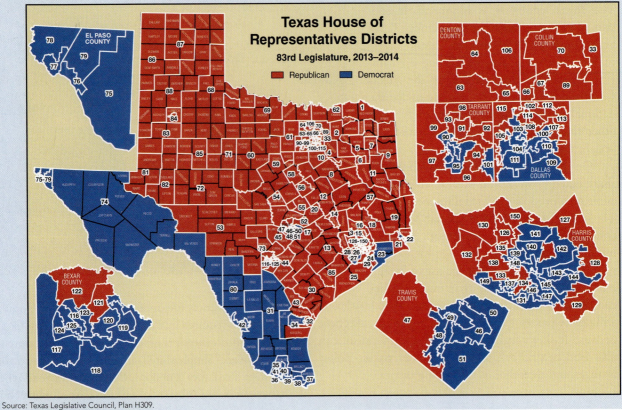

Source: Texas Legislative Council, Plan H309.

FIGURE 7-2

Texas Senate Districts
83rd Legislature, 2013–2014

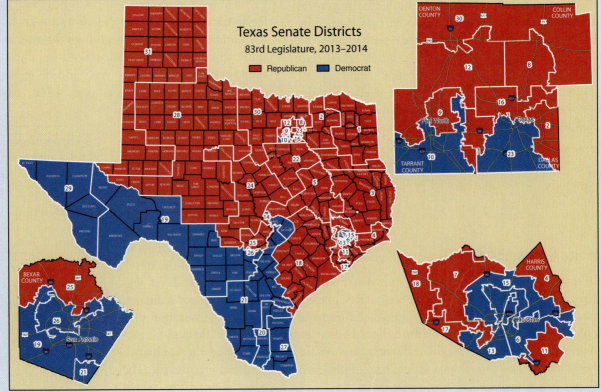

Source: Texas Legislative Council, Plan S172.

means that its membership is made up of persons who hold other offices. The members are the lieutenant governor, the speaker of the house, the attorney general, the comptroller, and the commissioner of the Texas General Land Office.

The Size of Districts The average population of an electoral district for the Texas House of Representatives in 2011 was 171,165. Each house member represented 32,000 more people than she or he did a decade earlier. Representing an average of 828,216 residents, each Texas senator served about 156,000 more people in 2011 than in 2000. Texas Senate districts contain more people than the districts that elect members of the U.S. House of Representatives.

The population of legislative districts can deviate plus or minus 5 percent from the average, but not much more. When districts deviate too much from the mean, Texas must justify these deviations to the U.S. Justice Department. The once-per-decade redistricting ritual goes more or less unnoticed by many members of the general public. For the political practitioner and the political activist, however, it may resemble a life-or-death struggle.

7–1b Gerrymandering

The way districts are drawn at any level of government determines, to a large extent, the political, ideological, and ethnic makeup of the legislative body. With redistricting, political careers may be made or broken, public policy determined for at least a decade, and the power of ethnic or political minorities neutralized.

A district drawn in such a way as to give candidates from a certain party, ethnic group, or faction an advantage is known as a **gerrymander.** Gerrymandering increases or reduces the political power of specific groups of voters. The relative influence of political parties, ethnic groups, ideological combatants, and individual politicians is therefore at stake. (See Figure 7–3 below.)

Cracking and Packing

Three basic gerrymandering techniques are widely used. One is to diffuse a concentrated political or ethnic minority among several districts so that its votes in any one district are negligible. This is known as **cracking.** A second tactic, known as **packing,** is used if the minority group's numbers are great enough when diffused to affect the outcome of elections in several districts. The minority is therefore concentrated, or "packed," in one district, ensuring that it will influence only one election and that its effect on other districts will be minimal.

> **gerrymander** A district or precinct that is drawn specifically to favor some political party, candidate, or ethnic group.
>
> **cracking** A gerrymandering technique in which concentrated political or ethnic minority groups are spread among several districts so that their votes in any one district are negligible.
>
> **packing** A gerrymandering technique in which members of partisan or minority groups are concentrated into one district, thereby ensuring that the group will influence only one election rather than several.

FIGURE 7–3

The Process of Gerrymandering

The schematic on the left shows an example of no gerrymandering, with the blue dots representing a given number of people in one party and the red dots representing the same number of persons in the other party in four equally competitive districts. The figure on the right shows how the same population can be gerrymandered to guarantee a three-to-one advantage in representation for the blue voters.

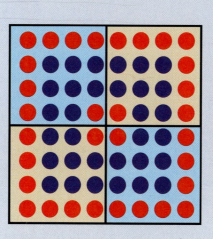
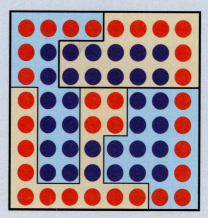

Pairing A third gerrymandering tactic is a **pairing** technique that places two or more **incumbents'** residences or political bases into the same district, thereby ensuring that one of the two legislators will be defeated. Pairing can be used to punish legislators who have fallen from grace with the legislative leadership.

As the technique of pairing illustrates, gerrymandering can be used to protect the "right kind" of incumbents—those who support the legislative leadership or the agenda of powerful special interests. Although the federal courts prohibit racial gerrymandering, they are reluctant to become involved in political gerrymandering.

7–1c Redistricting after the 2010 Census

Texas has experienced some very contentious debates over redistricting in the past few decades. As the state's minority population has grown, so has the demand for minority political representation. But minority groups are not the only populations growing in influence.

Politically, the state's citizens have grown more Republican. More and more policymakers are Republicans as well. After the 2010 elections, Republicans controlled both the Texas House and the Texas Senate with much larger majorities than before. As a result, following the 2010 census, Republicans were able to redraw district boundaries that were favorable to the Republican Party.

Disputes over the 2010 Redistricting Organizations representing minority groups sued the state, charging that new district boundaries did not create new Latino districts, even though a majority of the state's net growth was in its Hispanic population. Latino groups and Republicans were able to come to an agreement on the Texas Senate maps. The Texas House and congressional district maps, however, were not settled in time for the regularly scheduled Texas primary.

Because Texas has a history of racial discrimination, it is one of several states covered by certain provisions of the federal Voting Rights Act. Under these provisions, Texas is required to obtain federal preclearance for newly redrawn districts. Normally, states obtain such preclearance from the U.S. Department of Justice. Instead, after the 2010 redistricting (undertaken in 2011), Texas elected to take its case to the U.S. District Court for the District of Columbia. It did so because Texas Republicans did not trust the judgment of a Justice Department that was part of the Obama administration.

Pending a ruling by the District of Columbia court, a federal district court in San Antonio drew temporary district boundaries so that primary elections would not be delayed any further. Typically, Texas primaries are usually held in early March, but in 2012 they were held on May 29. The initial boundaries drawn by the San Antonio court were rejected by the United States Supreme Court in January 2012. The Supreme Court ruled that the district court had departed too far from the lines drawn by the legislature and that, pending a definitive ruling on the legislative maps, the Republican boundaries should stand unless they resulted in unmistakable discrimination. The San Antonio court then drew new maps closer to the original legislative plan, which were used in the 2012 primaries and the general election.[2]

In August 2012, the District of Columbia court finally ruled that the legislature's plans were discriminatory.[3] On the basis of that ruling, Texas will have to redistrict once again in time for the 2014 elections. Figure 7–4 on the facing page shows the current U.S. congressional districts in Texas.

An Independent Redistricting Commission?

During the heat of the redistricting controversy in the winter of 2011–2012, Texans were asked what they felt were the state's most pressing problems. While the expected issues of the economy, unemployment, and border security were at the top of the list, a surprising 5 percent of Texans polled pointed to legislative redistricting as one of the state's most important problems. It ranked in seventh place, ahead of gas prices and water supply.[4]

A sizeable number of Texans—42 percent—supported the creation of an independent redistricting commission to redraw legislative district lines. The creation of an independent, nonpartisan redistricting commission to reduce political considerations in the drawing of legislative district boundaries was supported by 29 percent of Republicans, 43 percent of independents, and 70 percent of Democrats.

Support for a nonpartisan redistricting commission can be explained, in part, by the sense that the current process was unfair to Democrats and members of minority groups. As word of the new district boundaries trickled out, Democratic legislators—and many of their Hispanic and African American constituents—feared that the new district boundaries would lead to a loss of political representation. Some

pairing Placing two incumbent officeholders in the same elective district through redistricting.

incumbent The current holder of an office.

FIGURE 7-4

U.S. Congressional Districts,
113th Congress, 2013–2014

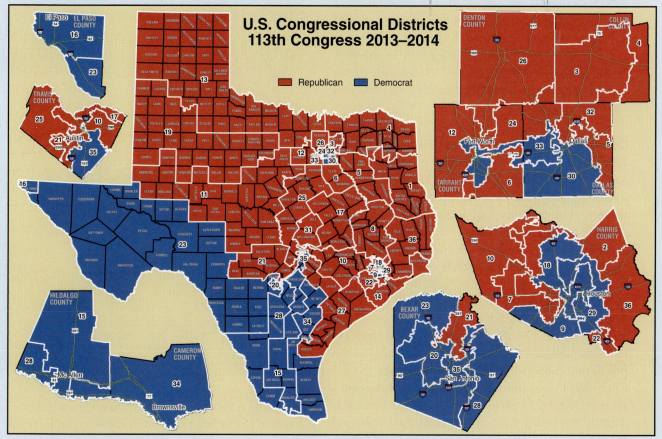

**U.S. Congressional Districts
113th Congress 2013–2014**

■ Republican ■ Democrat

Source: Texas Legislative Council, Plan C235.

people who support a redistricting commission may also believe that legislative redistricting efforts lead to less competitive races. Gerrymandering results in districts that are safe for only one of the major parties. It therefore contributes to a lack of competition, which, in turn, leads to the election of legislators who are either very conservative or very liberal. Moderates may be unrepresented, even though they are numerous.

7-1d Qualifications for Membership

Although legal, or formal, qualifications must be met before anyone can serve in the state legislature, rarely do these requirements prohibit serious candidates from seeking legislative seats. In fact, the criteria are broad enough to allow most Texas citizens to run for the legislature.

Formal Qualifications To be a Texas state senator, an individual must be a U.S. citizen, be a qualified voter of the state, be at least twenty-six years of age, and have lived in the state for the previous five years and in the district for one year prior to election. Qualifications for house membership are even more easily met. A candidate must be a U.S. citizen, be a qualified voter, be at least twenty-one years of age, and have lived in Texas for the two previous years and in the district for one year prior to being elected.

Informal Qualifications The most important requirements for holding legislative office in Texas are not the legal limitations, but the informal ones. Certain political, social, and economic criteria determine who is elected not just to the state legislature but also to offices at all levels of government—national, state, county, city, and special district.

Party Affiliation Until the 1990s, the Democratic Party was the dominant legislative party in Texas. Realignment has made Texas a strongly Republican state, however. By the end of 2004, Republicans had established dominance over all three branches of state government. The Republicans had two U.S. senators and a majority in the Texas delegation to the U.S. House of Representatives. Figure 7–5 alongside shows that it is increasingly advantageous to be a Republican candidate in Texas electoral politics.

Demographics: Descriptive Representation

Although not a majority, a plurality of Texans are Anglo American and Protestant. They tend to elect legislators who share these characteristics, just as voters in a predominantly Latino district typically elect a Latino legislator and those in an African American majority district usually elect an African American representative. When the people in legislative districts elect representatives that "look like" the people they represent, the legislative body is said to achieve *descriptive representation*.

Texas is one of the few states with a majority-minority population, meaning that the majority of the population consists of members of a minority group.[5] Currently, 45 percent of the Texas population is non-Hispanic white, 38 percent is Hispanic, 12 percent is African American, 4 percent is Asian American, and the remaining 1 percent is of some other racial or ethnic group.[6] Much of this diversity is also found in the Texas House, although the various racial and ethnic groups in the state are not precisely represented in the Texas House and Texas Senate.

DEMOGRAPHICS AND THE LEGISLATURE. Minority populations in Texas have experienced significant improvements in their levels of descriptive representation. In the 83rd Legislative Session, 22 percent of the members of the Texas House were Latino, 12 percent were African American, and 2 percent (three representatives) were Asian American. Women, who make up slightly more than one-half of the state's population, account for 21 percent of the representatives in the Texas House. The differences between the makeup of the state's population and the members of the Texas House vary for each group but are major improvements from the recent past.

The Texas Senate, by contrast, is 23 percent Latino, 6 percent African American, and 19 percent female. Although the non-Hispanic white population accounts for 45 percent of the state's population, 71 percent of the senators are non-Hispanic white. These discrepancies

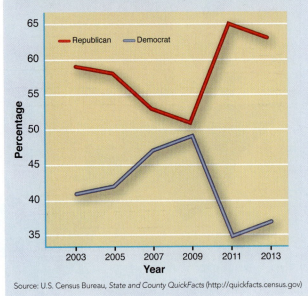

FIGURE 7–5

Partisanship in the
Texas House of Representatives

This figure shows the percentage of Democratic and Republican house members since Republicans gained control of the Texas House of Representatives in 2003.

Source: U.S. Census Bureau, *State and County QuickFacts* (http://quickfacts.census.gov)

are partly a function of gerrymandering and partly a function of low voter turnout in minority communities.

LATINOS. The Latino population in Texas has grown significantly since the Voting Rights Act of 1965. As a result, Latino levels of representation in the Texas House and Senate have also increased. Figure 7–6 on the facing page shows the percentage of the state's Latino population, as well as Latino members of the Texas House and Senate. As the state's Latino population has grown, so, too, have the shares of house and senate seats held by Latinos. Until recently, the percentage of Latino senators was greater than the percentage of Latino house members. Most Latino legislators are Democrats, but the number of Latino Republicans is growing.

AFRICAN AMERICANS. The percentage of African Americans in the Texas legislature has also risen since the Voting Rights Act of 1965. Figure 7–7 on the facing page shows the percentage of African Americans in Texas, as well as the percentage of African American representatives and senators. The African American population in Texas has remained at about 12 percent for the last several decades, with the proportion of house seats held by African Americans remaining relatively steady

FIGURE 7-6

The Latino Population
and Latino Representation in the Texas House and Texas Senate

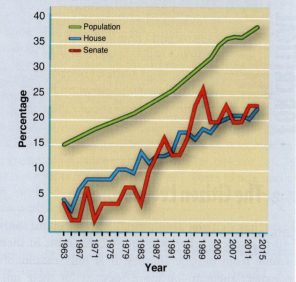

Source: U.S. Census Bureau, *State and County QuickFacts* (http://quickfacts.census.gov)

FIGURE 7-7

The African American
Population and African American Representation in the Texas House and Texas Senate

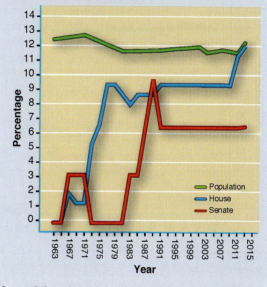

Source: U.S. Census Bureau, *State and County QuickFacts* (http://quickfacts.census.gov)

at 9 percent since 1972. The percentage of African Americans in the senate, however, leveled off at 6 percent beginning in the early 1990s. Although most African American lawmakers are Democrats, a few have been elected as Republicans.

ASIAN AMERICANS. Asian Americans account for a little more than 4 percent of the state's population. Nevertheless, three Asian-American members of the Texas House served in the 83rd Legislative Session—Dallas Republican Angie Chen Button and Houston Democrats Hubert Vo and Gene Wu.

WOMEN. Women have been involved in Texas politics for quite some time. Texans elected their first female governor in 1925 and have been sending women to the Texas legislature since the women's suffrage movement. In the mid-1970s, women began to win house seats with greater frequency. A similar pattern can be seen in the senate, beginning in the mid-1980s.

Still, women are by far the most underrepresented group in the Texas legislature. (See Figure 7–8 on the following page.) Although slightly more than one-half of the state's population is female, in 2012–2013 only 21 percent of Texas representatives and 19 percent of Texas senators were women.

Occupation Law is the most frequently represented profession in U.S. legislative bodies. In other democratic countries, the percentage of lawyers in legislative bodies is far smaller, and lawyers are viewed as just another professional group that might seek to advance its own interests. In the United States, however, the expectation that politicians will have a legal background is so woven into our political fabric that people who want political careers often become lawyers as a step toward that goal. In Texas's 81st Legislative Session, 29 percent of representatives and 39 percent of senators were lawyers.[7]

The occupations of the members of state legislative bodies are becoming more diverse, however. The number of lawyers serving in state legislatures has decreased somewhat. Reasons for this include the increasingly professionalized nature of state legislative assemblies. One study has determined that as legislative bodies enact ethics reform, the number of lawyers in the legislature diminishes.[8]

As lawyers are joined by lawmakers from other occupations, descriptive representation is enhanced.

to establish the per diem allowance, which it regularly increases, but only the voters can approve any increase in salary.

Lawmakers have not received a salary increase since 1975, and voters rejected the last attempt to increase their pay in 1991. Texas lawmakers are among the worst-paid large-state legislators in the country, but they have found ways to benefit from their contacts with interest groups to offset their living expenses.

Methods of Enhancing Legislative Income

Low legislative salaries create a situation where legislators must obtain their primary income from other sources. Legislators who are lawyers accept **retainers** from a variety of clients, including those who have lawsuits against state agencies. Lawyers and nonlawyers alike receive consulting fees from business clients and act to invest based on information that they gain from lobbyists and "insider information" from their own specialized knowledge about the prospects for pending legislation.

Texans thus oblige their legislators to seek additional income, yet ask few questions about the nature or sources of this income. People tend to be loyal to those who pay them, and it is not the public that furnishes most of the legislators' incomes.

Arguments in Favor of Higher Pay

Some reformers believe that legislators' pay should be increased and their outside income strictly limited. In the present system, the potential for conflict between the public interest and the interests of lawmakers' private businesses or their employers is obvious. Higher pay would not guarantee honest legislators, but it would enable the conscientious ones to perform their legislative duties without having to turn to sources of outside income that might compromise their ability to represent the people who elected them.

7-2c The Limited Session

The Texas legislature meets on the second Tuesday in January in odd-numbered years for a 140-day session. It is the only legislature in the ten most populous states to meet only every two years. In these short, infrequent sessions, the volume of legislation can be overwhelming. Most bills are passed or killed with little consideration, but they still consume valuable time that could

be used more judiciously. Conversely, many important bills are never granted a legislative hearing.

Special Sessions

The short biennial sessions and the increasingly complex problems of a modern society make thirty-day special sessions, which can be called only by the governor, more common. They are, however, unpopular with both the general public and the legislators. The public views their $1.2 million price tag as wasteful, and legislators are put out by being called away from their homes, families, and primary occupations. Furthermore, opponents of certain bills often intentionally kill the legislation by neglect in the regular session and will fight a special session to reconsider the corpse.

The Problem of Time Constraints

Because most of the legislative work is performed during the regular session, time becomes critical. Legislators find it increasingly difficult to maintain even rudimentary knowledge of the content of much of the legislation that must be considered, whether in committee or on the floor. These time constraints dictated by the limited session, combined with inadequate staff support and weak legislative research institutions such as the Office of House Bill Analysis, serve to isolate individual legislators and deepen their reliance on the information provided by lobbyists, administrators, and the legislative leadership.

Bills of limited scope or on trivial matters are a further drain on legislative time. For example, bills regulating the size of melon containers or minnow seining in a specific county do affect public policy, but they could easily be delegated to an executive department or administrative agency.

The limited biennial session tends to work against deliberative, orderly legislative practice and ultimately against the public interest. Texas legislators cannot possibly acquaint themselves in only 140 days with the immense volume of legislation presented to them. Few legislators have personal knowledge of any particular subject under consideration unless they are employed, retained, or hold investment interests in the particular field.

Although forty-five states have regular annual sessions to conduct state business, Texans refuse to accept annual sessions. Texans' general belief is that the legislature does more harm than good when it is in session and a longer session will simply give legislators more time for mischief.

Favors to Constituents

Often, bills are introduced as a favor to an interested constituent or interest group by a friendly legislator. When these bills lack legislative, interest group, or administrative support, as is often the case, they have no chance of passage or even serious committee consideration.

Resolutions by legislators to congratulate a distinguished constituent, a winning sports team, or a scout troop for some success are common. Legislators usually pay little attention to this legislation, but it is important to the recipients.

Demonstrating the lack of legislative scrutiny, one such resolution was passed unanimously by the Texas House on April Fools' Day 1971—a congratulatory recognition of Albert DeSalvo for his "noted activities and unconventional techniques involving population control and applied psychology." The house later withdrew this recognition when it discovered that DeSalvo was in fact the "Boston Strangler," an infamous serial murderer.

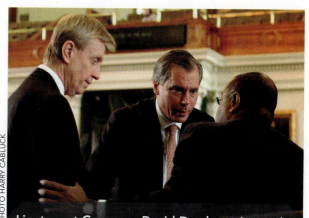

Lieutenant Governor David Dewhurst (center) meets with senators in Austin. He is the presiding officer of the state senate and has extensive authority in that chamber.

AP PHOTO HARRY CABLUCK

The End-of-Session Crunch Historically, much odious legislation was passed in the final days of a session. Because of procrastination and delaying tactics by legislators, the end-of-session flow of legislation became a deluge. Under these conditions, legislators simply did not have time for even the most rudimentary review of important last-minute legislation.

In 1993, the Texas House adopted new rules to deal with the end-of-session legislative crunch. During the last seventeen days, the house may consider only bills that originated in the senate or that received previous house approval. The new rules also gave house members twenty-four hours to study major legislation before floor action. These reforms have diminished the volume of last-minute legislation and allowed legislators some time to become better acquainted with bills.

7–3 Organization of the Texas Legislature

The legislature has several institutions that affect its operations during and after the session—the presiding officers, the legislative committees, and the legislative staff.

7–3a The Presiding Officers

The most visible individuals in the Texas legislature are the two presiding officers—the lieutenant governor in the senate and the speaker of the house of representatives. Each exercises tremendous power.

The Lieutenant Governor The presiding officer in the Texas Senate is the lieutenant governor, who serves as the senate president. Although not officially a senator, the lieutenant governor is in the unique position of being a member of both the legislative branch and the executive branch. The lieutenant governor is elected in a statewide, partisan election and can have a party affiliation that is different from that of the governor or other members of the Texas executive branch. In the event the office becomes vacant through death, disability, or resignation, the senate elects one of its members to serve as lieutenant governor until the next regular election. The senators have adopted rules that grant the lieutenant governor extensive legislative, organizational, procedural, administrative, and planning authority.

The election of the lieutenant governor for a four-year term attracts far less public attention than the power of the office merits. In fact, the lieutenant governor is one of the most powerful officials in Texas government. Organized interests are aware of the importance of the office, however, and contribute sizable sums to influence the election.

Lieutenant governors in most states, like the vice president in the federal government, are neither strong executives nor strong legislative officials. Some states have either eliminated the office or have the governor and lieutenant governor run as a team. In other states, the governor and other executives monopolize the executive function. Meanwhile, the upper chamber, where the lieutenant governor usually presides, is often too protective of its legislative powers to include that officer in the real power structure. Although many lieutenant governors exercise a hybrid executive-legislative function, their actual powers do not approach those enjoyed by the lieutenant governor of Texas.

The Speaker of the House

The Texas House of Representatives, in a recorded majority vote of its members, chooses one of the representatives to serve as its presiding officer. The campaign for this post can be very competitive and may attract candidates from all parts of the ideological spectrum. Because the vote for speaker is not secret, the winning candidate often takes punitive action against opponents and their supporters. As a result, incumbent speakers, until recently, faced almost no opposition.

SPEAKER TOM CRADDICK. In 2002, Republicans gained a majority in the Texas House. They then ousted the Democratic speaker and elected the first Republican speaker since Reconstruction, Tom Craddick. After 2002, the Republicans enjoyed a fairly narrow majority until their 2010 landslide victory gave them overwhelming dominance in the house.

Regardless of the size of the Republican majority, the speaker has been a member of the Republican Party since 2002. That is not to say, however, that incumbent Republican speakers have gone unchallenged. In fact, Republican speakers have experienced challenges from both the left and the right.

During the 80th Legislative Session (2007), Speaker Craddick was harshly criticized for his autocratic style. After Republicans lost seats in the house in 2008, many of his fellow Republicans turned on him, and in 2009 Republicans and Democrats joined together to elect Republican Joe Straus as their new speaker.

SPEAKER JOE STRAUS. During the 82nd Legislative Session (2011), Speaker Straus himself faced a challenge from members of his own party who criticized

Representative Joe Straus, R.-San Antonio, has been speaker of the house since 2009, but his moderate image has caused problems among the more conservative members of the house. How is the speaker's bargaining position affected by the need to win a majority of fellow representatives to get reelected?

him for not being conservative enough. Straus is a relatively moderate Republican from San Antonio, and some Republicans have dubbed him as a RINO (Republican in Name Only).[10] After the 2010 Republican state convention, Speaker Straus was accused by several conservative Republicans of being too cozy with Democrats.[11]

Although speakers traditionally do not attract much opposition, Straus's moderate views have continued to create problems within his own party. So far, house Republicans' attempts to oust the speaker have failed because the speaker has built a successful coalition of Republicans and Democrats.

Threats to Joe Straus's speakership came on the heels of a truly impressive Republican sweep in the 2010 elections, which gave the Republicans a 102- to 48-seat advantage in the Texas House. With so many Republican seats, Straus might have anticipated greater support. Most of the gains, however, came from the highly energized Tea Party movement. The new conservative Republican legislators did not necessarily agree with Straus's moderate positions. As a result, in an effort to placate the growing conservative wing of his own party, Straus has moved further to the right. This did not, however, stop Tea Party Republicans from recruiting a challenger to run against the speaker in his San Antonio district in the 2012 primaries.

The Speaker's Team

Typically, house members who support the winning candidate for speaker can become a part of the **speaker's team,** even if they are members of the opposition party. Team status may include membership on a prestigious committee or even a committee chair or vice chair appointment. Presiding officers typically rely on members of the other party to chair or vice chair a substantial number of committees. Team members also may attract campaign contributions and other assistance for their own political campaigns, and they may gain lobbyist support for their legislative initiatives. This team policy is known as the "no-party" system. Representatives are elected as party members but achieve leadership status by supporting the winning candidate for speaker. In an attempt to curtail abuses of power, speaker candidates who use threats or promises of important appointments can be charged with "legislative bribery." The law is difficult to enforce, though, and the speaker's supporters are usually appointed to important committees.

Funds raised and spent for a speaker's campaign are part of the public record. Candidates for speaker are required to file a complete statement of loans, campaign contributions, and expenditures with the secretary of state. No corporation, labor union, or organization may contribute, and individual contributions are limited to $100. All expenditures greater than $10 must be reported. These requirements are an attempt to reduce the influence of lobbyists and interest groups on the speaker's race by limiting and making public their campaign contributions. However, the support of The Lobby (the major political and economic interest groups in Texas) is still a practical necessity for a representative who wants to become speaker.

The No-Party System

The Texas legislature historically has been organized on the basis of ideology, rather than political party. Under this no-party system, party affiliation has less significance than ideology and interest group ties. Political party caucuses do not fill positions of power as they do in the U.S. Congress. Instead, members of the minority party may join the speaker's team, serve on important committees, and even chair committees.

In recent years, however, the parties have become more intensely polarized. As a result, the legislature has become more partisan. For example, in 2009 Speaker Joe Straus appointed eighteen Democrats to chair the thirty-four standing committees in the Texas House. Another fifteen Democrats served as vice chairs. Because of conservative threats to his leadership in 2011, however, Straus reduced the number of Democratic committee chairs in his team to eleven, and many of these were for less influential committees. The Texas Senate also has committee chairs from both parties. Would Texas be better off if the speaker's team system were replaced by a full-fledged system of party organization? We examine that question in the *Join the Debate* feature on page 155.

7–3b Legislative Committees

Legislative committees are necessary for any orderly consideration of proposed legislation. As we explained earlier, because of the volume of legislative proposals offered each session, legislators cannot possibly become familiar with all bills—not even all the major ones. They therefore organize themselves into committees for the division of labor necessary to ensure that at least someone knows something about each piece of proposed legislation. Committees serve as the workhorses of the Texas legislature. The numerous types of legislative committees in the Texas House and Texas Senate include standing, conference, joint, and select committees.

Standing Committees

Standing committees are permanent committees that initially consider most legislation after it is introduced. They hold hearings on selected bills and *mark them up*—rewrite them—to meet the wishes of the committee majority. However, most bills lack significant support and simply expire in standing committees for lack of action. For most legislation, these committees are the place bills go to die. In short, standing committees act as screening mechanisms to filter out bad bills or bills that have little or no political support.

SUBSTANTIVE AND PROCEDURAL COMMITTEES. The two types of standing committees are substantive and procedural committees. *Substantive standing committees* consider bills and monitor administrative behavior in a specific subject matter area, such as taxation,

speaker's team
Members of the Texas House who supported the speaker in his or her run for the office and who obtained favorable committee appointments.

standing committee
A permanent committee that functions throughout the legislative session.

education, or agriculture. The Texas House also has several *procedural standing committees* that regulate the flow of legislation, pass resolutions, conduct investigations, and the like. A chair and a vice chair head every committee. Each legislator serves on at least one committee, and some serve on several.

SUBCOMMITTEES. Many of the standing committees have established subcommittees for further specialization. **Subcommittee** members are a subset of the total committee membership and are usually the first to become familiar with a bill. The subcommittees hold initial hearings, mark up legislation, and then report their work to the standing committee. Subcommittees have their own chairs and vice chairs.

Other Committee Types In addition to standing committees and their subcommittees, a variety of special committees can be classified based on function, membership, and longevity. They include conference, select, and joint committees. (See Table 7–1 below.)

Conference committees are temporary committees created to reach a compromise on house and senate versions of a bill. Members are appointed to resolve differences when a bill is passed by the two houses in different forms.

Whereas the function of standing committees is to draft legislation, *select committees* are charged with such tasks as studying a problem and making recommendations to the legislature. The Select Committee on Federal Legislation, created by Speaker Joe Straus to monitor the activities of the federal government in January 2010, is an example of this type of committee.

Standing and select committees usually include members from only one chamber, whereas conference and **joint committees** consist of members from both chambers. Some special committees may even include members of the public. Conference and select committees tend to be temporary, or **ad hoc,** committees, whereas standing and joint committees are longer lasting.

Interim committees meet when the legislature is not in session to consider proposed legislation for the next legislative session or to study a particular problem that has arisen since the last session.

7–3c Legislative Staff

The legislature provides only minimal funds for hiring competent staff. Monthly staff allotments are $11,925 for House members and $35,625 for senators, who are also reimbursed for other "reasonable and necessary" office expenses. These funds are for staff salaries and office expenses, not personal use. House members usually have about three or four staff people, whereas the average senate staff size

TABLE 7–1

Types of Committees in the Texas Legislature

	Standing	Conference	Joint	Select
Function	Lawmaking authority	Lawmaking authority	Advisory	Advisory
Longevity	Permanent	Temporary	Permanent	Temporary
Membership	From one chamber only	From both the house and the senate	From both the house and the senate	May include members of one chamber, members of both chambers, or members of the legislature and nonlegislators
Examples	House: Agriculture and Livestock Committee Senate: Criminal Justice Committee		Legislative Budget Board	House Select Committee on Emergency Preparedness

Should the Texas Legislature Be Organized by Party?

In the U.S. House of Representatives, the U.S. Senate, and most state legislative chambers around the country, one party sits on the left side and the other party sits on the right. The majority party picks its leaders (who also lead the chamber), chooses all committee chairpersons, and determines which members of the majority party will serve on each committee. The party out of power chooses its leaders and determines which minority party members will fill the minority's allotted committee positions.

Texas is different. Of course, there are Republicans and Democrats, but the house and senate are organized under a no-party system. There are no majority or minority leaders in Texas. The speaker of the house and the lieutenant governor in the senate may—and do—appoint both Republicans and Democrats as committee chairs, no matter which party has the majority.

In the house, the speaker is usually a member of the majority party, but members of the minority may vote with the speaker so that they can join the *speaker's team*. In return, minority party members hope to obtain favorable committee assignments. As a result of their desire to become team players, many members of the minority are no longer really part of the opposition.

Texas Needs Clear Opposition Parties

Texans would be better off with true opposition parties in the two houses of the legislature. The majority party should be able to propose specific policy alternatives. The minority should then be able to develop and articulate a rival political philosophy.

If the Texas House and Senate were organized by political party, Texans would be better informed. The press would make sure of that. Indeed, citizens and journalists would see both sides of policy issues and could better evaluate the legitimacy and desirability of two competing policy proposals rather than just one.

The minority party could control which of its members filled its allotted committee seats. As a result, members of the minority would not need to make political compromises in order to join the presiding officer's team. If they were not dominated by the presiding officers, senators and representatives would have more independence in representing their constituents.

The Current System Is Worth Keeping

The reason the Texas legislature wasn't originally organized by political party is because for much of the state's history, the Democrats had overwhelming majorities. As a result, ideological divisions tended to run right through the middle of the Democratic Party. Members of the legislature were inclined to identify themselves as conservatives, moderates, or (rarely) liberals, not so much as Democrats or Republicans. Then, conservative Democrats ruled the roost with the help of Republicans. Now, Republicans rule with the assistance of conservative Democrats.

The no-party system arose by historical accident, but it is worth keeping. If you want to know why, take one look at the U.S. Congress today. Partisanship there has reached such absurd levels that one party will regularly oppose measures it supports in principle—just because the other party proposed them. Congress is deadlocked, unable to pass legislation the nation needs to recover from the recent economic crisis. Texas doesn't have that problem. Let's hope it never does.

FOR CRITICAL ANALYSIS How important is political opposition in a democracy?

is slightly more than seven. Some senators have as many as fourteen staff members, while others have as few as four.[12]

The Consequences of Limited Staff Support

Neither individual legislators nor legislative committees have professional staff comparable to that of special interest groups. With minimal staff support, "expert" testimony and arguments by interest group lobbyists and agency liaisons can mislead legislators. Powerful interests and administrative agencies have a distinct advantage when they can monopolize information and expertise, and create a situation in which legislators must remain dependent on them for research data, advice, and other services.

Both legislative houses have established nonpartisan institutions to provide information to legislators. Former House Speaker Pete Laney created the House

Bill Analysis Department as part of legislative operations. Renamed the House Research Organization by Speaker Craddick, it provides bill analyses, floor reports, focus reports, and interim news to legislators and the public.[13]

The Senate Research Center was formed in 1979 as the Senate Independent Research Group. It currently provides research and bill analysis to the Texas senate and the lieutenant governor's office. The center's staff also attend meetings and conferences of other governmental entities and report to the senators on their content.

Barriers to Increased Staff Spending Whenever the legislature considers increasing appropriations to hire competent staff for individual legislators and, even more important, for committees, both the general public and the special interests voice strong opposition—the former out of lack of knowledge and the latter out of self-interest.

Ironically, legislators who report a surplus in their expense accounts are acclaimed by the press and their constituents as conscientious guardians of the public treasury, whereas, in fact, their ignorance of proposed legislation may cost taxpayers millions of dollars. By contrast, legislators who use their allotted funds to become informed about pending legislation are often suspected of wasting the money—or stealing it.

Texas legislative committees lack year-round professional staffs, which could give the legislators sources of information and services independent of those provided by interest groups, administrators, and the legislative leadership. Texas senators have enough staff to research some legislation each session, but representatives are not as fortunate. Texas spends less than 0.3 percent of total state expenditures on legislative staff salaries, services, and accommodations.

FOR CRITICAL THINKING

Given the short legislative sessions in Texas, could the power of the presiding officers be a positive factor? Why or why not?

7–4 Leadership and the Legislative Process

The presiding officers—the lieutenant governor in the senate and the speaker of the house of representatives—dominate every step in the legislative process, from initial committee consideration to scheduling and floor debate to negotiation of differences between the senate and house versions of a bill.

7–4a The Powers of the Presiding Officers

The rules of each house, formal and informal, give the presiding officers the procedural power to do the following:

- Appoint most committee members and committee chairs.
- Assign bills to committees.
- Schedule legislation for floor action.
- Recognize members on the floor for points of order and amendments.
- Interpret the procedural rules when conflict arises.
- Appoint the chairs and members of the conference committees.

Furthermore, statutes grant the presiding officers nonprocedural, institutional power to appoint the members and serve as joint chairs of the Legislative Budget Board and Texas Legislative Council, and to determine the members of the Legislative Audit Committee and the Sunset Advisory Commission.

The appointive power of the presiding officers means that the action of a committee on specific legislation is usually predictable. The presiding officers can also use the power of appointment to reward friends and supporters as well as to punish opponents. Interest groups often attempt to influence the presiding officers to assign sympathetic legislators to standing committees that have jurisdiction over legislation vital to their interests. Power in the Texas legislature is thus concentrated in the offices of the lieutenant governor and the speaker of the house.

7–4b Membership in the Standing Committees

As we discussed earlier, standing committees do much of the legislative work in both chambers of the Texas legislature. The presiding officers' power to appoint committee members and chairs gives the speaker and lieutenant governor considerable influence over their work and, therefore, considerable influence over policy decisions.

House Committee Membership The speaker appoints the total membership as well as the chair and vice chair of all house procedural committees, such as the Calendars, Rules, Ethics, and Redistricting committees. The Calendars Committee controls the flow of most legislation from the committees to the house floor. The speaker uses his or her influence with the Calendars Committee to determine when or whether bills are heard on the house floor.

The speaker also appoints the total membership as well as the chair and vice chair of the powerful twenty-seven-member Appropriations Committee and the chairs of the five Appropriations subcommittees. The Appropriations Committee strongly influences all state spending and has important budget and oversight functions as well.

For nonprocedural committees other than Appropriations, a limited seniority system in the house determines up to one-half of a committee's membership, and the speaker appoints the other half. The speaker also appoints the committee's chair and vice chair, which ensures the speaker's influence. Besides controlling the Calendars and Appropriations committees, the speaker must have strong allies on the powerful Ways and Means Committee and the State Affairs Committee.

Senate Committee Membership The lieutenant governor officially appoints all members and chairs of all senate committees. In practice, an informal seniority system allows senators to choose their preferred committee until one-third of the committee's positions are filled. This guarantees senior senators a seat on some of the more powerful committees, such as Finance, Jurisprudence, and State Affairs. The chairs of standing committees, at their discretion, may appoint subcommittees from the committee membership.

The Importance of Committee Assignments Because the relative power of a committee varies, a legislator's committee assignments directly affect the legislator's influence in the legislature. Serving on an important committee, especially as its chair, gives a legislator a strong bargaining position with administrators, lobbyists, and other legislators. Legislators negotiate intensely to get choice committee assignments, and they rely on various coalitions, compromises, and deals to get them. Conflict in the process is unavoidable, and Texas legislators have resolved a large part of it by concentrating power over committee selection in the presiding officers.

Selection of Committee Chairs Owing to the chair's power over the committee's organization, procedure, and the jurisdiction of its subcommittees, the fate of much public policy is determined when the chair is selected. A presiding officer's power to appoint committee chairs is like a magnet attracting legislators to his or her team. If legislators want to "get along," they "go along" with the presiding officers. The influence that presiding officers have over other legislators also increases their bargaining position with interest groups. Lobbyists who can help get sympathetic legislators appointed to important committees have earned their salary. At the same time, the lobbyist owes the presiding officer a real favor for appointing the "right" committee member or chair.

The appointive power of the presiding officers, although significant, is not absolute. They often appoint as chairs key committee people who have political power in their own right, such as members with close ties to a powerful special interest group. The presiding officers may thus establish a reciprocally beneficial relationship with some of the more powerful members of the legislature. They can usually count on the loyalty of the chairs, who, in turn, depend on the presiding officer's support.

Committee Jurisdiction The presiding officers in the Texas legislature assign bills to specific standing committees, and the officers have considerable discretion when making these assignments because committee jurisdiction in the Texas legislature is often poorly defined. Texas's presiding officers do not hesitate to assign a bill they oppose to a committee they know will kill it. Likewise, they assign bills they support to committees that will report favorably. Because the presiding officers can stack the committees to their liking, this can be easily achieved.

Presiding officers may press a committee to kill a bill for several reasons:

- The backers and financial supporters of the presiding officer may view the bill as a threat to their economic or political well-being.
- The presiding officer and his or her team may feel that the bill's legislative and interest group supporters have been uncooperative in the past and should be punished.
- The supporters of the bill may either refuse or be unable to match the bargaining offers of the bill's opponents.
- The presiding officer and his or her supporters may feel that the bill, if it became law, would take funds away from programs that they favor.

- The presiding officer may simply think that the bill is bad public policy.

Committee members may negotiate with the presiding officers by promising substantial changes to a bill, by supporting legislation that the leadership team favors, or by opposing a bill that the leadership wants to defeat. A politically knowledgeable leadership that astutely uses its powers can help consolidate committee support for its policies.

7–4c Standing Committees' Powers and Functions

Committees have been called "little legislatures" because they normally conduct the real legislative business of compromise and accommodation. Standing committees may totally rewrite a bill, **pigeonhole** it (bury it in committee), or **mark up** the bill by substantially altering it by adding or deleting major provisions. Rarely does a committee report a bill in the form in which it was originally introduced.

Division of Labor Because several thousand bills are introduced into the Texas legislature each session, a division of labor is necessary. Every bill introduced during the legislative session is referred to a committee, which conducts public hearings where witnesses—both for and against—may be heard, debates held, and bills marked up. Because standing committees do the basic legislative work, the general membership relies heavily on them for guidance in deciding how to vote on a bill when it is considered on the floor.

Competency Where a seniority system is used, committee members and chairs are usually returned to the same committee posts each session, and legislators can thus become reasonably informed, if not expert, in a given subject. This expertise is important because committee members must evaluate the arguments of interest group representatives and administrative officials concerning the merits of proposed legislation.

pigeonhole To kill a bill in standing committee.

mark up To rewrite a bill in standing committee, often substantially altering it by adding or deleting major provisions.

AP PHOTO/HARRY CABLUCK

Standing committees do much of the legislative work of ignoring or pigeonholing bills lacking significant support, gathering information in public hearings, and rewriting or marking up legislation to make essential political compromises that make a bill's passage possible.

Because Texas legislators operate under a limited seniority system, the expertise of committee members may be gained outside the formal structures of government. For example, if the primary occupation of a legislator is banking, that particular lawmaker may be more sensitive to interests of the banking industry than to those of the public. The same problem arises with regard to any industry—oil, real estate, the law, or insurance. Sometimes, legislators are not initially involved in an occupation that benefits from their committee activity, but based on legislative experience, they may later become active in the businesses under the jurisdiction of their committees.

The Pigeonhole Standing committees act as a screening system when they bury bills. A legislator may introduce a bill as a favor to some group or constituent, knowing full well that it will be killed in committee (and that the committee will take the blame). The presiding officers assign bills to hostile committees with the expectation that they will be totally rewritten, if not pigeonholed. Legislators not serving on a committee may bargain with standing committee members to pigeonhole a bill because they are ideologically opposed to it, because their interest group supporters oppose it, or simply because they want to avoid voting on a controversial bill.

Bills that are pigeonholed may be extracted from committees, but it is usually difficult to so. Legislators are reluctant to press for discharging a bill from committee even when they support it. They see the **discharge process** as a threat to the privileges of the entire committee system—privileges that they, too, enjoy.

In the Texas Senate, a single senator may use another tactic to delay committee hearings for up to forty-eight hours by **tagging** a specific bill. If a senator notifies the chair of a senate committee that he or she wants forty-eight hours' advance notice before hearings are held on a bill, the committee may take no action on the bill within that period. Tagging delays the legislative progress on the bill and is effective only because of the short legislative session. A senator may use the tagging privilege only once, but it enables a single senator effectively to kill a bill late in the session or to demand negotiations with the bill's sponsors in exchange for removing the tag.

Bureaucratic Oversight

In the United States, legislatures function as watchdogs over the executive branch—that is, the legislature "oversees" the administrative **bureaucracy** that executes the law and implements public programs. The vehicle for **bureaucratic oversight** is usually a legislative committee hearing where legislators investigate the activities of an agency to determine whether it is administering the laws as the legislature intended and whether new or revised legislation is needed.

Ostensibly, the committees are watching out for the public good by checking on whether the bureaucrats perform their duties in ways consistent with the public interest. More often than not, standing committees serve as the legislative advocates for the bureaucrats' interests and viewpoints. As part of the iron-triangle power structure described in Chapter 6, legislative committees often lack any incentive to put state agencies under critical scrutiny, and short, infrequent legislative sessions make continuous legislative oversight of state agencies impossible.

7–4d Scheduling the Legislative Process

The flow of legislation from the standing committees to debate and final vote in the entire house or senate is scheduled on a **calendar.** Scheduling is important in any legislative body, but in Texas it is paramount because of the legislature's short sessions. Timing is also of strategic importance because, in the process of negotiation, any of the following situations may develop:

- Supporters may want floor consideration of a bill delayed until they can muster the necessary votes to get it passed.
- Opponents think that they have the necessary votes

to defeat the bill, but that opposition might erode if the supporters are given time to consolidate their forces.

- Conversely, supporters may want early consideration of a bill because the opposition appears to be gaining strength.

Given these political calculations, the presiding officers can use their influence over scheduling to expedite or to hinder the progress of legislation and to reward allies or punish enemies.

The House Calendars

The House Calendars Committee or the Local and Consent Calendars Committee schedules legislation by placing it on one of the following house calendars:

- The Emergency Calendar.
- The Major State Calendar.
- The Constitutional Amendments Calendar.
- The General State Calendar.
- The Local, Consent and Resolutions Calendar.
- The Resolutions Calendar.
- The Congratulatory and Memorial Resolutions Calendar.

While the speaker exercises no direct formal control over house calendars, he or she is careful to appoint members and chairs of the two calendars committees who can be persuaded to accommodate the speaker's wishes. Unimportant or trivial bills are placed on special schedules and are usually disposed of promptly with little debate on the house floor, but the process is not so automatic for major or controversial legislation. When or whether such legislation is scheduled is a decision largely determined by the speaker and the Calendars Committee chair.

The Senate Calendar Officially, the senate has a calendar system that advances bills systematically. A

---

discharge process
A rarely used legislative process for rescuing a bill pigeonholed in a standing committee.

tagging A senate rule that allows a senator to demand a forty-eight hours' advance notification before a standing committee holds hearings on a particular bill.

bureaucracy The system of unelected officials administering government policies and programs.

bureaucratic oversight The legislative function of monitoring agency activities to make sure the agencies are administering the laws according to legislative intent.

calendar In the context of the Texas legislature, the scheduled list of bills reported out of committee and ready for consideration by the house or the senate.

senate rule requires that bills be placed on the calendar and then considered on the senate floor in the same chronological order in which they were reported from the committees. In practice, bills are taken off the calendar for senate floor consideration by a **suspension of the rule,** which requires a two-thirds majority vote of the entire membership of the senate.

THE TWO-THIRDS RULE. The process goes something like this: The first bill placed on the senate calendar each session is called a **blocking bill,** usually a bill dealing with a trivial matter that senators have no interest in passing. The blocking bill is never taken up on the senate floor. Its only purpose is to stop floor consideration of any other bills except by the two-thirds vote to suspend the rule requiring chronological consideration of bills.

This time-honored practice affects the senate's entire legislative process because it allows just eleven senators to block a bill. The irony is that although only a simple majority is necessary for final passage in the senate, a two-thirds majority is necessary to get the bill to the floor for consideration. The two-thirds rule is designed to protect the minority from the majority.

The rule is also a means whereby the senate can kill a bill without having a floor vote for or against—the bill simply fails to reach the floor in a rules-suspension vote and thus dies on the calendar. Although lobbyists are keenly interested in these votes, the general public is usually unaware that a vote even occurred or where individual senators stood on the issue.

The two-thirds rule is also a tool that can be used to enhance the powers of the presiding officer. The lieutenant governor may keep a bill from reaching the floor of the senate by simply persuading eleven members to vote against it. Any coalition of eleven senators can, of course, achieve the same result—occasionally against the wishes of the lieutenant governor.

SUSPENDING THE TWO-THIRDS RULE. During the 2011 session, eleven senators were prepared to block passage of a bill requiring Texans to show state-issued photo identification before voting. The lieutenant governor and a majority of senators therefore adopted a rule to specifically exempt the bill from the two-thirds rule. In 2011, the senate passed the voter ID bill (SB 14) by a simple majority over strong objections. Opponents believed the ID requirement would disparately affect the elderly and minorities, because members of those populations are less likely to have a photo identification card. As noted earlier, the voter ID law was ruled unconstitutional by the U.S. District Court for the District of Columbia in August 2012.

7–4e Floor Action

Floor action refers to action by the entire house or the entire senate to debate, amend, and pass or defeat legislation. To take official action, each legislative chamber requires a **quorum** of two-thirds of its members to be present. On several occasions, a determined minority opposed to a scheduled action has used quorum-busting tactics by deliberately absenting themselves, thus denying their chamber the quorum necessary to proceed on legislation.

During floor action, the Texas Constitution requires that bills must be "read on three consecutive days in each house." The purpose of the requirement was to ensure that laws would not be passed without adequate opportunity for debate and understanding. Bills are read once upon being introduced, before they are assigned to a committee by the presiding officer. In practice, though, the entire bill is seldom read at this time. Instead, a caption or a brief summary is read to acquaint legislators with the subject of the bill. The bill is read the second time before floor debate in each house, and if an entire bill is to be read, it is usually on this second reading.

The constitutional requirement that a bill be read on three separate days may be suspended by a four-fifths vote of the chamber in which the bill is pending. The senate routinely suspends this provision and gives each bill an immediate third reading after its second-reading passage. The house, however, rarely suspends this provision. A simple majority is required for passage on the third reading, but amendments must have a two-thirds majority.

House Floor Action As bills reach the floor of the house, a loudspeaker system allows the members and

---

suspension of the rule The setting aside of the rules of the legislative body so that another set of rules can be used.

blocking bill A bill placed early on the senate calendar that will never be considered by the full senate.

floor action The entire senate or house acting as a whole to debate, amend, pass, or defeat proposed legislation.

quorum The number of members that must be present to conduct official business.

visitors to follow the debate on the floor. The **floor leaders** are the representatives who take center stage to rally support or opposition to a bill during floor action. They usually stand at the front of the chamber, answer questions, and lead debate on the bill. Microphones located elsewhere in the room serve other lawmakers who wish to speak or ask questions. Representatives are each allotted ten minutes to speak, but few of them use even this limited privilege.

The consideration of bills on the floor of the house would seem to be a study in confusion and inattention. Throughout the process, members of the house may be laughing, talking, reading papers, or sleeping at their desks. One might think that because many members know very little about the bill under consideration, floor debate should be an excellent opportunity for both proponents and opponents of the legislation to convince fellow legislators to vote for or against the bill. Actually, eloquent speeches seldom change votes on major legislation because most legislators already have well-defined positions long before the bill reaches the floor. Legislators may know little of the specific content of specialized legislation that has generated little statewide interest, but they are still prepared to vote for or against it based on the advice of lobbyists or fellow legislators.

POINTS OF ORDER. Presided over by the speaker, floor action is usually routine, but it can become quite dramatic and debate can become intense when major legislation is brought up for a vote. Representatives opposing the legislation may bring up points of order that require rulings by the speaker. A **point of order** is a representative's objection that the rules of procedure are not being followed during floor action. If the speaker sustains the point of order late in the session, there may not be time to correct the error, and the bill dies. In 1997, one legislator raised points of order that killed some eighty bills at the end of the session.

CHUBBING. Late in the session, opponents may attempt to delay action on a bill in an effort to run out the clock on the session. Unlike state senators, representatives do not have the privilege of unlimited debate, but they have developed other strategies to forestall legislative action. For example, knowing that a bill they oppose is scheduled to come up for debate, opponents may engage in **chubbing** by slowing down the whole legislative process, debating preceding bills for the maximum allotted time, peppering the bill's sponsors with trivial questions, and proposing so many amendments and raising so many points of order that the house never addresses the bill to which they ultimately object.

THE MECHANICS OF VOTING. When it is time to vote, house members insert cards that allow them to push buttons to record an "aye," "no," or "present" vote on a large electronic scoreboard by means of green, red, and white bulbs next to each legislator's name. As votes are cast, the bill's supporters and opponents walk up and down the aisles pleading with either one finger (vote "yes") or two fingers (vote "no").

Until recently, lawmakers decided many bills by **voice vote** only, which meant that many of their votes were not recorded so voters had no way of knowing how their representatives voted on many bills. A state constitutional amendment passed in November 2007 ended this practice by requiring **recorded votes** on final passage of all bills.

THE PROS AND CONS OF RECORDED VOTES. The use of recorded votes, which became a political issue in the 79th (2005) and 80th (2007) Legislative Sessions, can be viewed from several perspectives. The most important argument in favor is that voting records are necessary for constituents to know how their representatives and senators voted on the issues. Without this information, voters cannot make informed decisions on election day. Democracy may be reduced to choices based on television images, mudslinging, and trivialities.

Alternatively, recorded votes can become political weapons wielded unfairly against legislators in campaigns. A legislator may be strongly opposed to one provision in an important bill and may unsuccessfully work, lobby, and argue against this measure in committee and

floor leader A legislator who is responsible for getting legislation passed or defeated.

point of order A formal objection that the rules of procedure are not being followed on the house floor. Often made to postpone or defeat a bill.

chubbing Slowing the legislative process by maximizing debate, amendments, and points of order on minor bills to prevent consideration of a more controversial bill scheduled later on the calendar.

voice votes Votes that are not reported in the official journal.

recorded votes Votes in which the vote of each member is recorded in the official journal.

on the floor of the chamber. Yet, if the bill contains other provisions that the legislator views as important and worthwhile, he or she may vote for the entire bill despite the objectionable provision. Political opponents may then pluck this provision from the total bill and use it as a campaign issue to defeat the legislator. These rivals know that the legislator cannot deny having voted for the objectionable provision, but they conveniently fail to point out that it was a small part of a much larger bill. This is an unfair but effective campaign tactic.

Because the final recorded vote may not be a measure of the legislator's efforts for or against the legislation, test votes on amendments or procedural issues often provide more information on where legislators actually stand. Despite recent reforms, these more important votes, which occur in the second reading, may continue to be hidden through voice voting unless the chamber provides exceptions to the rules.

Senate Floor Action The senate scene may be similar to that in the house in one sense—few members are paying attention to the debate. Although debate time is not limited in the senate as it is in the house, debates even on important bills are usually much shorter in the senate. The fact that legislation is brought up for senate debate by a two-thirds vote means that most major compromises have been made before the legislation reaches the senate floor and that there is widespread support for its passage.

FILIBUSTERS. In the U.S. Senate, a minority of senators may **filibuster** a bill. That is, they may use the Senate's tradition of unlimited debate to block passage of a bill. Sixty senators, however, can agree to invoke **cloture** to limit debate. Filibusters are so frequent in the U.S. Senate that it is often simply assumed that sixty votes will be required to pass a bill.

In the Texas Senate, members are much less likely to resort to a filibuster. Still, senators may use a filibuster to attract public attention to a bill that is sure to pass without the filibuster or to delay legislation in the closing days of the session. In fact, just the *threat* of a filibuster may be enough to compel a bill's supporters to change the content of the bill to reach a compromise with the dissatisfied senator.

If a filibuster does occur, it means it was impossible to reach a compromise, usually

AP PHOTO/HARRY CABLUCK

Nearly a dozen members of the Texas Senate, foreground, meet on the chamber floor in Austin. Many times, lawmakers will gather in private groups to be briefed on a bill or to try to work out a compromise. The senate has a long-standing tradition of not debating bills on the floor unless the measure has the support of two-thirds of the members.

filibuster An attempt by a senator to delay a bill by unlimited debate.

cloture A parliamentary move to stop legislative debate and force a floor vote; also known as *closure*.

because a sufficient number of senators strongly favored the bill and refused to be intimidated by the threat of a filibuster. For example, Democratic senator Wendy Davis of Fort Worth used a filibuster to protest the billions of dollars in spending cuts to public education passed in the 82nd Legislative Session. The filibuster is credited with forcing Governor Rick Perry to call a special session to address education spending.

One reason that filibusters are far less important in the Texas Senate than in the U.S. Senate is that a member may not yield the floor to another senator who wants to continue the filibuster. In the Texas Senate, the floor is controlled by the lieutenant governor, so only one senator may filibuster as long as he or she can physically last, and then the vote is taken.

VOTING IN THE SENATE. Usually after a modest amount of debate, the Texas Senate takes a vote without the benefit of an electronic scoreboard. Senators vote by holding up a single finger for a "yes" vote and two fingers for a "no" vote. A clerk records the vote, and only a simple majority is necessary for passage.

7–4f Conference Committees' Powers and Functions

A unique byproduct of bicameralism is the need to resolve differences between similar bills passed by the two chambers. A conference committee is appointed for each bill to resolve these differences.

Conference Committee Members In Texas, conference committees consist of five members from each chamber, appointed by their respective presiding officer. A compromise proposal must win the support of a majority of the committee members from each house to be reported out of the committee. Because the members of the conference committee may strengthen, weaken, or even kill a bill, the attitudes of the legislators appointed to the committee are crucial to the various interests involved. This affords the presiding officers, as well as the conference committee members, enviable bargaining positions. To determine the acceptability of proposed compromises, the members of the committee must remain in contact with interested legislators, lobbyists, administrators, and the presiding officers. Bargaining before the selection of the committee is common, and it continues within the committee during deliberations.

Passing the Compromise After a bill has been reported out of the conference committee, it may not be amended by either chamber but must be accepted or rejected as it is written or sent back to the conference committee for further work. In practice, due to the volume of legislation that must be considered in the limited time available, the Texas legislature tends to accept **conference committee reports** on most legislation.

7–4g How a Bill Becomes a Law

Bills may be introduced in either the house or the senate or, to speed the process, in both chambers at the same time. Let us consider the example of a bill that is introduced in the senate before it is sent to the house of representatives. The numbers in Figure 7–9 on the following page correspond to the numbers in the following discussion list.

> **conference committee report** A compromise between the house and senate versions of a bill reached by a conference committee.

1. *Introduction to the senate.* Only a senator may introduce a bill in the senate, and only a representative may do so in the house. It is not difficult to find a legislator who is willing to perform this somewhat clerical function. More difficult is finding a sponsor who will devote political skill and bargaining prowess to help get the bill through the legislative process. Upon introduction, the bill is assigned a number—for example, Senate Bill 13 (SB 13). The first bill introduced in the house of representatives would be designated HB 1.

2. *Assignment to a committee.* The lieutenant governor assigns bills to committees in the senate. For many bills, the lieutenant governor can choose from two or more committees. It is very important to supporters of a bill that the chosen committee does not oppose the spirit of the legislation. If possible, proponents of the bill and their allies will gain the lieutenant governor's support and get a friendly committee assignment in exchange for their support of or opposition to a bill of particular interest to the lieutenant governor.

3. *Senate committee action.* Supporters and opponents of the bill are allowed to testify in subcommittee and committee hearings. Witnesses are often lobbyists or bureaucrats affected by the bill. The subcommittee then marks up the bill (makes changes) and sends it to the committee, where it may be further marked up. Some senate committees do not have subcommittees. If that is so, the entire committee initially hears testimony and marks up the bill. The committee may then report on the bill favorably or unfavorably or may refuse to report on it at all.

4. *Senate calendar.* As described earlier, the senate has only one calendar of bills, and it is rarely followed. In the usual procedure, a senator makes a motion to suspend the regular calendar order and consider a proposed bill out of sequence. For this parliamentary maneuver to succeed, prior

FIGURE 7–9

How a Bill Becomes a Law

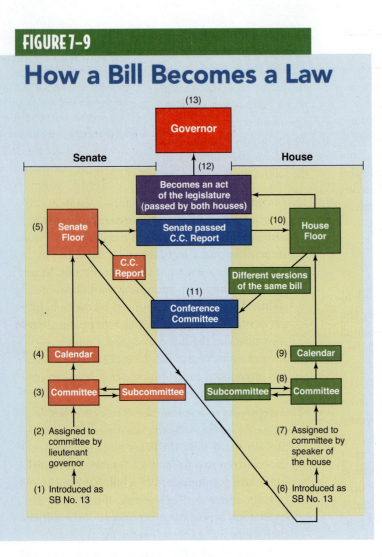

"talk the bill to death" or force a compromise. If a bill is successful in reaching the senate floor, it has already cleared its major obstacle (the two-thirds majority necessary for senate consideration) and will usually be passed in some form. Only a simple majority is necessary for a bill to pass.

The senate may also form itself into a **committee of the whole,** at which time the lieutenant governor appoints a senator to preside. Only a simple majority rather than the usual two-thirds is necessary to consider legislation, and the lieutenant governor may debate and vote on all questions. Otherwise, the senate rules are observed. No journal is kept of the proceedings.

6. *Introduction to the house.* After the senate passes a bill, the bill is sent to the house of representatives. A procedure similar to that in the senate is followed there.

7. *Assignment to a committee.* It is the responsibility of the speaker of the house to assign each bill to a committee. The speaker, like the lieutenant governor, has some freedom of choice because of the vague jurisdiction of house committees.

8. *House committee action.* Committee action in the house is similar to that in the senate. Each bill is assigned to a committee and then to a subcommittee, which may want to hold public hearings. The subcommittee as well as the committee may amend, totally rewrite, pigeonhole, or report favorably or unfavorably on a bill.

9. *House calendars.* A bill that is either reported favorably by the committee or receives a favorable minority report by the required number of committee members is placed on one of the house calendars by one of the calendars committees. This establishes the approximate order in which the whole house will consider the legislation. If the calendars committees fail to assign the bill to a calendar, they may be forced to do so by the action of a simple majority of the house. If a bill has the blessing of the speaker, however, it is sure to be promptly placed on the appropriate calendar.

10. *House floor.* The speaker of the house has the power to recognize representatives on the house floor and also to interpret the rules and points of order. Although the speaker may be overruled,

arrangements must be made for the lieutenant governor to recognize the senator who will make the motion. If two-thirds of the senators agree to the motion, the bill, with the blessings of the lieutenant governor, is ready for action on the senate floor.

5. *Senate floor.* The president of the senate (the lieutenant governor) has the power to recognize senators who wish to speak, to vote in the event of a tie, and to interpret rules and points of order. Rarely do members of the senate overrule these interpretations.

The Texas Senate permits unlimited debate, but this policy is not meant to imply that the senate is a deliberative body, because it is not. Such a luxury is impossible due to the short legislative session. Unlimited debate could, however, lead to a filibuster—an attempt to

committee of the whole The entire senate acting as a committee to allow it to relax its rules and expedite legislation.

this seldom happens. The size of the house necessitates that debate be more limited than in the senate—usually ten minutes for each member. Bills may be amended, tabled (which usually kills the measure), killed outright, or sent back to committee. Legislation may be passed by a simple majority of members present.

11. *Conference committee.* If the house changes the senate-passed version of a bill, a conference committee is necessary to resolve the differences between the two houses. The lieutenant governor appoints five senators and the speaker appoints five representatives to sit on the committee. The compromise bill must be approved by a majority of both the senators and the representatives before it can be reported out of the conference committee.

12. *Final passage.* The bill is sent first to the chamber where it originated and then to the other chamber for final approval. Neither may amend the reported bill but rather must accept it, reject it, or send it back to the conference committee. The conference committee report is sent to the governor after passage in both the house and the senate.

13. *The governor.* The governor has several options. First, she or he may sign a bill into law. Second, the governor may choose not to sign, in which case it becomes law in ten days if the legislature is in session or in twenty days if the legislature is not in session. Third, the governor may choose to veto the act, but the veto can be overridden by a two-thirds vote in each house.

The governor must either accept or veto the complete act unless it contains provisions for appropriating funds. In appropriations acts, the governor may strike out an item of appropriation, but she or he does not have a reduction veto to reduce spending for an item. Also, the governor may not veto riders on appropriations bills that do not authorize state spending.

The governor may use the veto late in the legislative session without fear of the legislature's overriding it, because a veto cannot be overridden in a subsequent session. If the governor signs an act of the legislature, it will become law in ninety days—or sooner if it appropriates funds or the legislature has designated it as emergency legislation.

14. *Certification.* If the act requires the expenditure of funds, the comptroller of public accounts must certify that adequate revenue is available for its implementation. If revenue is lacking, the act goes back to the legislature, where either

adequate funds are provided or it is approved by a four-fifths majority in each chamber. If neither option is successful, it cannot be implemented.

7–4h The Role of the Governor

The Texas Constitution gives the governor a considerable role in the legislative process. The governor may veto any bill and can use the item veto on appropriations. These formal powers place the governor in a strong bargaining position, and the governor's support for or opposition to specific programs is an important factor. The governor's influence with The Lobby and the threat to veto constitute the most useful instruments to achieve changes in the substance of a bill while it is still in the legislature. Of course, the governor has lost a battle with the legislative leadership if he or she is forced to veto a bill after attempting to influence it.

In fact, a coalition consisting of the governor, the lieutenant governor, and the speaker is the norm, with each sharing influence over the legislative process. The governor also has the support of friendly interest groups that can often be enlisted to influence the presiding officers and other legislators. A governor who tends toward activism can exercise substantial influence over legislation. If the governor chooses a passive legislative role, however, his or her influence is significantly decreased.

FOR CRITICAL THINKING

The Texas Senate suspended the two-thirds rule so that the voter ID bill could pass with a simple majority. *Given increased party polarization, do you think such violations of tradition may become more common in the future? Why or why not?*

7–5 Institutional Tools of Leadership

Taken as a whole, the procedural tools of leadership give the presiding officers enough authority, both formal and informal, to exercise fundamental control

Learning Outcome 7–5

Identify and describe the various legislative boards and committees at the disposal of the legislative leadership.

over the legislative process. Complementing their procedural powers, institutional powers give the lieutenant governor and speaker influence over actual policy implementation, further enhancing their bargaining position with economic and political players who seek to influence the state's public policy.

7–5a The Legislative Budget Board

Most states, the U.S. government, and most countries have only one budget. Texas has two. Each agency in state government presents its budget requests to both the governor's office and the powerful **Legislative Budget Board (LBB).** The board then provides the governor and the legislature with a draft of the appropriations bill. The LBB has broad authority for strategic, long-range planning, bill analyses, and policy-impact analyses of education, criminal justice, and financial policies.

The LBB consists of ten members, including the lieutenant governor and the speaker, who serve as joint chairs. The remainder of the board is composed of the chairs of the Senate Finance Committee and the House Ways and Means and Appropriations Ccommittees, who serve as automatic members, and two house members and three senate members appointed by their respective presiding officer. The LBB operates continuously, even when the legislature is not in session, under the management of an administrative director appointed by the board.

Control of the board gives the two presiding officers strong influence over state spending from the budgeting stage through the final appropriations stage. LBB staff members assist appropriating committees and their chairs and serve as watchdogs overseeing to some extent the expenditures of the executive agencies and departments.

7–5b The Legislative Council

Another instrument of influence is the fourteen-member **Legislative Council,** made up of six senators, the chair of the House Administration Committee, five other representatives, and the lieutenant governor

and speaker, who serve as joint chairs. The lieutenant governor appoints the senate members, and the speaker appoints the house members. With the exception of the speaker and lieutenant governor, the appointees' terms end with the beginning of the regular legislative session. The presiding officers govern the council during the regular session.

The Legislative Council, its director, and staff function as a source of information and support to the legislature, state agencies, and other governmental institutions. It also provides research, computing, and printing support for legislators and helps them draft legislative proposals. The council staff plays a key role in the redistricting process.

7–5c The Legislative Audit Committee

The **Legislative Audit Committee** appoints and supervises the state auditor, who with the consent of the senate, heads the State Auditor's Office. The six-member Legislative Audit Committee is composed of the lieutenant governor, the chair of the Senate Finance Committee, one senator chosen by the lieutenant governor, the house speaker, and the chairs of the House Appropriations Committee and Ways and Means Committee.

The authority of the Office of the State Auditor is both broad and deep. Under the direction of the committee, any entity receiving funds from the state can be audited. This includes state agencies and departments, and even colleges and universities. A variety of audits—including financial, compliance, economy and efficiency, effectiveness, and special—may be conducted.

7–5d The Sunset Advisory Commission

The Texas Sunset Act reevaluates the need for more than 150 statutory state agencies on a twelve-year cycle to determine the need for their continuance. Those agencies not specifically renewed by the legislature are automatically terminated—that is, their "sun sets." Many of those that are reauthorized by legislation are given altered scope and authority.

The twelve-member **Sunset Advisory Commission** enforces the act. The lieutenant governor appoints five senators and one public member, and the speaker appoints five representatives and one public member to the commission. Public members are appointed for two-year terms and legislators for four-year staggered terms. The commission chair is appointed by the presiding officers and alternates between senate and house members. The agency's chief executive officer is appointed by the commission.

Legislative Budget Board (LBB) The body responsible for proposing the legislature's version of the biennial budget.

Legislative Council The body that provides research support, information, and bill-drafting assistance to legislators.

Legislative Audit Committee The body that performs audits of state agencies for the legislature.

Sunset Advisory Commission A body that may recommend restructuring, abolishing, or altering the jurisdiction of an agency.

In the Sunset Advisory Commission's more than thirty-year history, it has abolished more than fifty-two state agencies, saving taxpayers hundreds of millions of dollars. In recent years, however, abolishing state agencies has proven politically unpopular. As a result, the Sunset Advisory Commission has worked to improve and reorganize state agencies, rather than abolish them completely.

FOR CRITICAL THINKING

Would you like to see more Texas administrative agencies abolished? Why or why not?

TEXANS IN
CONFLICT The Legislature

The general public is seldom aware of legislative events in Austin. Rare exceptions are when a scandal spreads over the state, such as the Sharpstown Bank scandal of the 1970s or the delinquent property tax scandal of the 1990s. Although public involvement is stimulated by a scandal, it is often limited to finding guilty parties rather than making serious inquiries into the need for reform. Citizens who monitor the legislature, however, have sharply conflicting opinions about its institutions. Some of the controversies include the following:

- Is gerrymandering an acceptable part of the political game—or should Texas try to create a nonpartisan redistricting system?

- Are the powers of the presiding officers excessive—or are they essential to the functioning of the legislative process?

- Should the Texas legislature become more professional, with higher pay, larger staffs, and annual sessions—or would such steps distance the members from the general public?

- Is increased political partisanship likely to alter traditional legislative procedures in Texas—or will tradition win out in the end?

TAKE ACTION

Consider volunteering to work on a political campaign or as an intern for a member of the Texas House or Senate. Here's how to identify candidates running for public office:

- Visit the Texas secretary of state's Web site by searching on "texas sos." Then click on a link that lists the candidates for the next primary or general election.

- View the list of candidates on the Texas Democratic and Republican parties' Web sites by typing "texas democrats" or "texas gop" into your search engine.

- For valuable information on candidates, visit the League of Women Voters of Texas by entering "lwvtexas."

You also might explore these legislative internship opportunities for Texas students:

- Investigate the Texas Legislative Internship Program by searching on "tlip."

- Look into the Moreno Rangel Legislative Leadership Program, which provides internship opportunities to Latino/Latina undergraduate and graduate students, by typing in "moreno rangel intern."

- Consider the Senator Gregory Luna Legislative Scholars & Fellows Program at "luna fellows."

- Check with your own university. Many universities have their own legislative internship programs.

- Call your representative in the Texas House or Senate for additional internship opportunities. For a listing of Texas House members, check "texas house," and for a listing of Texas Senate members, see "texas senate."

STUDY TOOLS

Ready to study?

- Review what you've read with the quiz below. Check your answers on the Chapter in Review card at the back of the book. For any questions you miss, read the corresponding Learning Outcome section again to prepare for class and your exam.
- Rip out and study the Chapter in Review card.

. . . Or you can go online to CourseMate

at www.cengagebrain.com for these additional review materials:

- Practice Quizzes
- Key Term Flashcards or Crossword Puzzles
- Audio Summaries
- Simulations, Animated Learning Modules, and Interactive Timelines
- Videos
- American Government NewsWatch

Quiz

1. The redrawing of district boundaries specifically to favor some political party, candidate, or ethnic group is known as _____.
   a. reapportionment   b. redistricting   c. gerrymandering

2. A change in the number of U.S. representatives allotted to Texas following each ten year census is known as _____.
   a. redistricting   b. reapportionment   c. gerrymandering

3. Although there have been major improvements in representation of certain historically underrepresented groups in the Texas legislature in recent years, which of the following groups is overrepresented in the Texas legislature, particularly in the senate?
   a. women   b. Anglos   c. Hispanics

4. Texas legislators receive an annual salary of _____ and meet biannually for terms of _____ days.
   a. $42,000; 240   b. $24,000; 140   c. $7,200; 140

5. As stipulated in the Texas Constitution, members of the Texas House of Representative serve terms of _____, while members of the Texas Senate serve terms of _____. The maximum number of terms a member can serve is _____.
   a. two years; four years; unlimited
   b. two years; six years; unlimited
   c. two years; four years; two consecutive terms

6. Perhaps the most significant consequence of Texas's short legislative session is that:
   a. very little legislation gets passed.
   b. Texas legislators pay closer attention to the process and are more professional than their counterparts in the U.S. Congress.
   c. Texas legislators have less experience, less knowledge of the issues, and must rely on information from special interests more than do members of Congress.

7. The legislative officer who is generally considered one of the most powerful persons in the Texas legislature and who presides over the senate is the _____, who is _____.
   a. speaker of the house; elected in statewide elections
   b. lieutenant governor; elected in statewide elections
   c. lieutenant governor; appointed by the governor

8. Identify the type of ad hoc committee that specifically meets to resolve differences between Senate and House versions of the same legislation.
   a. conference committee
   b. joint committee
   c. interim committee

9. The name for permanent committees that function throughout the legislative session is _____.
   a. subcommittees
   b. conference committees
   c. standing committees

10. To be sent to the governor for signature into law, a bill must be approved after _____ reading(s) in both the house and the senate.
    a. one   b. two   c. three

11. Which of the following is NOT a power of the speaker of the house?
    a. Veto of legislation being debated on the house floor
    b. Appointment of committee members and committee chairs
    c. Scheduling of legislation for floor action

12. The _____ rule permits an individual Texas Senator to delay a bill in committee for forty-eight hours upon request.
    a. two-thirds   b. tagging   c. first reading

13. The _____ Committee is a special procedural committee whose members are appointed by the Texas Speaker of the House. The committee schedules floor debate for bills that have already been approved by other committees.
    a. Conference   b. Standing   c. Calendars

14. What is the purpose of the Sunset Advisory Commission?
    a. To re-evaluate the need for state agencies every twelve years
    b. To re-evaluate how well laws passed by the legislature are working every ten years
    c. To monitor ethical procedures and the behavior of legislative members

15. Identify the ten-member board that bears responsibility for proposing the legislature's version of a two-year budget.
    a. Legislative Council
    b. Legislative Audit Committee
    c. Legislative Budget Board

The Executive Branch

ERICH SCHLEGEL/THE NEW YORK TIMES

★ Learning Outcomes

The **Learning Outcomes** labeled 1 through 6 are designed to help improve your understanding of the chapter. After reading this chapter, you should be able to:

8–1 Describe the informal requirements to become governor of Texas, the line of succession if a governor leaves office, and the duties of the gubernatorial staff.

8–2 Discuss the governor's legislative tools of persuasion, including the veto, and executive tools of persuasion, such as appointive powers.

8–3 Demonstrate knowledge of the administrative structure of the Texas executive branch, including the functions of the attorney general, the comptroller, and other key administrators.

8–4 List the major characteristics of bureaucracies and ways in which reformers have tried to make bureaucracies more efficient.

8–5 Describe how bureaucracies relate to clientele interest groups, and define the Iron Texas Star model.

8–6 Discuss the problem of bureaucratic accountability, and ways in which agencies have been made account-able to the people, the legislature, and the executive branch.

Remember to visit page 199 for additional Study Tools

CONFLICT

Should Texas Recognize IDs Issued by Mexico?

AP PHOTO/KIICHIRO SATO

The Mexican government issues an identity card called the *matricula consular*, which is also known as the consular identification, or CID, card. Mexico will issue this identity card to any of its citizens living in the United States. Applicants must appear in person at a Mexican consular office and present a Mexican birth certificate or an official Mexican identification document that contains a photograph. The *matricula* card resembles a U.S. state driver's license and has a variety of security features to prevent forgery.

Under most circumstances, the state of Texas does not accept the *matricula* card as a valid form of identification. Several Texas cities, counties, colleges, and police departments, however, including those of Dallas and Houston, have accepted it as valid identification. Some banks accept this card as identification when opening a bank account—the U.S. Department of Treasury has ruled that the *matricula* card is an acceptable form of ID for financial institutions. Between September 3, 2012 and August 31, 2013, Texas residents with a *matricula* card were able to register or transfer vehicle titles at the Texas Department of Motor Vehicles.

Currently, thirty states accept these cards as a legitimate form of photo identification for citizens of other countries in some contexts. Other states reject the ID. Arizona recently decided that the state and Arizona local governments could no longer recognize photo ID cards issued by foreign consulates. Indiana has even attempted to ban private businesses such as banks from accepting the ID. Should the state of Texas and its local governments accept the Mexican consular identification cards for more purposes—or should we follow the lead of Arizona and Indiana and refuse them?

Accept the IDs—We Are a Bicultural State

To be sure, there are Texans who do not like the fact that our state is bicultural, bilingual, and even binational, but that is the reality. The best way to regularize the status of the large number of Mexican immigrants residing and working in Texas is to let them become part of the system. A secure ID that makes no statements about the immigration status of the holder helps immigrants deal with private businesses. It could also help them in interactions with the police and with other government agencies.

Some argue that recognition of the *matricula* card makes life too easy for undocumented immigrants. After all, legal immigrants do not need the card because they have other acceptable forms of identification. But immigration laws are federal laws. Enforcement of immigration laws is properly the responsibility of the federal government, not the state of Texas. Our state government should not get involved with immigration issues at all.

Matricula Cards Are Just Too Easy to Get

Those who are against the acceptance of *matricula* cards argue that they are not secure, for several reasons. They can be forged too easily. Mexican officials in U.S. consular offices do not adequately check the documents used to obtain such cards. Indeed, historically, Mexican officials have been susceptible to corruption, which might call the validity of a *matricula* card into question. In addition, Mexico has no unified database of cardholders that could be checked by Texas officials.

It is true that possession of a *matricula* card says nothing about the cardholder's immigration status. But there is no question that recognition of the card makes life much easier for illegal immigrants who want to stay and work in Texas. The state government has not only the right, but also the responsibility to uphold national immigration laws. If Texas allows illegal immigrants to readily integrate themselves into mainstream society, Texas and America become worse off.

Where do you stand?

1. What groups might favor use of the *matricula* card, and what groups would oppose its acceptance?
2. How much of a problem do you think exists with the forgery of U.S. state drivers' licenses?

Explore this issue online

- If you look for "matricula consular" using a search engine, you will discover that debate on the issue is dominated overwhelmingly by activists opposed to illegal immigration.
- To hear the other side of the story, search on "justice for immigrants." That is the name of a group founded by the Roman Catholic Church, but the search phrase brings up other pro-immigrant pages as well.

Introduction

The executive branch is the part of government that administers the law and implements public policy. When a highway is built, when a police officer writes a ticket, when taxes are collected, or when a public school teacher conducts a class, an executive (or administrative) function is being performed. Executive-branch employees check gas pumps and meat scales for accuracy. They license morticians, insurance agents, and doctors. They check food for purity. The executive branch of government enforces public policies and is responsible for the day-to-day management of the government. Almost all of a citizen's contacts with the government are with the executive branch.

The most distinctive characteristic of the Texas executive branch is that no one is officially in charge of the administrative apparatus.[1] As in many other states, the administration of laws in Texas is divided among a variety of elective and appointive positions. Although an agency director heads each executive department, no single official in Texas government has ultimate responsibility for the actions of the Texas bureaucracy. No single official can coordinate either planning or program implementation among the many agencies, commissions, and departments. The officer who comes closest to filling that role, however, is the governor.

Texas Governor Rick Perry (center) participated in the ribbon-cutting ceremony for a highway in Caldwell County. It will be the first highway in the United States with an 85 MPH speed limit.

BOB DAEMMRICH/BOB DAEMMRICH PHOTOGRAPHY, INC./CORBIS

8–1 The Office of Governor

⭐ **Learning Outcome 8–1**

Describe the informal requirements to become governor of Texas, the line of succession if a governor leaves office, and the duties of the gubernatorial staff.

Although the Texas Constitution designates the governor as chief executive, the executive branch is splintered into various offices and agencies that are often beyond the governor's effective control. The division of Texas executive power is largely based on the democratic theory, dating back to President Andrew Jackson (1829–1837), that most major officeholders should be elected.

8–1a The Powers of the Governor

The legislature has recently strengthened the governor's administrative influence over several agencies, but the continued preference for decentralized government by powerful special interest groups, bureaucrats, the legislative leadership, and the general public ensures the survival of the *weak governor system* in Texas.

The lack of administrative authority does not mean the governor's office has no potential for meaningful political power. The governor has legislative powers, access to the media, influence over his or her party, and the ability to make appointments to boards, commissions, and the judiciary. These powers allow an astute, savvy officeholder to exert significant influence on both legislative and administrative policy.

Established interest group support and the willingness to penalize opponents are also important factors in a governor's influence. A long-serving governor who has the support of powerful interest groups can wield a dominant influence over the enactment and implementation of public policy. Such a governor will have appointed most members of administrative boards and commissions, convinced legislators that he or she will punish errant behavior, and have his or her authority backed by the political and financial muscle of special interests.

In a show of support, Governor Rick Perry and the governors of several other states tour a beef plant in South Sioux City, Nebraska. The plant produces a ground beef product that has been characterized as "pink slime" by opponents. The corporation that owns the plant also has operations in Texas.

exercised the power of the office. In reality, Governor Richards was the first woman to serve as the governing Texas chief executive.

Elected state treasurer in 1982, Ann Richards was the first woman to win a statewide election in Texas since Governor Ferguson. Richards became governor in 1990 after hard-fought and bitter primaries and general election contests, disproving the assumption that Texans will not support a woman for high office. Richards was also an exception to several other informal criteria for becoming Texas's governor. Her political views ranged from moderate to liberal, and she had been divorced and was a recovering alcoholic.

Occupation and Age The typical governor has usually been successful in business or law. In fact, more than one-half of the governors who have served since 1900 have been lawyers. He or she will probably be between forty and sixty years of age, have a record of elective public service in state government or some other source of name recognition, and be a participant in service, social, and occupational organizations.

Party Affiliation Texas was a two-party state for top-of-the-ticket elections for president, U.S. senator, and governor for more than two decades, although it was basically Democratic for most other offices. It became a complete two-party state with the 1990 election of two Republicans to the lower-level offices of state treasurer and commissioner of agriculture.

THE TRIUMPH OF THE REPUBLICANS. Texas had effective two-party politics for only a few years before it completed its evolution into a Republican one-party state. Republicans first swept statewide offices in 1998, electing the governor, lieutenant governor, and all lower-level administrators, including the members of the Texas Railroad Commission.

Statewide elective offices provide political experience and name recognition that can serve as a springboard to higher office. In 1998, Rick Perry moved from being commissioner of agriculture to lieutenant governor, and in 2002 he was elected governor. That same year, Attorney General John Cornyn was elected to the U.S. Senate.

The Republican primary is a joust between conservative-to-moderate candidates, with the more

8–1b The Necessary Qualifications to Become Governor

To become governor, a candidate must meet formal or legal qualifications, as well as the informal qualifications that are imposed by the state's political culture. As is usual with elective offices, the legal requirements for becoming governor are minimal. One must be thirty years of age, an American citizen, and a citizen of Texas for five years before running for election. While the formal qualifications for governor are easily met, the informal criteria are more restrictive.

Race and Religion Since the Texas Revolution, governors have all been white Protestants. They have usually been Methodist or Baptist, and also Anglo American, with family names originating in the British Isles.

Gender The governor is historically male. The only female governor of Texas before Ann Richards (1991–1995) was Miriam A. Ferguson, who served for two nonconsecutive terms (1925–1927 and 1933–1935). She ran on the slogan "Two Governors for the Price of One" and did not really represent a deviation from male dominance in Texas politics, for it was clear that her husband, former governor James E. Ferguson,

conservative candidate usually winning. Republican gubernatorial candidates usually have the campaign funds to outspend their Democratic opponents. As a result, they can purchase name recognition and a positive political image. They can also define the issues of the campaign.

THE DEMOCRATS' DISADVANTAGE. The Democratic gubernatorial primary is usually a match between pro-business moderates and more liberal candidates. The Democratic nominee must forge a shaky coalition of business leaders, ethnic minorities, unions, intellectuals, teachers, conservationists, and consumer advocates. Even then, a Democratic candidate has little chance of prevailing in the general election because Texas has become reliably Republican in statewide elections.

Financial Support Money is a critical factor in any serious campaign for Texas governor. Although the candidate who spends the most does not always win the office, a hefty bankroll is necessary for serious consideration. Challengers will usually spend more

> ## "I'm from Texas, and one of the reasons I like Texas
> is because there's no one in control."
>
> ~ WILLIE NELSON ~
> SINGER AND SONGWRITER

than incumbents to buy name recognition. Paul Taylor, president of the Alliance for Better Campaigns, commented that "the legacy is a political culture in which we auction off the right to free speech thirty seconds at a time to the highest political bidder."[2]

8–1c Tenure, Removal, and Succession

As in forty-seven other states, Texas governors serve a four-year term. Unlike most states, however, there is no limit on the number of terms that a Texas governor may serve. As Governor Rick Perry has demonstrated, unlimited terms can be one of the governor's greatest sources of power to overcome the constitutional restrictions on the power of the office. If the governor is reelected repeatedly, he or she will be able to appoint members to every state board, establish working relationships with powerful lobbyists and campaign contributors, and win powerful allies in the legislature. Without such benefits, the powers of the governor are relatively limited, as we explain in the *How Texas Compares* feature below.

HOW TEXAS COMPARES

The Governor's Power

Compared with the average state governor, the governor of Texas has less authority to actually see that the laws are administered. In fact, the Texas governor's combined administrative and legislative powers rank thirty-fourth among the fifty states. By comparison, Utah's governor ranks first and Vermont's ranks fiftieth.

Using a one- to five-point scale, with five representing the greatest power, a 2007 study ranked the institutional powers of U.S. governors in several important categories.[3] With an institutional rating of 3.2, the Texas governor ranked above only ten other state governors and slightly below the average of 3.5.

The study also ranked the governors on personal power, awarding Texas's governor a personal power ranking of 3.8, above the governors in twelve other states but slightly below the average of 3.9.

FOR CRITICAL ANALYSIS

- How can Texas's governor use personal political power to overcome the formal legal and institutional limits on the office? From your reading of this chapter, identify ways in which the executive branch could be restructured to give the governor more institutional power.
- Would Texas benefit from having a stronger governor? Why or why not?

The governor may be removed from office only by **impeachment** by the Texas House of Representatives and conviction by the Texas Senate. Impeachment is the legislative equivalent of indictment and requires only a simple majority of members present. Conviction by the senate requires a two-thirds majority. If the office of governor becomes vacant, the lieutenant governor fills the post for the remainder of the elected term. The next in the line of succession is the president pro tempore of the senate, followed by the speaker of the house, the attorney general, and the chief justices of the Texas Courts of Appeals in numerical order by district.

If the lieutenant governor becomes governor, the Texas Senate elects a senator as acting lieutenant governor. This individual serves both as lieutenant governor and as senator until the next general election.

8–1d Compensation

The governor's salary is set by the legislature. At present, it is $150,000 yearly and stands in marked contrast to the low salaries paid to Texas legislators. Although the governor's salary is among the highest in the nation for state governors, several other Texas state officials earn more.

The governor has a mansion and an expense account to keep it maintained and staffed. He or she also has a professional staff and a security detail with offices in the capitol or the mansion. The modern chief executive depends heavily on staff to carry out the duties of office.

8–1e Staff

The governor's increased involvement in legislative affairs and appointments—and the increasing demands on government by the general public—weigh heavily on the governor's time and resources. The Texas governor, like all executives in modern government, depends on others for advice, information, and assistance when making decisions and recommendations. A good staff is a key ingredient for successful service as chief executive. The governor's staff, although primarily responsible for assisting with the everyday duties of the office, also attempts to persuade legislators, administrators, and representatives of various local governments to follow the governor's leadership in solving common problems.

impeachment The official indictment of an officeholder for improper conduct in office.

Evaluation of Political Appointees Among the most important concerns of the governor's staff are political appointments. Each year, the governor makes several hundred appointments to various boards, commissions, and executive agencies. He or she also fills newly created judicial offices and those vacated because of death or resignation. Staff evaluation of potential appointees is necessary because the governor may not personally know many of the individuals under consideration.

Legislative Liaisons Legislative assistants act as liaisons between the office of the governor and the legislature. Their job is to stay in contact with key legislators, committee chairs, and the legislative leadership. These assistants are, in practice, the governor's lobbyists. They keep legislators informed and attempt to persuade them to support the governor's position on legislation. Often, the success of the governor's legislative program rests on the staff's abilities and political expertise.

Budget Recommendations and Planning Some administrative assistants head executive offices that compile and write budget recommendations. Others manage and coordinate activities within the governor's office. Staff members also exercise administrative control over the governor's schedule of ceremonial and official duties.

The governor is the official planning officer for the state, although coordination and participation by affected state agencies are voluntary. The planning divisions also help to coordinate local and regional planning among councils of government in an effort to bring the work of these jurisdictions into harmony with state goals. In addition, national and state funds are available through the governor's office to assist local units of government in comprehensive planning.

Texas Political
SOCIAL MEDIA

Like all major politicians, Texas governor Rick Perry has an active presence on social media. To find his Facebook page, search "rick perry." To follow him on Twitter, try "governor perry."

FOR CRITICAL THINKING

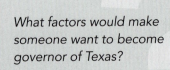

What factors would make someone want to become governor of Texas?

8–2 The Governor's Powers of Persuasion

LearningOutcome 8–2

Discuss the governor's legislative tools of persuasion, including the veto, and executive tools of persuasion, such as appointive powers.

The governor's ability to influence policy depends on his or her bargaining skills, persuasiveness, and ability to effectively broker deals between competing interests—the tools of persuasion. Thus, the **informal (extralegal) powers** of the office are as important as its **formal (legal) powers**—those granted by the constitution or by law. Still, the governor's ability to use informal power is largely determined by the extent of the formal powers.

Compared to governors of other states, the governor of Texas has weak formal powers. Some Texas governors, however, have been able to exert substantial influence on policy formulation and even on policy execution when the formal and informal powers are enhanced by other factors, including the following:

- A strong personality.
- Political expertise.
- Prestige.
- A knack for public relations and political drama.
- Good relations with the press.
- Supporters with political and economic strength.
- A favorable political climate.
- Good luck.

8–2a Legislative Tools of Persuasion

Ironically, the most influential bargaining tools that the Texas governor has are legislative. How these tools are used largely determines the governor's effectiveness.

The Veto One of the governor's most powerful formal legislative tools is the **veto.** After a bill has passed both houses of the legislature in identical form, it is sent to the governor. If signed, the bill becomes law. If vetoed, the bill is sent back to the legislature with a message stating the governor's reasons for opposition. The legislature has the constitutional power to override the governor's veto by a two-thirds vote, but, in practice, vetoes are usually final.

Because legislative sessions in Texas are short, the vast majority of important bills are passed and sent to the governor in the final days of the session. The governor does not need to take any action on the legislation for ten days when the legislature is in session (twenty days when it is not in session). Therefore, the governor can often wait until the legislature has adjourned to ensure that a veto will not be overridden. It is so difficult to override a veto in Texas that this has happened only once since World War II.

No Pocket Veto The Texas governor, however, lacks the pocket veto that is available to many other chief executives, including the president of the United States. The pocket veto provides that if the executive chooses to ignore legislation passed at the end of a session, it dies without ever taking effect. By contrast, if the Texas governor neither signs nor vetoes a bill, it becomes law. By not signing a bill and allowing it to become law, the governor may register a protest against the bill or some of its provisions.

The Item Veto The most important single piece of legislation enacted in a legislative session is the appropriations bill. If it were vetoed in its entirety, funds for government operations would be cut off, and a special session would be necessary. Like most states, however, Texas gives the governor an item veto, which allows the governor to veto funds for specific items or projects without killing the entire bill.

If used to its fullest potential, the item veto is a very effective, negative legislative tool. Funding is necessary to administer any law. By vetoing an item or a category of items, therefore, the governor can, in effect, kill programs or whole classes of programs. The Texas governor cannot, however, reduce the appropriation for a budgetary item, as some governors may. Because the appropriations bill is usually passed at the end of the session, the item veto is virtually absolute.

The Budgetary Impact of the Item Veto There is little evidence that governors across the country have used the item veto as an effective tool for responsible fiscal management. States with governors who have the item veto have about the same level of per capita state spending as those without it. In 2011, Texas governor Rick Perry used the item veto only to kill funding for legislative proposals that had not

informal (extralegal) powers Powers that are not stated in rules, by law, or by the constitution, but are usually derived from formal powers.

formal (legal) powers Powers stated in rules, by law, or by the Constitution.

veto The executive power to reject a proposed law unless a legislative supermajority votes to override.

Republican presidential candidate Texas Governor Rick Perry signs a copy of his book *Fed Up!*

The governor can also use this powerful informal tool to influence bureaucrats. Agency representatives are very active in the legislative process, often seeking increased funding for programs and projects or seeking authorization for new ones. Because of this, the governor may be able to influence the administration of existing programs by threatening to withhold funds or veto bills actively supported by an agency. The agency's legislative liaison personnel (its lobbyists) may also support the governor's legislative program in exchange for support (or neutrality) for agency-supported bills.

The threat of veto can also be used to consolidate lobbyist support for the governor's legislative proposals. Lobbyists may offer to support the governor's position on legislation if the governor will agree not to veto a particular bill that is considered vital to the interests of their employers. The governor can thus bargain with both supporters and opponents of legislation in order to gain political allies.

Bargaining The governor's bargaining with legislators, lobbyists, and administrators is often intense, as various political forces attempt to gain gubernatorial neutrality, support, or opposition for legislation. If the governor has not made particular legislation an explicit part of his or her legislative program, avenues are open for political bartering. The governor can support or oppose the particular legislation to rally support for measures that really are in the governor's legislative program. Whoever seeks the governor's support must be willing to give something of real political value in return.

All sides of the negotiation want to gain as much as possible and give as little as possible. There is, of course, a vast difference in political resources among politicians, just as among interest groups. What the governor brings to the bargaining table depends on several political factors:

1. *The depth of the governor's commitment to the bill.* If the governor is committed to a position, because of either a political debt or an ideological belief, this support or opposition may not be open to negotiation.
2. *Timing.* Politicians often try to be the player who tips the scales for the winning side.
3. *The political and financial support the governor receives during a campaign.* This does not mean that all campaign contributions buy political decisions, but they do increase the chances that contributors will get a favorable hearing.

become law during the session. In other words, Perry used the item veto as a housekeeping operation to cut spending that did not fund any existing program.

Although there is little evidence that the item veto is an effective tool for financial discipline, governors certainly can use it as a bargaining chip with legislators. For example, in 2005, when Governor Perry item-vetoed the entire $35.3 billion appropriation for the Texas Education Agency (one-fourth of state spending), he put pressure on the state legislature to pass his own version of educational spending in a thirty-day special session. This forced the legislature to act, because without a compromise between the governor and the legislature, Texas public schools would have closed.

The Threat of a Veto An informal legislative power of the governor not mentioned in the constitution or the law is the **threat of veto.** Both the veto and the item veto are negative tools that simply kill bills or programs—they do not let the governor shape legislation. By threatening to use these formal powers, though, the governor can often persuade the legislative supporters of a bill to change its content or face the probability of a veto.

threat of veto The informal power of the Texas governor to threaten to veto legislation.

4. *Future campaign support.* Bargaining may involve financial or political support for the reelection or advancement of an ambitious politician.

5. *The identity of the bill's supporters and opponents.* The governor may not want to align with a political group that is unpopular with financial supporters or the general electorate—for example, advocates for the legalization of marijuana or a graduated state income tax.

6. *The amount of firm legislative support for or opposition to the proposal.* Even if the chief executive is inclined to support a particular position, backing a losing cause could mean loss of prestige.

7. *Political benefits.* Some groups may be more willing or more able than others to pay a high price for the governor's support. Thus, an important consideration is the relative strength of the supporters and the opponents of a bill and their ability to pay their political and financial debts. For example, because medical patients in Texas have no organization and few political allies, their interests are not as well represented as those of the Texas Medical Association, health maintenance organizations, and insurance companies, which have strong organizations and ample political and financial resources.

8. *The danger of alienating interests that could provide postgubernatorial economic opportunities or political assistance.* Some governors may have extensive investments and are unlikely to make political decisions that could mean personal financial loss.

Pre-session Bargaining

If the governor, the legislative leadership, concerned administrators, and special interest groups can arrive at successful bargains and compromises before the legislative session begins, the prospect for passage of a proposal is greatly enhanced. This practice is called **pre-session bargaining**.

Pre-session bargainers seek compromises, but harmonious relationships seldom develop immediately. Powerful and often competing political forces may force the continuation of bargaining throughout the legislative session. Failure to reach an amicable settlement usually means either defeat of a bill in the legislature or a veto by the governor.

There are several advantages if advance agreement can be reached on a bill:

- The advocates of the bill are assured that both the legislative leadership and the governor are friendly to the legislation.

- The governor need not threaten a veto to influence the content of the bill. This keeps the chief executive on better terms with the legislature.
- The legislative leaders can guide the bill through their respective houses, secure in the knowledge that the legislation will not be opposed or vetoed by the governor.

Special Sessions

The constitution gives the governor exclusive power to call the legislature into special session and to determine the legislative subjects to be considered by the session. The legislature may, however, consider any nonlegislative subject, such as confirmation of appointments, resolutions, impeachment, and constitutional amendments, even if the governor does not include it in the call. Special sessions are limited to thirty days, but the governor may call them as often as he or she wants.

Often, when coalitions of legislators and lobbyists request a special session so that a "critical issue" can be brought before the legislature, other coalitions oppose consideration of the issue and therefore oppose the special session. Because there is seldom any legislation that does not hurt some and help others, the governor has an opportunity to use the special session as a bargaining tool. The governor may decide whether to call a special session on the basis of a concession or support to be delivered in the future. The supporters and opponents of legislation may also have to bargain with the governor over the inclusion or exclusion of specific policy proposals in the special session.

Of course, if the governor has strong feelings about a proposal, he or she may be determined to call (or not to call) a special session. If the governor thinks that an issue is critical, the attention of the entire state can be focused on the proposal during the special session much more effectively than during the regular session.

Message Power

As a constitutional requirement, the governor must deliver a state-of-the-state message at the beginning of each legislative session. This message includes the outline for the governor's legislative program. Throughout the session, the governor may also submit messages calling for action on individual items of legislation. The receptiveness of the legislature to the various messages is influenced by the governor's popularity,

> **pre-session bargaining**
> Negotiations that let the governor and legislative leaders reach necessary compromises before the legislative session.

interest groups, and legislators. Interest groups would continue to influence administrative appointments and removals in "their agencies," just as they now influence appointments to the boards and commissions under the present system. The governor would also have problems enforcing the accountability of agencies that have allies among powerful interest groups and legislators.

8–6d Bureaucratic Responsibility

To whom is a Texas administrator really accountable? The answer is, in all probability, to the clientele interest groups that benefit from the service programs the administrator provides. Agency officials are often obligated to administer the law and make policy decisions in ways that are favorable to the goals and aspirations of their political allies among private economic interests.

Appointees to boards and administrative positions are usually chosen from the industry concerned, and the policy decisions they make tend to benefit the most influential operatives in the industry. In turn, when government employees leave government service, many find jobs in the industry where their expertise lies. It is understandable that many administrators feel more directly accountable to the economic powers they affect than to the public at large.

open-meetings laws
Laws that require meetings of government bodies that make decisions concerning the public interest to be open to public scrutiny with some exceptions.

open-records laws Laws that requires the records of all government proceedings to be open for the examination of the public.

whistleblowers
Employees who expose corruption, incompetence, and criminal acts by government employees.

ombudsperson An official who hears complaints of employees and citizens concerning government administrators or policy administration.

Open Meetings and Open Records One way to obtain greater accountability is enhanced openness. A basic concept of democracy is that policy made in the name of the people should be made in full view of the public. Texas has made great strides in this area. **Open-meetings laws** require that meetings of government bodies at all levels

> ## "You want moral leadership?
> Try the clergy. It's their job."
>
> ~ MOLLY IVINS ~
> POLITICAL COMMENTATOR

of government be open to the general public, except when personnel, land acquisition, or litigation matters are discussed. The laws prohibit unannounced sessions and splitting up to avoid a quorum, and they require that public notice be posted for both open and closed sessions. However, these laws are continuously tested by policymakers, who feel more comfortable operating behind closed doors.

Openness is further encouraged by the state's **open-records law,** which requires that the records of all government proceedings be available to the public for only the expense involved in assembling and reproducing them.

The Internet can contribute to openness with records being posted online, in addition to making it easier for Texas residents to access forms and other bureaucratic information. We discuss e-government in the *Texas Politics and the Bureaucracy* feature on the facing page.

Whistleblowers and Ombudspersons Another source of openness is **whistleblowers**—government employees who expose bureaucratic excesses, corruption, or discrimination. These employees should be commended and protected from retribution, but too often they are instead exiled to the bureaucratic equivalent of Siberia or fired for their efforts. To its credit, Texas has a whistleblowers law that bans agencies from acting against employees who report law violations. But enforcement is difficult and time-consuming, and whistleblowers often suffer.

Reformers argue that the appointment of **ombudspersons** at every level of government would give individuals increased access to the bureaucracy in cases of real or imagined administrative injustice. In this way, administrative error, injustice, or oversight could be rectified. Ombudspersons usually lack authority to force administrative compliance, but they can bring the complaints to the proper authorities and represent the individual's interests within the administration.

In the end, however, the lack of public accountability by Texas administrators cannot be blamed wholly on poor organization or the lack of consumer- or citizen-oriented agencies. No amount of reorganization and no number of consumer agencies can overcome the willingness of an indifferent public to accept bureaucratic errors, inefficiency, excesses, favoritism, or corruption.

E-Government in Texas

Among the states, Texas is a leader in on-line information, presentation, and service. See for yourself by visiting texasonline.com, the state's portal and clicking through the various sites. You'll discover that having on-line access to the Texas government fosters openness and accountability. The Internet is "delivering" government in this state.

E-Knowledge, E-Service, and E-Governance

A way to evaluate the quality of e-government is to look at the strengths of three basic elements: (1) e-knowledge, (2) e-service, and (3) e-governance. If you examine the online presence of state, county, and local governments in Texas, you will find all three of these elements present for the state, the 254 countries, and thousands of cities.

E-knowledge means that you can find government regulations, required documents, officials' duties, and more online. In the area of e-services, state sites help Texas residents and businesses by providing them with job information, local maps, and instructions about procedures, such as vehicle registration. There are online forms, polls, surveys, chat rooms, and places to file complaints. In the domain of e-governance, the variety of government-to-citizen connections is impressive. Links on Web sites provide e-mail addresses and other contact information for officials and policy-making bodies.

The State's Online Services

Texas's Web site lists e-services in numerous categories. They include searchable license records databases, government forms, industry permits, and instructions on filing court documents. If you want to start a business, you can find how to register it online. Additionally, there is a Spanish version of most Web pages.

If you need to obtain an occupational license, you can find out how by going to texasonline.com. If you are interested in employment with state government, you can find that information, too.

And Then There Are the Cities

Every major city in Texas has its own Web page. Most of the mid-sized and smaller cities do, too. Often, you can pay utility bills and parking tickets on such Web sites. Each city's code of ordinances is also available online. If you want to work for a city's police or fire department, you can look at promotional videos and then find out the requirements for the position.

FOR CRITICAL ANALYSIS In what ways does the Internet make city, county, and state governments more accountable to the people?

FOR CRITICAL THINKING

Why do you think that citizens of Texas pay relatively limited attention to the activities of their state government?

CONFLICT The Executive Branch

The Texas plural executive, in which voters choose multiple executive officers and the members of various boards, came into being under the Constitution of 1875. The framers of that document wanted to abolish the centralization of power in state government experienced under Reconstruction governor Edmund J. Davis. That was more than 135 years ago, however. Today, many people do not know Governor Davis, but the plural executive marches on.

A key reason that it does is that Texans, like other Americans, are highly resistant to the idea that they could lose the right to vote for a particular official. Even those who admit that they never pay attention to the behavior of officeholders at the bottom of the ballot want to hold on to the right to "throw the rascals out." Whatever changes the future may bring to the Texas executive, the "long ballot" will probably stay. There are executive-branch topics that divide Texans, however. They include the following:

- Would state government be more efficient if the governor had more power over unelected boards and agencies—or would the concentration of power in the governor's office be dangerous?

- When the governor plays a role in national politics, does this help Texas—or does it merely distract the governor from his or her proper duties?

- Is it appropriate for agencies to seek to benefit the industries that they regulate—or do such practices harm the broader public?

- Does the privatization of government functions spur efficiency—or the foundation of a new spoils system?

TAKE ACTION

Use state agencies to protect your rights as a consumer.

- Contact the Consumer Protection Division of the Office of the Attorney General to learn about your rights and how to exercise them. Copies of the Deceptive Practices Act and consumer brochures are available. The office also provides instructions on how to file a complaint as well as a copy of a consumer complaint form. Search on "texas consumer protection" or write to Consumer Protection Division, Office of the Attorney General, P.O. Box 12548, Austin, TX 78711. The Texas consumer protection hotline is (800) 621-0508.

- Work with private organizations that advocate for consumer rights. For example, get tips on all types of insurance from Texas Watch at "texas watch."

- To support a cleaner environment for Texas, check Texas Public Employees for Environmental Responsibility by searching on "txpeer." Write letters to elected officials, and organize study groups to become more aware of environmental concerns.

Ready to study?

- Review what you've read with the quiz below. Check your answers on the Chapter in Review card at the back of the book. For any questions you miss, read the corresponding Learning Outcome section again to prepare for class and your exam.
- Rip out and study the Chapter in Review card.

. . . Or you can go online to CourseMate

at www.cengagebrain.com for these additional review materials:

- Practice Quizzes
- Key Term Flashcards or Crossword Puzzles
- Audio Summaries
- Simulations, Animated Learning Modules, and Interactive Timelines
- Videos
- American Government NewsWatch

Quiz

1. Texas governors in the last three decades have been primarily:
   a. white, male, Protestant, Republican.
   b. white, male, Protestant, Democrat.
   c. Hispanic, male, Catholic, male, Democrat.

2. Effective Texas governors tend to be those who:
   a. settle for the limited role assigned to them under the fragmented constitutional system of government.
   b. skillfully use interpersonal political skills, the media, and appointment powers to overcome the limited formal powers of the office.
   c. overpower the lieutenant governor with their formal powers.

3. Which of the following is one of the few formal executive powers that the Texas governor possesses that the U.S. president does not possess?
   a. the veto
   b. the line-item veto
   c. appointment powers

4. The Texas governor's formal powers vis-à-vis other state governors can best be described as:
   a. stronger than most other governors.
   b. about the same as most other governors.
   c. weaker than most other governors.

5. The Texas governor's power to remove most executive officials is:
   a. subject to majority approval by the senate.
   b. subject to two-thirds approval by the senate.
   c. unlimited.

6. A distinctive aspect of the executive branch in Texas is that:
   a. it is very centralized.
   b. the governor appoints most major executive officials.
   c. it is a plural executive.

7. The _____ is the executive official who serves as Texas's accountant, is elected statewide, certifies the official budget for the state of Texas, and has the power to audit state agencies for waste and fraud.
   a. attorney general
   b. secretary of state
   c. comptroller of public accounts

8. Of the following, which is NOT true of the position of the Texas attorney general?
   a. Issues nonbinding but influential legal interpretations of Texas law.
   b. The position has traditionally been an important stepping stone to the governorship.
   c. Is appointed by the governor.

9. "The federal government employs more workers than state and local governments."
   a. true.   b. false.

10. What is the term used to describe a system that gives public officials considerable discretion in employment and promotion to reward political friends and supporters?
    a. spoils system
    b. civil service system
    c. private system

11. An *ideal* bureaucracy is NOT characterized by:
    a. expertise.   b. political loyalty.   c. neutrality.

12. The model of policy making in Texas by a coalition of interests including interest groups, the lieutenant governor, standing committees, the governor, administrators, and boards and commissions is:
    a. the spoils system.
    b. the merit system.
    c. the Iron Texas Star.

13. Groups that directly benefit from government agency programs and have disproportionate influence on the policy process are known as:
    a. clientele interest groups.
    b. administrators.
    c. non-profits.

14. "One of the chief mechanisms by which the governor exercises control over the bureaucracy is that the Texas executive branch has a cabinet system of governance."
    a. true.   b. false.

15. _____ are officials who hear complaints of employees and citizens concerning government administrators or policy administrators.
    a. Ombudspersons   b. Legislative staffers   c. Whistleblowers

TX.GOV

9

Texas Judiciary

★ LearningOutcomes

The **Learning Outcomes** labeled 1 through 4 are designed to help improve your understanding of the chapter. After reading this chapter, you should be able to:

9–1 Identify the differences between criminal and civil cases, and the differences between original and appellate jurisdiction.

9–2 Explain how the courts are organized in Texas, and identify the jurisdiction of each major type of court.

9–3 Understand the role of grand juries and trial juries, and analyze the responsibilities of citizens in the legal system in Texas.

9–4 Compare the most common methods of judicial selection in the United States with the methods that Texas uses to select judges.

Remember to visit page 219 for additional Study Tools

BOB DAEMMRICH/THE IMAGE WORKS

CONFLICT

Is It Right That Judges Are Elected in Our State?

The founders of this country were concerned that too great a degree of popular control over government would lead to "mob rule." As a result, they attempted to insulate various institutions from direct elections. In particular, federal judges are appointed for life.

In contrast, in Texas and in many other states, judges are elected by the people. Popular election raises a number of issues, however. Elected judges, such as those in Texas, may receive campaign contributions and then make decisions that involve the very parties that made those contributions. Is that constitutional? The United States Supreme Court has ruled that elected judges must excuse themselves from a case when a conflict of interest is severe enough. Campaign contributions aside, there is the broader question of whether judges should be accountable to their constituents or independent from political pressure.

Then there is the issue of partisan voting. Among the twenty-two states that choose judges through elections, Texas is one of only seven in which judges run as candidates of political parties. The result is that judicial campaigns now resemble other election campaigns in Texas. Competition between the two major parties has created the following lineup: Defense attorneys in civil (as opposed to criminal) cases typically contribute to Republican judicial candidates. Plaintiffs' attorneys usually give to the Democratic candidates. Judicial campaigns are more expensive than they used to be, and they can be mean spirited, with plenty of negative ads.

Let the People Rule

Let's face it—judges cannot be insulated from politics. If the people of a state do not elect their judges, then the usual alternative is to have the governor appoint them. But appointments by the governor are always highly political. Governors tend to appoint supporters of their own party. If politics is going to play a role in judicial selection, then the people ought to have a direct say. Let voters decide whether a judicial candidate has the right approach to crime. Let them determine whether the candidate is too easy or too tough in business liability cases.

Let us not forget that a part of the judicial process involves jury trials. We let ordinary individuals participate in jury decisions, so why shouldn't judges respond to the public as well? Judges who do not face the electorate become removed from the people. Do not let judges end up living in a legal never-never land where abstractions matter more than the real world. It takes elections to provide us with the kinds of judges that we really want and need in Texas.

Just Look at Who Supports Elected Judges

Election campaigns require money. Most judges or would-be judges are not wealthy enough to pay for their own campaigns. For a seat on the Texas Supreme Court, candidates' spending currently approaches $1 million. Pro-business Republican judicial candidates have won the greater share of seats in recent years. They inevitably raise more contributions than their Democratic opponents. Doesn't that mean that these winning judges are beholden to their business supporters? How can they be capable of meting out impartial justice?

How neutral in any event can the Texas Supreme Court be when most, if not all, of its members are affiliated with one political party—today, the Republicans? Partisan judicial elections mean that interest groups use the elections to promote their causes. In Texas, interest groups have established tight financial relationships with judicial candidates. It is no surprise that, in Texas, incumbent judicial candidates usually receive about 60 percent of the vote.

Where do you stand?

1. What are the arguments in favor of switching to non-partisan judicial elections?
2. When one party controls all the seats on the Texas Supreme Court, is it still possible for litigants to expect fair rulings? Why or why not?

Explore this issue online

- To learn more about the Texas court system, type "texas courts" into your Internet search engine. The "Web Central" page of the Texas Courts Online Web site provides basic information on the court system. To look up particular cases, click on "Case Search."

Introduction

American society has increasingly turned to the judiciary to find answers to personal, economic, social, and political problems. Courts are often asked to determine our rights and answer important legal questions that touch almost every aspect of our lives.

For example, what level of privacy should we expect in our cars, offices, and homes? What treatment should people of different racial, gender, and age groups expect? In a divorce proceeding, with which parent should the children live? Should an accused person go to jail, and if so, for how long? Should a woman be allowed to terminate her pregnancy? Should a patient be allowed to refuse potential life-saving treatment? These are among the thousands of questions asked and answered daily by courts in the United States.

In fact, we are considered one of the most litigious societies in the world. We have about one-quarter of the world's lawyers—there are more than 1 million attorneys in the United States today.[1] Whereas 1 out of approximately every 700 people was a lawyer in 1951, that figure is now 1 out of about 260 people. In comparison, Japan has almost 27,000 lawyers, or 1 for every 4,700 people.[2]

Texas clearly fits into this general pattern of using the courts often—it ranks eighteenth among the states in terms of litigation. In recent years, Texas was found to have 292 people per attorney. The state also has more than 2,700 courts and approximately 3,400 justices or judges. These courts dealt with more than 9 million cases in 2011—on average, almost one case for every three residents of the state.[3]

9–1 Basic Judicial Concepts

LearningOutcome 9–1
Identify the differences between criminal and civil cases, and the differences between original and appellate jurisdiction.

In recent years, Texas courts have heard important or controversial cases involving topics such as flag burning, the death penalty, school desegregation, school finance, sexual orientation, the welfare of children in a polygamist sect, and one of the largest civil cases in history in which Texaco was found liable to Pennzoil for more than $8.5 billion. All of these cases have certain factors in common—basic judicial concepts apply.

9–1a Civil and Criminal Cases

In the American legal system, cases are generally classified as either civil or criminal. Table 9–1 on page 204 shows the most important differences between these two types of cases.

Civil Cases A **civil case** concerns private rights and remedies and usually involves private parties (*Smith v. Jones*) or organizations, although the government may occasionally be a party to a civil case. A personal-injury suit, a divorce case, a child-custody dispute, a breach-of-contract case, a challenge to utility rates, and a dispute over water rights are all examples of civil suits.

civil case A case that concerns private rights and remedies. A successful civil plaintiff may receive relief in the form of a court order requiring that that the defendant make financial restitution to the plaintiff or undertake a certain course of action.

State district judge Kevin Fine displays his tattoos at his office in Houston. Fine used his experience of beating drug addiction in his election campaign. Houston's Harris County sends more convicts to death row than any other in the United States, and Fine faced a torrent of criticism when he declared the death penalty unconstitutional.

AP PHOTO/*HOUSTON CHRONICLE*, NICK DE LA TORRE

Criminal Cases A **criminal case** involves a violation of penal law. If convicted, the lawbreaker may be punished by a fine, imprisonment, or both. The action is by the state against the accused (*State of Texas v. Smith*). Typical examples of criminal actions range from arson, rape, murder, and armed robbery to embezzlement, speeding, and jaywalking.

The Burden of Proof One of the most important differences between civil and criminal cases is the **burden of proof**—the duty and degree to which a party must prove its position. In civil cases, the standard used is a **preponderance of the evidence.** This means that whichever party has more evidence or proof on its side should win the case, no matter how slight the differential is.

In a criminal case, however, the burden of proof falls heavily on the government or prosecution. The prosecution must prove that a defendant is guilty **beyond a reasonable doubt.** The evidence must overwhelmingly, without serious question or doubt, point to the defendant's guilt. Otherwise, the defendant should be found "not guilty."

9–1b Original and Appellate Jurisdiction

Two important types of jurisdiction are original and appellate jurisdiction.

Original Jurisdiction The authority to try a case for the first time is called **original jurisdiction.** Legal rules of procedure are followed in hearing witnesses, viewing material evidence, and examining other evidence—such as documentary evidence—to determine guilt in criminal cases or responsibility in civil cases. The judge oversees procedure, but evaluating evidence is the jury's job (unless the right to a jury trial has been waived, in which case the judge weighs the evidence). The verdict or judgment is determined, and the remedy set. A trial involves the determination of fact and the application of law.

Appellate Jurisdiction The power of an appellate court to review the decisions of a lower court is called **appellate jurisdiction.** Such appeals do not involve a new trial. Rather, the appellate court reviews the law as it was applied in the original trial. Many appeals are decided by review of the record (transcript) of the case and the lawyers' **briefs** (written arguments). Sometimes, lawyers may appear and present oral arguments.

Appellate proceedings are based on law (legal process), not fact. Witnesses and material or documentary evidence are not consulted. A reversal does not necessarily mean that an individual who was convicted is innocent, only that the legal process was improper. Consequently, that person may be tried again, and questions of **double jeopardy** (being prosecuted twice for the same offense) are not involved because the individual waives the right to claim double jeopardy by appealing the case.

Criminal and Civil Cases Arising from the Same Incident
Sometimes, an action may lead to both criminal and civil proceedings. Suppose that in the course of an armed robbery, the thief shoots a clerk at a convenience store. The state could prosecute for the robbery—criminal action—and the clerk could sue for compensation for medical expenses, lost earning power, and other damages—civil action.

These dual proceedings are not unusual. A famous case involved former football star O.J. Simpson, who was tried in California for the alleged murder of his ex-wife, Nicole Brown Simpson, and her friend Ronald Goldman. Simpson was found not guilty in a criminal trial, but he was later held liable for damages in a civil proceeding.

criminal case A case that involves a violation of criminal law. The plaintiff is the state, even if private parties have experienced injury. If the state proves its case, the court will impose a punishment on the defendant.

burden of proof The duty of a party in a court case to prove its position.

preponderance of the evidence The amount of evidence necessary for a party to win in a civil case. Proof that outweighs the evidence offered in opposition to it.

beyond a reasonable doubt The standard used to determine the guilt or innocence of a person criminally charged. The state must provide evidence of guilt such that jurors have no doubt that might cause a reasonable person to question whether the accused was guilty.

original jurisdiction The authority of a court to consider a case in the first instance. The power to try a case, as contrasted with appellate jurisdiction.

appellate jurisdiction The power of an appellate court to review and revise the judicial action of an inferior court.

brief A written argument prepared by a lawyer that supports the lawyer's position. The brief summarizes the facts of the case, the pertinent laws, and the application of those laws to the facts.

double jeopardy A second prosecution for the same offense after acquittal in the first trial.

TABLE 9–1

Major Differences between Civil and Criminal Cases

Civil and criminal cases involve very different concepts of law based on different court procedures, who brings the case, and the consequences that result from court decisions.

Civil Cases	Criminal Cases
• Civil cases deal primarily with individual or property rights and involve the concept of responsibility but not guilt.	• Criminal cases deal with public concepts of proper behavior and morality as defined in penal law. A plea of guilty or not guilty is entered.
• The plaintiff, or petitioner, who brings suit is often a private party, as is the defendant or respondent.	• The case is initiated by a government prosecutor on behalf of the public.
• The dispute is usually set out in a petition.	• Specific charges of wrongdoing are spelled out in a grand jury indictment or a writ of information.
• A somewhat relaxed procedure is used to balance or weigh the evidence. The side with the preponderance of the evidence wins the suit.	• Strict rules of procedure are used to evaluate evidence. The standard of proof is guilt beyond a reasonable doubt.
• The final court remedy is relief from or compensation for the violation of legal rights.	• The determination of guilt results in punishment.

FOR CRITICAL THINKING

Is it appropriate to bring action in civil court when a defendant has been found not guilty in a criminal proceeding? Why or why not?

9–2 Court Organization

Figure 9–1 on the facing page shows the organizational structure of the Texas court system and the various types and levels of courts. It is important to note that some courts within this rather large and complicated system have overlapping jurisdictions.

9–2a Municipal Courts

The state authorizes incorporated cities and towns to establish municipal courts. City charters or municipal ordinances provide for their status and organization.

Legally, municipal courts have exclusive jurisdiction to try violations of city ordinances. They also handle minor violations of state law—class C misdemeanors, for which punishment is a fine of $500

de novo Latin for "anew." A trial *de novo* is a new trial conducted in a higher court (as opposed to an appeal). In *de novo* cases, higher courts completely retry cases. On appeal, higher courts simply review the law as decided by the lower courts.

or less and does not include a jail sentence. (Justice of the peace courts have overlapping jurisdiction to handle such minor violations.) Most municipal court cases in Texas involve traffic and parking violations (see Figure 9–2 on page 206).[4]

Appeals versus Trials *de novo* The Texas legislature has authorized city governments to determine whether their municipal courts are *courts of record*. Normally, they are not. When they are so designated, however, records from such courts are the basis of appeal to the appropriate county court. Only slightly more than 1 percent of all cases are appealed from municipal courts. Otherwise, where records are not kept, defendants may demand a completely new trial—trial **de novo** (Latin for "anew")—in overworked county courts, where most such cases are simply dismissed. Where it is available, drivers frequently use this procedure to avoid traffic convictions and higher auto insurance rates.

A trial *de novo* is a new trial conducted in a higher court as opposed to an appeal. In *de novo* cases, higher courts completely retry cases. On appeal, higher courts simply review the law as decided by the lower courts.

People who favor the court-of-record concept point to the large amount of revenue lost because trials *de novo* usually result in dismissal. Opponents of the concept argue that municipal courts are too often

LearningOutcome 9–2

Explain how the courts are organized in Texas, and identify the jurisdiction of each major type of court.

FIGURE 9–1

The Court Structure of Texas

This organizational chart arranges Texas courts from those that handle the least serious cases (bottom) to the highest appeals courts (top).

Source: Office of Court Administration, Texas Judicial Council, "Annual Report for the Texas Judiciary, Fiscal Year 2011," www.courts.state.tx.us/pubs/AR2011/jud_branch/1-court-structure-chart.pdf.

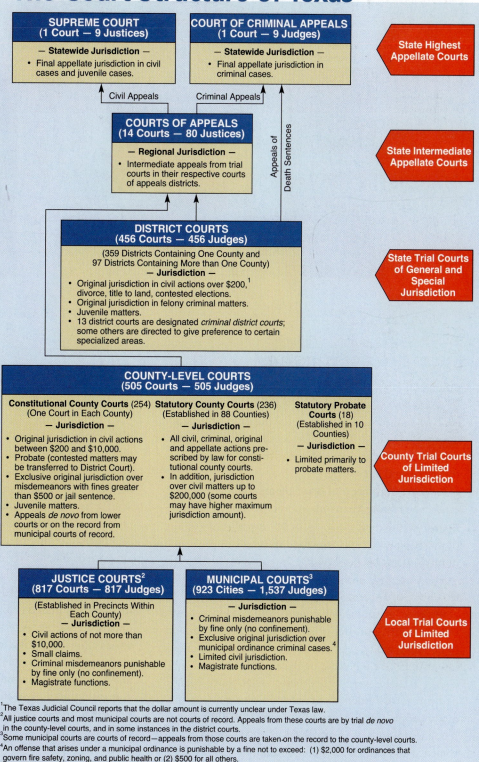

SUPREME COURT
(1 Court — 9 Justices)

— Statewide Jurisdiction —
• Final appellate jurisdiction in civil cases and juvenile cases.

COURT OF CRIMINAL APPEALS
(1 Court — 9 Judges)

— Statewide Jurisdiction —
• Final appellate jurisdiction in criminal cases.

State Highest Appellate Courts

Civil Appeals | Criminal Appeals

Appeals of Death Sentences

COURTS OF APPEALS
(14 Courts — 80 Justices)

— Regional Jurisdiction —
• Intermediate appeals from trial courts in their respective courts of appeals districts.

State Intermediate Appellate Courts

DISTRICT COURTS
(456 Courts — 456 Judges)

(359 Districts Containing One County and 97 Districts Containing More than One County)
— Jurisdiction —
• Original jurisdiction in civil actions over $200,[1] divorce, title to land, contested elections.
• Original jurisdiction in felony criminal matters.
• Juvenile matters.
• 13 district courts are designated *criminal district courts*; some others are directed to give preference to certain specialized areas.

State Trial Courts of General and Special Jurisdiction

COUNTY-LEVEL COURTS
(505 Courts — 505 Judges)

Constitutional County Courts (254)
(One Court in Each County)
— Jurisdiction —
• Original jurisdiction in civil actions between $200 and $10,000.
• Probate (contested matters may be transferred to District Court).
• Exclusive original jurisdiction over misdemeanors with fines greater than $500 or jail sentence.
• Juvenile matters.
• Appeals *de novo* from lower courts or on the record from municipal courts of record.

Statutory County Courts (236)
(Established in 88 Counties)
— Jurisdiction —
• All civil, criminal, original and appellate actions prescribed by law for constitutional county courts.
• In addition, jurisdiction over civil matters up to $200,000 (some courts may have higher maximum jurisdiction amount).

Statutory Probate Courts (18)
(Established in 10 Counties)
— Jurisdiction —
• Limited primarily to probate matters.

County Trial Courts of Limited Jurisdiction

JUSTICE COURTS[2]
(817 Courts — 817 Judges)

(Established in Precincts Within Each County)
— Jurisdiction —
• Civil actions of not more than $10,000.
• Small claims.
• Criminal misdemeanors punishable by fine only (no confinement).
• Magistrate functions.

MUNICIPAL COURTS[3]
(923 Cities — 1,537 Judges)

— Jurisdiction —
• Criminal misdemeanors punishable by fine only (no confinement).
• Exclusive original jurisdiction over municipal ordinance criminal cases.[4]
• Limited civil jurisdiction.
• Magistrate functions.

Local Trial Courts of Limited Jurisdiction

[1]The Texas Judicial Council reports that the dollar amount is currently unclear under Texas law.
[2]All justice courts and most municipal courts are not courts of record. Appeals from these courts are by trial *de novo* in the county-level courts, and in some instances in the district courts.
[3]Some municipal courts are courts of record—appeals from those courts are taken on the record to the county-level courts.
[4]An offense that arises under a municipal ordinance is punishable by a fine not to exceed: (1) $2,000 for ordinances that govern fire safety, zoning, and public health or (2) $500 for all others.

operated as a means of raising revenue rather than achieving justice. The fact that municipal courts collected $751 million in 2011 lends some support to the latter argument.[5]

Qualifications of Municipal Judges Judges of the municipal courts meet whatever qualifications are set by the city charter or ordinances. Some city charters require specific legal training or experience, while

FIGURE 9-2

Cases Filed in Municipal Courts,
Year Ending August 31, 2011

Traffic Cases Added

Non-parking (88.6%)

Parking (11.4%)

Traffic 5,809,973 (82.3%)

All Cases Added
7,062,830 (100%)

Non-traffic 1,252,857 (17.7%)

Non-Traffic Cases Added

State law (71.8%)

City ordinance (28.2%)

Source: *Texas Judicial System Annual Report*, 2011. Activity Report for Municipal Courts (Austin: Office of Court Administration, Texas Judicial Council, 2011), www.courts.state.tx.us/pubs/AR2011/mn/2-mn-courts-overall-activity.pdf.

others say very little about qualifications. Judges may serve for one year or indefinitely. Most are appointed for two-year terms but serve at the pleasure of the governing bodies that have selected them. Furthermore, these judges' salaries are paid entirely by their respective cities and vary widely.

Where statutes authorize them, some cities have established more than one municipal court or more than one judge for each court. In view of the volume of cases pending before these courts, the need for a number of judges is obvious.

Public Confidence in Municipal Courts Public confidence in municipal courts is low. Out-of-town, out-of-county, and out-of-state residents often expect to be found guilty, regardless of the evidence presented. Interestingly, 41.6 percent of all cases filed in municipal courts in 2011 were settled before trial.[6] Such a large percentage of settlements could indicate guilt or that many people fear that the legal process will not be fair. It could also indicate people's desire to avoid the inconvenience and expense of going through a trial.

9-2b Justices of the Peace

The *justice of the peace* courts in Texas are authorized by the Texas Constitution, which requires that county commissioners establish at least one and not more than eight justice precincts per county—a *precinct* is

the district from which a justice of the peace is elected for each four-year term.

County commissioners determine how many justices of the peace shall be elected, based on population, and where their courts shall sit. Changes are made continuously, making it difficult to determine the number of justices of the peace at any given time. The Texas Judicial Council estimated that there were more than 816 justices of the peace in 2011.[7]

The functions of the justice of the peace courts are varied. They have jurisdiction over criminal cases where the fine is less than $500. Original jurisdiction in civil matters extends to cases where the dispute involves less than $10,000. Justices of the peace courts may issue warrants for search and arrest, serve ex officio as notaries public, conduct preliminary hearings, perform marriages, serve as coroners in counties having no medical examiner, and conduct small claims courts. Figure 9–3 on the facing page shows that most cases filed in justice of the peace courts were criminal or involved traffic violations.[8]

Qualifications and Objectivity All these functions are performed by an official whose only qualification is to be a registered voter. No specific statutory or constitutional provisions require that a justice of the peace must be a lawyer. A justice of the peace who is not a licensed attorney is required by statute to take a forty-hour course in the performance of the duties of

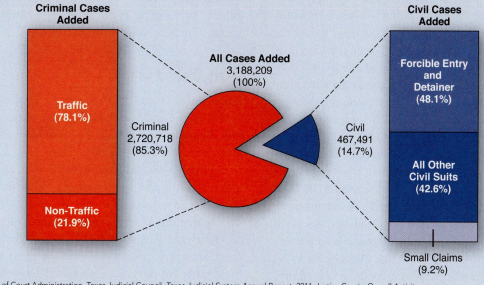

FIGURE 9-3

Justice of the Peace Courts:
Categories of Cases Filed, Year Ending August 31, 2011

Criminal Cases Added

Traffic (78.1%)

Criminal 2,720,718 (85.3%)

Non-Traffic (21.9%)

All Cases Added 3,188,209 (100%)

Civil 467,491 (14.7%)

Civil Cases Added

Forcible Entry and Detainer (48.1%)

All Other Civil Suits (42.6%)

Small Claims (9.2%)

Source: Office of Court Administration, Texas Judicial Council, *Texas Judicial System Annual Report, 2011*: Justice Courts, Overall Activity.

the office, plus a twenty-hour course each year thereafter at an accredited state-supported institution of higher education.

Serious questions have arisen as to the constitutionality of this provision because it adds a qualification for the office not specified in the constitution. Also, salaries of justices of the peace vary a great deal from county to county, and even from justice to justice within the same county.

Negative Popular Perceptions The public's perception of justices of the peace is often not flattering. Many justices are regarded as biased, untrained in the law, and generally incompetent. Skepticism about receiving a fair trial may be a major factor in the settlement of a high percentage of cases before trial. If a person appears before a justice of the peace in a county other than that of his or her home, the general assumption is that fairness is the exception rather than the rule.

Justices of the peace who are conscientious, objective, and fair find it difficult to overcome the stereotype, which is reinforced by the activities of justices who act as coroners. Though the function of the coroner is to determine the cause of death in specified cases, for decades stories have been told about such determinations that left more questions than answers.

Defenders traditionally refer to the justice courts as the "people's courts" and maintain that eliminating these courts would remove the close contact with

the public that many treasure. To eliminate them, it is argued, would put judicial power in the hands of professionals and would ignore the amateur status of these courts, which depend to a considerable extent on common sense law. This is consistent with the widely held view that government is best when it is closest to the people. Critics counter that incompetence and bias are not justified simply because these courts are close to the people.

9–2c County Courts

Each of the 254 counties in Texas has a *county court* presided over by a *county judge,* sometimes referred to as the *constitutional county court* and the constitutional county judge. The Texas Constitution requires that the county judge be elected by voters for a four-year term and be "well informed in the law of the state"—a rather ambiguous stipulation. Thus, the constitution does not require that a county judge possess a law degree.

Salaries are paid by the county and vary greatly. County courts handle probate and other civil matters in which the dispute is between $200 and $10,000. Their criminal jurisdiction is confined to serious misdemeanors for which punishment is a fine greater than $500 or a jail sentence not to exceed one year.

County Courts-at-Law A constitutional county judge also has administrative responsibilities as presiding officer of the commissioners' court, the governing body for Texas counties and not a judicial entity at all. Therefore, the judge may have little time to handle judicial matters. The legislature has responded to this by establishing—in some, but not all Texas counties—county courts-at-law to act as auxiliary or supplemental courts. The qualifications of the judges of the statutory county courts-at-law vary according to the statute that established the particular court. In addition to residence in the county, a court-at-law judge usually must have four years of experience as a practicing attorney or judge.

Various state laws determine whether these courts have either civil or criminal jurisdiction or both. Their civil jurisdiction involves cases of less than $100,000. Their criminal jurisdiction includes misdemeanors that are more serious than those tried by justices of the peace and municipal courts, and misdemeanors that include a jail sentence or a fine in excess of $500. More than two-thirds of cases disposed of in county-level courts are criminal (see Figure 9–4 below). Cases involving theft and driving while intoxicated or under the influence of drugs are the most common. Civil cases include probate matters and suits to collect debt.

The Competence of County Courts Administration of justice is very uneven in Texas county courts. Although many of the judges are competent and run their courts in an orderly manner, others regard their courts and official jurisdictions as personal fiefdoms, paying little attention to the finer points of law or accepted procedures. Opportunities for arbitrary action are compounded if the county judge is performing as the chief administrative officer of the county as well as a judicial officer.

9–2d District Courts

District courts are often described as the *chief trial courts* of the state, and as a group, these courts are called *general trial courts*. The names of these courts and their jurisdictions vary. They include constitutional district courts, civil district courts, and criminal district courts, and total more than forty jurisdictions.

Currently, there are 456 district courts, all of which function as single-judge courts. Judges, elected for four-year terms by the voters in their districts, must be at least twenty-five years of age, a resident of the district for two years, and a citizen of the United States. Candidates must have been licensed practicing lawyers or judges for a combined total of four years. Texas pays $125,000 of the salary of each district judge, and although each county may supplement the salary, the combined salary must be at least $1,000 less than that received by justices of the courts of appeals.

District Court Jurisdiction District courts possess jurisdiction in felony cases, which comprise

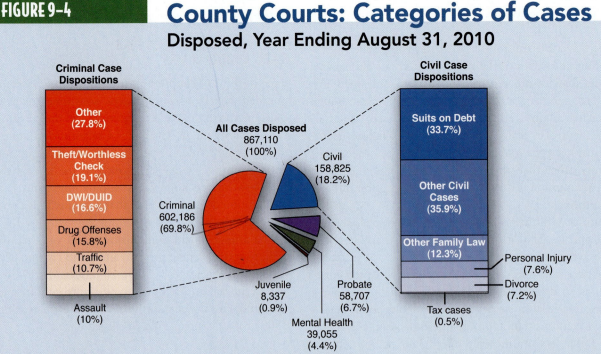

FIGURE 9–4

County Courts: Categories of Cases
Disposed, Year Ending August 31, 2010

Criminal Case Dispositions
- Other (27.8%)
- Theft/Worthless Check (19.1%)
- DWI/DUID (16.6%)
- Drug Offenses (15.8%)
- Traffic (10.7%)
- Assault (10%)

All Cases Disposed 867,110 (100%)

- Criminal 602,186 (69.8%)
- Civil 158,825 (18.2%)
- Juvenile 8,337 (0.9%)
- Mental Health 39,055 (4.4%)
- Probate 58,707 (6.7%)

Civil Case Dispositions
- Suits on Debt (33.7%)
- Other Civil Cases (35.9%)
- Other Family Law (12.3%)
- Personal Injury (7.6%)
- Divorce (7.2%)
- Tax cases (0.5%)

Source: Office of Court Administration, Texas Judicial Council, *Texas Judicial System Annual Report, 2010*: County-Level Courts, Summary of Activity by Case Type; updated stats and labels for graph: www.txcourts.gov/pubs/AR2010/AR10.pdf.

approximately one-third of their caseload.[9] Civil cases in which the matter of controversy exceeds $200 may also be tried in district courts, and such cases constitute the greatest share of their workload (see Figure 9–5 below). In addition, juvenile cases are usually tried in district courts. Although most district courts exercise both criminal and civil jurisdiction, the tendency in metropolitan areas is to specialize in criminal, civil, or family law matters.

Plea Bargaining The caseload for these courts is so heavy that **plea bargaining** is often used to dispose of criminal cases. Plea bargaining refers to a situation in which the prosecutor and defense attorney negotiate an agreement whereby the accused pleads guilty to a less serious crime than originally charged or in return for a reduction in the sentence to be served.

This process saves the state a tremendous amount of time and money. For example, it is often estimated that about 90 percent of criminal cases are disposed of in this way. If plea bargaining were not used in many urban areas, court delays would be increased by months if not years. Although efficient, this practice raises many issues concerning equity and justice because it often encourages innocent people to plead guilty and allows guilty people to avoid less punishment than provided by the law.

Likewise, many civil lawsuits are resolved by negotiated settlements between the parties. At times, this may be an appropriate and just recourse. In many urban areas, however, there is such a backlog of cases before the courts that it can take years for a matter to be heard and settled. As a result, litigants often choose to settle their case out of court for reasons other than justice.

> **plea bargaining**
> Negotiations between the prosecution and the defense to obtain a lighter sentence or other benefits in exchange for a guilty plea by the accused.

9–2e Courts of Appeals

Fourteen *courts of appeals* hear intermediate appeals in both civil and criminal cases from district and county courts in their area. In fact, only a small percentage of trial court cases are appealed, and even fewer are reversed. In 2011, the courts of appeals disposed of 11,936 cases, and the appeals courts reversed the decision of the trial court in only 700 of those cases.[10]

The state pays each chief justice $140,000 and each associate justice $137,500. Counties may pay a supplement to appeals judges. Appeals judges are elected from their districts for six-year terms (see Figure 9–6 on the following page) and must be at least thirty-five years of age, with a minimum of ten years of experience as a lawyer or judge.

FIGURE 9–5   **District Courts: Categories of Cases**
Disposed, Year Ending August 31, 2010

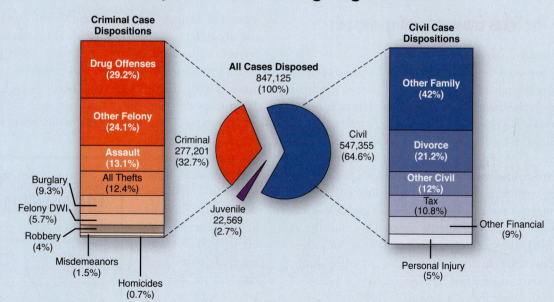

Source: Office of Court Administration, Texas Judicial Council, *Texas Judicial System Annual Report, 2010*: District Courts, Summary of Activity by Case Type. www.courts.state.tx.us/pubs/AR2010/dc/4-summary-of-activity-by-case-type.pdf.

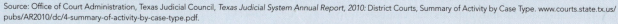

FIGURE 9-6

Appeals Court Districts

Fourteen courts of appeals serve the geographical areas shown on this map. These courts handle both criminal and civil appeals from district courts in their area.

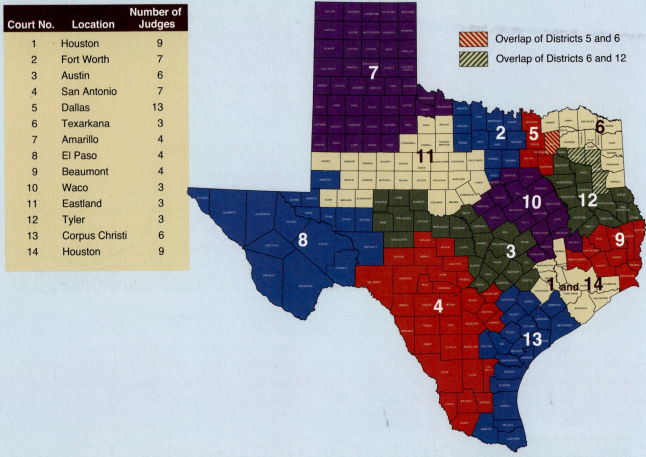

Court No.	Location	Number of Judges
1	Houston	9
2	Fort Worth	7
3	Austin	6
4	San Antonio	7
5	Dallas	13
6	Texarkana	3
7	Amarillo	4
8	El Paso	4
9	Beaumont	4
10	Waco	3
11	Eastland	3
12	Tyler	3
13	Corpus Christi	6
14	Houston	9

Overlap of Districts 5 and 6

Overlap of Districts 6 and 12

Source: Texas Legislative Council, Courts of Appeals Districts, www.tlc.state.tx.us/redist/pdf/COA05_map.pdf; Office of Court Administration, Annual Report for the Texas Judiciary: 2011, p. 31.

9-2f The Texas Court of Criminal Appeals

Texas has a dual system of courts of last resort. The Texas Supreme Court is the highest state appellate court in civil matters, and the Texas Court of Criminal Appeals is the highest state appellate court in criminal matters. Only Oklahoma has a similar system.

Although most criminal cases decided by the fourteen courts of appeals do not advance further, some are heard by the court of criminal appeals, which consists of a presiding judge and eight judges. Criminal court judges are elected statewide in partisan elections for six-year overlapping terms. They must be at least thirty-five years of age and be lawyers or judges with ten years of experience. The presiding judge of the court of criminal appeals receives a salary of $150,000. Other judges receive $137,000.

The court of criminal appeals has exclusive jurisdiction over automatic appeals in death penalty cases.

Since the United States Supreme Court restored the use of capital punishment in 1976, Texas has executed far more citizens than any other state. As of January 2012, the state had executed 478 people since 1976. Since 1990, the average has been approximately 13 prisoners a year.[11]

Death penalty cases have led to a number of headline stories. These include controversies regarding the use of lethal injection, persons who were juveniles at the time of their crime, those who received poor legal counsel, and persons who might actually be innocent of the crime in question.[12]

Texas Political SOCIAL MEDIA

The Innocence Project of Texas works to exonerate those wrongfully convicted of serious crimes in Texas. Find its Facebook page by searching on "innocence texas."

9–2g The Texas Supreme Court

The Texas Supreme Court is the final court of appeals in civil and juvenile cases. Original jurisdiction of the court extends to the issuance of writs and the conduct of proceedings for involuntary retirement or removal of judges. All other cases involve appellate jurisdiction. The court also has the power to establish rules for the administration of justice—rules of civil practice and procedure for courts having civil jurisdiction. In addition, it makes rules governing licensing of members of the state bar.

The supreme court consists of one chief justice and eight associate justices, all elected statewide after their nomination in party primaries. Three of the nine justices are elected every two years for six-year terms. A Texas Supreme Court justice must be at least thirty-five years of age, a citizen of the United States, a resident of Texas, and a lawyer or judge of a court of record for at least ten years. The salary of the chief justice is $152,500, and the salary of associate justices is $150,000.

The Texas Supreme Court spends much of its time deciding which petitions for review will be granted. Generally, the court only takes cases it sees as presenting the most significant legal issues. The supreme court, at times, plays a policymaking role in the state. For example, in 1989 the court unanimously declared in *Edgewood v. Kirby* that the huge disparities between rich and poor school districts were unacceptable and ordered changes in the financing of Texas's public schools.[13] The supreme court has also made important decisions about oil, gas, and water rights.[14] Is it appropriate for the courts to play such as policymaking role? We examine that question in the *Join the Debate* feature on the following page.

COURTESY OF THE SUPREME COURT OF TEXAS

Texas Supreme Court justices (back row, left to right) Eva Guzman, Phil Johnson, David Medina, Paul Green, Don Willett, and Debra Lehrman, (front row, left to right) Nathan Hecht, Chief Justice Wallace Jefferson, and Dale Wainwright (who resigned in 2012).

FOR CRITICAL THINKING

What steps might be taken to improve the reputation of the lowest-level Texas courts, that is, the municipal courts and justice of the peace courts?

9–3 Juries in Texas

Juries are an important and controversial aspect of the American judicial system. Some people argue that juries are beneficial because they allow for community input and the use of common sense in the legal system. Others claim that they often do not fairly represent the community and that the reasons for their decisions are often inappropriate or suspect. What is certain is that while millions of Americans serve on juries every year, the frequency of their use is declining, and they decide relatively few cases in our legal system.[15]

Learning Outcome 9–3

Understand the role of grand juries and trial juries, and analyze the responsibilities of citizens in the legal system in Texas.

9–3a Grand Juries

In Texas, when a person is accused of a crime, the matter is likely to be taken to a twelve-member **grand jury.** Some states do not have grand juries, but in those that do, the size ranges from five to twenty-three members.)

grand jury In Texas, twelve persons who sit in pretrial proceedings to determine whether sufficient evidence exists to try an individual and therefore return an indictment.

Should Judges Be Banned from "Legislating from the Bench"?

Judges are expected to be neutral. That is to say, judges are supposed to apply the law impartially when issuing verdicts. The law that they apply may be based on the federal constitution, a state constitution, or legislation passed by the appropriate lawmaking body. Legislatures make policy and put that policy into effect by passing laws. Presidents and governors have some input due to their veto powers, but in principle, no one else should be making policy decisions.

Judges, Keep Your Hands Off Policy

Those who are concerned about judicial policymaking argue that whether judges are elected or appointed, they are supposed to apply the law as it is written. A judge's personal preferences should not influence the court's decision. A Texas judge who personally believes, say, that marijuana should be legalized has a duty to uphold any Texas laws that make possession or sale of marijuana a crime. If a judge believes that Texas businesses are overregulated, she or he nonetheless must uphold regulations that are on the books. Every judge in Texas has a duty to uphold the law as it is written when she or he decides cases or issues rulings.

It's Impossible to Avoid Judicial Policymaking

Those who consider judicial policymaking to be inevitable point to the way in which laws in Texas are often written. Frequently, legislation contains language such as *reasonable* or *appropriate*. What are such words supposed to mean? A bill that contains a word such as *reasonable* might as well contain an explicit statement that "the exact meaning of this statute will be left up to the executive and the courts."

So, Texas judges have to take a stand on certain issues when interpreting the law. Legislating from the bench is here to stay. Let us just make sure that Texas judges act in a manner that is consistent with what the majority of Texans really want.

FOR CRITICAL ANALYSIS In California, the voters themselves can make laws by voting on initiatives and referendums. (We described these institutions in Chapter 3 on page 52.) Lino A. Graglia, a law professor at the University of Texas, believes that Texas should have a California-style initiative and referendum system precisely to rein in "lawmaking judges." Would this be a good or bad idea? Why?

Indictments The grand jury does not determine the guilt or innocence of the accused but rather whether there is sufficient evidence to bring the accused to trial. If the evidence is determined to be sufficient, the accused is indicted. An **indictment** is sometimes referred to as a **true bill** by the grand jury, and the vote of at least nine of the twelve grand jurors is needed to indict. If an indictment is not returned, the conclusion of the grand jury is a **no bill.**

At times, a grand jury may return indictments simply because the district attorney asks for them. In fact, grand juries return true bills in approximately 95 percent of the cases brought before them.[16]

This high indictment rate is attributable at least in part to the fact that the accused cannot have an attorney in the room during questioning.

Some grand juries, known as *runaway* grand juries, may consider matters independently of the district attorney's recommendation. In general, prosecutors do not like a grand jury to be so assertive and are likely to refer only routine matters to it. To bypass it, the prosecutor may refer cases to a second grand jury meeting simultaneously or postpone action for another, more favorable grand jury.

Choosing Grand Juries
The process of selecting the grand jury has come under criticism in recent years. Because it can be chosen by a grand jury commission (of three to five members) appointed by the district judge, the grand jury panel might not be truly representative of the county's citizenry. A total of fifteen to twenty people are nominated by the commission, and twelve are selected to become the grand jury for the

indictment, or **true bill** A formal written accusation issued by a grand jury against a party charged with a crime when it has determined that there is sufficient evidence to bring the accused to trial.

no bill A grand jury's refusal to return an indictment filed by the prosecutor.

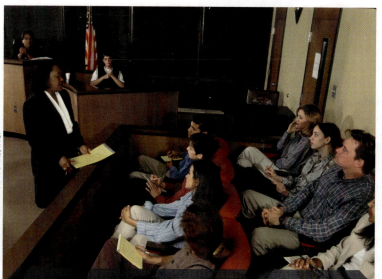

An attorney addresses the jury in a civil trial. Why have civil suits become so common in Texas?

Juries in Civil Cases Although not required by the U.S. Constitution, the parties to a civil case in Texas generally decide whether a jury trial will be held. If a jury is to be used in a civil case in district court, the party requesting it pays a nominal fee to see that a jury panel is called. After the panel is summoned, the per diem allowance for each juror is paid from public funds, which can entail considerable expense to the public if a trial becomes lengthy. County courts have six-person juries, whereas twelve people are on juries at the district court level.

Choosing Trial Juries A *venire*, or jury panel, is randomly selected from among those individuals who have registered to vote and hold a Texas driver's license or a Texas identification card. Jurors must be literate citizens at least eighteen years of age and qualified to vote, and must not have been indicted or convicted for a theft or felony.

Exemptions for jury service are now severely restricted. Persons older than seventy years of age, students in active attendance, and women with custody of a child younger than the age of ten are automatically exempt from jury service but may serve if they desire. Fathers have sought to claim the same exemption when they are legally responsible for children. Other excuses from jury service are at the discretion of the judge.

In cases that receive a great deal of publicity, a special venire may consist of several hundred persons. Jury selection (known as *voir dire*) may last days or weeks, sometimes even longer than the trial itself.

Challenging Jurors If either side believes that a prospective juror has a preconceived opinion about a defendant's guilt or innocence, the prosecutor or defense attorneys may bring a **challenge for cause.** Challenges for cause extend to any factor

term of the court. In some counties, grand juries are chosen through random selection by computer.

The Information and Prosecutorial Discretion

An alternative to a grand jury indictment is an **information,** which is used for minor offenses not punishable in the state penitentiary. Filed by the prosecutor with the appropriate court, an information must be based on an investigation by the prosecutor after receiving a complaint and a sworn affidavit that a crime has been committed.

The district attorney may determine whether or not a person indicted for a crime will be prosecuted. Some district attorneys will prosecute only if the odds are high that a conviction can be secured. This improves their statistical record, which can be taken to the voters when reelection time comes. Other prosecutors may take most indicted persons to trial, even if the chances for conviction are low. This may prove politically costly, however, and can make the prosecutor appear ineffective.

9–3b Petit (Trial) Juries

A jury in a criminal or civil trial is known as a **petit jury.** Trial by jury in criminal cases is a right guaranteed by the Texas Constitution and the Sixth Amendment of the U.S. Constitution. Even if the accused waives the right to a trial by jury, expecting to be tried by a judge, the state may demand a jury trial in felony cases.

information In the context of criminal justice proceedings, a written accusation filed by the prosecutor against a party charged with a minor crime. It is an alternative to an indictment and does not involve a grand jury.

petit jury A trial jury for a civil or criminal case.

challenge for cause A request to a judge that a certain prospective juror not be allowed to serve on the jury for a specific reason, such as bias or knowledge of the case.

Justice Eva A. Guzman speaks after being sworn into the Texas Supreme Court by Texas Governor Rick Perry at the Texas State Capitol in January 2010.

shown that the vast majority of the public knows little about its rulings and actions.[19] If most Americans know very little about the U.S. Supreme Court—the court that receives the most media attention in this country—how much do voters know about state and local courts? A voter in Texas could be asked to choose candidates running for the Texas Supreme Court, the court of criminal appeals, the courts of appeals, district courts, county courts, and justices of the peace.

In addition to the findings of systematic research, an abundance of anecdotal evidence suggests that most voters in Texas are unaware of candidates' qualifications or experience. As a result, many people do not vote in judicial elections at all, and those who do often select candidates based on some type of name recognition. They may vote for judicial candidates with names similar to those of movie stars, historical figures, or other famous persons.[20]

Partisanship A voter who has no knowledge of the views or backgrounds of the candidates on the ballot may make a choice based on the candidates' political party affiliation. In Texas, this appears to be a common approach for making selections in judicial elections.

Where judicial campaigns are competitive, the Republican judicial candidate usually has a distinct political advantage. Democrats nonetheless have had some success at the local level in some counties. In large,

politically competitive metropolitan counties, both of the major parties have been able to sweep to power in a good year. Democrats took all judicial positions in Dallas County in 2006 and surged in Harris County in 2008. In 2010, Democrats again swept all the races in which they competed in Dallas County, but Republicans won nearly as many judicial positions in Harris County as they had lost in the previous election.[21]

It has been argued that because judges, especially at the appellate level, make significant policy decisions, it is reasonable for voters to select judges on the basis of political party affiliation.[22] Party affiliation may provide accurate information concerning the general ideology and thus the decision-making pattern of judges. Even if this is true, however, voting based solely on a candidate's political party can lead to controversial results.

Campaign Contributions Because voters often look for simple voting cues (such as name familiarity or party identification), candidates often want to spend as much as possible to make their name or candidacy well known. In recent years, spending in judicial races has increased dramatically. Candidates need to win two elections—their party's nomination and the general election. In modern politics, this can be expensive.

For more than a decade, Republican candidates have dominated the race for campaign contributions. For example, in 2006 a Democratic challenger was outfunded 368 to 1 ($937,000 to $2,549) by the Republican justice. In 2008, the three Republican incumbents raised more than $2.8 million, whereas their Democratic challengers raised just more than $1 million. Not surprisingly, the Republican candidates were successful.[23]

JUSTICE FOR SALE? In addition to questions of fairness or the advantages of incumbency in raising campaign finances, many critics have also asked whether justice is for sale in Texas. More directly, individuals and organizations often appear before judges after contributing to the judges' election campaigns. Do such contributions affect a judge's impartiality? In 1998, a study found that 40 percent of campaign contributions to supreme court justices came from sources with cases before the court.

In 2008, Texas Supreme Court incumbents running for reelection received half their support from lawyers, law firms, and lobbyists. More recently, a public advocacy group sued Texas over this system, claiming that it violates due process and the right to a fair trial. The group cited surveys indicating that 83 percent of the Texas public, 79 percent of Texas lawyers, and

48 percent of Texas judges believe that campaign contributions significantly affect judicial decisions.[24]

THE UNITED STATES SUPREME COURT RULES ON CAMPAIGN CONTRIBUTIONS.

In 2009, the United States Supreme Court weighed in on the question of judicial bias when litigants had significantly influenced the election of judges hearing their cases. In *Caperton v. A. T. Massey Coal Co., Inc.,* the Court held that the chairman of Massey Coal had created such a question by donating $3 million to help finance the successful election of a new justice to the Supreme Court of Appeals of West Virginia.

The possible conflict of interest arose because Massey had a $50 million civil suit appeal pending before the court at the time. It was later decided in Massey's favor by a three-to-two vote, with the new justice voting with the majority. A five-to-four U.S. Supreme Court majority reversed and remanded the case holding that "there is a serious risk of actual bias . . . when a person with a personal stake in a particular case had a significant and disproportionate influence in placing the judge on the case."[25]

THE CASE OF *CITIZENS UNITED V. FEDERAL ELECTION COMMISSION.*

Recently, the issue of corporate campaign financing became politically salient again. In 2010, the United States Supreme Court decided the case of *Citizens United v. Federal Election Commission* A divided Court, in a five-to-four decision, ruled in favor of Citizens United, a nonprofit organization accused of violating the Bipartisan Campaign Reform Act of 2002.

The ruling upheld disclosure requirements for corporate campaign contributions, but removed all financial restrictions on those contributions, allowing for individuals and corporate entities to donate unlimited funds to political action committees (PACs). The decision affected campaign-finance laws at the state level and began a debate about whether corporations will have increased influence on elected officials.[26]

In 1995, Texas passed the Judicial Campaign Fairness Act, which set limits on contributions to judicial candidates from law firms, individuals, and PACs. That law continues to be enforced but is facing numerous legal challenges under *Citizens United.*[27] For a more detailed discussion on the issue of campaign financing, refer to the section titled "Campaign Finance" on page 86 in Chapter 4 of this text.

TRIAL LAWYERS VERSUS BUSINESS INTERESTS.

Part of the debate over the impropriety of campaign contributions involves a battle between plaintiffs' attorneys and defense attorneys in civil cases. Texas has traditionally been a conservative, pro-business state. This perspective has usually been reflected in the decisions of the judiciary, which has often favored big business and professional groups such as the medical profession. Plaintiffs' lawyers and their related interest group, the Texas Trial Lawyers Association, have made a concerted effort in the past few decades to make the judiciary more open to consumer suits, often filed against businesses, doctors, and their insurance companies.

The plaintiffs' lawyers poured millions of dollars into the political funds of candidates they believed would align more favorably with their perspective. Defense and business attorneys responded with millions of dollars of their own contributions. Both groups of lawyers often appear before the very judges to whom they have given these large sums of money.

> **"I dearly love the state of Texas, but I consider that** a harmless perversion on my part, and discuss it only with consenting adults."
>
> ~ MOLLY IVINS ~
> POLITICAL COMMENTATOR
> 1944–2007

9–4c Minority Representation

A final criticism of the current partisan elective system involves diversity and minority representation. In 2011, of the state's ninety-eight appellate judges, only ten were Latino and three were African American. Within the district courts, only 81 of 456 judges were Latino or African American. Out of the total of 4,294 statewide judges, 1,097 were female.[28]

Minorities and women are still underrepresented when compared to their white male counterparts. The system thus continues to be sharply criticized by minority and women's groups.

FOR CRITICAL THINKING

Why might researchers find that the merit plan is just as political a process as judicial elections are?

CONFLICT The Courts

Court decisions can affect the lives of millions. For example, in 1973 the United States Supreme Court, in *Roe v. Wade,* held that the constitutional right to privacy included the right to have an abortion. Over time, courts in the United States have established a reputation with the public for dispensing justice in a fair and reasonable manner. Even in Texas, the courts are relatively more popular (or perhaps less unpopular) than other governmental institutions. This is so despite concerns about unprofessionalism in the lower courts and the effects of campaign contributions at the higher levels. Still, Texans are at odds over the courts in a number of ways, including the following:

- Should judges defer to the decisions of legislatures and administrative agencies whenever possible—or should they strictly police the constitutionality of legislative and executive decisions?

- Is plea bargaining a beneficial way of streamlining the judicial process—or is it a dangerous source of injustice?

- Are campaign contributions in judicial elections a form of free speech—or are they a thinly veiled form of bribery?

- Is the merit plan for choosing judges an improvement over judicial elections—or does it merely deprive the people of their right to vote?

TAKE ACTION

- If you are concerned by the impact of campaign contributions in judicial elections, support independent courts by searching on "justice at stake." On the state drop-down menu, click on "Your State National Map" and then click on the state of Texas.

- The American Judicature Society supports the independence, ethics, and unbiased selection of judges. Find it by typing in "ajs.org."

- Track money and corporate influence in Texas politics at "texans for public justice."

- Team up with groups that advocate using the courts to protect consumers, workers, and patients, such as the Texas Trial Lawyers Association. Search on "ttla."

- Be an intelligent juror. Check out the jury selection system by visiting the site of the Lone Star Fully Informed Jury Association. Enter "fija texas."

STUDY TOOLS

Ready to study?

- Review what you've read with the quiz below. Check your answers on the Chapter in Review card at the back of the book. For any questions you miss, read the corresponding Learning Outcome section again to prepare for class and your exam.
- Rip out and study the Chapter in Review card.

... Or you can go online to CourseMate

at www.cengagebrain.com for these additional review materials:

- Practice Quizzes
- Key Term Flashcards or Crossword Puzzles
- Audio Summaries
- Simulations, Animated Learning Modules, and Interactive Timelines
- Videos
- American Government NewsWatch

Quiz

1. The difference in the burden of proof in a civil case as opposed to a criminal case is that in a civil case it is _____.
   a. beyond a reasonable doubt
   b. a preponderance of the evidence
   c. probable cause

2. Which of the following accurately describes the nature of a civil case?
   a. It is always a case brought by the government against an individual or group of individuals.
   b. It is always a case decided by a jury instead of a judge.
   c. It is usually brought by private parties and involves the concept of responsibility, not guilt.

3. The power of an appellate court to review and revise the judicial action of an inferior court is called _____ jurisdiction.
   a. original   b. appellate   c. remedial

4. The legal principle that an individual may not be prosecuted twice for the same offense is called:
   a. double jeopardy.   b. true bill.   c. prior restraint.

5. "All judges in Texas, regardless of level, are required to have a law degree."
   a. true   b. false

6. What is the state court of last appeal for *criminal* cases?
   a. The Texas Supreme Court
   b. Texas Court of Criminal Appeals
   c. The district court where the crime was allegedly committed

7. Which of the following courts have the lowest level of jurisdiction as measured by monetary damage requirements or seriousness of the crime?
   a. municipal courts
   b. justice of the peace courts
   c. county courts

8. A new trial conducted by a higher court, as opposed to an appeal, is referred to as a(n) _____.
   a. original jurisdiction trial
   b. appellate trial
   c. trial *de novo*

9. _____ is the term used to describe twelve persons who sit in pretrial proceedings to determine whether sufficient evidence exists to try an individual and therefore return an indictment.
   a. Grand jury   b. Petit jury   c. Hung jury

10. The right to a trial by jury in a criminal case is
    a. guaranteed by the U.S. Constitution but not the Texas Constitution.
    b. guaranteed by both the U.S. Constitution and the Texas Constitution.
    c. guaranteed by the Texas Constitution but not by the U.S. Constitution.

11. Both the prosecution and the defense in a criminal case are permitted a limited number of challenges, called _____, to bar a prospective juror from serving without having to give a reason why.
    a. indictments
    b. challenges for cause
    c. peremptory challenges

12. Texas selects its judges by which of the following methods?
    a. partisan elections
    b. nonpartisan elections
    c. the merit (Missouri) plan

13. "There is no significant evidence that the merit plan of judicial selection produces less political or significantly more competent judges than do judicial elections."
    a. true   b. false

14. The judicial selection method used by more states than any other is _____.
    a. partisan elections
    b. nonpartisan elections
    c. the merit (Missouri) plan

15. What has generally been the impact of the Supreme Court's ruling in the case *Citizens United v. FEC* in 2010?
    a. It has limited the appearance of corruption in judicial elections.
    b. It has increased the traditional power of trial lawyers over business interests.
    c. It has undermined efforts at the local, state, and national level to limit political contributions.

Law and Due Process

★ Learning Outcomes

The **Learning Outcomes** labeled 1 through 6 are designed to help improve your understanding of the chapter. After reading this chapter, you should be able to:

10–1 Give examples of major types of civil law cases, and describe important controversies in civil law.

10–2 Identify the major types of crime and the major factors that contribute to the making of a criminal.

10–3 Describe how the due process of law applies to searches and arrests in criminal cases.

10–4 List the major steps that take place before a criminal trial and how they relate to the rights of the accused.

10–5 Explain the processes involved in a trial, and describe the adversary system.

10–6 Define and evaluate the functions of correctional institutions.

Remember to visit page 240 for additional Study Tools

BOB DAEMMRICH / THE IMAGE WORKS

CONFLICT

Does Texas Execute Too Many People?

The death penalty was handed down in this country even before we had prisons. In 1608, a man named George Kendall was executed by a Virginia firing squad on charges of spying for Spain. Since Kendall's time, more than eighteen thousand Americans have been executed. In the 1700s, citizens were executed for robbery, forgery, and illegal tree cutting. In more recent times, Texas has led the nation in executions. Indeed, Texas currently accounts for about 37 percent of all executions nationwide. Only Oklahoma executes a larger percentage of its residents than Texas.

As it happens, Texas juries are no more likely to impose the death penalty in murder cases than are juries in other states. The difference is that Texas follows through with the punishment. It executes a larger share of its death-row prisoners than does any other state. Texas authorities have executed almost 45 percent of those sentenced to death between 1997 and today. Still, the question remains: Are too many people executed in Texas?

MARJORIE COTERA/DAEMMRICH PHOTOGRAPHY/THE IMAGE WORKS

Texas Executions Do Not Reflect Changing Times

As far back as 1764, the Italian jurist Cesare Beccaria asserted, "The death penalty cannot be useful because of the example of barbarity it gives men." Five states—Connecticut, Illinois, New Jersey, New Mexico, and New York—have abolished the death penalty in the last decade. Many other states rarely, if ever, carry out executions. In spite of the high execution rate in Texas, murder rates remain high. In fact, no statistical relationship between executions and lower murder rates has ever been proved.

Unlike imprisonment, an execution cannot be undone, and there are reasons to believe that some individuals recently executed in Texas were, in fact, innocent. Consider also the other nations that permit capital punishment—China, Iran, North Korea, and Saudi Arabia—are not ones that we want to emulate. If Texas continues to employ the death penalty, it should be reserved for the most extreme cases only.

Texans Have a Right to Justice

When someone takes another's life, in Texas or in any other state, why shouldn't the killer's life be taken in return? In arguments about the death penalty, there are two lives to think about. Too much emphasis is placed on the convicted murderer, the one who is to be executed. Often, the victim is all but forgotten. The death penalty provides a degree of finality that allows the families of victims some small measure of peace.

Life imprisonment without the possibility of parole is not always an acceptable alternative, given that parole may still be possible, despite the sentence. It's also important to note that the death row population in Texas does not reflect racial discrimination. In Texas, African Americans who are convicted of murder are actually less likely to find themselves on death row than are whites.

There is also a freedom issue here. When one person kills another, the victim obviously has no freedom at all. Why then should his or her killer have the freedom to live after the murder?

Where do you stand?

1. Even if you generally oppose capital punishment, do you think that there are certain murders that are so heinous that those who commit them should not be allowed to live? Explain.
2. Are potential murderers likely to understand the odds that they will be executed if caught and convicted? Why or why not?

Explore this issue online

- Typing "capital punishment" into a search engine is enough to provide you with a wide variety of resources on the issue. They begin with a Wikipedia article and continue through a series of debate sites and a collection of court cases. The site of the Death Penalty Information Center is one of many hosted by opponents. Pro-Death Penalty.com, in contrast, supports executions.

Introduction

As we mentioned in Chapter 9, there are substantial differences between criminal and civil law. **Civil law** deals largely with private rights and individual relationships, obligations, and responsibilities. **Criminal law** is concerned with public morality—concepts of right and wrong as defined by government. Punishment under criminal law can include fines, imprisonment, or even the death penalty, as discussed in the *Texans in Conflict* feature at the beginning of this chapter.

Criminal cases are prosecuted by public officials (usually county or district attorneys) in the name of the public. Civil suits are brought by **plaintiffs,** who are usually private citizens or corporations, although agents of government occasionally initiate civil suits when seeking to enforce antitrust laws, abate public nuisances, or pursue other noncriminal matters.

Perhaps the most important distinction between civil and criminal law is the way each is handled by the courts. In criminal law, the aim is punishment; in civil law, the **remedy** (the means used to redress an injury) is relief or compensation. For example, criminal law might punish a thief, but the civil law remedy for the unlawful seizure of property might be the return of the property to its rightful owner.

10–1 Civil Law

The primary focus of civil law is defining and civilizing interpersonal relationships. It also seeks to enforce legitimate contracts between parties and assigns responsibilities for personal injuries. We will provide a sample of some civil laws, but you should remember that Texas civil law fills volumes of printed matter. Its civil statutes are organized into twenty-eight codes, ranging from the Agriculture Code to *Vernon's Texas Statutes and Codes Annotated*. It is impossible to discuss the state's civil laws in detail—even the most competent Texas attorneys tend to specialize in narrow fields of law.

10–1a Types of Civil Law

Civil law in the United States today is based in large part on centuries-old English *common law*. (We first discussed common law and statutory law in Chapter 3.) Common law is judge-made law. Whether written or unwritten, it is based on **precedents,** or previous case decisions. If the essential elements of a current case are like those of a case already decided, the judge makes the same decision as was made in the earlier case. The principle of following these precedents is called **stare decisis,** and over the years, these cumulative decisions have formed the basis of common law. In contrast, *statutory law* is law that has been passed by legislative bodies and written in codebooks. Legislatures have incorporated many common law principles into civil statutes and thereby reduced the need to rely directly on common law.

10–1b Major Civil Law Topics

As noted, the number of different issues addressed by civil law is great. We can describe only a few of the more important ones here.

Family Law The family is protected by civil law in Texas. For example, even if a man and a woman have not participated in a formal ceremony of marriage in the presence of an authorized officer of a religious organization or a judge, the law may nevertheless recognize the existence of a marriage. A man and a woman who live together, agree they are married, and publicly present themselves as husband and wife have a *common law marriage*. Their children are legitimate, and the marriage can be terminated through a legal divorce. Divorce action must, however, be taken within one year of separation, or the marriage will be treated as if it never existed.

Texas courts may require alimony between the filing and granting of a divorce or when one spouse is

LearningOutcome 10–1

Give examples of major types of civil law cases, and describe important controversies in civil law.

---

civil law The branch of law that spells out the duties that individuals in society owe to other persons or to their governments, excluding the duty not to commit crimes.

criminal law The branch of law that defines and governs actions that constitute crimes. Generally, criminal law has to do with wrongful actions committed against society for which society demands redress.

plaintiff The party initiating a civil lawsuit.

remedy The relief or compensation given to an innocent party to enforce a right or address the violation of a right.

precedent A court decision that furnishes an example or authority for deciding subsequent cases involving identical or similar facts and legal issues.

stare decisis A common law principle under which judges normally are obligated to follow the precedents established by prior court decisions. (Pronounced *ster*-ay dih-*si*-sis.)

incapable of self-support and the marriage has existed for at least ten years. As a *community property state,* Texas requires that a couple divide property acquired during marriage equally, and one spouse is not usually responsible for the other's support after divorce. Children, however, have the right to be supported by their parents, even if the parents are divorced. Either parent may be given legal custody of the children, but the other parent also may be responsible for part of their support. Parents who are delinquent in child support may now have their state licenses, including driver's licenses, revoked.

Real Estate Law Titles to real property, such as land and buildings, are registered in the office of the county clerk, and the legitimate use of any property by its owner is enforceable in the courts. A person cannot lose title to a *homestead* in a civil suit except to satisfy tax liens, home-improvement loans, mortgage loans for the initial purchase of the property, or home equity loans. The protected family homestead includes the home and two hundred acres of land in rural areas or ten acres in the city.

Wills and Inheritance Even in death, property rights are protected—a person may control transfer of his or her estate through a will. If a will exists at the time of death, the courts (usually the county courts) **probate** the will, which means they determine that it is the last and valid will of the deceased. If someone dies *intestate* (without leaving a will), civil law defines the right to inherit among various relatives. If there are no living relatives, the property passes to the state.

Property Law The right to inherit, bequeath, sell, lease, or transfer property is protected by law, but the rights of ownership do not include the privilege of misuse. The right to own a gun does not convey the right to use it as a weapon in murder. The privilege of opening an industrial plant does not include the right to pollute. The regulation of private property for public purposes is one of the oldest functions of law.

Texas law includes thousands of provisions regulating private property, and it establishes hundreds of courts and administrative agencies to elaborate, interpret, and enforce those regulations. Texas regulatory agencies include the Railroad Commission, the Commissioner of Insurance, the Finance Commission, the Public Utilities Commission, and occupational licensing boards. Their administrative regulations—administrative law—have the same binding effect as civil law and are usually enforced by civil courts.

Corporate Law Corporations secure permission from the state to conduct business. The secretary of state issues them a **charter,** which defines their structure, purposes, and activities. For corporations chartered in other states ("foreign" corporations), the secretary of state also issues permits to operate in Texas. Civil law holds that when a new corporation is chartered, a new legal person is created—one who can sue, be sued, or be fined for criminal activity.

Labor Law When two parties enter into a valid contract, the courts will enforce the terms of the contract. However, certain kinds of contracts are not enforceable in the courts—for example, most contracts with minors. Texas's **right-to-work law** also forbids contracts between labor and management that establish a **union shop,** in which management agrees to require all new employees to join the union, or alternatively, to pay representation fees to the union. Texas also bans the **closed shop,** in which management agrees to hire only persons who were members of a particular union before they were hired. (The closed shop has also been illegal nationally since 1947, however.) Texas is generally considered to be inhospitable to unions.

Slander and Libel Civil law also protects a person's reputation against false and malicious statements. **Slander** (spoken

Texas Political SOCIAL MEDIA

Twitter can be useful in locating a variety of sites dealing with Texas laws and crime. In the Twitter search box, enter "texas laws," "texas courts," or "texas crime."

probate The procedure for proving the validity of a will.

charter The organizing document for a corporation or a municipality.

right-to-work law A law that bans unions from collecting dues or representation fees from workers that they represent but who have not actually joined the union.

union shop A workplace in which management requires all new employees to join a union or pay a representation fee to the union as a condition of employment (illegal in Texas).

closed shop A workplace in which the employer is limited to hiring individuals who were members of a particular labor union before they are hired.

slander A public utterance that holds a person up for contempt, ridicule, or hatred.

defamation) or **libel** (published defamation) may result in a lawsuit to recover monetary compensation for damage to one's reputation and earnings potential. In a recent twist, the law extends protection against libel to vegetables—farmers may sue people who make unfounded allegations against their products.

Negligence Failure to act with the prudence or care that an ordinary person would exercise—**negligence**—may result in someone's bodily harm or other injury, and negligent persons are liable for damages. If a personal-injury lawsuit results, it is a **tort** action (a case involving a private or civil wrong or injury other than a breach of contract).

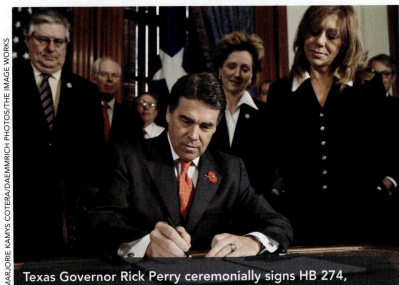

Texas Governor Rick Perry ceremonially signs HB 274, which brings tort reform to Texas courts.

MARJORIE KAMYS COTERA/DAEMMRICH PHOTOS/THE IMAGE WORKS

libel A published report of a falsehood that injures a person's reputation or character.

negligence Failure to act with the prudence or care that an ordinary person would exercise.

tort A private or civil injury or wrong other than a breach of contract.

tort reform Efforts to limit liability in civil cases.

punitive damages Judgments in excess of actual damages intended to punish a defendant in a civil suit.

no-fault insurance An insurance plan allowing the insured person to collect from the individual's own insurance company regardless of who is at fault in a vehicular accident.

liability insurance Insurance against negligence claims such as those arising from auto accidents.

10–1c Issues in Civil Law

In Texas, issues surrounding civil lawsuits have become a significant source of controversy. Efforts to change civil law concerning suits have been a major topic in Texas's election campaigns and have occupied much of the legislature's time and energy.

Tort Reform Insurance companies, corporations, medical practitioners, and others have argued that society has become too litigious (inclined to go to court to settle differences). They have asserted that "frivolous" lawsuits have overcrowded court dockets, and that excessive damages awards have unnecessarily driven up insurance premiums and other business costs. As a result, Governor Rick

Perry and most Republican leaders joined with groups representing defendants in civil actions, the Texas Civil Justice League, Texans for Lawsuit Reform, insurance companies, and a wide range of business and medical interest groups to urge **tort reform.**

Because of the power of this political alliance, Texas has (1) restricted lawsuits by prison inmates, (2) given judges the power to dismiss frivolous lawsuits, (3) limited liability in civil cases involving multiple defendants, and (4) capped jury awards for **punitive damages** (judgments in excess of actual damages that are intended to punish the defendant). In 2003, Texans narrowly approved a constitutional amendment to allow the legislature to limit claims for pain and suffering and punitive damages. We discuss tort reform in the *Join the Debate* feature on the facing page.

Liability Insurance Automobile insurance is one aspect of tort reform that the Texas legislature has not seriously considered. A **no-fault insurance** plan would allow an insured person to collect damages from the individual's own insurance company regardless of who is at fault in an accident. Under Texas's **liability insurance** plan, an expensive and time-consuming legal effort is often required to determine which of the individuals involved in an accident is to blame and thus legally responsible for damages. With no-fault insurance, insurance company costs for court trials could be substantially reduced, and the resulting savings could presumably be passed on to policyholders. At least a dozen states use limited no-fault insurance programs.

Has Tort Reform Gone Too Far in Texas?

Tort reform advocates contend that too many lawsuits are frivolous. They claim that in most states, the tort system is too expensive, clogs up the courts, and rewards trial attorneys too generously. (Under a typical arrangement, the lawyer receives one-third of any settlement.) Studies show that tort costs have grown nationally since 1950. They have fallen as a percentage of GDP since 2001, however, and are now at their lowest level since 1984. Perhaps tort reform has had some effect. Still, the argument over it continues to rage in Texas.

Tort Reform in Texas Addressed a Real Problem

Those who supported the recent limits on lawsuits have made several arguments against the previous system. One argument is that excessively generous settlements in the past drove up the cost of insurance for everyone, because most tort claims are actually paid by insurance companies.

Reform advocates also blame lawsuits for rapidly increasing health-care costs. In a 2005 survey by the *Journal of the American Medical Association*, 93 percent of physicians reported practicing "defensive medicine" to protect themselves against lawsuits. Unnecessary MRIs and CAT scans were ordered by 43 percent of those surveyed. Others avoided risky procedures and patients with complex ailments or those who might sue. According to a 2004 Harvard study of medical malpractice, half of all malpractice costs are eaten up in administrative overhead. Moreover, most patients victimized by negligence do not receive compensation. Only one malpractice claim is filed for every eight injuries attributable to negligence. Finally, malpractice insurance premiums have fallen an average of 17 percent in states adopting tort reform.

Don't Limit the Right to Demand Justice

Consumer and patients' rights groups argue that isolated anecdotal examples of lawsuit abuse should not be used as a justification to restrict the fundamental right to trial by jury. Only a jury that hears all evidence presented by both sides can make an appropriate judgment in cases of extreme negligence and abuse of an individual's rights. Almost 200,000 people die each year as a result of medical negligence. We need a robust system to compensate victims for their losses and to deter future wrongdoing. Opponents of tort reform also see it as an attack by big business on laws that protect consumers against defective products and deceptive practices.

Tort reform makes lawyers reluctant to take the risk of bringing costly and time-consuming lawsuits against well-funded corporations. Under the new Texas "loser pays" system, if either party refuses an out-of-court settlement and the jury awards damages significantly different from the settlement offer, the loser must pay all of the winner's legal expenses.

Finally, savings from tort reform may increase insurance company profits instead of reducing premiums. In Texas, tort reform created $600 million in annual savings for insurance companies. Before reform, the companies paid out seventy cents in damages for each dollar in premiums. After reform, they paid out only fifty-eight cents.

FOR CRITICAL ANALYSIS Civil lawsuits have become an important issue in Texas judicial elections. Corporations, insurance firms, and health professionals contribute to candidates who are inclined to limit damages. Consumer groups, patients' rights groups, and trial lawyers rally around candidates who may be friendlier to their causes. Is this dynamic due to tort reform—or simply a result of the Texas system of judicial elections? Explain your answer.

Eminent Domain Since the time of the Republic, Texas constitutions, like the U.S. Constitution, have required that owners be given "adequate" or "just" compensation when the government takes their private property for "public use"—that is, when the government exercises its right of **eminent domain.** Just compensation has long been interpreted to mean fair market value. Recently, however, the meaning of *public use* has become controversial. In 2005, the United States Supreme Court interpreted public use to include private commercial development as long as it benefits the community as a whole. In its ruling, the Court approved seizing private residences in Connecticut to make way for a resort hotel, office buildings, and posh apartments.[1]

eminent domain The power of a government to take land for public use from private citizens for just compensation.

STUDY TOOLS

Ready to study?

- Review what you've read with the quiz below. Check your answers on the Chapter in Review card at the back of the book. For any questions you miss, read the corresponding Learning Outcome section again to prepare for class and your exam.
- Rip out and study the Chapter in Review card.

... Or you can go online to CourseMate

at www.cengagebrain.com for these additional review materials:

- Practice Quizzes
- Key Term Flashcards or Crossword Puzzles
- Audio Summaries
- Simulations, Animated Learning Modules, and Interactive Timelines
- Videos
- American Government NewsWatch

Quiz

1. The major difference between civil law and criminal law is that:
   a. only civil law uses the adversarial system.
   b. one of the two major parties in a criminal law case is the *plaintiff.*
   c. civil law involves disputes betweens private citizens, not violations of public morality prosecuted by the state.

2. Which of the following would NOT be an example of a civil law case?
   a. A dispute over who owns a particular piece of property.
   b. A woman arraigned for selling sexual services where such services are banned.
   c. A lawsuit by workers who feel they have been wrongly denied their wages.

3. The conflict over the government's authority to take an individual or company's property as long as it pays "just compensation" is a conflict over what is known as:
   a. eminent domain.   b. tort.   c. *stare decisis.*

4. Very serious crimes, such as robbery, are classified as:
   a. capital crimes.   b. misdemeanors.   c. felonies.

5. Which profile best fits an individual more likely to be a criminal?
   a. Male, white, rural, younger.
   b. Female, minority, urban, older.
   c. Male, minority, urban, younger.

6. What legal device do the courts use to enforce the Fourth Amendment's prohibition against "unreasonable searches and seizures" against law enforcement officers who violate it?
   a. the exclusionary rule
   b. *stare decisis*
   c. a writ of *habeas corpus*

7. *Miranda* warnings, which are required of law enforcement officials when they take a criminal suspect into custody, exist primarily to:
   a. make sure that a suspect gets an attorney.
   b. keep a suspect from feeling forced into making a confession.
   c. let judges know that due process is being followed.

8. "The majority of, though not all, criminal cases end up going to trial."
   a. true   b. false

9. Which of the following is NOT a major purpose of the "arraignment" stage of the pre-trial phase of the criminal process?
   a. To interrogate the accused.
   b. To explain the charges against the accused.
   c. To set bail.

10. What is the name used to describe the legal system in English-speaking countries in which two contesting parties present opposing views and evidence in a court of law?
    a. the inquisitorial system
    b. the common law system
    c. the adversarial system

11. In a Texas criminal trial, where the accused has the right to a jury trial, a jury can only find the accused guilty by a verdict of _____.
    a. two-thirds of the jurors
    b. three-fourths of the jurors
    c. all of the jurors

12. The theory of incarceration that emphasizes the discouragement of other would-be lawbreakers is known as:
    a. punishment.   b. deterrence.   c. rehabilitation.

13. One of the major arguments cited by opponents of the criminal justice system as it presently exists in Texas is that it:
    a. deters too harshly.
    b. doesn't permit the use of probation.
    c. doesn't show any evidence of rehabilitation or deterrence.

Public Policy in Texas

MARJORIE KAMYS COTERA/DAEMMRICH PHOTOGRAPHY/THE IMAGE WORKS

★ Learning Outcomes

The **Learning Outcomes** labeled 1 through 5 are designed to help improve your understanding of the chapter. After reading this chapter, you should be able to:

11–1 Detail the major sources of revenue for the state, and summarize the debate over progressive and regressive tax rates.

11–2 Explain how the legislature appropriates funds, and describe the major purposes of state spending.

11–3 Discuss the systems that govern public K–12 and higher-education institutions in Texas, and describe major political issues dealing with education.

11–4 Provide details about major health and human services policies in Texas, including Medicaid, the new Affordable Care Act, unemployment insurance, and cash welfare.

11–5 Describe the development of the Texas highway system, as well as current problems with funding road work.

Remember to visit page 268 for additional **Study Tools**

241

CONFLICT

Should Texas Adopt School Vouchers?

School vouchers are grants to families to help pay for private school tuition. Parents can apply these vouchers toward tuition or, in some cases, even use them for home-schooling expenses. By offsetting the cost of private school tuition, vouchers allow families to choose which school their children attend. In other words, education vouchers imply school choice. Without vouchers, families that wish to send their children to alternative private institutions have to pay the full cost in addition to paying their property taxes, which support the public school system.

In 1990, Milwaukee was the first major city that offered vouchers for K–12 education (K–12 refers to the system of kindergarten, elementary, and secondary schools). More than one-quarter of Milwaukee students receive such vouchers to attend schools that are not part of the public school system. Cleveland is another city with a voucher system, which began in 1995.

In 2005, the Texas legislature considered a school voucher plan to allow some children to leave under-performing public schools and to transfer to private schools. State funding would have followed the children to whatever schools they attended. The plan found strong support among religious and economic conservatives. Additional support for a Texas education voucher system was found in poorer, central city, and minority neighborhoods. The 2005 effort failed, but state senators planned to raise the issue again in 2013.

The Voucher System Is Not for Texas

Opponents of the proposed Texas voucher system included parents of children in better-performing public schools, as well as groups such as the Texas Federation of Teachers and the Parent-Teacher Association.

Opponents charge that vouchers would damage public schools by draining their financial resources. Such a system would also drain some of the public schools' best students, leaving these schools to educate students with special problems. Moreover, public funds should not be used to subsidize special private privileges. If educational vouchers were adopted, opponents argue private schools should then offer open admissions, open meetings, and open records policies, just as public school systems must do.

There is also the issue of separation of church and state. In Texas, 85 percent of private schools are religious, with the largest number being Catholic schools. How can state taxpayer dollars be used for students attending religious schools? Despite the United States Supreme Court's approval of the Cleveland voucher plan, such programs seem to violate the spirit of the U.S. Constitution. The state should not be supporting any religion. In any event, such a school voucher system in Texas would probably violate the Texas Constitution, which prohibits appropriations for the benefit of any sect or religious society.

Let Competition Reign—Support Vouchers

With an educational voucher system, Texas parents would be able to send their children to schools that compete with the public school system. That just makes good sense because competition usually brings out the best in people and enterprises. If the public schools wanted to maintain their enrollments, they would have to improve their performance to compete with private schools.

The legal arguments against a Texas school voucher system are unlikely to stand up. In 2002, the United States Supreme Court ruled that the Cleveland voucher program was not in violation of the establishment clause of the U.S. Constitution because the program gives funds to parents, not to religious organizations. Because parents and students choose the school, educational vouchers do not favor religious over nonreligious schools. Similarly, a plan that gives vouchers directly to parents should not violate the Texas Constitution.

The poorest-performing public schools continue to perform poorly because their students do not have a choice, unless their parents have the money to send them to private schools—which few parents do. That is certainly not fair. School choice would allow parents to select schools based on their children's educational needs rather than on the neighborhoods in which they live.

Where do you stand?

1. How might a voucher program in Texas affect cultural diversity?
2. Why do you think so few cities and states currently have an educational voucher system?

Explore this issue online

- Entering "school vouchers" into your favorite Internet search engine will bring up a wide variety of arguments about the topic, both pro and con.
- If you type in "school vouchers texas," you will narrow the focus. Find out how the Texas legislature is dealing with this issue.

Introduction

The Texas legislature finally passed and sent to the governor a $173.5 billion budget for fiscal years 2012 and 2013. Counting one dollar every second without resting for weekends, holidays, or coffee breaks, it would take about 5,501 years to count these appropriations! Texas has the third-largest state budget, exceeded only by those of California and New York.

Until recently, Texas state expenditures rose steadily. Each successive budget was larger than the preceding one, resulting in a long succession of record expenditures. Figure 11–1 below shows that inflation and population increases explain much of the historical growth in state spending.

Texas's population has grown more rapidly than that of most other states. In the absolute number of new residents added during the last ten years, no other state comes close. Each new person had to be served, protected, and educated. Of course, the demands of a larger population for state services were offset by the fact that more people were also paying taxes to support those services. Adjusted for population and inflation, state spending grew at an average annual rate of 0.8 percent over the last twenty years.

The 2012–2013 budget, however, abruptly reversed that historical trend and represented the first real decline in state spending in generations. Texas's budget cuts were largely the result of the Great Recession of 2007–2009 and the slow economic recovery in its aftermath. Rather than raise taxes to make up for revenue shortfalls, Texas's conservative state legislature took the unprecedented action of cutting already-lean state spending by a dramatic 14.6 percent (after adjusting for inflation and population growth).

11–1 Revenues

Later in this chapter, we will discuss some of the ways in which the state spends its money. For now, let's look at where the funds come from. Surprisingly, much state revenue comes from sources other than state taxes. During the 2012–2013 fiscal years, 44 percent of estimated

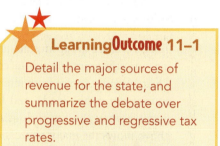

LearningOutcome 11–1

Detail the major sources of revenue for the state, and summarize the debate over progressive and regressive tax rates.

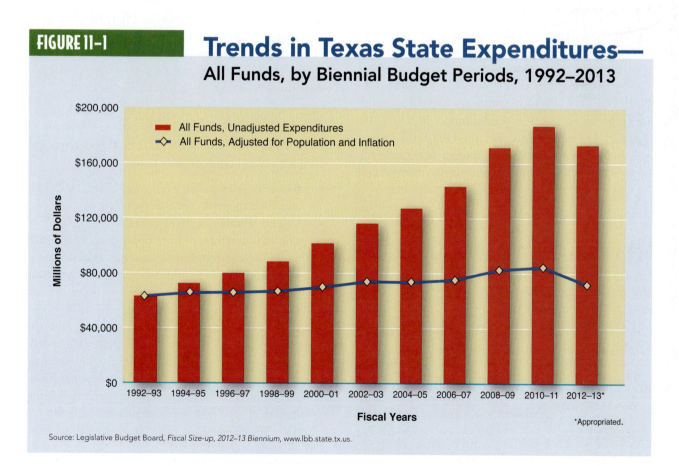

FIGURE 11–1

Trends in Texas State Expenditures—
All Funds, by Biennial Budget Periods, 1992–2013

- All Funds, Unadjusted Expenditures
- All Funds, Adjusted for Population and Inflation

Millions of Dollars

Fiscal Years: 1992–93, 1994–95, 1996–97, 1998–99, 2000–01, 2002–03, 2004–05, 2006–07, 2008–09, 2010–11, 2012–13*

*Appropriated.

Source: Legislative Budget Board, *Fiscal Size-up, 2012–13 Biennium*, www.lbb.state.tx.us.

FIGURE 11–2

This figure shows that Texas's largest single revenue source is federal funding and that the state tax producing the most revenue is the general sales tax.

Source: Legislative Budget Board, *Fiscal Size-up, 2012–13 Biennium*, p. 29.

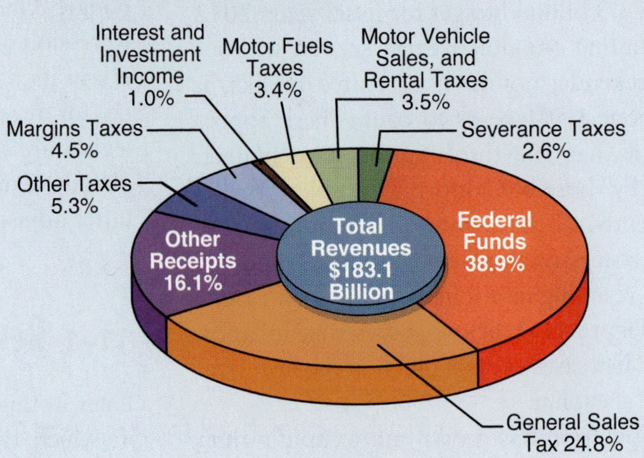

Sources of Estimated State Revenues, 2012–2013 Budget Period

Texas revenues are from state taxes, while federal funding—mostly grants-in-aid—accounts for 38.9 percent. The remainder comes from interest on investments, revenues from public lands, and licenses, fees, and other minor nontax sources such as the lottery. Figure 11–2 above shows the major sources of Texas state revenues.

11–1a Taxation

Governments rely on a variety of taxes, and each level of government—national, state, and local—tends to specialize in levying certain types of taxes.

National Taxes With the ratification of the Sixteenth Amendment to the U.S. Constitution in 1913, the national government was able to establish the income tax. Individual and corporate income taxes immediately became the national government's major source of funding and today provide about 56 percent of federal tax revenues, with most of the remainder coming from payroll taxes for Social Security and Medicare.

State Taxes Property taxes were once the major source of state revenue, but property values collapsed during the Great Depression of the 1930s and so did property tax revenues. At the same time, demands for economic assistance and other public services skyrocketed.

Forced to seek other sources of revenue, states came to rely on various sales taxes. Texas adopted a tax on cigarettes in 1931, on beer in 1933, and on distilled spirits in 1935. Additional selective sales taxes were adopted in the 1940s and 1950s, but it became apparent that a more general, broadly based tax would be necessary to provide needed revenue. In 1961, Texas adopted a general sales tax on most items sold. At the same time, Texas drastically reduced state taxes on property. It then abandoned the property tax altogether, which was used thereafter exclusively by local governments.

TYPES OF SALES TAXES. Most state tax revenue in 2012–2013 came from various sales taxes. Texas has adopted several types of sales taxes:

- **General sales taxes** are broad-based taxes collected on the retail price of most items.
- **Selective sales (excise) taxes** are levied on the sale, manufacture, or use of particular items, such as liquor, cigarettes, and gasoline. Because these taxes are usually included in the item's purchase price, they are often considered to be **hidden taxes.**
- **Gross-receipts taxes** are taxes on the total gross revenue (sales) of certain enterprises. A broadbased *margins tax* (also known as the *franchise tax*) applies to the gross sales of most corporations and limited partnerships after taking a deduction for the cost of goods or personnel. Small companies, sole proprietorships, and general partnerships are exempt.

general sales tax
A broad-based tax collected on the retail price of most items.

selective sales (excise) taxes Taxes levied on specific items only.

hidden taxes Taxes included in the retail prices of goods and services.

gross-receipts tax A tax on the gross revenues of certain enterprises.

SALES TAX REVENUES. The general sales tax—6.25 percent on retail sales of most items—yielded 24.8 percent of the state's revenues in 2012–2013. The margins (franchise) tax brought in 4.5 percent. Motor fuels excise taxes yielded 3.4 percent, and motor vehicle sales and rental taxes, 3.5 percent. Once a major source of state revenue, **severance taxes** (production taxes on oil and natural gas) now account for only 2.6 percent of revenues. Texas also collects special taxes on a range of items and activities, such as tobacco, alcohol, registration of motor vehicles, hotel and motel occupancy, and insurance company operations.

Texas Governor Rick Perry ceremonially signs a new law at a Target store in 2009. This legislation adds school supplies to the list of items that are exempt from sales tax during the annual sales tax holiday.

Local Taxes Many services that are financed by the state government in other states are left to local governments in Texas. The state government has also imposed many mandates (required services) on local governments, especially school districts, without funding them. As a result, state taxes remain low in Texas, but local taxes are higher than in many states.

Property taxes are the major source of revenue for virtually all local governments—cities, counties, and special districts. **Ad valorem taxes,** which are assessed according to value, may be applied to two major types of property: **real property** (land and buildings) and **personal property** (other tangible possessions, such as furniture and automobiles).

Most Texas local governments primarily tax real property. A central appraisal authority in each county determines property values for all taxing units in the county according to uniform state standards and procedures. The tax rate is set by local policymaking bodies—city councils, county commissioners' courts, and boards of trustees for special districts.

Local governments also impose other taxes. For operating expenses, most Texas cities have adopted a 1 percent city sales tax applied to items taxable under the state general sales tax. Cities in counties with populations of more than 500,000 may also collect an additional sales tax up to 1 percent for economic development projects. Mass transit authorities and other special districts also collect sales taxes, but total local sales taxes are capped at 2 percent. Other local revenue sources include miscellaneous taxes, user fees, and federal grants.

11–1b The Politics of Taxation

As with all public policy, the state's tax policy is designed by elected politicians who make decisions based on which groups will be most affected by different types of taxes. Arguments are usually phrased in terms of the "public interest." Still, tax questions mobilize millions of dollars in campaign funds, millions of campaign hours, and thousands of lobbyists. These forces are not trying to settle some abstract academic argument. The contest is over real resources.

The Tax Base: Who Should Pay? Not all taxes are equally effective in raising funds. **Tax rates** may be raised or lowered in percentage terms, but simply raising a tax rate may not guarantee

severance tax A tax on raw materials (such as oil and natural gas) when they are extracted from their natural state.

ad valorem tax A tax assessed according to value, such as the tax on real property and personal property.

real property Land and buildings.

personal property Tangible possessions other than real estate.

tax rate The amount of tax given as a percentage of the value of a taxable item or activity.

increased revenues if people cut back on purchases of the taxed item.

Tax rates can affect the **tax base**—the range of items subject to the tax. Excessive property taxes may discourage construction and repair of buildings. High income taxes are believed to discourage general economic activity and individual initiative, undermining the tax base in a very broad way. To raise necessary revenue, a tax must not discourage too much of the activity that produces the revenue.

Most governments tax a wide variety of items and activities because they have found that **broad-based taxes**—those paid by a very large number of taxpayers—are most effective at raising revenue. Such broad-based taxes include property taxes, general sales taxes, and income taxes.

In the battle over taxation, the decision about *what* to tax is really a decision about *whom* to tax and how heavily. Those with influence on decision makers try to get special tax treatment for themselves and other taxpayers in similar circumstances. What seems to motivate almost every group is the belief that the best tax is the one paid by somebody else. The three most common political rationalizations for taxing various people differently are (1) to regulate their behavior, (2) to tax them according to the benefits they receive, and (3) to tax them according to their ability to pay.

REGULATORY TAXES. Taxes do more than simply pay for the services of government. They can serve as a tool for social or economic control. Rewarding approved behavior with a lower tax rate or punishing socially undesirable action with a higher tax rate can have a definite effect on conduct.

State **regulatory taxes** are sometimes called *sin taxes*. High taxes are placed on items such as alcohol or tobacco in an attempt to discourage their use. Texas has an excise tax on alcoholic beverages, and its cigarette tax of $1.41 per pack is close to the national average.

Texans continue to drink, smoke, and frequent strip clubs (which are also taxed), so sin taxes do not entirely prevent the sinner from sinning. They do substantially increase the share of the tax burden borne by the sinner, however. The most vocal advocates of alcohol and tobacco taxes are often those who abstain. Still, regulatory taxes may have some positive effect—research suggests young people can be deterred from smoking by the high price of cigarettes.

BENEFITS RECEIVED. On the surface, nothing would seem fairer than taxation according to benefits received—let those who benefit from a public service pay for it. An example of a **benefits-received tax** in Texas is a 20-cent-per-gallon tax on gasoline. Three-fourths of the income from gasoline and diesel fuel taxes is directed into the Texas Highway Trust Fund. This fund also receives the state's share of license plate fees (although most of these fees are retained by the counties). Texas drivers, therefore, pay for the roads they use in proportion to the fuel they consume.

Although not strictly a tax, tuition paid by students in state colleges and universities is largely determined on the basis of the benefits-received principle. Although much of the cost of public college education in Texas is paid out of state and local tax revenues, in recent years an increasing share has been paid by tuition. The presumption is that students should pay a larger share of the cost of a service from which they greatly benefit. Likewise, revenues from hunting and fishing permits are used for wildlife management.

ABILITY TO PAY. Most taxes are rationalized on the basis of taxpayers' ability to pay them. The most common **ability-to-pay taxes** are levied on property, sales, and income. An argument for property taxes is that the more valuable a person's property, the wealthier he or she is and hence the greater his or her ability to pay taxes. The payment of sales taxes is directly proportional to how much you buy. Income taxes are based on the assumption that the more a person earns, the greater is that person's ability to pay.

No tax base is fully adequate as a measure of a person's ability to pay. A retired person may own a house that has risen drastically in value. Yet that person may also be living on a small, fixed income. The income tax also has its limits. Exemptions often allow taxpayers to avoid much of the tax. Sales taxes are in some ways even more troubling. While they appear to fall on all spending equally, they actually weigh more heavily on lower-income groups than on the wealthy. Upper-class families spend large sums on items that are not subject to sales tax, while most of the goods purchased by the poor are taxed.

tax base The object or activity taxed.

broad-based tax A tax designed to be paid by a large number of taxpayers.

regulatory tax A tax imposed with the intent of discouraging undesirable activities.

benefits-received tax A tax assessed according to the services received by the payers.

ability-to-pay taxes Taxes apportioned according to taxpayers' financial capacity.

Progressive and Regressive Tax Rates Some taxes, such as federal income taxes, have **progressive tax rates** because the tax rates go up as income increases. Liberals and other supporters of progressive taxation argue that persons with greater incomes can better afford to pay higher tax rates and that lower-income persons should be left with enough of their incomes to maintain the necessities of life. Lower-income persons also spend a larger share of their incomes on consumption, which is the largest driving force in the economy.

Such arguments have not convinced Texans, who adopted a state constitutional amendment that forbids a state income tax unless voters approve. Even then, it can be used only for education and property tax relief.

REGRESSIVE TAX RATES. By contrast, Texas has **regressive tax rates,** whereby the rates decline as income increases. For example, the state general sales tax (6.25 percent, among the highest in the nation) is proportional to the value of sales, but because of patterns of consumption, the effective rate actually declines as a person's income increases. Table 11–1 alongside shows that if a family's income increases, so does its general sales tax payment. That fact seems reasonable—one would expect the purchases of taxable items to increase as income increases. But note that as income increases, an ever-smaller *percentage* of that income is used for taxable purchases. More money is saved, invested, or spent on tax-exempt items.

Thus, despite exemptions for certain essential items, the effective rate of the Texas general sales tax declines as income increases. A working-class individual with an income of $25,000 pays an effective sales tax *rate* that is more than twice as high as an individual with an income of $190,000 annually. Similarly, taxpayers pay a smaller percentage of their incomes in property and excise taxes as their incomes increase.

TAX SHIFTING. Even business taxes may be regressive for individuals because of *tax shifting.* Businesses must include their tax burden as part of their operating cost, and much of that cost is shifted to customers in the form of higher prices. When property taxes increase, landlords raise rents. When business taxes are imposed, prices of consumer items usually increase as those taxes are passed on to customers as hidden taxes. Thus, many business taxes become, in effect, consumer taxes and, like other *consumer* taxes, regressive relative to income.

PUTTING IT ALL TOGETHER. Taking into account all state and local taxes and tax shifting, Texas has one

TABLE 11–1

Texas's General Sales Tax Paid in Dollars and as a Percentage of Taxable Income, 2011*

Notice that as income increases, sales tax payments in dollars increase, but the tax rate declines as a percentage of income.

Taxable Income	Texas General Sales Tax	Percentage of Taxable Income
$ 10,000	$ 269	2.69
25,000	439	1.76
35,000	526	1.50
45,000	602	1.34
55,000	699	1.22
65,000	731	1.12
75,000	789	1.05
85,000	844	0.99
95,000	895	0.94
110,000	963	0.88
130,000	1,055	0.81
150,000	1,137	0.76
170,000	1,217	0.72
190,000	1,291	0.68
1,000,000	1,655	0.17

*For single individuals.
Source: Internal Revenue Service, *Form 1040, 2011*, p. A-12.

of the most regressive tax structures among the fifty states. Table 11–2 on the following page shows the impact of major state and local taxes on Texas families. Those with the lowest household incomes paid 6 percent of their income in general sales taxes—more than four times the percentage that upper-income households paid. These households also paid an effective school property tax rate more than three times as high as that of upper-income households. And, for those with the lowest household incomes, the gasoline tax represents more than eight times the burden that it does for the upper-income households. Lower-income families even bear a disproportionate share of the state's franchise tax on business.

progressive tax rates
Tax rates that increase as income increases. For example, the federal income tax is assessed using progressive rates.

regressive tax rates
Tax rates that effectively decrease as income increases. These rates place more of a burden on low- and middle-income taxpayers than on wealthier ones.

TABLE 11-2

Texas's Major State and Local Taxes as a Percentage of Household Income, Fiscal 2013*

Look across each row in the table to see how major state and local taxes burden low- and middle-income taxpayers more than they do upper-income taxpayers.

Tax	Lower Income	Lower–Middle Income	Middle Income	Upper–Middle Income	Upper Income
General sales tax	6.0%	3.4%	2.9%	2.5%	1.3%
Franchise (margins) tax	1.0	0.6	0.5	0.4	0.3
Gasoline tax	0.8	0.5	0.4	0.3	0.1
Motor vehicle sales tax	0.6	0.4	0.4	0.3	0.2
School property tax	5.3	2.9	2.4	2.2	1.6

*Estimates based on an economic model that takes into account the effect of tax shifting. Household incomes are categorized by quintiles from the lowest one-fifth to the highest one-fifth, each representing 1,919,580 households.

Source: Texas Comptroller of Public Accounts, *Tax Exemptions and Tax Incidence*, February, 2011, pp. 44–63.

STATE-BY-STATE COMPARISONS. Consistent with Texas's conservative political culture, state taxes are lower and more regressive than in most other states. Figure 11–3 on the facing page shows that including local taxes and even the taxes that Texans pay in other states, Texans paid only 7.9 percent of personal income in all state and local taxes. Residents of only five states paid less.

ARGUMENTS FOR REGRESSIVE TAXES. Although they usually oppose business taxes, conservatives and high-income groups who support other regressive taxes also argue that taxes on higher-income individuals should be kept low to allow them to save and invest to stimulate the economy. They argue that applying higher rates to higher incomes is unfair and that sales and property taxes are easier to collect, harder to evade or avoid, and generally less burdensome than progressive income taxes. Some advocate a national sales tax, also known as the *fair tax*, to replace the progressive federal income tax.

11–1c Other Revenues

Much of the state's revenue comes from federal grants-in-aid. A smaller amount is generated from nontax revenues such as licenses, fees, and borrowing.

Federal Grants For the 2012–2013 biennium, Texas will have received about $71 billion in federal funds, which represents 38.9 percent of state revenues. Much of what Texas spends for health and human services and for transportation originates as federal grants, which we discussed in depth in Chapter 2.

Borrowing and Other Revenues At the beginning of each legislative session, the comptroller of public accounts reports to the legislature the total amount of revenues expected from current taxes and other sources. The legislature can, in turn, appropriate no more than this amount unless it enacts new tax laws. The two exceptions to this general limit are that (1) the legislature, by a nearly impossible four-fifths vote, may borrow in emergency situations, and (2) voters may amend the Texas Constitution to provide for the issuance of bonds for specific programs.

State bonds are classified as (1) **general-obligation bonds** (to be repaid from general revenues), which have been used to finance prison construction, the veterans' real estate programs, water development, and higher education, and (2) **revenue bonds,** which are to be repaid with the revenues from the service they finance, such as higher-education bonds financed by tuition revenue.

Other nontax revenues that account for a small share of Texas's income include the following:

- The lottery.
- Various licenses, fines, and fees.
- Dividends from investments.
- The sale and leasing of public lands.

general-obligation bonds Bonds to be repaid from general taxes and other revenues. Such bond issues usually must be approved by voters.

revenue bonds Bonds to be repaid with revenues from the projects they finance, such as utilities or sports stadiums.

FIGURE 11-3

Rankings of State and Local Tax
Burdens among the Fifty States

This figure shows the percentage of income residents paid to state and local governments in all fifty states and is based on a model that takes into account tax shifting. The state's ranking is noted in the parentheses below the state's percentage.

Source: The Tax Foundation.

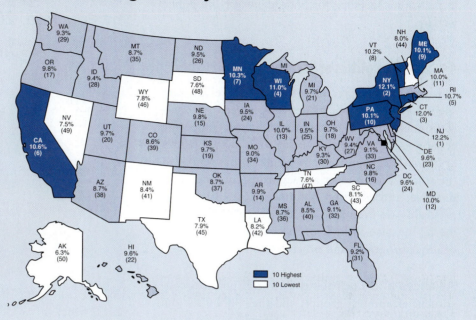

WA 9.3% (29) | MT 8.7% (35) | ND 9.5% (26) | MN 10.3% (7) | WI 11.0% (4) | MI 9.7% (21) | NH 8.0% (44) | VT 10.2% (8) | ME 10.1% (9) | NY 12.1% (2) | MA 10.0% (11) | RI 10.7% (5) | CT 12.0% (3) | NJ 12.2% (1) | PA 10.1% (10) | DE 9.6% (23)

OR 9.8% (17) | ID 9.4% (28) | WY 7.8% (46) | SD 7.6% (48) | NE 9.8% (15) | IA 9.5% (24) | IL 10.0% (13) | IN 9.5% (25) | OH 9.7% (18) | WV 9.4% (27) | VA 9.1% (33) | MD 10.0% (12) | DC 9.6% (24)

NV 7.5% (49) | UT 9.7% (20) | CO 8.6% (39) | KS 9.7% (19) | MO 9.0% (34) | KY 9.3% (30) | NC 9.8% (16)

CA 10.6% (6) | AZ 8.7% (38) | NM 8.4% (41) | OK 8.7% (37) | AR 9.9% (14) | TN 7.6% (47) | SC 8.1% (43)

TX 7.9% (45) | LA 8.2% (42) | MS 8.7% (36) | AL 8.5% (40) | GA 9.1% (32)

AK 6.3% (50) | HI 9.6% (22) | FL 9.2% (31)

■ 10 Highest □ 10 Lowest

11–2 State Spending

LearningOutcome 11–2

Explain how the legislature appropriates funds, and describe the major purposes of state spending.

11–2a The Appropriations Process

It is through the **appropriations** process that the legislature legally authorizes the state to spend money to provide its various programs and services. Appropriations bills follow the same steps (described in Chapter 7) as other legislation. They pass through standing committee consideration, floor action, conference committee compromise, final voting, and then approval by the governor.

The U.S. Congress and most state legislatures work with a budget plan submitted by the chief executive as they begin the appropriations process. Texas is different. During most of the legislative process, the recommendations of the Legislative Budget Board carry greater weight than those of the governor because they tend to reflect the wishes of the legislature's powerful presiding officers. The governor may use the line-item veto to strike particular parts of the appropriations bill, but the governor rarely vetoes a significant share of state spending. Texas's governor is not truly the state's chief budget officer.

Unlike the national government, most states require that either their governor submit a balanced budget or the legislature pass one. Texas's restrictions against borrowing are more effective than most—state debt per capita in Texas is just over a third of the national average for states.

Texas ranks forty-seventh among the fifty states in overall per capita spending—25 percent below the national average. Texas's per capita

appropriations process
The process by which a legislative body legally authorizes a government to spend specific sums of money to provide various programs and services.

Having examined the revenue side of state policy, we now turn to the appropriations process and the politics of state spending.

expenditures for education ranked thirty-third among the fifty states, and for hospitals, it ranked twenty-fifth. The state ranked near the bottom (forty-fourth) in per capita spending for both highways and public welfare.

11–2b The Politics of State Spending

A wide variety of factors affects the level of state spending and complicates efforts toward rationalization. Nowhere is the conflict between competing economic interests more visible than in the budgetary process. Behind the large figures that represent the state's final budget are vigorous conflict, compromise, and coalition building. Most of society's programs are evaluated not only according to their merits but also in light of the competing demands of other programs and other economic interests.

Alliances and Logrolling Powerful political constituencies, interest groups, and their lobbyists join forces with state agencies to defend the programs that benefit them. This alliance between administrative agencies and interest groups brings great pressure to bear on the legislative process, especially targeting the powerful House Appropriations Committee, the Senate Finance Committee, and the presiding officers. Individual legislators trade votes among themselves, a process called *logrolling*, to realize increased funding to benefit their districts or their supporters.

Where the Funds Are Spent The pattern of spending is, in a sense, a shorthand description of which problems the state has decided to face and which challenges it has chosen to meet. The budget shows how much of which services the state will offer and to whom. Figure 11–4 alongside shows how Texas spent its state revenues in the 2012–2013 biennium.

The most costly service in Texas is education, which accounted for 42 percent of the state budget. Health and human services, including Medicaid and social services, were the second-most expensive, accounting for 31.9 percent. Transportation, primarily highways, consumed 11.4 percent. These three services take up more than four-fifths of the state's budget. A variety of miscellaneous services use up the remainder.

K–12 systems School systems in which students progress from kindergarten to the twelfth grade.

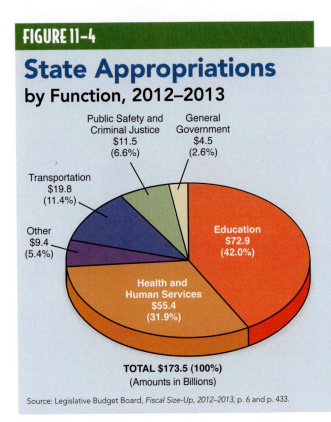

FIGURE 11–4

State Appropriations
by Function, 2012–2013

Public Safety and Criminal Justice $11.5 (6.6%)

General Government $4.5 (2.6%)

Transportation $19.8 (11.4%)

Other $9.4 (5.4%)

Education $72.9 (42.0%)

Health and Human Services $55.4 (31.9%)

TOTAL $173.5 (100%)
(Amounts in Billions)

Source: Legislative Budget Board, *Fiscal Size-Up, 2012–2013*, p. 6 and p. 433.

FOR CRITICAL THINKING Education takes up the largest share of the state budget because most students—at both the K–12 and the college level—attend public institutions. *Why do you think that Americans—including Texans—have made education primarily a public function?*

11–3 Education

The educational system in Texas includes elementary and secondary schools (the public schools) and the college and university system (higher education). Public school systems are commonly referred to as **K–12 systems** because students progress from kindergarten to the twelfth grade. Private K–12 systems exist as well.

LearningOutcome 11–3

Discuss the systems that govern public K–12 and higher-education institutions in Texas, and describe major political issues dealing with education.

11–3a Elementary and Secondary Schools

Public schools were accepted institutions in the North by the early nineteenth century, but they did not take root in the South (including Texas) until after the Civil War. Not until the Constitution of 1876 provided that alternate sections of public land grants would be set aside to finance schools did the state begin to commit itself to locally administered, optional public schools.

Meaningful state support for public education began with a compulsory attendance law, enacted in 1915, and a constitutional amendment that provided for free textbooks in 1918. In 1949, the Gilmer-Aikin laws increased state funding and established the Texas Education Agency (TEA), which carries out the state's educational program.

Recent Trends Sweeping changes in education resulted when the 1984 legislature established state-wide **accountability** standards for student performance and teacher competence. As president George W. Bush did when he took the use of high-stakes testing nationwide with his No Child Left Behind Act.

The standards used to measure public school performance are sometimes controversial. Still, there has been a recent trend toward using these standards to introduce market forces into the public school system. Some teachers and administrators receive merit pay—bonuses for improved student achievement.

To introduce the element of competition among schools, the state legislature authorized the State Board of Education to establish schools with innovative program charters that can recruit students from across existing school district boundaries. Many conservative state legislators now also favor adding even more school competition through *privatization* by providing vouchers to help students buy their education from private organizations, including churches and businesses. (We discussed vouchers in the chapter-opening *Texans in Conflict* feature on page 242.)

Today, public elementary and secondary education has grown from an underfinanced local function into a major state–local partnership. The TEA administers about 27 percent of all state expenditures, helping local school districts educate the approximately 90 percent of Texas students who enroll in public K–12 schools. Public policy decisions affect the lives of these 5 million students and the approximately 330,000 teachers who teach them.

Public School Administration As in other states, the Texas public school administration has three basic aspects:

1. Substantial local control in a joint state–local partnership.
2. Emphasis on professional administration supervised by laypersons.
3. Independence from the general structure of government.

STATE ADMINISTRATION. The Texas Constitution, the legislature, and the State Board of Education (SBOE) have established the basic decision-making organizations and financial arrangements for public education in the state. The legislature approves the budget for the state's share of the cost of public education and sets statutory standards for public schools, but many policy decisions are left to the SBOE, the TEA, and local school districts.

Members of the SBOE are elected to four-year overlapping terms in fifteen single-member districts, and together they establish general rules and guidelines for the TEA. The SBOE approves organizational plans, recommends a budget to the governor and the Legislative Budget Board, and implements funding formulas established by the legislature. It sets curriculum standards, establishes guidelines for operating public schools, and requires management, cost accounting, and financial reports from local districts. The SBOE leaves most routine managerial decisions to the commissioner of education.

The commissioner is appointed by the governor with the advice and consent of the senate to serve as the state's principal executive officer for education. With a number of assistant and associate commissioners and professional staff, the commissioner carries out the policies and regulations established by the legislature and the SBOE for public school programs.

LOCAL ADMINISTRATION. Texas's 1,029 regular independent school districts (more than any other state) are the basic structure for local control. Voters in independent school districts elect seven or nine school board members (depending on the district's population) for either three- or four-year terms. Board members may run at large or in single-member electoral districts. These trustees set the district's tax rate and determine school policies within the guidelines established by the TEA. They approve the budget, contract for instructional

accountability The responsibility for a program's results—for example, using measurable standards to hold public schools responsible for their students' performance.

An enthusiastic kindergarten student in a Texas public school raises her hand to answer a question.

supplies and construction, and hire and fire personnel. Their most important decision is the hiring of a professional superintendent, who is responsible for the executive or administrative functions of the school district.

Elected state and local school boards usually follow the recommendations of professional administrators—the commissioner at the state level and the superintendents locally. Most educational decisions are made independently of general government. Nevertheless, one should not conclude that independence from general government, localization, or professionalism keeps education free of politics. On the contrary, elected boards, especially the SBOE, have become quite politically assertive in recent years.

11–3b The Politics of Public Education

One of the most important decisions concerning public education is what education should seek to accomplish. Should it promote traditional views of society, reinforce the dominant political culture, and teach acceptable attitudes? Or should it teach students to be independent thinkers, capable of evaluating ideas for themselves? Because the Texas state educational system determines the curriculum and selects textbooks, it must address these fundamental questions.

The Curriculum Most of the basic curriculum is determined by the SBOE. Some school districts supplement the basic curriculum with a variety of elective and specialized courses, but it is in the basic courses—history, civics, biology, and English—that students are most likely to be exposed to issues that may fundamentally affect their attitudes.

How should a student be exposed to the theory of evolution? Should sex education courses offer discussion of artificial birth control or present abstinence as the only reliable birth control method? In the social sciences, should the political system be pictured in ideal terms or as it actually operates, with all its flaws? How should the roles of women and minorities be presented? How should elective Bible courses be taught and by whom?

Historically, vocational, agricultural, and home economics programs were viewed as burial grounds for pupils who had failed in the traditional academic programs. Today, almost one-half of high school students are enrolled in career and technology programs, and one in five are in family and consumer sciences. Although program titles have changed, much remains to be done to meet the need for highly skilled technical workers who possess other practical life skills.

The Curriculum and the Culture Wars After adopting controversial science and literature curriculum revisions in recent years, Texas's State Board of Education caused an even louder uproar in 2010 when it largely ignored the advice of professional educators and voted along party lines to establish social studies curriculum standards for the upcoming decade. Critics charged that the SBOE had hijacked the state's educational apparatus to impose a conservative, Christian fundamentalist political agenda on public school students.[1]

Critics focused on standards that require teaching the political beliefs of conservative icons like Phyllis Schlafly, Newt Gingrich, the now-disbanded Moral Majority, and the National Rifle Association. Meanwhile, students will be taught that Senator Joseph McCarthy's anticommunist crusade may have been justified. Confederate president Jefferson Davis's inaugural address will be taught alongside Abraham Lincoln's speeches, and the role of slavery as a cause of the Civil War is downplayed.

Students will evaluate how the United Nations undermines U.S. sovereignty and learn about the devaluation of the dollar, including the abandonment of the gold standard. The curriculum standards emphasize biblical and Judeo-Christian influences on the nation's founders and the benefits of free enterprise, which is mentioned more than eighty times in the curriculum requirements. For more details on controversies surrounding the SBOE, see the *Texas Politics and Public Policy* feature on the following page.

Textbooks The SBOE selects a list of approved textbooks that the state may buy for public school courses, and like the curriculum, the textbook selection process generates intense political battles between conservative groups, such as the Texas Public Policy Foundation and Texas Freedom Works, and liberal groups, such as the Texas Freedom Network. The conservatives have dominated the battle, and some publishers have withdrawn their text offerings or changed the content of their texts to satisfy the SBOE.

Legally, the SBOE can only determine the accuracy of textbooks, but it has used this power to pressure publishers to submit texts that reflect the political and religious values of its members. One publisher eliminated references to "fossil fuels formed millions of years ago" from a science text because that phrase conflicts with the religious belief that the world is only a few thousand years old. Another eliminated sections asserting that Osama bin Laden's actions were inconsistent with commonly accepted Islamic teachings (even though this is the official policy view of the U.S. government).

Faculties Although the state board for educator certification establishes standards for qualification, conduct, and certification of public school teachers, actual hiring of teachers is a local matter. Most districts do not follow a publicly announced policy of hiring or dismissing teachers because of their political viewpoints, but in many districts teachers are carefully screened for their attitudes.

Salary and working conditions are perpetual issues of dissatisfaction among teachers. Increasing public demands for accountability have added reporting and other paperwork to teachers' workloads. Education does not compare favorably among the professions to begin with, and Texas teachers earn less than public school teachers in other states. The National Education Association reported an average salary for Texas teachers of $49,017 in 2011–2012, 13 percent below the national average. One-third of beginning teachers leave the profession by their fifth year.

Teachers have also objected to the practice of basing retention, promotion, and salary decisions on test results. Tests in use include the Texas Assessment of Knowledge and Skills (TAKS), the new State of Texas Assessments of Academic Readiness (STAAR), and the National Assessment of Education Progress ("The Nation's Report Card"). Teachers' groups have objected to the use of these test results on the ground that they do not accurately measure the full range of teachers' contributions to student development. Further, these groups believe that their use causes faculty to "teach to the test," ignoring skills and subjects that are not included in standardized tests.

> **"The activist is not the man who says the river is dirty.** The activist is the man who cleans up the river."
>
> ~ ROSS PEROT ~
> TEXAS BUSINESSMAN

Students The number of students attending Texas public schools has been increasing at a rate of about 2 percent per year, and that increase is expected to continue for the next decade. Texas's students are also becoming more ethnically diverse and are increasingly from low-income backgrounds—50 percent of public school students are Latino, and 13 percent are African American.

The changing student population presents a challenge to the public schools because a significant achievement gap exists between the performance of Anglo students and that of African Americans and Latinos. Scores on standard state performance tests, such as STAAR and TAKS, indicate that the achievement gap is closing. In 2011, however, Anglo pass rates were still 21 percent higher than those of African Americans and 15 percent higher than Latinos' rates.

Public School Finance In 2011–2012, expenditures for current public school operations in Texas amounted to $8,908 per student, 22 percent below the national average. In general, how good are Texas public schools when compared to those of other states? We examine that question in the *How Texas Compares* feature on page 255.

The distribution of school funds is governed by extremely complex rules and mathematical formulas

God, Man, and the State Board of Education

What is taught in the Texas public schools has a major impact on the thinking of future generations of Texans. What, if anything, should be taught in our public schools about the relationship between "God and man" (or in less dated language, "God and humanity")? Did God create humans, or did they evolve from lower life forms? Here, we have one of the most contentious issues in Texas public education.

The Classroom as a Battleground

Right or left, political or not, religious or not, everyone sees the classroom as a battleground in the war to shape children's minds. And, of course, Texas has a school board that probably has more power over curriculum issues than the board in any other state. The fifteen members of the Texas State Board of Education approve what is taught in all Texas public schools. These board members decide which textbooks to buy.

There are national implications for decisions made by the Texas State Board of Education, too. Because Texas is a very large state with centralized adoption and purchase of textbooks, many textbook publishers will try very hard to conform to the standards required in Texas. Because it is expensive to produce alternative versions of textbooks for other states, the majority of states end up using textbooks written for Texas schoolchildren.

Biology as Contested Terrain

Should Charles Darwin's theory of evolution be taught in Texas? Or should the doctrine of creationism be taught alongside Darwin's theory or as the only valid theory? The United States Supreme Court has weighed in repeatedly on this issue. Darwinism is central to modern biological science. Creationism, however, is a religious doctrine that cannot be taught as fact or as an alternative to evolution in the public schools.[2]

Darwin deduced that humans evolved from lower life forms. Creationists argue that a supernatural being created the universe and everything in it. In particular, conservative Christian creationists believe that the *Book of Genesis* is actual fact: God created each species of animal at once, independently of all others. God also created humans to exercise dominion over all other life forms.

A currently popular version of creationism is the theory of intelligent design—considered an alternative to Darwinism. Intelligent design advocates do not explicitly identify the *intelligent designer*, though the term is clearly another name for God. In 2005, a federal judge ruled that intelligent design was a restatement of creationism and that teaching it violated the separation of church and state.[3]

The State Board of Education Has Its Views

Seven members of a Christian conservative voting bloc on the State Board of Education have, over time, attempted to promote creationism by questioning the strength of the evidence for evolution. They argue that fossil records show gaps in evolution. A few years ago, the board successfully voted to require students to "analyze, evaluate, and critique" evolution and other theories, as well as to examine "all sides" of issues in science.

In a more recent battle, the fight over religion moved to the standards for social science textbooks. Some religious conservatives believe that America was created by God to carry out his mission, and that the Declaration of Independence and the Constitution are divinely inspired and based on biblical principles. They also believe that these concepts should be communicated to students.

FOR CRITICAL ANALYSIS Why do most scientists reject the theory of intelligent design? In what ways might such scientists be wrong?

that occupy six chapters and more than 75,000 words in the Texas Education Code. Although public school accountants and financial officers must understand the nuances of these rules to maximize funding for their districts, we need to understand only the system's most basic features to debate public school finance. There are three basic sources of public school funding—federal, state, and local.

HOW TEXAS COMPARES

Ranking Texas Public Schools among the Fifty States

Several indicators are frequently used to measure states' educational efforts and their outcomes, but you should be extremely careful in interpreting the meaning of state rankings among the fifty states.

One measure of resources available to educate students is total state and local expenditure per student: Texas ranks forty-fourth. This statistic, however, fails to take into account the growth rate in student enrollment. Because Texas has one of the fastest-growing school systems in the nation—three times the national average—it must devote a considerable amount of resources to the construction of new physical facilities and the development of new school programs.

The rankings of average teacher salaries are not always fair indicators of educational inputs because they do not take into account large variations in the cost of living from state to state. Nor do state rankings by percentage of adults who have graduated from high school adequately measure public school performance because many Texas residents migrated to the state (and in many cases, to the nation) after their education was completed.

Even comparisons of high school graduation rates are suspect because states currently use different methods of reporting graduation and dropout rates.

Finally, comparisons of SAT scores among the fifty states are questionable because not all students take the test. States in which a large share of students are encouraged to take the test might be expected to have lower average scores than those states where only a select few high-achieving students are tested.

Although no single statistic adequately evaluates the resources and performance of Texas public schools, their consistently low ranking on a variety of measures indicates that they do not compare favorably to public schools in much of the nation. Table 11–3 below shows a series of such measurements.

TABLE 11–3

How Texas Ranks in Education

Measure	Texas's Rank
Population and Resources:	
State and local expenditures per pupil in public schools	44th
Percentage of population under age 18	2nd
Current expenditures per student	38th
Average teacher salary	33rd
Results:	
Percentage of population older than age 25 with high school diploma	50th
High school graduation rate	43rd
Scholastic Aptitude Test (SAT) scores	45th

Source: Data derived from *Texas on the Brink, How Texas Ranks among the 50 States*, 2011, A Report from the Texas Legislative Study Group.

 **FOR CRITICAL ANALYSIS** Is there any way to determine objectively how much spending on education is enough? Is this simply a political decision?

STATE FUNDING. Funding comes from a variety of state sources. The Permanent School Fund was established in 1854. It invests income derived from rentals, sales, and mineral royalties on Texas's public lands. Only the interest and dividends from this permanent endowment may be spent. Earnings from the Permanent School Fund and one-fourth of the motor fuels tax make up the Available School Fund, some of which is used for textbooks. The remainder is distributed to local school districts based on average daily student attendance. Basing distribution of state funds on attendance focuses a school district's attention on truancy.

The Foundation School Program (FSP) accounts for the largest portion of state and local funding by far. State funds from general revenues, a margins tax on business (the franchise tax), and a portion of tobacco taxes are distributed to districts according to formulas based on district and student characteristics. The FSP is structured as a state–local partnership to bring some financial equality to local districts, despite vast differences in local tax resources.

LOCAL FUNDING. Local funding comes primarily from property taxes. The county appraisal authority determines the market value of property for all local governments within the county, and local district boards then set the property tax rate per $100 of property value. Local school district trustees may set the property tax rate for maintenance and operations no higher than $1.17 per $100 valuation.

These property taxes are used to pay about 53 percent of the FSP's basic operating expenses, with the state paying for the remainder. The state supplements local funds to ensure that each district has a basic allotment per student of $4,765 and guarantees that each additional cent in local tax rates above the minimum must yield at least $31.95 per student.

The system of basic allotments and guaranteed yields is designed to provide some financial equity among local school districts. Local revenues from property taxes vary so much among school districts, though, that the state has also been forced to establish certain *recapture* requirements. Richer districts such as those with taxable property of more than $319,000 per student may, under certain circumstances, be required to share their local revenue with poorer districts. They may choose one of several mechanisms to provide aid directly to poorer districts, but most send money to the state for redistribution.

School Finance Reform The current finance system resulted from four decades of struggle, litigation, and failed reform efforts. Because the old state funding system failed to overcome significant inequalities resulting from heavy dependence on local property taxes, a lawsuit attacking the Texas system of educational finance was filed in federal court. Parents of several students in the Edgewood Independent School District in San Antonio charged that funding inequalities violated the Fourteenth Amendment to the U.S. Constitution, which guarantees that no state shall deny any person the equal protection of the laws. Ultimately, the United States Supreme Court declined to strike down Texas's system of school finance because it failed to find a fundamental U.S. constitutional right to equally funded public education.[4]

THE *EDGEWOOD V. KIRBY* CASE. The battle over inequality then shifted to the state level. In 1987, a state district court challenged the funding system under a variety of provisions in the Texas Constitution guaranteeing a suitable and efficient school system. The wealthiest school district had property wealth per student seven hundred times greater than the poorest district, and the court cited numerous other disparities resulting from heavy reliance on local property taxes.

In 1989, the Texas Supreme Court unanimously upheld the lower court decision in *Edgewood v. Kirby* that the funding system was unconstitutional.[5] After a series of aborted attempts and adverse court rulings, the legislature enacted the current system as its best effort at **school finance reform.** Revenues per student now depend primarily on the tax rate (the "tax effort" made by the district). The state guarantees that a particular local property tax rate will produce a specific amount of revenue or the state will make up the difference.

Part of the revenue shifting comes from the recapture requirement that wealthier districts share their revenues with poorer districts. The recapture requirement outraged some parents and school officials, who described the system as "socialistic" or a "Robin Hood" plan that interfered with local control and the right to educate their children.

LINGERING DISPARITIES. Despite the changes, some disparity still exists in revenues per student among school districts. For example, the Dallas Independent School District still has $20,700 more in revenue for a class of twenty students than does the Huntsville Independent School District. Yet, ironically, the poorer school district's students perform better on standard tests.

Despite more equalized revenues, suburban school districts like Plano and Alamo Heights continue to have far more students passing TAKS than do urban school districts such as Dallas and Houston, which include the largest share of minority students and those from economically disadvantaged families. Table 11–4 on the facing page shows that students' TAKS scores—and the factors sometimes thought to

school finance reform
Changes in the public school financial system resulting from a Texas Supreme Court ruling that significant inequality in school financial resources violated the state constitution.

TABLE 11–4

Selected Texas School District Profiles

This sample of school district profiles is arranged by size of enrollment. Column 6 shows that some financial inequity remains among school districts. Reviewing Columns 5 and 6, you will notice that there is little relationship between the percentage of students meeting the TAKS standard and district revenues per student. Now look at Columns 3 and 4 to see if the percentage of minority students or economically disadvantaged students relates to the TAKS scores in Column 5.

1. School District	2. Enrollment	3. Percentage Minority	4. Percentage Economically Disadvantaged	5. Percentage Meeting 2011 TAKS Standard	6. Revenue per Student
Houston I.S.D.	203,294	92.2%	80.6%	73%	$ 7,701
Dallas I.S.D.	156,784	95.4	87.1	67	8,101
Plano I.S.D.	55,294	55.8	24.6	88	7,670
Edgewood I.S.D.	11,904	99.5	92.6	59	8,293
Huntsville I.S.D.	6,243	57.1	62.1	71	7,066
Alamo Heights I.S.D.	4,744	40.6	22.4	87	8,206
West Orange-Cove I.S.D.	2,529	74.7	84.9	53	7,609
Wink-Loving I.S.D.	356	41.0	34.3	77	15,728
Statewide	4,912,385	68.8	59.2	76	10,328

Source: Texas Education Agency, *Academic Excellence Indicator System, 2010–11.*

affect them—vary dramatically from district to district in Texas. Besides per-student revenues, ethnicity and family incomes are major variables that seem to determine public school outcomes.

School Privatization Adjustments to the school funding system will continue indefinitely. Among recent proposals for school finance changes are various voucher plans to use public funds to enable students to attend private and parochial schools. We discussed the voucher proposal in the chapter-opening *Texans in Conflict* feature.

Short of vouchers for students to attend private schools, several programs offer school choice and foster competitiveness within the public school system. Local school districts have established magnet schools. Charter schools and district home rule are also available options. Opponents of such innovations can point to research indicating that, on average, students perform no better in private schools than they do in public schools.

11–3c Higher Education

Like public schools, higher education is a major state service, accounting for 12 percent of state expenditure during the 2012–2013 budget period. Figure 11–5

on the following page shows that public institutions enroll 90 percent of all students in Texas higher education. These institutions include thirty-eight general academic institutions and universities, nine health-related institutions, and one technical college with four campuses. Fifty public community college districts operate more than eighty campuses.

Administration of Colleges and Universities

The Texas Higher Education Coordinating Board (THECB) was established in 1998 to coordinate the complex system of higher education in Texas. Its eighteen members are appointed by the governor with the advice and consent of the senate, and they serve six-year terms. The board appoints a commissioner of higher education to supervise its staff. Together, the board and staff outline the role of each public college and university, and plan future needs for programs, curricula, and physical plants.

UNIVERSITY SYSTEMS IN TEXAS. Boards of regents or trustees set basic policies for their institutions, within the limits of state law and the rules and guidelines established by the THECB. These governing boards provide for the selection of public university administrators, including systemwide administrators to state universities under the **top 10 percent rule** than under traditional admission criteria. As of 2011, however, only 75 percent of those who enter the University of Texas at Austin are admitted through the top 10 percent rule, which in practice has turned the program into a top 8 percent rule for that campus.

In 2003, the United States Supreme Court overturned the Fifth Circuit Court's ruling and again allowed race to be considered in college admissions policies under limited circumstances.[8] Administrators at the University of Texas at Austin therefore reestablished affirmative action policies for the 25 percent of incoming students not covered by the 10 (really 8) percent rule. The Supreme Court was scheduled to rule on the constitutionality of the university's current affirmative action program during its 2012–2013 term.[9]

FOR CRITICAL THINKING

Have decisions by the Texas state legislature affected your college experience or the experiences of your friends or relatives? If so, how?

11–4 Health and Human Services

The second-most costly category of state spending is health and human services. These programs include Medicaid, public assistance, and a variety of other programs. In 2012–2013, these programs cost $55.4 billion, or 31.9 percent of the state's total budget. About 60 percent of this funding

LearningOutcome 11–4

Provide details about major health and human services policies in Texas, including Medicaid, the new Affordable Care Act, unemployment insurance, and cash welfare.

originates as grants from the federal government.

Figure 11–7 on the facing page shows that the Texas Health and Human Services Commission

provides a variety of social services, including Medicaid, the Children's Health Insurance Program (CHIP), and Temporary Assistance to Needy Families (TANF). The commission also coordinates planning, rule making, and budgeting among its four subsidiary social-service agencies: the Department of Aging and Disability Services, the Department of Assistive and Rehabilitative Services, the Department of Family and Protective Services, and the Department of State Health Services.

11–4a Private-Sector Health Insurance

Nationally, about 56 percent of the nonelderly are covered by employment-based insurance, whereas only 49 percent have employment-based health insurance in Texas. Texas ranks forty-third among states, including the District of Columbia, in the percentage of people with employer-sponsored insurance.

In 2012, one of every six Americans and one in four Texans had no health-insurance coverage. Texas had the nation's highest percentage of uninsured residents. In 2010, about 6.1 million Texans, or 25 percent of the state's nonelderly population, were uninsured, including more than one in six Texas children.

Employer-Based Health Insurance Although about 19 percent of nonelderly Texans have some sort of public insurance coverage such as Medicaid or CHIP, most others rely on private insurance companies to pay for their medical expenses. As noted, employer-sponsored plans cover 49 percent of Texans. Private individual policies cover 4 percent. The state itself pays private insurance companies for part of the premiums for its employees and teachers.

As a result, businesses, government, and individuals have been seriously affected by health-insurance premiums that have skyrocketed. Between 2001 and 2010, premiums across the nation rose by an average of 104 percent. By 2010, the average health-insurance premium cost for employer-sponsored family coverage in Texas was $14,526, somewhat above the national average.[10] High premium costs have caused some businesses to drop coverage for their employees, and many individuals have chosen not to buy private coverage, leaving Texas as the state with the largest share of uninsured persons in the nation.

The Uninsured Population The fact that many Texans are uninsured poses problems for individuals,

FIGURE 11-7

Texas Health and Human Services Agencies

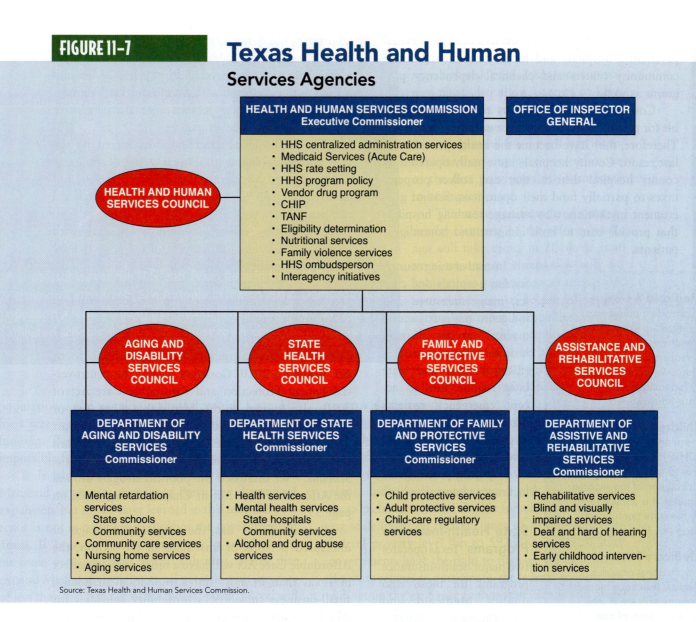

Source: Texas Health and Human Services Commission.

businesses, and state and local governments, which bear extra costs to pay for uncompensated care. Medical providers of all types have been forced to raise fees for paying patients to cover losses resulting from unpaid medical services to the uninsured.

Costs that are not reimbursed are passed on to Texans in the form of higher taxes and insurance premiums. In 2005, Texas's insured families spent an extra $1,551 in premiums to cover the unpaid health-care bills of the uninsured. Meanwhile, rising premiums have caused private employers to drop employee insurance coverage altogether, thereby compounding the problem.[11]

11-4b Government Health Programs

While some oppose government involvement in providing health care, such involvement has existed for a very long time. In the United States, the federal government began to provide hospital care to non-government sailors in 1798. Today, health care has evolved into a growing public–private partnership.

The state has three levels of involvement in health care: (1) In some instances, the state is the direct provider of health services to special populations. Prison inmates are one example. (2) In other instances, the state is the payer but not the provider. Medicaid, for example, pays for medical services provided by private practitioners. (3) The state also acts as a regulator and buyer of private health insurance.

Direct Health Services Texas's Department of Health Services provides personal health services for special populations. For example, the health department operates a lung and tuberculosis hospital in San Antonio and a general services hospital in Harlingen.

STUDY TOOLS

Ready to study?

- Review what you've read with the quiz below. Check your answers on the Chapter in Review card at the back of the book. For any questions you miss, read the corresponding Learning Outcome section again to prepare for class and your exam.
- Rip out and study the Chapter in Review card.

. . . Or you can go online to CourseMate

at www.cengagebrain.com for these additional review materials:

- Practice Quizzes
- Key Term Flashcards or Crossword Puzzles
- Audio Summaries
- Simulations, Animated Learning Modules, and Interactive Timelines
- Videos
- American Government NewsWatch

Quiz

1. "The majority of Texas state revenues come from federal funding."
   a. true   b. false

2. The major sources of revenue for the state government in Texas are:
   a. sales taxes.
   b. severance taxes.
   c. income taxes.

3. A tax that places a heavier burden on low- and middle-income taxpayers than on wealthier ones is called a _____ tax.
   a. progressive
   b. regressive
   c. neutral

4. Which of the following absorbs the greatest amount of state government spending in Texas?
   a. transportation
   b. public safety and criminal justice
   c. education

5. The process by which individual legislators trade votes among themselves to fund local projects that benefit their constituents is called _____.
   a. tagging   b. logrolling   c. appropriations

6. Compared to the federal government and most other states, Texas carries:
   a. more debt per capita.
   b. about the same debt per capita.
   c. less debt per capita.

7. Which agency is the highest authority for K–12 public education in the state of Texas?
   a. Texas Education Agency
   b. State Board of Education
   c. Parent-Teacher Association

8. A student must be in the top _____ percent of his or her high school class to be automatically accepted to a public university or college in Texas.
   a. 5   b. 10   c. 20

9. _____ has/have been a persistent theme in the politics of the K–12 academic curriculum.
   a. Culture wars
   b. Math competency
   c. Literacy

10. What is the difference between a welfare program and a social-insurance program?
    a. Welfare programs require recipients to pay in to receive benefits and are not means tested.
    b. Social-insurance programs require recipients to pay in to receive benefits and are not means tested.
    c. Welfare programs do not require recipients to pay in to receive benefits and are not means tested.

11. Which of the following is a health-care program that helps insure children of parents with incomes less than 20 percent of the poverty rate who do not qualify for Medicaid?
    a. TANF   b. CHIP   c. Medicare

12. What feature does NOT characterize the Affordable Care Act of 2010?
    a. a phased-in federal monopoly on the provision of health care
    b. incentives to expand Medicaid coverage
    c. a prohibition against insurance companies denying coverage to children with preexisting conditions

13. Unemployment insurance:
    a. typically provides benefits for only twenty-six weeks.
    b. is based on need rather than previous earnings.
    c. is funded by an income tax on individuals.

14. Which of the following lists of state functions is in order from most expensive to least expensive?
    a. health care, transportation, education
    b. transportation, education, health care
    c. education, health care, transportation

15. "Texas has been one of the more aggressive states in adopting mass transit and stricter rules concerning pollution and fuel efficiency for automobiles."
    a. true   b. false

Local Government

AARON M. SPRECHER/BLOOMBERG/GETTY IMAGES

★ Learning Outcomes

The **Learning Outcomes** labeled 1 through 5 are designed to help improve your understanding of the chapter. After reading this chapter, you should be able to:

12–1 List the various types of local government in Texas.

12–2 Explain the different ways in which municipalities are organized and how they conduct elections.

12–3 Discuss the property tax as a source of municipal revenue, and evaluate controversies surrounding economic development, unfunded mandates, and annexation.

12–4 Identify the major county officials, and describe the issues resulting from the ways in which counties are organized.

12–5 Consider the uses of special districts and the danger that voters will not be able to monitor them effectively.

Remember to visit page 291 for additional Study Tools

CONFLICT

Should Texas Public Schools Require Uniforms?

Individuality reigns in the decisions that young people have made for the last few generations, especially when it comes to how they dress. This can create problems—some kids pressure their less-than-rich parents to buy them $300 sneakers. Other teenagers take part-time jobs that interfere with their schoolwork, just to buy the latest designs in clothes and shoes.

Most schools, even public ones, have at least a simple dress code. Some do not allow students to wear shorts. Others have restrictions on how low jeans can hang. Still others restrict how short girls' skirts can be. Imposing school uniforms on public school children is the most rigorous form of dress code. Private schools can easily establish dress codes, and many of them do require uniforms, especially for younger students. A broad-based uniform requirement in a public school district is another matter.

How effective is a school uniform requirement in improving student performance and reducing negative behavior? Even the experts disagree.

Stop the Insane Clothing Competition

Proponents of school uniforms argue that today's young people experience too much competitive pressure to dress well. School uniforms, in contrast, create a sense of social equality among all students. Someone from a poor family will not stand out in the crowd when all students are wearing the same uniform, and wealthier students cannot display their good fortune. Students and teachers are less likely to form personal biases when everyone dresses alike. Uniforms are also less expensive than the latest, trendiest clothes.

School uniforms also build team spirit. Whenever students wear uniforms in public, they necessarily represent their school. This fact by itself can affect student behavior. Uniforms create a sense of discipline and purpose.

Studies at some public schools have found that when uniforms are required, discipline problems are reduced. Other studies suggest that school uniforms encourage a stronger work ethic, because students are more aware of the roles they are expected to play while in uniform.

Just because many students dislike uniforms does not mean that a school uniform policy is not for the best. A number of schools in Dallas and Houston require uniforms, and both Lubbock and Midland have recently considered the concept.

Isn't This a Free Country?

No government in the United States ought to be able to tell its citizens how to dress. If parents want to send their children to private schools that require uniforms, that is their right. A public school system should not have such a policy. According to Dr. Alan Hilfer of Maimonides Medical Center in Brooklyn, "Clothes are a source of expression for children, and as kids get older, they become increasingly resentful of uniforms." Uniform policies violate students' right to free expression. If everyone wears the same uniform, students are less able to engage in self-discovery.

School uniforms can also create a false sense of security. It is a fine ideal that students should be respected for their speech, behavior, and actions, rather than how they look. But what happens when these students enter the real world? People are, in fact, judged on their appearance.

Studies have shown no correlation between the implementation of school uniform policies and improved academic outcomes. In some cases, there may actually be a negative correlation between the use of uniforms and disciplinary problems. The spirit that underlies uniform requirements can also push school administrators toward zero-tolerance policies, under which students are disciplined for any rule infraction, no matter how minor.

Where do you stand?

1. Does a public school district have the right to impose a uniform policy on its students? Why or why not?
2. Would you have been better off in high school had you been required to wear a uniform? Why or why not?

Explore this issue online

- You will find plenty of debates on school uniforms by entering "school uniforms pro con" into an Internet search engine.
- Dress codes, as opposed to full uniforms, may not do very much to discourage certain clothing display, as you can see if you search on "dress code swag texas" and watch the videos.

Introduction

Should a city place red-light cameras at high-traffic intersections? Or pass antiloitering laws to curb the presence of the homeless? Or make it a crime for landlords to rent to undocumented immigrants? How should counties provide for mentally ill prisoners or fund the burial of indigents with no known next of kin? These issues are just a few that have been placed on the agendas of local governments throughout the nation, including Texas.

12–1 Types of Local Government

Local governments are primarily responsible for law enforcement, mass transit, sewage treatment, flood control, and emergency services. Many issues that are nationwide in scope, such as reducing traffic fatalities, homelessness, immigration, mental health, and poverty, also have an important local dimension.

> ★ **LearningOutcome 12–1**
> List the various types of local government in Texas.

12–1a The Number and Types of Local Governments

The sheer number of local governments across Texas and the rest of the nation can challenge even the most interested members of a community who want to contact local officials occasionally or on a routine basis. Pressing concerns might range from the need for better street lighting and more police to an increase in the number of homeless families. See Table 12–1 below for a comparison of local governments in Texas and in the United States as a whole.

Anyone who lives in a metropolitan area is likely to be governed by two **general-purpose governments**—a municipal and a county government—which provide a wide range of public services. In addition, numerous *special districts* exist, such as school districts, hospital districts, metropolitan transit authorities, and municipal utility districts. A special district is a limited-purpose local government that provides a narrow range of services not provided by general-purpose local governments. Examples of special districts include municipal utility districts, hospital authorities, and transit authorities.

12–1b Popular Attitudes toward Local Government

According to the Pew Research Center, the American public has a more positive view of local governments than of the national and state governments. Also, more than 70 percent of the public "follow local news closely."[1] Although information about local governments is available in a variety of print and electronic media, adequately covering thousands of local governments is no small challenge. Political scientist Doris A. Graber has observed that when it comes to local media, "Reporting, of necessity, becomes highly selective and superficial."[2]

Nor can the public always depend on political parties to provide information and generate interest about local governments. In Texas, political parties do not nominate candidates below the county level. Municipal and special district elections are nonpartisan—that is, no mention of party affiliation is placed on the ballot. It is not surprising that in the absence of party labels, voter turnout tends to be low in municipal and special district elections.

In an effort to shed more light on the inner workings of local government, the following sections examine the various institutional features of cities, counties, and special districts. We also look at issues and trends facing local government. Finally, given the growing interest in finding regional solutions to local problems, we discuss the role of councils of government (COGs) at the local level.

TABLE 12–1

Local Governments and Public School Systems, United States and Texas, 2007

	Total	County	Municipal	Township or Other	Special Districts	School Districts
United States	89,476	3,033	19,492	16,519	37,381	13,051
Texas	4,835	254	1,209	0	2,291	1,081

Source: U.S. Census Bureau, "2007 Census of Governments."

> **general-purpose government** A municipal or county government that provides a wide range of public services.

12–2 Municipalities

Cities hire police and fire fighters to protect the community. Cities also enforce building and safety codes, pass anti-litter ordinances, issue garage sale permits, maintain recycling programs, launch anti-graffiti programs, impound stray animals for the safety of the community, and enforce curfews. These are just a few examples of how cities routinely affect our day-to-day lives.

LearningOutcome 12–2

Explain the different ways in which municipalities are organized and how they conduct elections.

Cities also become involved in high-profile, controversial issues. For example, in 2012 the U.S. Fifth Circuit Court of Appeals struck down an ordinance passed in a Dallas suburb, Farmers Branch, that banned the rental of apartments to illegal immigrants.[3] In 2010, Arizona passed a controversial state law that required police officers who stopped individuals for lawful reasons to check their immigration status if they suspected the individuals were in the country illegally. In reaction to the Arizona law, the Austin City Council passed a resolution banning (with some exceptions) city employee trips to Arizona and official business dealings with the state.

general-law city A city, usually with a population of five thousand or fewer, with a structure and organization prescribed and limited by state law.

home-rule city A city with a population greater than five thousand that has exercised its legal option to write its own charter using any organizational structure that complies with state law.

charter The organizing document for a corporation or a municipality.

12–2a Cities and the State

All local governments are bound by federal and state laws as well as the constitutions of the United States and Texas. The relationship between state and local governments follows from the fact that states, including Texas, have a *unitary system of government* (see Chapter 2). Municipalities—like counties, special districts, and school districts—are creatures of the state and have only as much power as the Texas Constitution and the Texas legislature grant them.

Texas has seen a marked increase in the number of municipalities in the state since the 1950s (see Table 12–2 below).

12–2b General-Law and Home-Rule Cities

Texas cities are classified as either general-law or home-rule cities. A **general-law city** is an incorporated community, usually with a population of five thousand or fewer, with a structure and organization prescribed and limited by state law. A city with a population of more than five thousand may, by majority vote, become a **home-rule city.** This means that it can adopt its own **charter** and structure its local government as it sees fit, so long as charter provisions and local laws (also called *ordinances*) do not violate national and state constitutions and laws.

The Texas Constitution allows a home-rule city whose population has dropped to five thousand or less to retain its home-rule designation. According to the Texas Municipal League, the majority of Texas cities—about 75 percent—are general-law cities.

Direct Democracy at the Municipal Level Home rule permits local voters to impose their will directly on government through initiative, referendum, and recall, and most home-rule cities have all three provisions. With the *initiative* power, after a campaign obtains a designated percentage of signatures of registered voters, it can force a sometimes-reluctant city council to place a proposed ordinance on the ballot. If the proposal passes with a majority vote, it becomes law. Texas cities have used initiatives to resolve the following issues:

- Should the city allow stores within the city limits to sell beer and wine?

TABLE 12–2

Municipal Governments in Texas, 1952–2007

1952	1962	1972	1982	1992	2002	2007
738	866	981	1,121	1,171	1,196	1,209

Sources: U.S. Census Bureau, "2002 Census of Governments"; and U.S. Census Bureau, "2007 Census of Governments."

- Should the city freeze the property tax exemption for senior citizens and people with disabilities?
- Should the city increase the local minimum wage?
- Should the city impose a cap on the property tax rate?

A *referendum* is similar to an initiative, but the measure in question is placed on the ballot by the legislative authority, not through a signature drive. Voters who want to remove an existing ordinance could petition the council to hold a referendum to determine whether the law should remain in effect. For example, College Station and Houston voters approved removing red-light cameras from intersections through referendum votes. Smoking bans were put on the ballot in Lubbock and Baytown. In both cases, voters decided to retain the ban. Finally, voters can, by petition, force the council to hold a **recall election** that would permit voters to remove the mayor, a member of the council, or any other elected municipal official.

The Limits of Home Rule Although home-rule cities have wider latitude than general-law cities in organizing their day-to-day operations, they must still contend with state limitations on their authority. For example, state law determines the specific dates on which municipal elections can be held. Voters are free to amend city charters, but the Texas Constitution permits cities to hold charter elections only every two years. An election establishing a metropolitan transit authority can be held only in cities that meet a population requirement determined by the Texas legislature.

Local governments in Texas are subject to "sunshine" laws, such as the Public Information Act and the Open Meetings Act. Because Texas is covered under the "pre-clearance" requirement of the federal Voting Rights Act, all state and local election law changes must first be approved by the U.S. Justice Department or a federal district court in Washington, D.C.

> **"Texas may be the one place where people actually still have bootstraps,**
> and we expect folks to pull themselves up by them."
>
> ~ JULIAN CASTRO ~
> MAYOR OF SAN ANTONIO

12–2c Forms of Government

The three most common forms of municipal government are the council-manager, mayor-council, and commission systems.

The Council-Manager System In a **council-manager system,** an elected city council makes laws and hires a professional administrator who is responsible for both executing council policies and managing the day-to-day operations of city government. The administrator serves at the pleasure of the council (see Figure 12–1 on the following page).

ORIGINS OF THE COUNCIL-MANAGER SYSTEM. The council-manager system was initiated as a reform during the Progressive Era (1900–1917). Reformers were attempting to substitute "efficient and businesslike management" for the then-prevalent system of boss rule, in which politics was the key consideration in city hall decisions. The council-manager system was seen as a means of separating politics from the administration of city government. Critics charge, however, that voters are shortchanged when they do not directly elect the chief executive officer of the city.

THE POWERS OF THE CITY MANAGER. The powers of the city manager come from the city charter and from the council's delegation of authority through direct assignment and passage of ordinances. For example, the city manager is responsible for selecting key personnel and for submitting a proposed budget to the council for its approval. The city council will likely seek the manager's opinion on a wide variety of matters, including what tax rate the city should adopt, whether or not the city should call a bond election, and the feasibility of recommendations made by interest groups.

Texas Political SOCIAL MEDIA

Texas cities ranging from Killeen to College Station have Facebook pages with information about local activities. Sometimes, though, the right Facebook page is a little hard to track down. For Dallas, try "dallas city hall." For Houston, search on "houston mayor."

recall election An election, called by citizen petition, that permits voters to remove an elected official before the official's term expires.

council-manager system A form of government that features an elected city council and a city manager who is hired by the council. The council makes policy decisions, and the city manager is responsible for the day-to-day operations of the city government.

FIGURE 12-1

Common Forms
of Municipal Government

Council-Manager Form

Voters

City Council

City Manager

Mayor

Departments

Strong Mayor–Council Form

Voters

Mayor

Council

Appoints with approval of the council

Department Heads

Commission Form

Voters

City Commission

Departments

Weak Mayor–Council Form

Voters

Council

Mayor

Other officials

Departments

---

council-manager system. Two former mayors of these cities—Henry Cisneros of San Antonio and Ron Kirk of Dallas—went on to become members of the federal cabinet.

The Mayor-Council System
Although most Texas cities now use a council-manager system, a few, including Houston and Pasadena, use a **mayor-council system** to govern their cities. The mayor-council system has many variations, which are generally classified according to the relative power of their mayors. These variations include the strong-mayor form and the weak-mayor form.

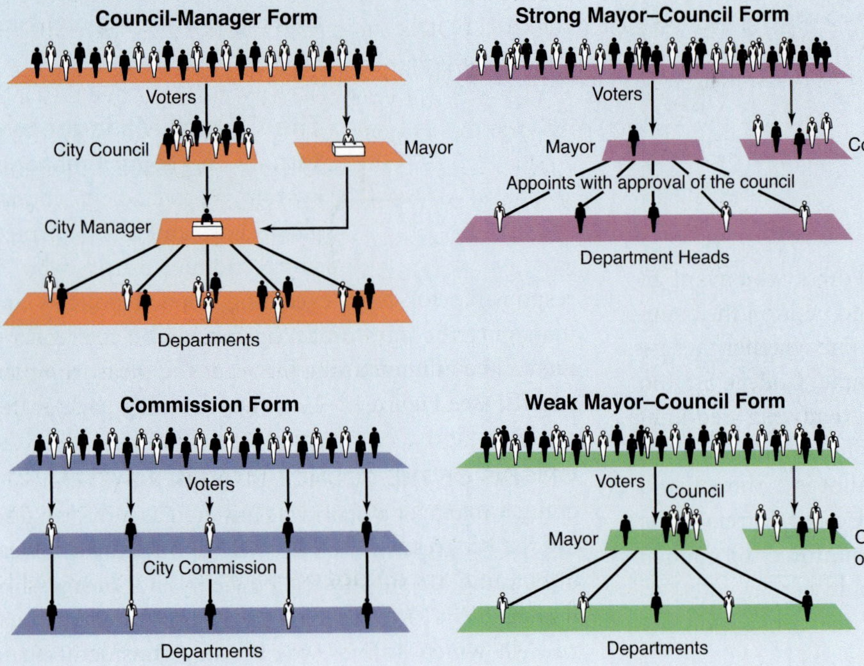

But these issues are ultimately up to the council, and the city manager is expected to implement whatever decisions the council makes.

THE ROLE OF THE MAYOR. In a council-manager form of government, the mayor may be either selected by the council from among its members or independently elected by the voters. The mayor presides over council meetings, has limited or no veto power, and has for the most part only the same legislative authority as members of the council.

The mayor also has important ceremonial powers, such as signing proclamations and issuing keys to the city to important dignitaries. Although the office is institutionally weak, a high-profile mayor can still wield considerable political influence, even under the council-manager system. San Antonio and Dallas both use the

mayor-council system
A form of municipal government consisting of a mayor and a city council. This form includes both strong-mayor and weak-mayor variations.

strong-mayor form
A form of municipal government in which substantial authority over appointments and budgets is lodged in the mayor's office. The mayor is elected by voters in a citywide election.

THE STRONG-MAYOR FORM. In the **strong-mayor form** (see Figure 12–1 above), the mayor, who is chosen in a citywide election, is both the chief executive and the leader of the city council. She or he makes appointments, prepares the budget, and is responsible for the management of city government. The mayor also sets the council agenda, proposes policy, and in many cities may veto council actions.

Critics of the strong-mayor form fear that it makes the office too powerful. The mayor may act out of political motives rather than distributing services fairly and efficiently. This system conjures up the image of nineteenth-century urban political machines led by mayors who appointed political cronies as department heads, hired campaign workers as city employees, and awarded contracts to supporters.

The old-fashioned strong-mayor form of government did not die out, but it was often restructured to include an independently elected city comptroller (or controller), who serves as a check on the mayor. Houston, for example, elects a city controller who serves as the chief financial officer for the city. Rules were also adopted to require that contracts be awarded to the lowest satisfactory bidder. Other restrictions on

AP PHOTO/DAVID J. PHILIP

Houston mayor Annise Danette Parker.

this form that are in place today include nonpartisan elections and ethics and campaign-finance laws.

THE WEAK-MAYOR FORM. The **weak-mayor form** (see Figure 12–1 on the facing page) lacks unified lines of authority because the mayor and council share administrative authority. Power is, in effect, decentralized. It is difficult, however, for voters to know which officials to hold accountable when problems and mismanagement occur. This type of government is usually found in small cities and is not common in Texas.

The Commission System

The **commission system** (see Figure 12–1 on page 274) is another approach to running a city. In this form of government, voters elect one set of officials who act as both executives and legislators. Together, the commissioners are the municipal legislature, but individually, each administers a city department. A manager or administrative assistant may be employed to assist the commissioners, but ultimate administrative authority still remains with the elected commissioners.

Commissioners may possess technical knowledge about city government because they supervise city departments. Coordination is difficult, however, because power in the city bureaucracy is fragmented among separately elected commissioners. Likewise, the checks-and-balances system is impaired because commissioners serve both legislative and executive functions—commissioners adopt the budget for the departments that they administer.

Mayors and city council members are usually elected for terms according to the city charter, usually two years. Municipal elections are scheduled at a different time from the state general elections. Election rules usually require that candidates receive a majority of the vote. If no candidate receives more than 50 percent of the vote, a runoff election is required.

Cities have employed a number of strategies in an attempt to guarantee fair and honest elections. Public financing of campaigns is one such plan, and we describe it in the *How Texas Compares* feature on the following page. Another strategy is to hold nonpartisan elections.

Nonpartisan Elections In Texas, all city elections are *nonpartisan*, meaning that parties do not nominate candidates or officially campaign for them. Advocates of nonpartisan elections contend that municipal issues transcend traditional party divisions and that party labels are irrelevant. They argue that the two parties are overly polarized and that qualified candidates should not be excluded simply because they belong to the minority party.

Several other states use partisan elections to select city officials. Supporters of partisan elections argue that party labels provide voters with useful cues as to how a candidate will govern. In nonpartisan elections, voters often take their cues from well-financed campaigns or from the ethnicity of the candidates. Parties are useful because they help narrow the field of potential candidates. Dozens of candidates sometimes clutter Texas municipal election ballots. Parties mobilize more voters and generate greater public interest than do nonpartisan campaigns. Critics of nonpartisan elections argue that they are dominated by low-visibility special interests. These interests may have much to gain from city contracts and have enough money to flood the airwaves with campaign ads.

While all municipal elections are nonpartisan in Texas, cities have the choice to use an at-large or a single-member district system—a choice that has generated considerable legal and political controversy.

weak-mayor form
A form of municipal government in which an elected mayor and city council share administrative responsibilities, often with other elected officers.

commission system
A form of government in which individual members of the commission head city departments and collectively act as a city council to pass ordinances.

FIGURE 12-3

Cities and Counties Served
by Public Transportation Systems

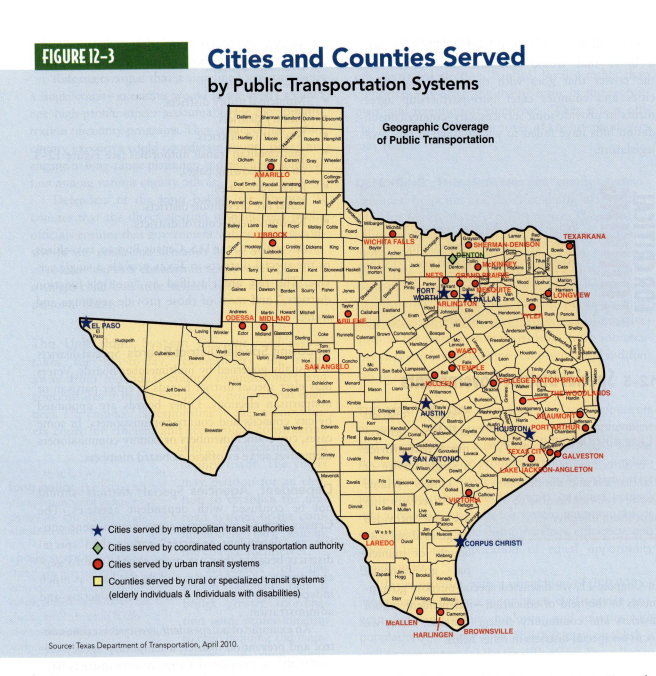

Geographic Coverage of Public Transportation

★ Cities served by metropolitan transit authorities
◆ Cities served by coordinated county transportation authority
● Cities served by urban transit systems
▢ Counties served by rural or specialized transit systems (elderly individuals & Individuals with disabilities)

Source: Texas Department of Transportation, April 2010.

12–5b Reasons for Creating Special District Governments

Providing a service through a special district rather than a general-purpose government is appealing to many residents for a variety of reasons. A city or county may have limited revenue because of a downturn in the economy, the loss of a major industry, unfunded mandates, or fewer federal dollars. The general-purpose government may have reached its state-mandated sales tax ceiling of 2 percent.

Only a small area within a city or county may need the service. Why tax the entire jurisdiction? A district may be created for the benefit of "underserved areas," as is the case with library districts in Texas that serve rural and suburban areas.

The demand for a service may also extend beyond a single jurisdiction, calling for a special district that is multicity or multicounty in scope. For example, a river authority with the power to govern the use of water throughout the river's watershed will need to transcend existing political boundaries. Likewise, flood control districts deal with a problem that crosses conventional political boundaries.

Municipal utilities districts (MUDs) are often created at the insistence of developers who want to provide water and sewerage for the subdivisions they establish outside city service areas. Special districts are an attractive option as an alternative revenue source.

12–5c Issues and Trends

Although special districts provide valuable public services not provided by general-purpose governments, reformers charge that they are often too small to be efficient, too low profile to be visible to the public, and too numerous to be readily held accountable by voters.

Multiple Governments

Although special districts can be dissolved when a municipality annexes the area and provides it with services, the trend in Texas and across the rest of the nation has been toward the proliferation of special district governments. The sheer number of special district governments and their small size create serious challenges.

Hidden Governments

Special districts are sometimes called *hidden governments,* because the actions of district officials and employees are less visible than if a county or city provided the services. When special district elections are held at times or places other than those for general elections, voter turnout is quite low.

The Cost of Borrowing

Because special districts are often small, they may purchase goods and services in limited quantities, paying higher prices than larger governments. In addition, if special districts have little or no authority to tax, they are forced to borrow money by issuing *revenue bonds.* These bonds are paid from fees collected for the service provided. *General-obligation bonds,* in contrast, are paid from tax revenue.

Investors consider revenue bonds to be less safe than general-obligation bonds. A proposed project may fail to pay for itself. It can then become impossible for the district to repay the bond. General-obligation bonds backed by governmental taxing power are more secure.

As a result, residents of special districts that issue revenue bonds are forced to pay higher interest rates just to service the bonded indebtedness. Even when special districts issue general-obligation bonds, these bonds may receive a lower rating than those of larger, general-function governments. Low ratings also increase borrowing costs.

Inefficiency

A study of special-purpose governments in more than three hundred U.S. metropolitan areas concluded that the special district approach to governing is more costly than the general-purpose approach. Moreover, social welfare functions—such as hospitals, housing, and welfare—tend to receive more funding in metropolitan areas with fewer special districts. Housekeeping functions such as fire protection, natural resources, and police protection tend to receive more funding when special districts are more common. The same is true of development functions that include airports, water, and highways.[7]

As an alternative to inefficient special districts, reformers advocate consolidation of small special districts into larger ones. The need for special districts can also be reduced by transferring their functions to general-purpose governments. Finally, reformers urge general-purpose governments to negotiate inter-local agreements to deal with problems that transcend city and county boundaries.

12–5d Councils of Government

Councils of government (COGs) are not governments. Instead, they are voluntary regional groupings of local governments that attempt to coordinate government activities and share information. Encompassing all parts of the state, twenty-four Texas COG regions focus on such major issues as homeland security, economic development, aging, emergency communications and preparedness, and environmental quality.

By bringing local officials together, COGs provide a base for the exchange of ideas and knowledge. Although COGs do not solve the problems that local governments face, they do encourage local officials to recognize the magnitude of these problems and cooperate to manage some of them.

FOR CRITICAL THINKING *Would consolidation of larger cities and counties promote efficiency, or would it instead create government behemoths that are remote from the citizenry? Explain your thinking.*

CONFLICT Local Government

Many questions of interest to Texans are, in fact, local ones. The police or sheriff's department, the public schools, even trash collection—all are local responsibilities. It is common for voters to pay much less attention to local governments than to the state and especially the national governments. But if you have a local concern, it is often much easier to get something done about it than it would be at the state or national level. Does a local intersection need a stop sign? Are local ordinances too hard on the homeless? Do municipal garbage trucks refuse to pick up cat litter? You may be able to get results on such issues. Local issues can also divide Texans, of course. Some of the broader issues of local governance follow:

- Is heavy reliance on the property tax a way to ensure sound local financing—or is it an unfair burden on the citizenry?
- Are the relatively permissive annexation laws in Texas a boon to rational governance—or a threat to local democracy?
- Should Texas counties be allowed to enjoy home rule—or would such a step create more problems than it would solve?
- Is the long ballot an expression of democracy—or does it merely shield elected officials from accountability?

TAKE ACTION

- Attend a city council meeting or a county commissioners court meeting. Sign up to speak during the time set aside for public comments. Let city or county officials know what improvements you think can be made in your community.
- Participate in a local campaign. Candidates need volunteers to help organize campaign rallies and get-out-the-vote drives, stuff envelopes with campaign literature, work phone banks, and pass out campaign literature. You will find the names of city council candidates listed on the election

ballot at the official Web sites of Texas cities. For county elections, you will find the candidates by going to the official Web sites of county governments.

- Apply for membership on a city advisory board or commission. Go to your city's official Web site and check out the many boards and commissions that offer you the chance to advise the city council and city officials on matters of importance to your community, such as health, education, transportation, housing, and ethics.

STUDY TOOLS

Ready to study?

- Review what you've read with the quiz below. Check your answers on the Chapter in Review card at the back of the book. For any questions you miss, read the corresponding Learning Outcome section again to prepare for class and your exam.
- Rip out and study the Chapter in Review card.

. . . Or you can go online to CourseMate

at www.cengagebrain.com for these additional review materials:

- Practice Quizzes
- Key Term Flashcards or Crossword Puzzles
- Audio Summaries
- Simulations, Animated Learning Modules, and Interactive Timelines
- Videos
- American Government NewsWatch

Quiz

1. Which political party holds the overwhelming majority of elected municipal (city) offices in Texas?
   a. Democratic Party
   b. Republican Party
   c. Elections for municipal public office are nonpartisan.

2. What are the three major types of local governments in Texas?
   a. county, municipal, and special district
   b. federal, municipal, and special district
   c. state, county, and municipal

3. Local government is _____.
   a. more popular than federal or state government in American public opinion
   b. about as popular as federal or state government in American public opinion
   c. less popular than federal or state government in American public opinion

4. A city with a population of more than 5,000 is eligible to become what kind of city under the Texas Constitution?
   a. a general-law city
   b. a home-rule city
   c. a special district city

5. The form of municipal government that includes an elected city council that makes laws and hires a professional administrator who is responsible for both executing council policies and managing the day-to-day operations of city government is the _____.
   a. mayor-council system
   b. strong-mayor system
   c. council-manager system

6. A major criticism of at-large elections is that they:
   a. require cumulative voting.
   b. do not adequately promote diverse representation and minority viewpoints.
   c. require term limits.

7. Which of the following is NOT an important source of municipal revenue?
   a. sales tax
   b. property tax
   c. income tax

8. When the federal or state government imposes a requirement that a lower level of government, such as a county or city, provide a certain service but does not provide funding, it has imposed:
   a. a mandate.
   b. an unfunded mandate.
   c. a direct regulation.

9. Which of the following is commonly used by cities to promote economic development and attract businesses and jobs?
   a. mandates   b. public debt   c. tax abatement

10. All of the following are criticisms of the Texas system of county government EXCEPT that:
    a. it is rigid and inflexible.
    b. it places far too much centralized power in the hands of the state government.
    c. it permits frequent use of the spoils system in hiring.

11. The elected, policy-making body that governs counties is the:
    a. county commissioners court
    b. county assembly
    c. constitutional county court at-large

12. Which of the following is a typical function of county government?
    a. recording land titles and deeds
    b. running small claims courts
    c. exercising veto powers over city governments

13. The official who presides over the commissioner's court and is elected to a four-year term is the:
    a. county mayor.   b. county judge.   c. county sheriff.

14. Voluntary regional groupings of local governments that attempt to coordinate regional government activities and share information are known as:
    a. special districts.
    b. dependent agencies.
    c. councils of government.

15. Which of the following is NOT an example of a function performed by a special district?
    a. airport authorities
    b. hospital authorities
    c. criminal courts

4LTR Press solutions are designed for today's learners through the continuous feedback of students like you. Tell us what you think about **TX.GOV** and help us improve the learning experience for future students.

YOUR FEEDBACK MATTERS.

Complete the Speak Up survey in CourseMate at
www.cengagebrain.com

Follow us at
www.facebook.com/4ltrpress

NOTES

Chapter 1

1. Daniel J. Elazar, *American Federalism: A View from the States,* 3rd ed. (New York: Harper & Row, 1984), pp. 94–99.
2. Ibid.
3. Information for this section is adapted from Donald W. Meinig, *Imperial Texas: An Interpretive Essay in Cultural Geography* (Austin, Texas: University of Texas Press, 1969).
4. "Texas Border Region," July 1998, p. 3; Jorge Bustamante, "A Conceptual and Operative Vision of the Population. Problems on the Border," in *Demographic Dynamics on the U.S.-Mexico Border,* eds. John R. Weeks and Roberto Ham Chande (El Paso, Texas: Texas Western Press, 1992).
5. Elizabeth York Enstam, "Women and the Law," *The Handbook of Texas Online,* published by the Texas State Historical Association, www.tshaonline.org.
6. Ibid.
7. Women of the West Museum, "Western Women's Suffrage—Texas," theautry.org/research/women-of-the-west.
8. Ibid.
9. Ibid.
10. Enstam, "Women and the Law."
11. *Roe v. Wade,* 410 U.S. 558 (1973); Sarah Weddington, *"Roe v. Wade," The Handbook of Texas Online,* www.tshaonline.org/handbook/online/articles/jrr02.
12. Christopher Long, "Ku Klux Klan," *The Handbook of Texas Online,* www.tshaonline.org/handbook/online/articles/vek02.
13. *Grovey v. Townsend,* 295 U.S. 45 (1935).
14. *Smith v. Allwright,* 321 U.S. 649 (1944).
15. *Plessy v. Ferguson,* 163 U.S. 537 (1896).
16. *Sweatt v. Painter,* 339 U.S. 629 (1950).
17. *Brown v. Board of Education of Topeka,* 347 U.S. 483 (1954).
18. George B. Green, "Mansfield School Desegregation Incident," *The Handbook of Texas Online,* www.tshaonline.org/handbook/online/articles/jcm02.
19. Frank R. Kemerer, *"United States v. Texas," The Handbook of Texas Online,* www.tshaonline.org/handbook/online/articles/jru02. For more information on desegregation, see CORE-online.org.
20. Alicia A. Garza, "Raymondville Peonage Cases," *The Handbook of Texas Online,* www.tshaonline.org/handbook/online/articles/pqreq.
21. www.justiceformypeople.org/drhector.html.
22. V. Carl Allsup, "Felix Longoria Affair," *The Handbook of Texas Online,* www.tshaonline.org/handbook/online/articles/vef01.
23. V. Carl Allstrop, *"Delgado v. Bastrop ISD," The Handbook of Texas Online,* www.tshaonline.org/handbook/online/articles/jrd01.
24. V. Carl Allstrop, *"Hernández v. State of Texas," The Handbook of Texas Online,* www.tshaonline.org/handbook/online/articles/jrh01.
25. See Robert E. Hall, "Pickets, Politics and Power: The Farm Worker Strike in Starr County," *Texas Bar Journal* 70, no. 5 (2007).
26. *Lawrence v. Texas,* 539 US 558 (2003).

Chapter 2

1. *Arizona v. United States,* 567 U.S. ___ (2012).
2. James Madison, *Federalist Paper* No. 10, November 23, 1787.
3. *McCulloch v. Maryland,* 17 U.S. 316 (1819).
4. Edward S. Corwin, "The Passing of Dual Federalism," *Virginia Law Review* 36, no. 1 (1950), p. 4.
5. *Annals of Congress: The Debates and Proceedings in the Congress of the United States,* "History of Congress," 42 vols. (Washington, D.C.: Gales & Seaton), pp. 1834–1856.
6. *New York v. Miln,* 36 U.S. 102 (1837).
7. Corwin, *op. cit.,* p. 2.
8. Ibid., p. 19.
9. *Aguilar v. Texas,* 378 U.S. 108 (1964). The first cases to incorporate the Fourth Amendment were *Wolf v. Colorado,* 338 U.S. 25 (1949), and *Mapp v. Ohio,* 367 U.S. 643 (1961).
10. *Pointer v. Texas,* 380 U.S. 400 (1965).
11. Another question worth pondering in this discussion is the clause in the Constitution that states, "[N]o Attainder of Treason shall work Corruption of Blood, . . . " (Article III, Section 2). The Constitution outlaws the punishment of offspring for crimes committed by the parents. It has generally been understood that the blood of the child is not corrupted by the sins of the father or the mother.
12. David Rauf, "Berman: 14th Amendment Does Not 'Apply to Foreigners,'" *Houston Chronicle,* February 2009, blog.chron.com/texaspolitics/2009/02/berman-14th-Amendment-does-not-apply-to-foreigners.

13. *Plessy v. Ferguson,* 163 U.S. 537 (1896).
14. *Sweatt v. Painter,* 339 U.S. 629 (1950).
15. *Brown v. Board of Education of Topeka,* 347 U.S. 483 (1954).
16. As quoted in Allen G. Breed, "Candidates' Talk of States' Rights Raises Issue of Whether Term Has Shed Baggage," *Washington Post,* January 26, 2012.
17. U.S. Advisory Commission on Intergovernmental Relations, *Federal Preemption of State and Local Authority* (draft report), 1989.
18. John Kinkaid, "From Cooperative to Coercive Federalism," *Annals of the American Academy of Political and Social Sciences* 509 (1990), pp. 139–152.
19. Rick Perry, "Governor's Initiatives," June 2010, governor.state.tx.us/initiatives/10th_amendment.
20. National Center for Missing & Exploited Children, "Analysis of Amber Alert Cases in 2010," 2011, p. 24, www.amberalert.gov/pdfs/10_amber_report.pdf.
21. Ibid., p. 9.
22. Robin A. Cohen, "State, Regional, and National Estimates of Health Insurance Coverage for People under 65 Years of Age: National Health Interview Survey, 2004–2006," in Centers for Disease Control, *National Health Statistics Reports,* no. 1 June 19, 2008, www.cdc.gov/nchs/data/nhsr/nhsr001.pdf.
23. American Wind Energy Association, "Wind Energy Facts: Texas," January 2012, www.awea.org/learnabout/publications/upload/4Q-11-Texas.pdf.
24. The Environmental Working Group.
25. The GoodGuide Scorecard, www.goodguide.com.
26. Ibid.
27. Ibid.
28. Richard Dunham, "George W. Bush Defends No Child Left Behind Reform from Attacks by Rick Perry, Others," *Houston Chronicle,* January 12, 2012.
29. Texas Association of Counties, *Unfunded Mandates Initiatives,* February 25, 2011, www.county.org/resources/legis/ufm.asp.
30. Paul Burka, "Abbott on the Legal Case against Health-Care," Burkablog, March 30, 2010, www.texasmonthly.com/blogs/burkablog.
31. Seung Min Kim, "Study: Insured Pay 'Hidden Tax' for Uninsured Health-Care," *USA Today,* May 29, 2009.
32. Kaiser Family Foundation, statehealthfacts.org.
33. Families USA, "Health Reform Central: From the States," www.familiesusa.org/health-reform-central/from-the-states/from-the-states.html.
34. Burka, *op. cit.*
35. *National Federation of Independent Business v. Sebelius,* 567 U.S. ___ (2012).
36. Joseph W. Singer, "Same Sex Marriage, Full Faith and Credit, and the Evasion of Obligation," *Stanford Journal of Civil Rights and Civil Liberties* 1 (2005).

Chapter 3

1. Earlier fatality estimates were lower, at about 618,000. Recent, more rigorous calculations place the figure between 650,000 and 850,000 soldiers. See David Hacker, "A Census-Based Count of the Civil War Dead," *Civil War History* 57, no. 4 (December 2011), pp. 306–347.
2. *Texas v. White,* 74 U.S. 700 (1869).
3. *San Antonio Independent School District v. Rodriguez,* 411 U.S. 1 (1973).
4. *Edgewood v. Kirby,* 777 S.W. 2d 391 (Tex. 1989).
5. Jeffrey R. Lax and Justin H. Phillips, "The Democratic Deficit," unpublished paper, Midwestern Political Science Association meeting, 2010.

Chapter 4

1. *Texas v. Holder,* ___ F.Supp.2d ___ (D.D.C. 2012).
2. Raymond E. Wolfinger and Steven Rosenstone, *Who Votes?* (New Haven, Conn.: Yale University Press, 1980). Also see Sydney Verba and Norman H. Nie, *Participation in America* (New York: Harper & Row, 1972).
3. Note that some Republican-controlled legislatures have tried to repeal Election-Day registration and were successful in Montana and Maine, though voters in Maine overturned the decision in a referendum. Efforts to repeal are still under way in Wisconsin. In Democratic-controlled Connecticut, conversely, there are moves to institute Election-Day registration.
4. For more information on measuring turnout, see the United States Elections Project at elections.gmu.edu.
5. G. Bingham Powell, Jr., "American Voter Turnout in Comparative Perspective," *American Political Science Review* 80 (March 1986), pp. 17, 23. Switzerland, the only country studied where turnout is lower than in the United States, was not included in this computation.
6. See Glenn Mitchell II and Christopher Wlezien, "The Impact of Legal Constraints on Voter Registration, Turnout, and the Composition of the American Electorate," *Political Behavior* 17 (June 1995), pp. 179–202.

Iron Texas Star model, 192–193
jurisdiction of, 157–158
membership appointments,
    156–158, 157
pigeonhole, 158–159
powers and functions of, 158–159
procedural, 154
selection of committee chairs, 157
seniority system, 158
subcommittees, 154
substantive, 153–154
Stanford, R. Allen, 228–229
Staples, Todd, 184
Stare decisis, 222
State Board of Education (SBOE),
    186, 251
on creationism and evolution, 254
curriculum and, 252–253, 254
textbook selection and, 253, 254
State boards, interest groups advising
    and serving on, 120–121
State conventions, 105
State government
    block grants, 31
    categorical grants, 31
    coercive federalism, 36–37
    cooperative federalism, 30–31
    federal aid and economic crisis, 31
    incorporation doctrine, 33–34
    powers of, 25, 26
        concurrent powers, 27
        reserved powers, 27
        separate-but-equal doctrine, 34–35
        state power over laws of illegal
            immigrants, 24, 34
        unfunded mandates, 37, 39
State of Texas Assessments of Academic
    Readiness (STAAR), 253
State-of-the-state message, 177–178
State police, use of, during
    Reconstruction, 49
Statute-like detail, 55
Statutory law, 52, 222
Stimulus package
    federal aid to states, 31
    Texas budget and, 31
Straus, Joe, 36
    as Speaker of the House, 152–153
Strayhorn, Carole, 13, 96
Strikes, jury selection, 234
Strong-mayor form, 274–275
Subcommittees, 154
Substantive standing committees,
    153–154
Succession, Texas right to secede from
    Union, 46
Suehs, Tom, 263
Suffrage, 14, 52
Sunset Advisory Commission
    appointment to, 156

membership and function of,
    166–167
role of, 195
Sunshine laws, 273
Supplemental Nutrition Assistance
    Program, 265
Supplemental Security Income (SSI),
    265
Supremacy clause, 28
Supreme Court, Texas, 57
    functions and power of, 211
    interest group influence, 124–125
    justices of, 211
    overview of, 211
    on public school funding, 211
Supreme Court, United States
    campaign financing, 88
    on campaign financing for judicial
        elections, 217
    campaign spending limits, 87
    eminent domain, 225
    equal rights cases, 15
    on health-care reform, 41, 262
    incorporation doctrine, 34
    judicial election contributions, 124
    Miranda rights, 231
    redistricting, 141
    separate-but-equal doctrine and,
        34–35
    sodomy laws, 19
    supremacy of federal government,
        28
    voter registration, 67
    white primary, 73
Suspension of the rule, 159
Sweatt, Heman, 17, 35
Sweatt v. Painter, 15, 17, 35
Swing voters
    defined, 110
    Latinos as, 110

T

Tagging, bill, 159
Taney, Roger, 30
Task Force on Unfunded Mandates, 39
Tax abatement, 280, 281
Tax assessor-collector, 77, 284
Tax base, 246
Taxes
    ability-to-pay tax, 246
    ad valorem tax, 245
    benefits-received tax, 246
    broad-based tax, 246
    consumer tax, 247
    during Davis administration, 49,
        50
    excise tax, 244
    fair tax, 248

hidden tax, 244
income tax, 30, 244
politics of, 245–248
progressive tax, 98, 247
property tax, 245, 256
public opinion on, 5
regressive tax, 247–248
regulatory taxes, 246
as revenue for Texas budget,
    244–248
sales tax, 244–245
severance, 245
sin tax, 246
tax base, 246
tax rates, 245–246
tax shifting, 247
Texas compared to other states, 5
Tax rate, 245
Tax shifting, 247
Taylor, Paul, 173
Tea Party movement
    formation of, 136
    inflexible spirit, 95
    Republican Party of Texas and,
        103
    success in Texas, 136
Temporary Assistance for Needy
    Families (TANF), 264
Tenth Amendment
    dual federalism and, 29–30
    reserved power of states, 27, 28
Term limits, 147, 277
Terrell Election Law, 73
Texan Association of Business, 118
Texans for Lawsuit Reform, 134, 224
Texans for Public Justice, 118, 129,
    132
Texas Abortion Rights Action League
    (TARAL), 99
Texas AFL-CIO, 118
Texas American Federation of
    Labor–Congress of Industrial
    Organizations (AFL-CIO), 134
Texas A&M System, 258
Texas Appraiser Licensing and
    Certification Board, 187
Texas Assessment of Knowledge and
    Skills (TAKS), 253
Texas Assn. of Home Health Care,
    134
Texas Assn. of Realtors, 134
Texas Association of Business, 134
Texas Association of Counties, 39
Texas Association of Realtors, 118,
    134
Texas Board of Pardons and Parole,
    237
Texas Bond Review Board, 186
Texas Border region
    binationality of, 11

drug trade, 13–14
economy of, 12
immigration and national security, 12–13
overview of, 11–14
Texas Cable & Telecom. Assn., 134
Texas Christian Life Commission, 118
Texas Civil Justice League, 224
Texas Commission on Environmental Quality (TCEQ), 37, 115, 187
Texas compared to other states
    constitution length, details, amendments, 60
    corruption risk, 128
    crime rate, 238
    education, 6
    environmental issues, 37, 38
    federal grants, 33
    governor's power, 173, 175
    health-care spending, 6
    judge selection process, 58, 215
    legislators' educational level and occupations, 149
    party competition, 109
    public financing and municipal elections, 276
    public safety, 6
    public school ranking, 255
    quality of life measures, 6
    state and local taxes, 248, 249
    taxes, 5
    tax revenue and spending, 6
Texas Constitution. *See* Constitution, Texas
Texas County Judges and Commissioners Association, 118
Texas Court of Criminal Appeals, 57, 210
    death penalty cases, 210
    function of, 210
Texas cultural regions
    Central Texas, 11
    East Texas, 8
    German Hill Country, 11
    Gulf Coast, 8–9
    North Texas, 10
    Panhandle, 10
    South and Southwest, 11–14
    Texas Border region, 11–14
    West Texas, 9–10
Texas Department of Agriculture, 184–185
Texas Department of Criminal Justice (DCJ), 237
Texas Department of Insurance, commissioner of, 185
Texas Department of Transportation, 188, 189
Texas Education Agency (TEA), 186, 251

duties of, 186
establishment of, 251
growing importance of, 186
Texas Equal Suffrage Association, 14
Texas Ethics Commission, 54, 126
    effectiveness of, 128
    lack of power, 131
    list of registered lobbyists, 126
Texas Farm Bureau, 118
Texas Farmers Union, 99
Texas Farm Workers Union (TFWU), 19
Texas Federation of Teachers, 242
Texas Freedom Network, 253
Texas Freedom Works, 253
Texas Grange, 49
Texas Higher Education Coordinating Board (THECB), 257–258
Texas Highway Department of Transportation (TxDOT), 265–266
Texas Highway Patrol, 181
Texas Highway Trust Fund, 246
Texas Legislative Council, 156
Texas Medical Assn., 134
Texas Medical Association, 134
Texas Motor Truck Association, 134
Texas Municipal League, 118, 134
Texas National Guard, 181
Texas Nature Conservancy, 118
Texas Public Policy Foundation, 253
Texas Racing Commission, 187
Texas Railroad Commission, 186
Texas Rangers, 16, 19, 46, 181
Texas Register, 123
Texas revenue
    federal aid to, 31–32, 33
    municipalities
        property tax, 278
        sales tax, 278
    by source for 2012-13, 31
    state budget, 243–249
        grants and borrowing, 248–249
        overview of sources of, 243–244
        taxes, 244–248
Texas Revolution, 12
Texas Right to Life movement, 117
Texas State Guard, 181
Texas State Teachers Association, 118, 134
Texas State University System, 258
Texas Tech System, 258
Texas Trial Lawyers Association, 118, 134, 217
Texas Two-Step, 106
Texas Workforce Commission (TWC), 264
Textbooks, 253, 254

Theft, 226
Third parties, difficulty of getting on ballot, 78–79, 96
Threat of veto, 176
Thurgood Marshall School of Law, 35
Ticket splitters, 110
Tipping, 110
Toomey, Mike, 133
Top 10 percent rule, 259–260
Top-two primary, 75
Tort reform, 224, 225
Tower, John, 100
Traditionalistic subculture, 7, 72
Transportation
    highway programs, 265–266
    mass transit, 266–267
    percent of state budget, 250, 265
    road commissioners, 283
    unit road system, 286
Trans-Texas Corridor (TTC), 188
Trial lawyers, 99
Trials
    adversary system of, 234
    appeals process, 235
    choosing jury, 234
    instructing jury, 234
    plea bargaining, 233–234
    post-trial proceeding, 235
    pretrial court activities
        arraignment and detention, 231–232
        grand juries, 232–233
        pretrial hearings, 233
    rehabilitation and punishment, 236–239
    sentencing defendant, 235
    special case of juvenile courts, 235–236
    verdict, 234–235
    waiving right to, 234
True bill, 212, 233
Truman, Harry, 99
Tucker, Thomas Tudor, 30
Turkey, voter turnout, 70
Twenty-fourth Amendment, 35, 71
Twenty-sixth Amendment, 68
Two-party system, as characteristic of American politics, 96
Two-thirds rule, 160
TXU Energy Retail Co., 134

U

Umbrella organizations, 135
Unauthorized immigrants, cost of, 13
Unemployment insurance, 263–264
Unfunded mandates, 37, 39, 280
Unfunded Mandates Interagency Work Group, 280

KEY TERMS

bicultural Encompassing two cultures. 12

binational Belonging to two nations. 11

conservatism A set of beliefs that includes a limited role for government in helping individuals and in economic affairs, and support for traditional values and lifestyles. 3

Creole A descendant of Spanish (or in some regions, French) immigrants to the Americas. 12

demographics Population characteristics, such as age, gender, ethnicity, employment, and income, that social scientists use to describe groups in society. 20

Hispanic An alternate word for *Latino* used officially by the U.S. government. 17

ideology A pattern of political beliefs about how society and the economy operate, including policy orientations consistent with that pattern; a set of beliefs consistent with a particular political perspective. 3

individualistic subculture A political subculture that views government as a practical institution that should further private enterprise but intervene minimally in people's lives. 7

internationality Having family or business interests in two or more nations. 11

Ku Klux Klan (KKK) A white supremacist organization. The first Klan was founded during the Reconstruction era following the Civil War. 16

Latino A person whose ancestors originated in a Spanish-speaking country. 17

liberalism A set of political beliefs that includes the advocacy of active government, including government intervention to improve the welfare of individuals and to protect civil rights. 4

maquiladora A factory in the Mexican border region that assembles goods imported duty-free into Mexico for export. A literal translation of the word is "twin plant." 12

Mestizo A person of both Spanish and Native American lineage. 12

Metroplex The greater Dallas–Fort Worth metropolitan area. 10

moralistic subculture A political subculture that believes government can be a positive force—one that values the individual but functions to benefit the general public. 7

SUMMARY

LearningOutcome 1–1 Analyze the relationships among political culture, public opinion, and public policy in Texas. **Political culture** describes the political values and beliefs of a people. Political culture includes various **ideologies,** or patterns of beliefs about how society and the economy should operate. The majority ideological perspective in Texas is **conservatism,** which holds that government should have a limited role in helping individuals and in economic affairs. It also includes support for traditional values and lifestyles. A minority ideology is **liberalism,** which advocates active government, including government intervention to promote the welfare of individuals and civil rights. These political views are reflected in **partisanship,** the tendency of Texans to identify with a particular political party. The Republican Party is the party of conservatism. Liberals tend to identify with the Democratic Party. Texan conservatism is also evident in measures of public opinion. **Public opinion** in Texas tends to be more conservative than in the rest of the country on average and results in overall support for more conservative **public policies.**

LearningOutcome 1–2 Distinguish among moralistic, traditionalistic, and individualistic political subcultures. Daniel Elazar has identified three major political subcultures in the United States. The **moralistic subculture,** predominant in the northern parts of the United States, believes that government can be a positive force that functions for the public good. The **individualistic subculture,** more pronounced in the Middle Atlantic and western states, holds that government should promote private enterprise but should otherwise play a limited role in people's lives. The **traditionalistic subculture,** strongest in the southern states, embraces government as an institution that should maintain the dominant social and religious values. Texas is a blend of the individualistic and traditionalistic subcultures.

LearningOutcome 1–3 Discuss the distinctive social, economic, and political characteristics of major Texas regions. Scholars have identified several distinct regions of Texas. East Texas is the most strongly southern, culturally and socially. The Gulf Coast, home to the economic giant, Houston, has been a major petrochemical and shipping area and has witnessed a great deal of economic distress since the 1980s. West Texas and the Panhandle host major oil-producing areas as well as cattle and agriculture. North Texas, which is dominated by the highly urban **Metroplex** (Dallas–Fort Worth), is more economically diverse and is a national banking and commercial center. Central Texas is home to the capital city, Austin, and the German Hill Country. South and Southwest Texas are characterized by their **internationality** and **binationalism,** thanks to their proximity to Mexico. They are distinctive for their **Creole** and **Mestizo** heritages, as well as South Texas's **ranchero culture.** Close economic ties have been forged in recent decades due to the proliferation of duty-free **maquiladora** factories and the negotiation of the **North American Free Trade Agreement (NAFTA)** in 1994.

LearningOutcome 1–4 Trace the struggle for equal rights in Texas by women, African Americans, Latinos, and gay men and lesbians. Texas has experienced a long history of discrimination against women and minority groups. The struggle for women's rights included the **suffrage** movement, culminating in the passage of the Nineteenth Amendment in 1920. Women struggled through the 1970s for equality in other civil rights and the debate over abortion rights continues in conservative Texas. African Americans suffered extreme discrimination under various legal devices, including social and legal segregation, exclusion from the dominant Democratic Party primary elections by so-called **white primaries,** and intimidation and violence at the hands of the **Ku Klux Klan (KKK).** A series of United States Supreme Court decisions and federal civil rights laws, as well as direct action by civil rights activists, ultimately dismantled the legal structures of racism, though

1

prejudice persists. Hispanics (Latinos) also experienced treatment as second-class citizens and ultimately benefited from the civil rights movement of the 1960s. Gay men and lesbians in Texas, while now enjoying a right to privacy to openly choose their partners, are still not fully protected by the Fourteenth Amendment like the aforementioned groups, and the Texas Constitution has been amended to ban same-sex marriage and domestic partnerships.

LearningOutcome 1–5 **Evaluate the social and cultural changes that are likely to define Texas's political future.** Texas politics has long been dominated by Anglo males, but projected demographics, the population characteristics such as age, gender, ethnicity, employment, and income, that social scientists use to describe groups in society, suggest this will be changing. A young and rapidly growing Hispanic population will constitute a majority of the population by 2040, resulting in greatly increased political influence and a probable change in focus on policy issues, most likely in a liberal direction, at least on economic issues. However, Hispanics and African Americans have much higher poverty rates and lower levels of education than Anglos, attributes associated with low voter turnout. So the political clout of this new majority population group could be delayed in making itself felt.

ANSWERS TO STUDY TOOLS QUIZ

1. b. (LearningOutcome 1–1)
2. b. (LearningOutcome 1–1)
3. c. (LearningOutcome 1–1)
4. c. (LearningOutcome 1–2)
5. b. (LearningOutcome 1–2)
6. a. (LearningOutcome 1–2)
7. b. (LearningOutcome 1–3)
8. c. (LearningOutcome 1–3)
9. b. (LearningOutcome 1–3)
10. b. (LearningOutcome 1–4)
11. a. (LearningOutcome 1–4)
12. c. (LearningOutcome 1–4)
13. c. (LearningOutcome 1–4)
14. c. (LearningOutcome 1–5)
15. a. (LearningOutcome 1–5)

North American Free Trade Agreement (NAFTA) A 1994 treaty calling for the gradual removal of tariffs and other trade restrictions among Canada, Mexico, and the United States. **12**

political culture A patterned set of ideas, values, and ways of thinking about government and politics. **3**

ranchero culture A quasi-feudal system whereby a property's owner, or *patrón*, gives workers protection and employment in return for their loyalty and service. The rancher, or *ranchero*, and workers all live on the *rancho*, or ranch. **12**

suffrage The right to vote. **14**

traditionalistic subculture A political subculture that views government as an institution to maintain the dominant social and religious values. **7**

The Valley An area along the Texas side of the Rio Grande known for its production of citrus fruits. **12**

white primary The practice of excluding African Americans from Democratic Party primary elections in Texas. First enforced by law and later by party rules, this practice was found unconstitutional in *Smith v. Allwright* (1944). **16**

KEY TERMS

block grants Federal grants to state or local governments for more general purposes and with fewer restrictions than categorical grants. **31**

categorical grants Federal aid to state or local governments for specific purposes, granted under restrictive conditions and often requiring matching funds from the receiving government. **30**

coercive federalism A relationship between the national government and states in which the former directs the policies that the states must adopt. **36**

commerce clause An enumerated power in Article I, Section 8, of the U.S. Constitution that gives Congress the power to regulate interstate commerce. **28**

concurrent powers Powers that are shared by both the national and state governments. **27**

confederal system A system of government in which member state or regional governments have all authority and any central institutions have only the powers that state or regional governments choose to give them. **25**

cooperative federalism A relationship in which the national government and the states are mutually complementary parts of a single government mechanism. **30**

delegated powers In relation to the U.S. Constitution, the powers granted to the national government. These include the enumerated powers found in Article I, Section 8, of the U.S. Constitution, as well as other powers that have evolved over time. **26**

devolution The surrender of powers to local authorities by a central government. **31**

dual federalism The understanding that the federal government and state governments are both sovereign within their respective spheres of influence. **29**

expressed powers Delegated powers that are explicitly listed in the U.S. Constitution. **26**

federal system A system of government in which governmental power is divided and shared between a national or central government and state or regional governments. **26**

SUMMARY

LearningOutcome 2–1 **Differentiate among federal, unitary, and confederal forms of government, and identify three types of powers found in the U.S. federal system.** Governments may be classified on the basis of their centralization. Unitary systems give central government ultimate authority, and any regional or local governments are subordinate to the central government. Confederal systems give member states or regional governments all authority and any central institutions have only the powers that state governments choose to give them. Federal systems divide and share governmental power between a national or central government and state or regional governments. The United States has a federal systems of government while all its constituent state governments have unitary system. Under the U.S. Constitution, the national government possesses delegated powers granted to it specifically by the Constitution, as well as other powers that have evolved over time. Delegated powers can be categorized as three different types. Expressed powers are those found in Article I, Section 8, and explicitly listed in the Constitution. Implied powers are delegated powers that are assumed to exist so that the government can perform the functions that are expressly delegated. These powers are granted by the necessary and proper clause in Article I, Section 8, of the U.S. Constitution. The third category, inherent powers, are those delegated powers that, while not always expressly granted, are necessary to ensure the nation's integrity and survival as a political unit. An example of such a power is the power to annex territory.

LearningOutcome 2–2 **Explain the constitutional bases and the development of dual federalism and cooperative federalism.** Federalism in the United States has not been a static institution but rather a dynamic process, with the general trajectory of power over time being more power going to the national government at the expense of the states. Until the Great Depression of the 1930s, the doctrine of dual federalism defined the federalism dynamic. This doctrine took a strict interpretation of the division of federal powers among delegated (federal), reserved (state), and concurrent (shared) powers. Because the Tenth Amendment to the Constitution specifies that all powers not delegated to the federal government are "reserved to the States, or the people," dual federalism is based on the understanding that the federal government and state governments are both sovereign within their sphere of influence. The division of powers between them was assumed to be fairly clear. The economic catastrophe of the 1930s, and the resulting weakness of states and local governments to respond effectively to it, initiated a transition to cooperative federalism, in which the national government and the states are mutually complementary parts of a single government mechanism. Through the use of categorical grants, the federal government has gained much greater influence over state and local policy. However, in the last three decades the federal government has devolved greater autonomy back to the states, as seen in the increasing transfer of much federal aid to the states and local governments in the form block grants, which allow these governments more flexibility in how they spend this money for a general purpose.

LearningOutcome 2–3 **Describe how federalism has affected the development of our civil liberties and civil rights, particularly through the rise of the incorporation doctrine and the fall of the separate-but-equal doctrine.** The expansion of federal power has also greatly expanded the scope of civil liberties and civil rights the states, including Texas, must respect. This is because the Fourteenth Amendment's due process clause, through creative judicial interpretation, has resulted in the doctrine of incorporation; the doctrine that under this clause most rights found in the Bill of Rights (which originally only applied to the national government) cannot be encroached upon by the states. Federal law was also key in contributing to the civil rights revolution that culminated in the 1960s. Southern states had long maintained, with the Supreme Court's support, the doctrine of separate-but-equal. After the Civil War and through the first half of the Twentieth Century, this embrace of states' rights in the name of racial segregation kept African Americans in Texas as second-class citizens through such devices as Jim Crow laws and the white primary. But in its landmark decision, *Brown v. Board of Education* (1954), the Supreme Court reversed its prior ruling and held that all government-sponsored racial segregation violates the Fourteenth Amendment's equal protection clause.

LearningOutcome 2–4 **Evaluate recent federalism controversies involving Texas, including those surrounding coercive federalism, unfunded mandates, health-care reform, and same-sex marriage.** Contemporary Texas politics has reflected the constant tension between states' rights and federal policy. While the national government has increasingly made use of block grants, it has also more aggressively asserted itself into traditional state concerns such as education, health care, and marriage. This relationship between the national government and the states, in which the former directs the policies that the states must adopt, has been labeled coercive federalism. Governor Rick Perry has bridled against recent Environmental Protection Agency regulations limiting carbon dioxide emissions of which Texas is a major producer. The national government is also increasingly using unfunded mandates, in which it imposes obligations on state governments without providing adequate funding to support the programs. One example is the No Child Left Behind Act. More recently, Texas joined with twenty-five other states in legal opposition to President Obama's health-care legislation, nicknamed "Obamacare." Finally, while the federal government currently opposes same-sex marriage with the DOMA, there is concern that litigation making its way through the federal court system could threaten Texans' conservative opposition to same-sex marriage, now embedded in the state constitution as a constitutional amendment.

ANSWERS TO STUDY TOOLS QUIZ

1. b. (LearningOutcome 2–1)
2. c. (LearningOutcome 2–1)
3. c. (LearningOutcome 2–1)
4. c. (LearningOutcome 2–1)
5. a. (LearningOutcome 2–2)
6. c. (LearningOutcome 2–2)
7. b. (LearningOutcome 2–2)
8. c. (LearningOutcome 2–2)
9. a. (LearningOutcome 2–3)
10. c. (LearningOutcome 2–3)
11. b. (LearningOutcome 2–3)
12. b. (LearningOutcome 2–3)
13. c. (LearningOutcome 2–4)
14. a. (LearningOutcome 2–4)
15. b. (LearningOutcome 2–4)

implied powers Delegated powers that are assumed to exist so that the government can perform the functions that are expressly delegated. These powers are granted by the necessary and proper clause in Article I, Section 8, of the U.S. Constitution. **26**

incorporation doctrine The doctrine that under the Fourteenth Amendment to the Constitution, most rights found in the Bill of Rights cannot be encroached upon by the states. **33**

inherent powers Delegated powers of the national government that, although not always expressly granted by the Constitution, are necessary to ensure the nation's integrity and survival as a political unit. An example of such a power not mentioned in the Constitution is the power to annex territory. **26**

Jim Crow laws State and local laws that promulgated racial segregation. **35**

necessary and proper clause The last clause in Article I, Section 8, of the U.S. Constitution, which gives Congress implied powers; also known as the *elastic clause.* **28**

police power A government's authority to legislate for the protection of the health, morals, safety, and welfare of the people. The term does not refer to law enforcement officers. **30**

reserved powers In relation to the U.S. Constitution, the powers that belong to the states. The legitimacy of these powers comes in part from the Tenth Amendment. **27**

separate-but-equal doctrine The doctrine resulting from the United States Supreme Court ruling in *Plessy v. Ferguson,* which legalized segregation. **34**

supremacy clause Article VI, Section 2, of the U.S. Constitution, which states that the U.S. Constitution, as well as laws and treaties created in accordance with the U.S. Constitution, supersede state and local laws. **28**

Tenth Amendment The section of the U.S. Constitution that reserves powers to the states. It reads as follows: "The powers not delegated to the United States by the Constitution, nor prohibited by it to the States, are reserved to the States respectively, or to the people." **28**

unfunded mandates Obligations that the federal government imposes on state governments without providing adequate funding to support the programs. **37**

unitary system A system of government in which one central government has ultimate authority, and any regional or local governments are subordinate to the central government. **25**

3 The Texas Constitution in Perspective

KEY TERMS

bicameral Consisting of two houses or chambers. Refers to a legislative body with two parts, such as a senate and a house of representatives (or state assembly). **54**

biennial regular sessions Regular legislative sessions scheduled by the constitution and held once every two years. **54**

budgetary power The authority to propose a spending plan to the legislative body. A limited power of the Texas governor because of the competing influence of the Legislative Budget Board. **56**

checks and balances A principle of American government in which each of the three branches is given powers that enable it to check (restrain or balance) the other branches. **53**

common law Law based on precedents (previous court rulings). The common law has been in continuous development in English-speaking countries since medieval times. **48**

community property Property acquired during marriage and owned equally by both spouses. **48**

deadwood State constitutional provisions voided by conflicting U.S. constitutional or statutory law. Also, provisions made irrelevant by changing circumstances. **52**

directive authority The power to issue binding orders to executive-branch agencies—severely limited in Texas. **56**

general-law charter A document authorizing the establishment of a city with a population below five thousand. The city's structure and organization are prescribed and limited by state law. **57**

home-rule charter A document organizing a municipality with a population greater than five thousand that allows it to use any organizational structure or institute any program that complies with state law. **57**

homestead An owner-occupied property, protected in Texas from forced sale under most circumstances. **48**

indirect appointive powers The authority to appoint supervisory boards but not operational directors for most state agencies. **56**

initiative A citizen-initiated ballot proposal that becomes law if passed. The initiative is permitted in some Texas cities but not at the state level. **52**

legitimacy The general acceptance of a government's right to govern. Also, the legality of a government's existence as established by a constitution. **47**

SUMMARY

LearningOutcome 3–1 **Identify Texas's historic constitutions and the cultural and political forces that shaped their distinctive features.** Texas's several constitutions reflect its changing fortunes in diplomacy and war. The first, the Constitution of 1836, reflected a newly independent country rejecting Mexican Catholic dominance and embracing separation of church and state. It imposed limits on the Republic's presidential powers and reestablished slavery. However, it did keep the Spanish-Mexican legal principles of **homestead** and **community property rights,** though the majority of the legal system incorporated English common law. The Constitution of 1845 facilitated Texas's transition from independent country to a new member of the United States. It placed severe restrictions on big business and introduced the **long ballot,** which Texas still uses today. The Civil War required the Constitution of 1861 to acknowledge Texas's secession from the United States and membership in the Confederacy. It prohibited the emancipation of slaves. By joining the losing side of the war, Texans were forced to abandon slavery and write a new constitution, that of 1866. It did not satisfy the Radical Reconstructionists in Congress, however, and Texas found itself under its penultimate governing document, the Constitution of 1869, and continued occupation by the Union military. This document greatly centralized the power of government, particularly that of the governor, whose police and appointment powers were considerable. It also excluded most of the prior political and social elites of Texas. Experience with the governorship of Edmund B. Davis, whom most Texans considered tyrannical, led directly to the reactionary principles of the Constitution of 1876. Influenced heavily by the Texas Grange, this, our final and present constitution, strives in almost every way to fragment power among the branches and within each branch through an enormous number of checks and balances, a plural executive, and numerous constitutional restrictions on the power of government.

LearningOutcome 3–2 **Identify the rights protected by the Texas Bill of Rights and those also protected by the U.S. Constitution, and describe the restriction on Texas voters.** Unlike the U.S. Constitution, the Texas Constitution begins with a Bill of Rights, which is strongly indicative of the priorities of its framers in limiting government power. It is a generous list of liberties generally consistent with and in some cases more extensive than the U.S. Bill of Rights. Texas citizens today have double protection for their rights since the doctrine of incorporation applies most of the U.S. Bill of Rights to the states. People can always sue in federal court if state courts fail to protect their rights. Because the U.S. Constitution establishes only minimum standards, Texas courts have used both Texas's constitution and **statutory law** (legislature-passed law). Texas law has been more generous in its protection of free speech and some privacy rights. It has an equal rights amendment (which failed to pass at the national level) and forbids the suspension of *habeas corpus* for any reason. While Texas is fairly typical in its requirements for **suffrage** (the right to vote), its constitution, like the constitutions of some other states, does not provide for the direct democracy measures of **initiative, referendum,** or **recall.**

LearningOutcome 3–3 **Describe separation of powers, checks and balances, the three branches of state government, and the three types of local government in Texas.** In broad outline, the structure of the Texas government mirrors that of the U.S. government. It features **separation of powers** into three branches (legislative, executive, and judiciary) and a series of **checks and balances** where each branch is given powers that allow it to balance or restrain the other branches. Given its historical context, however, the Texas Constitution goes even further than the U.S. Constitution in purposefully fragmenting government power. The legislature is **bicameral,** or two-chambered, consisting of the House of Representatives and Senate. It meets in **biennial regular sessions** (every two years) for 140 days, though the governor may call

special sessions as needed. Compared to the U.S. Constitution and most other state constitutions, the Texas Constitution is extremely detailed in its provisions, making frequent constitutional amendments necessary to handle matter that in other states could be handled by ordinary legislative action. Its length is also explained by the existence of many **deadwood** provisions that no longer have any legal validity. Texas has a plural executive characterized by a chief executive, the governor, who must share power with several other independently statewide-elected executive officials. This makes the Texas governor a relatively weak governor in terms of formal powers. While the governor has relatively robust veto powers, including the **line-item veto,** his or her **appointment** and **removal powers** are rather weak. The executive branch also consists of a broad array of boards and agencies, some appointed by the governor but others whose members are independently elected. Power is fragmented in the judiciary as well since Texas has a dual supreme court system with a Supreme Court for civil cases and a Court of Criminal Appeals for criminal cases. In contrast to many other states, Texas judges are elected in **partisan elections** where judges run as Republicans, Democrats, or members of third parties. The Texas Constitution makes local governments subordinate to the state and assigns many responsibilities to local governments. The three general types of local government designated and described are **general-law charters, home-rule charters,** and **special districts.**

LearningOutcome 3–4 **Explain the process of amending and revising the Texas Constitution and the reasons that amendments are frequently necessary.** Amending the Texas Constitution requires a two-thirds proposal by both chambers of the legislature and **ratification,** or approval, by a majority popular vote. The Texas Constitution is criticized for being too long, too detailed, and requiring too many amendments (474 to date). Because it is so detailed and long, and contains deadwood provisions, it can be confusing. The many restrictions on legislative action means amendments are sometimes the only way to make important policy changes. Amendments also serve as a convenient way for well-organized interest groups to protect their policy preferences since voter attention and participation in elections with constitutional amendment proposals tend to be very low.

ANSWERS TO STUDY TOOLS QUIZ

1. c. (LearningObjective 3–1)
2. b. (LearningObjective 3–1)
3. a. (LearningObjective 3–1)
4. b. (LearningObjective 3–2)
5. c. (LearningObjective 3–2)
6. a. (LearningObjective 3–2)
7. b. (LearningObjective 3–3)
8. c. (LearningObjective 3–3)
9. b. (LearningObjective 3–3)
10. b. (LearningObjective 3–4)
11. b. (LearningObjective 3–4)
12. a. (LearningObjective 3–4)

line-item veto Executive authority to strike out sections of a bill and allow the remainder to become law. Limited in Texas to appropriations bills. **56**

long ballot A ballot that permits the election of a large number of independent executive and judicial officers. If a chief executive has the power to appoint most executive and judicial officers, the result is a *short ballot.* **48**

merit plan A method of selecting judges based on the candidate's qualifications rather than politics. Also known as the *Missouri Plan.* **58**

partisan elections Elections in which candidates are nominated by political parties. **57**

plural executive An executive branch with power divided among several independent officers and a weak chief executive. **55**

pocket veto The power to kill legislation by failing to sign it following the end of the legislative session. This power is not available to Texas's governor. **56**

ratification The approval of a constitutional amendment by a majority of voters. **59**

recall A special election to remove an official before the end of his or her term, initiated by citizen petition. Permitted in some Texas cities but not at the state level. **52**

reduction veto The power to reduce dollar amounts in an appropriations bill without deleting the clauses in question altogether. Texas's governor does not have this power. **56**

referendum A vote on a ballot proposal initiated by the state legislature. **56**

removal powers The authority to fire appointed officials. The Texas governor has limited removal powers, which extend only to officials the governor has appointed and are subject to the consent of two-thirds of the state senators. **56**

separation of powers The principle of dividing governmental powers among the legislative, executive, and judicial branches. **53**

special district A limited-purpose local government that provides a narrow range of services not provided by general-purpose local governments, such as cities or counties. Examples include municipal utility districts, hospital authorities, and transit authorities. **57**

special session A legislative session called by the Texas governor, who also sets its agenda. **54**

statute-like detail Detailed state constitutional policies of narrow scope. Often handled in other states by statutes passed by legislative bodies. **55**

statutory law Law passed by legislatures. **52**

suffrage The right to vote. **52**

writ of *habeas corpus* A court order requiring that an individual be presented in person and that legal cause be shown for confinement. The writ may result in release from unlawful detention. **52**

4 Voting and Elections

KEY TERMS

Australian ballot A ballot printed by the government (not by political parties) that allows people to vote in secret. **79**

chads The small pieces of paper produced in punching data cards, such as punch-card ballots. **82**

closed primary A type of primary in which a voter can participate only by voting for candidates of the party of which the voter is a member. **75**

crossover voting Voting by members of one political party in the other party's primary to influence the result. **75**

direct primary An election in which voters directly select the nominees from a political party who will run in the general election. The primary is "direct" because voters vote directly for candidates, and not for delegates who later choose the nominee. **73**

early voting The practice of voting before Election Day by mail, at more traditional voting locations such as schools, and at grocery and convenience stores. **82**

electronic voting Voting using touch screens similar to those in automated teller machines (ATMs). **83**

independent expenditures Funds that individuals and organizations spend to promote a candidate without working or communicating directly with the candidate's campaign organization. **87**

negative campaigning A strategy used in election campaigns in which candidates attack opponents' issue positions or character. **85**

office-block ballot A type of ballot used in a general election where the offices are listed across the top, in separate columns, and the candidates' names are listed in rows beneath each office. **78**

open primary A type of primary in which a voter can choose on Election Day in which party's primary the voter will participate. **74**

participation paradox The fact that individuals continue to vote even though their votes rarely influence the result of an election. **66** Calc

party-column ballot A type of ballot used in a general election on which all of the candidates from each party are listed in parallel columns. **77**

plurality vote An election rule that the candidate with the most votes wins,

SUMMARY

LearningOutcome 4–1 Explain the participation paradox in electoral politics. Voting is the defining characteristic of formal citizen participation in a democracy. The **participation paradox** refers to the puzzle of why individuals continue to vote even though their votes rarely influence the result of an election. The answer is that people vote for other reasons such as a sense of civic duty or psychic satisfaction, or because they wish to root for a particular party.

LearningOutcome 4–2 Describe the leading predictors of whether a person votes, some of the ways that the right to vote has been restricted in Texas, and why voting turnout is low in Texas. **Voter turnout** in the United States is measured by either the **voter-age population** or the **vote-eligible population.** Indicators predicting who will vote are the same in Texas as across the rest of the country. The three most prominent are age, education, and income. Older, more educated, and higher-income individuals have higher turnout rates. Other factors include the intensity of a person's interest in politics and whether an individual strongly identifies with one of the political parties. The more interested and more partisan the individual, the more likely she or he is to vote. Voter turnout in the United States is low compared to that in most other industrialized democracies. In Texas, voter turnout, as in the rest of the South, has been consistently lower than the national average. Texas also has a long history of legal restrictions that, collectively, served to depress voter turnout. These included the poll tax, restrictions on women's suffrage, the white primary, long residence requirements, and registration for jury duty as a condition of voting, among other legal factors. Although most legal barriers to voting have been removed, low voter turnout persists. The reasons for this are twofold and lie in Texas's socioeconomics and culture. First, while Texas has many wealthy individuals, it has a higher poverty rate than the national average and poor educational outcomes. Poor education and poverty are predictors of nonvoting. Texas is also heir to the traditionalistic heritage which emphasizes deference to political and social elites and downplays popular participation. Combined with the influence of Texas' individualistic subculture and its pro-business, anti-government orientation, it's no surprise that civic participation is not particularly prized or encouraged.

LearningOutcome 4–3 Discuss the differences among primary, general, and special elections, as well as between open and closed primaries. There are three types of elections in Texas: primary, general, and special. Elections are typically a two-step process. In the first, political parties hold **primary elections,** elections within a party to select a candidate for the general election. Texas has **direct primaries** in which voters directly select the candidates who will run in the general election. Generally speaking, primaries may be open or closed. In a **closed primary,** only members of a party may vote in that party's primary. In an **open primary,** voters may choose on Election Day in which party's primary they will participate. Primaries require a candidate to win office by a majority vote. If no candidate receives a majority of the vote, the top two candidates must compete in a **runoff primary** election to see who will be the candidate. Texas has direct, open primaries with runoff elections. Each party's candidate then competes in the **general election** which determines who will actually win public office. In general elections, candidates only need to win by a **plurality** vote. Voter turnout tends to very low in primary elections. General elections for state positions are held every other year on the first Tuesday after the first Monday in November of even-numbered years. Special elections, the third type of elections, serve contingent needs such as filling vacancies in elected legislative offices or for constitutional amendments. For vacancies, special elections are nonpartisan and do not require a primary. The winner of a special election must receive a majority of the vote.

LearningOutcome 4–4 Examine how elections are conducted in Texas. Most of the work of election administration takes place at the county though the secretary of state is the chief elections officer of the state. Texas uses the party-column ballot, which makes straight-party voting easier, rather than the office-block ballot. This works to the advantage of the two major parties. It also benefits the Republican Party since the party with the highest proportion of votes in the most recent gubernatorial election is listed in the first column. Ballot access rules ensure that Democrats and Republican candidates automatically appear but make it difficult for independent and third-party candidates to get on. Use of the secret, or Australian ballot, protects the integrity of elections. An important recent development in Texas elections is early voting, which begins on the seventeenth day before Election Day and ends the day before it and allows some voters to vote by mail.

LearningOutcome 4–5 Identify factors that provide the greatest advantages to candidates in Texas state elections, and discuss the difficulty of controlling spending in Texas campaigns. Primary elections are characterized by (a) low voter turnout, and (b) turnout by individuals who are very partisan and/or ideologically committed. Candidates attempting to win a primary therefore need to appeal to these kind of voters. In the general election, however, candidates have an incentive to present a more moderate image in order to appeal to independents and swing voters. Two key advantages in state elections are the advantage that accrues to the dominant party (in Texas that means the Republicans in most places) and the incumbency advantage, the numerous advantages enjoyed by the candidate running who is already in office. While Americans often criticize the negative tone of politics, negative campaigning is often and increasingly a successful campaign tactic. Election campaigns are becoming more expensive, especially at the state level. While candidates seek individual contributions, political action committees (PACs) representing powerful businesses and interest groups play a hugely influential role in collecting money for preferred candidates. The important role of money in campaigns raises questions about its role in influencing policymaking and the integrity of democracy generally. Texas has fewer limits on campaign contributions at the state level than exist at the federal level. Combined with Texas's low voter turnout, this only serves to reinforce the power of those individuals and groups with the money to join the political game.

regardless of whether that candidate has an absolute majority. **75**

political action committee (PAC) An organization that raises and then contributes money to political candidates. **86**

runoff primary A second primary election that pits the two top vote-getters from the first primary against each other when the winner in the first primary did not receive a majority. The runoff primary is used in states such as Texas that have a majority election rule in party primaries. **74**

soft money Money spent by political parties on behalf of political candidates, especially for the purposes of increasing voter registration and turnout. **87**

vote-eligible population (VEP) The total number of persons who are eligible to vote. Excludes noncitizens and felons whose eligibility to vote has not yet been restored. Includes citizens living abroad who can cast absentee ballots. **69**

voter turnout The percentage of those eligible to vote who actually vote. **68**

voting-age population (VAP) The total number of resident persons who are eighteen years of age or older, regardless of citizenship or felony status. **68**

ANSWERS TO STUDY TOOLS QUIZ

1. c. (LearningOutcome 4–1)
2. a. (LearningOutcome 4–2)
3. c. (LearningOutcome 4–2)
4. b. (LearningOutcome 4–2)
5. c. (LearningOutcome 4–2)
6. b. (LearningOutcome 4–3)
7. c. (LearningOutcome 4–3)
8. b. (LearningOutcome 4–3)
9. a. (LearningOutcome 4–4)
10. b. (LearningOutcome 4–4)
11. b. (LearningOutcome 4–5)
12. a. (LearningOutcome 4–5)
13. b. (LearningOutcome 4–5)

5 Political Parties

KEY TERMS

dealignment A process through which large numbers of voters refuse to identify with either of the two major parties and become increasingly independent of party affiliation. **110**

decentralization Exercise of power in political parties by state and local party organizations rather than by national party institutions. **95**

evangelicals Protestant Christians who believe that being "born again" is essential to salvation. Other characteristics are a strong regard for biblical authority, emphasis on the saving death and resurrection of Christ, and active sharing of the gospel. **102**

grassroots The lowest level of party organization. In Texas, the grassroots level is the precinct level of organization. **95**

partisan identification A person's attachment to one political party or the other. **108**

partisan realignment A transformation in which the major political parties experience a substantial change in the nature and number of their supporters. **108**

party platform The formal issue positions of a political party. Specifics are often referred to as *planks* in the party's platform. **102**

pragmatism The philosophy that measures should be judged on the basis of their practical results rather than on an ideological basis. **95**

precinct convention A gathering of party members who voted in the party's primary for the purpose of electing delegates to the county or district convention. **104**

presidential preference primary A primary election that allows voters in the party to vote for candidates seeking their party's presidential nomination. **106**

primary An election held by a political party to nominate its candidates. Texas party primary elections are usually held in the spring. **104**

single-member district system A system in which one candidate is elected to a legislative body in each election district. **96**

swing voters People who are willing to cast their ballots for either major party. Swing voters are often independents who are persuadable by either party's campaign. **110**

SUMMARY

LearningOutcome 5–1 **Describe the functions and chief characteristics of American political parties.** Although the U.S. Constitution does not mention political parties, they are central to every modern democracy. Political parties are broad-based coalitions of individuals whose primary goal is to win elections. They are vital linkage institutions because they provide a more permanent connection between citizens and their government than mere periodic elections and make it possible for citizens to participate in their government in a more meaningful way. Parties provide a variety of functions, among them (a) nominating and electing members to public office, (b) educating voters, (c) mobilizing voters at election time, (d) and holding office and running government when their members win elections. The American political party system is distinctive when compared to most other political systems due to three major features. It exhibits (a) pragmatism, the notion that policies should be judged on the basis of practical results rather than principles; (b) decentralization, with most of a party's power flowing from the state and local levels rather than national level; and (c) a two-party system as opposed to having multiple effective parties. This last feature results from several factors, but the most important is the use by every state of the single-member district system, which tends to strongly reinforce the dominance of the most successful, existing two parties. Some recent trends in the American party system, however, include a shift from pragmatism to increasing ideological polarization within the parties and a discernable movement in power toward the national party organizations.

LearningOutcome 5–2 **Distinguish between liberals and conservatives and between likely supporters of Texas Republicans and Democrats. Explain how the Republican Party became the dominant party in the state.** While a two-party system characterizes our electoral politics at the national level, Texas has an enduring tradition as a one-party state. This mostly reflects the traumatic experience of Texas and other southern states that lost the Civil War and experienced military occupation by the triumphant North. The Republican Party was the party of the North, so Texans and other white southerners voted overwhelmingly Democratic. Entrenched by the white primary system and lacking meaningful Republican competition, the Democratic Party became the only game in town. While both *conservative* and *liberal* factions existed within the party, the conservative faction practically always held the upper hand when it came to handling the levers of power. Conservatives favor limited government and support for business, and oppose active government efforts at equalizing socioeconomic outcomes, believing in individual responsibility. Liberals favor active government intervention in the economy and believe in policies that champion efforts to promote socioeconomic equality. Many conservatives, particularly Republican-identified evangelical Christians, believe the government should promote morality and "traditional" values, while liberals are inclined to think it is inappropriate for the government to intervene in the realm of personal values. Starting slowly in the 1960s, however, and accelerating in the 1990s, Texans began to switch from voting for the Democratic Party to voting for the Republican Party. By 1998, every statewide office was held by Republicans. Although several factors explain this dramatic shift in political allegiance, the general explanation is that a majority of Texans are conservative and no longer identified with the liberalism of the national Democratic Party. As historical memory has weakened, the more conservative party platform and policies of the Republican Party have proved more inviting for conservative Democrats who once found a home in the Democratic Party.

LearningOutcome 5–3 **Explain the differences between temporary and permanent party organizations in Texas.** To better understand party organization and dynamics in Texas, we can distinguish between the *temporary party organization* and the

9

permanent party organization. The former is a series of conventions convened to nominate candidates from within the party. The latter consists of the permanent leadership of the party at various levels who formulate party strategy and provide continuity between election campaigns. Those who vote in a party's primary election—the election held to select candidates for the general election—are eligible to attend their **precinct convention,** the main purpose of which is to adopt resolutions and choose delegates to send to the county or senatorial district convention. County convention delegates in turn vote on resolutions and delegates to be sent to the state convention. State conventions for both Republicans and Democrats take place in June of even-numbered years. The state convention performs a number of functions including the election of state party officers, the adoption of a party platform, and certification of the party's candidates for the general election. The state convention assumes added importance in election years when it must select candidates for the state's thirty-eight electoral college seats. Presidential candidates, however, are now voted for directly by voters in the **presidential preference primary,** greatly diminishing the role of national convention delegates. Parallel to the temporary party organization, the permanent party organization exists at the precinct (neighborhood), county, and state levels. The precinct committee and its chair are the workhorses of voter registration, education, and mobilization for elections. The county convention chair, chosen in the party primary, presides over the county executive committee and coordinates a variety of important activities that actually allow elections to take place. Overseeing all this, as well as serving as a liaison to the national party, is the state chair, the highest-ranking individual in the state's political party.

LearningOutcome 5–4 Define *realignment.* **Describe why a majority of Texas voters now identify with the Republican Party, and explain why more Texas voters may identify with the Democratic Party in the future.** Electoral fortunes change. While the Democratic Party in Texas enjoyed a seemingly impregnable dominance for roughly one hundred years, Texas is now an overwhelmingly Republican state with every statewide office (as of 2012) held by Republicans. In political science terms, Texas has undergone a **partisan realignment,** a massive transition in **partisan identification** and voting patterns from one party to another. While the majority of those Texans who now self-identify with a party identify as Republicans, a larger number of Texans self-identify with neither party, though a majority of these "independents" still lean toward the Republican Party. Support for Republican presidential candidates, alienation by Democratic civil rights policies in the 1960s and 1970s and its more liberal economic policies at the national level, and increased immigration to the state by individuals more sympathetic to Republican policies have all contributed over the last few decades to the Republican realignment. Republicans are also more likely to be white, educated, and upper income, making them more likely to vote. Since voter turnout in Texas has declined over the years, low voter turnout has primarily benefited the Republicans at the expense of the Democrats. Still, the increased tendency of voters to **ticket-split** (vote for candidates of different parties in the same general election) provides some evidence that Texas is undergoing **dealignment,** a disinterest among voters in identifying with either of the two major parties. Looking ahead to the coming decades, current Republican dominance may not be so secure. Texas's rapidly growing Hispanic population, a group that has strongly supported Democratic policies, presents the very real possibility that the predominantly white Republican Party is losing the battle of demographics.

ticket splitters People who vote for candidates of more than one party in a given election. **110**

tipping A phenomenon that occurs when the growing population of a group becomes large enough to change the political balance in a state, district, or county. **110**

two-party system A political system characterized by two dominant parties competing for political offices, in which third parties have little chance of winning. **97**

ANSWERS TO STUDY TOOLS QUIZ

1. c. (LearningOutcome 5–1)
2. a. (LearningOutcome 5–1)
3. c. (LearningOutcome 5–1)
4. b. (LearningOutcome 5–1)
5. c. (LearningOutcome 5–2)
6. b. (LearningOutcome 5–2)
7. c. (LearningOutcome 5–2)
8. b. (LearningOutcome 5–2)
9. a. (LearningOutcome 5–2)
10. a. (LearningOutcome 5–3)
11. c. (LearningOutcome 5–3)
12. a. (LearningOutcome 5–3)
13. b. (LearningOutcome 5–4)
14. b. (LearningOutcome 5–4)
15. b. (LearningOutcome 5–4)

6 Interest Groups

KEY TERMS

access The ability to contact an official either in person or by phone; often gained through campaign contributions. **132**

advocacy The promotion of a particular public-policy position. **116**

astroturf lobbying The fabrication of public support for issues supported by interest groups that gives the impression of widespread public support. **121**

conflict of interest The situation that exists when a public official is in a position to make a decision that might result in personal economic benefit or advantage. **121**

co-optation The capturing of a state institution by members of an interest group. In effect, state power comes to be exercised by the members of a private interest. **121**

delegate To legally transfer authority from one official or institution to another. **120**

discretion The power to make decisions on the basis of personal judgment rather than specific legal requirements. **120**

fragmentation The division of power among separately elected executive officers. A plural executive is a fragmented executive. **130**

implementation The carrying out by the executive branch of policies made by the legislature and rulings issued by the judiciary. **120**

interest group An organization that expresses the policy desires of its members to officers and institutions of government. Also known as a pressure group. **116**

iron triangle A working coalition among administrative agencies, interest groups, and legislative committees that share a common interest in seeing either the implementation or the defeat of certain policies and proposals. **136**

issue network Fluid alliances of individuals and organizations that are interested in a particular policy area and join together when policymaking topics affect their interests. **136**

late-train contributions Campaign funds given to the winning candidate after the election up to thirty days before the legislature comes into session. Such contributions are designed to curry favor with individuals the donors may not have supported originally. **133**

SUMMARY

LearningOutcome 6–1 **Define *interest groups,* and explain what they do.** An **interest group** is an organization that expresses the policy desires of its members to officers and institutions of government. Unlike political parties, their *primary* purpose of interest groups is to influence government, not to win elections, though the outcome of elections is often of keen interest to them. People join interest groups because organized groups of individuals, even small ones, can have a much greater influence on government than the mass of voters. Such organizations generally engage in **advocacy,** the promotion of particular policy positions. Interest group membership may also benefit individual social and career goals as well. Although interest groups engage in a variety of activities aimed at influencing government, the most effective is **lobbying,** direct contact between an interest group's representatives and officers of government.

LearningOutcome 6–2 **Describe the different types of interest groups.** While interest groups reflect a dizzying variety of motivations and backgrounds, they can generally be classified as economic, noneconomic, or some combination of the two. Economic interest groups, such as professional associations, businesses, education, local government, agriculture, and organized labor, generally seek financial benefits or favorable regulatory conditions for their members. Their goals may include low taxes, better wages and salaries, subsidies, lower or higher levels of regulation, or government contracts. Noneconomic interest groups in theory seek benefits for society as a whole, such as clean air and water, safety from crime and campaign-finance reform. Noneconomic interest groups have more difficulty organizing than economic interest groups do because of the free rider problem—there is little incentive for people to join (commit time, pay dues) such an organization if they will benefit from that organization's work anyway. To overcome this problem, noneconomic interest groups must rely on three factors: intense passion of their members, selective incentives (material goods such as T-shirts and magazine subscriptions), and social pressure. Governments themselves form and operate as interest groups. For example, local governments lobby state governments, which in turn lobby the federal government.

LearningOutcome 6–3 **Distinguish between direct and indirect forms of influencing government, and identify the different actors that that lobbyists attempt to influence.** Interest groups use varied tactics to influence policymakers. The most important, because it is usually the most effective, is lobbying. Lobbying is particularly effective because continuous personal contact can establish an influential relationship and because there are so many points within government at which such contacts can be made. It isn't just elected officials that may be persuaded, because the executive branch and its administrative agencies that **implement** laws and promulgate regulations, and because the legislature has great **discretion** to **delegate** how laws are carried out or to grant those agencies flexibility in how they are implemented, lobbyists have many opportunities to affect the policymaking process. Another frequent tactic of interest groups is to use the judicial system. Filing suit in court or giving financial and public support to other interest groups that already have done so is often a useful approach, particularly if attempts to influence the executive and legislative branches have been unsuccessful. In some cases, interest groups may be able to get members appointed to government agencies or commissions relevant to their interests. Organizing demonstrations, Grassroots mobilization, the mobilization of supporters to contact their representatives in the legislature (and its more sophisticated cousin "astroturfing"), are other direct tactics employed. Interest groups also engage in more subtle, indirect means of influencing the policy process, such as electioneering (that is, forming political action committees), conducting public information campaigns, and socializing with important political players.

LearningOutcome 6–4 **Describe the work of lobbyists, and explain what they do and do not have to report.** Lobbying has already been described as typically the most potent interest group tactic. This is particularly true in Texas where the existence of a part-time legislature makes lawmakers more reliant on lobbyists for information about a variety of policy issues about which they may have little knowledge and little time to educate themselves. With the state's legislative session lasting only 140 days in a regular session, lobbying must take place between sessions as well as during them to be effective. This allows lobbyists to establish the kind of personal rapport essential to their missions. Particularly important is securing the support of key committee members or presiding officers. When lobbying administrative agencies, lobbyists must take special care to follow the *Texas Register,* which gives advance notice of all rules and regulations intended to be implemented and those industries or groups that interact with regulatory agencies or commissions have ample opportunity to form cozy relationships with their members. "Judicial lobbying" is even more porous in Texas than at the federal level as Texas judges are elected and judicial campaigns can involve considerable fund-raising. The First Amendment and its equivalent in the Texas Constitution guarantees the right of free speech and peaceable assembly. But bribery is illegal. The Texas Ethics Commission regulates Texas's relatively loose lobbying laws. While it provides an enormous amount of information, critics point out it does little to rein in the undue influence of special interests.

LearningOutcome 6–5 **Identify some of the factors that affect the power of interest groups, and define** *revolving door, iron triangles,* **and** *issue networks.* Interest groups present a dilemma for Texas' political system. On the one hand, like political parties they are a valuable linkage institution for citizen-government contact. However, not all interest groups are created equal. Rather, some interest, especially well-financed corporate and professional interests, typically exercise a great deal more influence than organizations without such financial power. The low levels of voter turnout and knowledge in Texas just amplify this disparity. And the fact that Texas has functioned as a one-party state, first Democratic, now Republican, exacerbates interest group influence at the expense of voter input. As mentioned, the short legislative session in Texas makes legislators more reliant on the expertise of well-paid and well-prepared lobbyists, even to the point of writing bills. Moreover, the frequent movement of former legislators, executive staffers, administrators, and regulatory board members into the lobbying business where they then lobby the very individuals they used to work with, known as the **revolving door** phenomenon, creates at the very least the appearance the appearance of cooperation and certainly creates conflicts of interest. The fragmented structure of Texas government, particularly that of the executive branch, greatly facilitates this easy back-and-forth—usually in one predictable direction—between lobbying firms and government institutions. The dynamics of interest group power and their impact on democracy have many dimensions, but perhaps the classic one is that of **iron triangles.** Many fear that these close, mutually beneficial relationships among interest groups, legislators, and bureaucrats may become so tight that the public interest will be shut out almost entirely. In short, while interest groups play a valuable role in communicating the more intense interests of particular groups of citizens and can help educate government officials and the public, their influence often comes at a cost to what may be the greater public good.

lobbying Direct contact between an interest group representative and an officer of government. **115**

lobbyist In state law, a person who directly contacts public officials to influence their decisions. Registered lobbyists are paid to represent the interests of their employers. **116**

political movement A mass alliance of like-minded groups and individuals seeking broad changes in the direction of government policies. **136**

public interest The good of the whole society, without bias for or against any particular segment of the society. **121**

revolving door The interchange of employees between government agencies and the private businesses with which they have dealings. **129**

Texas Register The official publication of the state that gives the public notice of proposed actions and adopted policies of executive-branch agencies. **123**

umbrella organization A temporary or permanent organization created by interest groups to promote common political goals. **135**

ANSWERS TO STUDY TOOLS QUIZ

1. b. (LearningOutcome 6–1)
2. c. (LearningOutcome 6–1)
3. c. (LearningOutcome 6–2)
4. b. (LearningOutcome 6–2)
5. b. (LearningOutcome 6–2)
6. a. (LearningOutcome 6–2)
7. c. (LearningOutcome 6–3)
8. b. (LearningOutcome 6–3)
9. a. (LearningOutcome 6–3)
10. a. (LearningOutcome 6–4)
11. c. (LearningOutcome 6–4)
12. c. (LearningOutcome 6–4)
13. c. (LearningOutcome 6–5)
14. b. (LearningOutcome 6–5)
15. c. (LearningOutcome 6–5)

7 The Legislature

KEY TERMS

ad hoc Temporary. **154**

blocking bill A bill placed early on the senate calendar that will never be considered by the full senate. **160**

bureaucracy The system of nonelected officials administering government policies and programs. **159**

bureaucratic oversight The legislative function of monitoring administrators to make sure they are administering the laws according to legislative intent. **159**

calendar In Texas, the list of bills reported out of committee and ready for consideration by the house or the senate. **159**

chubbing Slowing the legislative process by maximizing debate, amendments, and points of order on minor bills to prevent ultimate consideration of a more controversial bill further down on the calendar. **161**

cloture A parliamentary move to stop legislative debate and force a floor vote. Also known as *closure*. **162**

committee of the whole The entire senate acting as a committee to allow it to relax its rules and expedite legislation. **164**

conference committee An ad hoc committee that meets to resolve differences between senate and house versions of the same legislation. **154**

conference committee report A compromise between the house and senate versions of a bill reached by a conference committee. **163**

cracking A gerrymandering technique in which concentrated political or ethnic minority groups are split into several districts so that their votes in any one district are negligible. **143**

discharge process A rarely used legislative process for rescuing a bill. **159**

ex officio Holding a position automatically because one also holds some other office. **141**

filibuster An attempt by a senator to delay a bill by unlimited debate. **162**

floor action The entire senate or house acting as a whole to debate, pass, or defeat proposed legislation. **160**

floor leader A legislator who is responsible for getting legislation passed or defeated. **161**

gerrymander A district or precinct that is drawn specifically to favor some political party, candidate, or ethnic group. **143**

incumbent The current office holder. **144**

interim committee A committee that meets between legislative sessions. **154**

SUMMARY

LearningOutcome 7–1 **Summarize the redistricting process, define *gerrymandering*, and describe the composition of the state legislature.** Texas has a bicameral legislature consisting of a 150-member House of Representatives and a 31-member Senate, both of which must agree on a proposed bill for it to become law. With the exception of the two U.S. Senate positions, legislators are selected from geographic districts into which the state is divided. Redistricting, the redrawing of boundaries of districts that elect U.S. representatives and state legislators, must be done after every ten-year census. This follows in part from the need for reapportionment, or the reallocation of U.S. representatives based on changes in state populations following the ten-year census. As interpreted by the Supreme Court, state governments must draw districts to reflect as closely as possible the principle of one-person, one vote, with districts having approximately equal populations. Nevertheless, redistricting provides opportunity for whichever party is in power to draw district boundaries that specifically favor a political party, candidate, or ethnic group. This is called gerrymandering. While three different tactics (cracking, packing, and pairing) can be used to accomplish this objective, the ultimate goal is to place one's political opponents at a disadvantage in forthcoming elections and help one's own party's incumbents maintain office without serious challenge.

LearningOutcome 7–2 **Evaluate the concept of a "citizen legislature" and the consequences of low compensation, short sessions, and small staffs.** Texas has a part-time legislature (also called, questionably, a "citizen legislature") that meets only 140 days every two years. As part-timers, Texas legislators are poorly paid, earning a salary of only $7,200 per year and a per diem allowance when the legislature is in session. The motivation of the Texas Constitution's architects in creating such a legislature was to ensure it would not be too powerful and that its members would not be professional politicians with too much time on their hands to pass too much legislation. Texas legislators must thus carry out their responsibilities while balancing the need to maintain their careers outside of government. The citizen legislature model, however, is often criticized for its negative effects on the legislative process, whether intended or not. Poor compensation and short sessions mean that legislators lack adequate time to research policy issues and review bills, making them dependent on The Lobby, a collective term describing the most politically and economically powerful groups in the state. That legislators have small staffs in contrast to their federal counterparts doesn't help. As a result, turnover in the Texas legislature tends to be high as its members often use it as a detour back to the private sector or as a stepping-stone to higher political office.

LearningOutcome 7–3 **Identify the presiding officers of the Texas House and Senate, and distinguish among the different types of legislative committees.** As in the U.S. Congress, presiding officers play a crucial role in moving legislation along and committees are where the majority of legislative work gets done. The presiding officer of the Texas House of Representatives is the speaker of the house who is chosen by majority vote by each incoming legislature. More powerful, however, is the lieutenant governor, who presides over the Texas Senate. Elected for a four-year term in a statewide election and straddling both the executive and legislative branches, the lieutenant governor is granted extensive authority under Senate rules to either advance or impede legislative agendas. Committees in both the house and senate fall into the categories of standing, ad hoc, conference, interim, and joint committees. As the name implies, standing committees are permanent committees charged with oversight of a specific policy area. Ad hoc and interim committees are temporary in nature, and conference committees serve the vital function of reconciling differing language in House and Senate versions of a bill so that it can eventually become law. Members of the House who have supported the speaker in his or her run for office may graduate to the **speaker's team** which carries with it the benefit of choice committee assignments or appointment as committee chairs.

LearningOutcome 7–4 **Explain the powers of the presiding officers and committee chairs, the ways in which legislators can delay or block bills, and how a bill becomes a law.** Both the speaker and lieutenant governor's powers can be summarized as including the authority to appoint most committee members and committee chairs, assign which bills go to which committees, schedule legislation for floor action, recognize which members may speak and offer amendments, and interpret procedural rules in the event of conflict. Both leaders also automatically serve on several key legislative boards and committees, including as joint chairs of the Legislative Budget Board. The legislative process begins with the introduction of a bill by a member of the house or senate. The presiding officers assign the bill to a committee where it may be delegated to a subcommittee for more detailed consideration. This is where a great deal of **mark up,** substantial alterations in the bill by adding or deleting various provisions, takes place. Most bills die in committee, but those that don't must be scheduled for reintroduction to the full chamber for debate and possible amendments. Scheduling is especially important because of the very short duration of the regular legislative session. In the house, the powerful Calendars Committee serves this function. A more complex set of rules constrict the legislative process and calendar in the senate and are intended to protect the minority from the majority. The **two-thirds rule** requires that proportion of senators to approve before a bill can actually reach the senate floor for debate. Other rules unique to the senate include **tagging,** which allows a senator to delay a bill's committee hearing for forty-eight hours, and the **filibuster,** in which a Senator may attempt to talk and delay a bill to death. Once a bill has been debated, amended, and approved by majority vote in the house or senate, it is still necessary that a bill with identical language emerge from both chambers in order to become law. Making sure this happens is the function performed by **conference committees** consisting of members of both chambers. Even when passed by both chambers, however, a bill still faces the possibility that it will be vetoed by the governor.

LearningOutcome 7–5 **Identify and describe the various legislative boards and committees at the disposal of the legislative leadership.** In addition to their procedural and appointment powers, the presiding officers of the Texas legislature can rely on the assistance of several boards, committees, and commissions in order to exert influence over the implementation of policy as well as its formulation. Among these is the important **Legislative Budget Board,** of which the speaker and lieutenant governor are joint chairs, that proposes the legislature's biennial budget and works with the governor's office to come to agreement on long-term fiscal policy. Other institutions include the **Legislative Council,** a body providing research, information, and bill-drafting assistance to legislators, the **Legislative Audit Committee,** with broad authority to audit the finances of state agencies and departments, and the **Sunset Advisory Commission,** which helps the legislature hold state bureaucracies accountable by reviewing their effectiveness or, in some cases, even the necessity of their existence.

ANSWERS TO STUDY TOOLS QUIZ

1. c. (LearningOutcome 7–1)
2. b. (LearningOutcome 7–1)
3. b. (LearningOutcome 7–1)
4. c. (LearningOutcome 7–2)
5. a. (LearningOutcome 7–2)
6. c. (LearningOutcome 7–2)
7. b. (LearningOutcome 7–3)
8. a. (LearningOutcome 7–3)
9. c. (LearningOutcome 7–3)
10. c. (LearningOutcome 7–4)
11. a. (LearningOutcome 7–4)
12. b. (LearningOutcome 7–4)
13. c. (LearningOutcome 7–5)
14. a. (LearningOutcome 7–5)
15. c. (LearningOutcome 7–5)

joint committee A committee that has members of both chambers. **154**

Legislative Audit Committee The body that performs audits of state agencies. **166**

Legislative Budget Board (LBB) The body responsible for proposing the legislature's version of the proposed biennial budget. **166**

Legislative Council The body that provides research support, information, and bill-drafting assistance to legislators. **166**

The Lobby A collective term for the most politically and economically powerful interest groups in the state. **149**

mark up To rewrite a bill in standing committee by altering major provisions. **158**

packing A gerrymandering technique in which members of partisan or minority groups are concentrated into one district, ensuring that they will influence only one election rather than several. **143**

pairing Placing two incumbent officeholders in the same elective district through redistricting. **144**

pigeonhole To kill a bill in standing committee. **158**

point of order A formal objection that the rules of procedure are not being followed on the house floor. Often made to postpone or defeat a bill. **161**

quorum The number of members that must be present to conduct official business. **160**

reapportionment The reallocation of U.S. representatives by state following a ten-year census. **141**

recorded votes Votes in which the vote of each member is recorded in the official journal. **161**

redistricting The redrawing of the boundaries of districts that elect U.S. representatives and state legislators. **141**

retainer Fee charged by a lawyer or other professional for ongoing services. **150**

speaker's team Members of the House who supported the speaker in his or her run for the office and obtained favorable committee appointments. **153**

standing committee A permanent committee that functions throughout the legislative session. **153**

subcommittee Division of a committee that considers specific subtopics of a committee's primary jurisdiction. **154**

Sunset Advisory Commission A body that may recommend restructuring, abolishing, or altering the jurisdiction of an agency. **166**

suspension of the rule The setting aside of the rules of the legislative body. **160**

tagging A senate rule that allows a senator to demand a forty-eight-hours' advance notice before a standing committee holds hearings on a particular bill. **159**

term limits Restrictions on the number of times or years that a politician can be reelected or hold a particular office. **149**

voice votes Votes that are not reported in the official journal. **161**

KEY TERMS

administrative law The rules and regulations written by administrators to carry out a law. **194**

administrative review The interpretation of a law and the development of rules and regulations for its implementation by administrative officers. All laws undergo administrative review. **193**

attorney general's opinion An interpretation of the constitution, statutory laws, or administrative laws by a state attorney general. **183**

blue-ribbon commission A group assembled by the governor (or the legislature) that may have both fact-finding and recommending authority. **178**

bureaucracy A complex, hierarchically structured administrative organization that carries out specific functions. **182**

cabinet system A system that allows the chief executive to appoint and remove top-level administrators, thereby giving the chief executive more control over the administration. **195**

chief of state The role of the governor when serving as the symbol of Texas. **180**

civil service (merit) system An employment system used by governments that takes merit into account in hiring and promotions. **190**

clemency powers The executive authority to grant relief from criminal punishment. In Texas, the governor's clemency powers are very limited. **181**

clientele interest groups The groups most concerned with the laws and policies being administered by a government agency. **191**

contract spoils The practice by which public officials award government contracts to benefit their campaign contributors, supporters, and allies. **190**

elective accountability The obligation of officials to be directly answerable to the voters for their actions. This allows elected administrators to ignore the wishes of the chief executive. **194**

formal (legal) powers Powers stated in rules, by law, or by the constitution. **175**

hierarchy A body of officials organized in ranks so that each official (except the top-ranking official) is subordinate to a superior. **188**

impeachment The official indictment of an officeholder for improper conduct in office. **174**

SUMMARY

LearningOutcome 8–1 Describe the informal requirements to become governor of Texas, the line of succession if a governor leaves office, and the uses of the gubernatorial staff. The executive branch is the part of government that administers law and implements public policy. It is responsible for the day-to-day management of government. At its pinnacle sits the governor who is elected to four-year terms without term limits. The present governor, Rick Perry, is the longest-serving governor in Texas history. The Texas Constitution establishes a weak governor system since the governor must share power with multiple independently elected executive officials and is relatively limited in his appointment powers. The overwhelming majority of Texas governors have been white, Protestant males, though Texas has had two, one-term white female governors. In recent years, governors have tended to be conservative Republicans, as have all statewide-elected executive officers. In the event that the governor's post becomes vacant, the lieutenant governor is first in the line of succession. He or she is also acting governor when the governor is out of state. Because the governor faces the complex task of overseeing a sprawling bureaucracy and maintaining a working relationship with the Texas legislature, he or she relies heavily on a competent staff that can evaluate political appointments, serve as legislative liaisons, and assist with budget formulation and planning.

LearningOutcome 8–2 Discuss the governor's legislative tools of persuasion, including the veto, and executive tools of persuasion such as the appointment power. Although the Texas governor's powers rank him among the weaker chief executives in the fifty states, skillful individuals occupying the office can exercise effective leadership. The governor's formal powers include the **veto,** the threat of which is often influential in extracting concessions from the state legislature. While the governor does not possess the **pocket veto,** allowing him to kill legislation at the end of a legislative session without signing it, he does possess a veto power the U.S. president does not have. The **line-item veto** allows the governor to veto specific funding for projects in appropriations bills without vetoing the entire bill. The governor may also call the legislature into **special sessions** to address specific issues of executive concern. The very visibility of the governor's office endows individuals occupying it with **message power.** Even though the governor's appointment powers are formally limited, many board and commission members are elected rather than appointed and he or she can only remove appointees with the approval of two-thirds of the senate. Governors who manage to stay in office for two or more terms are able to pretty much fill all appointed positions with individuals who are politically loyal and responsive to the governor's policy preferences. Longevity accrues power.

LearningOutcome 8–3 Demonstrate knowledge of the administrative structure of the Texas executive branch, including the functions of the attorney general, the comptroller, and other key administrators. The Texas Constitution creates a plural executive in which power is deliberately fragmented among several separately elected executive officials, rather than a unitary executive with a cabinet system typical of many other state governments and the federal government. This reflects a profound distrust of governmental power on the part of the constitutional framers and a resulting desire to decentralize executive power. The most prominent elected executive officials are the lieutenant governor, attorney general, state comptroller of public accounts, land commissioner, land commissioner, and agricultural commissioner. The secretary of state is the major cabinet-type official who is actually appointed by the governor. The position of attorney general has traditionally been an important stepping stone to higher political office and its responsibilities include the issuance of nonbinding but influential **attorney general's opinions**

and representation of the state in both civil and criminal lawsuits. Also critical to effective budgeting is the mission of the comptroller, who has the constitutional responsibility of certifying the state's biennial budget to make sure anticipated tax revenues match planned expenditures and final responsibility for tax collection for the state. In short, the comptroller is the accountant-in-chief for the state.

LearningOutcome 8–4 List the major characteristics of bureaucracies and ways in which reformers have tried to make bureaucracies more efficient. The Texas bureaucracy consists of more than two hundred separate institutions. A bureaucracy can be defined as a complex, hierarchically structured administrative organization that carries out specific functions. An ideal bureaucracy is characterized by hierarchy, a clear chain of command, neutrality in its application of rules, and expertise on the part of its employees. While the national government and many other states have adopted the civil service (merit) system in staffing their bureaucracies, Texas still makes extensive use of a spoils system with many public employees, especially at the top level, being appointed based on political loyalty. Texas has attempted to reign in the excesses of a politicized bureaucracy by instituting a board and commission system designed to insulate the bureaucracy from direct political influence. Board members not appointed by the present governor cannot be removed by the governor until their terms of office have expired. Even the governor's own appointees may only be removed with the approval of two-thirds of the senate.

LearningOutcome 8–5 Describe how bureaucracies relate to clientele interest groups, and define the Iron Texas Star model. Attempts to depoliticize the Texas bureaucracy have generally been unsuccessful, not entirely surprising in a political system with a part-time legislature which amplifies the influence wielded by powerful and well-funded interest groups. Observers have described Texas bureaucratic politics as the Iron Texas Star. Government agencies and their clients tend to share not only information, but common interests and values which render the agencies less effective as regulatory watchdogs. Clientele interest groups wield enormous influence, not only because of the close working relationships they forge with related bureaucracies, but because there is frequent movement between government agencies and the industries and other interest groups with which they deal (the revolving door).

LearningOutcome 8–6 Discuss the problem of bureaucratic accountability, and ways in which agencies have been made accountable to the people, the legislature, and the executive branch. In theory, bureaucracies are held responsive to the democratic process through elective accountability. The public interest, however, is often difficult to discern from periodic elections and few citizens keep track of the very detailed regulations of state agencies. Several mechanisms have been put in place that attempt to remedy this problem of democratic responsiveness, such as open-meeting laws, open-records laws, sunset laws, and the establishment of ombudspersons. The fragmented nature of the executive branch and its myriad boards, agencies, and commissions make effective citizen oversight through elections and constant vigilance more of an ideal than a reality.

ANSWERS TO STUDY TOOLS QUIZ

1. a. (LearningOutcome 8–1)
2. b. (LearningOutcome 8–1)
3. b. (LearningOutcome 8–2)
4. c. (LearningOutcome 8–2)
5. b. (LearningOutcome 8–2)
6. c. (LearningOutcome 8–3)
7. c. (LearningOutcome 8–3)
8. c. (LearningOutcome 8–3)
9. b. (LearningOutcome 8–4)
10. a. (LearningOutcome 8–4)
11. b. (LearningOutcome 8–4)
12. c. (LearningOutcome 8–5)
13. a. (LearningOutcome 8–5)
14. b. (LearningOutcome 8–6)
15. a. (LearningOutcome 8–6)

KEY TERMS

appellate jurisdiction The power of an appellate court to review and revise the judicial action of an inferior court. **203**

beyond a reasonable doubt The standard used to determine the guilt or innocence of a person criminally charged. The state must provide evidence of guilt such that jurors have no doubt that might cause a reasonable person to question whether the accused was guilty. **203**

brief A written argument prepared by a counsel supporting the counsel's position. The brief summarizes the facts of the case, the pertinent laws, and the application of those laws to the facts. **203**

burden of proof The duty of a party in a court case to prove its position. **203**

challenge for cause A request to a judge that a certain prospective juror not be allowed to serve on the jury for a specific reason, such as bias or knowledge of the case. **213**

civil case A case that concerns private rights and remedies. A successful civil plaintiff may receive relief in the form of a court order requiring that that the defendant make financial restitution to the plaintiff or undertake a certain course of action. **202**

criminal case A case that involves a violation of criminal law. The plaintiff is the state, even if private parties have experienced injury. If the state proves its case, the court will impose a punishment on the defendant. **203**

de novo Latin for "anew." A *de novo* trial is a new trial conducted in a higher court (as opposed to an appeal). In *de novo* cases, higher courts completely retry cases. On appeal, higher courts simply review the law as decided by the lower courts. **204**

double jeopardy A second prosecution for the same offense after acquittal in the first trial. **203**

grand jury In Texas, twelve persons who sit in pretrial proceedings to determine whether sufficient evidence exists to try an individual and therefore return an indictment. **211**

hung jury A jury that is unable to agree on a verdict after a suitable period of deliberation. The result is a mistrial. **214**

SUMMARY

Learning Outcome 9–1 **Identify the differences between criminal and civil cases, and the differences between original and appellate jurisdiction.** Almost every social, economic, and political question eventually finds its way to the court system. A fundamental distinction in the legal system is between civil cases and criminal cases. The former are usually brought by private parties and concern private rights and remedies. Litigants in such cases seek relief for injury, typically in the form of monetary damages. Criminal cases involve violations of penal law and are brought by the state against criminal defendants, and convictions carry with them the punishment by fines and/or imprisonment. Another important difference between civil and criminal cases concerns the burden of proof, the duty of a party in a court case to prove its position. In a civil trial, the plaintiff's burden is relatively easier, requiring only a showing that a preponderance of the evidence supports his or her case. Criminal trials, reflecting the seriousness of possible sanctions, impose a higher standard of proof on the government by requiring the prosecution to prove the defendant's guilt beyond a reasonable doubt. Parties in both civil and criminal cases have the right to appeal their cases to higher courts. A court with the authority to hear a particular case for the first time and decide issues of both law and fact is said to enjoy original jurisdiction. Courts with the authority to hear appeals have appellate jurisdiction. Upon reviewing a case from a lower court, appellate courts usually only consider whether the law was properly applied. They do not conduct a new trial.

Learning Outcome 9–2 **Explain how the courts are organized in Texas, and identify the jurisdiction of each major type of court.** Consistent with the overarching theme of the Texas Constitution, the Texas judiciary reflects a distrust of concentrated power and is therefore quite complex. Some courts have overlapping jurisdictions. The state recognizes municipal courts (courts run by cities and towns), which have jurisdiction over violations of city ordinances and minor violations of state law (misdemeanors). Some municipal courts are courts of record while others are not. Verdicts handed down in municipal courts that are not courts of record may be appealed to a county court for a completely new trial, called a trial *de novo*. The Texas Constitution requires at least one justice of the peace court for every county. Their jurisdiction is broad, including minor criminal cases, civil cases involving less than $10,000, and the power to perform marriages. Constitutional county courts exercise both judicial and administrative functions, and are supplemented in many counties by county courts-at-law that may have civil jurisdiction, criminal jurisdiction, or both. Civil jurisdiction is limited to cases involving less than $100,000, and criminal jurisdiction to serious misdemeanors punishable by jail time. At the state level, district courts are the courts of original jurisdiction for high-dollar civil cases and felony criminal cases. Over them are the courts of appeals exercising appellate jurisdiction. At the peak of the Texas judicial hierarchy are two supreme courts, one with final authority to review criminal cases and the other with final authority to review criminal cases. The former is the Texas Supreme Court and the latter the Texas Court of Criminal Appeals. While state judges must possess law degrees and pass the state bar exam, there are no uniform requirements regarding legal qualifications for municipal judges, justices of the peace, or county judges.

Learning Outcome 9–3 **Understand the role of grand juries and trial juries, and analyze the responsibilities of citizens in the legal system in Texas.** In contrast to most other democracies, ordinary citizens play an integral role in the United States legal system. This is particularly true in Texas where citizens are expected to both vote their judges into office and serve as jurors on grand juries in criminal matters and **petit (trial) juries** for both civil and criminal cases. The grand jury consists of twelve persons who attend pretrial proceedings to determine whether there is sufficient evidence to deliver an **indictment,** a written accusation charging an individual with a crime and establishing the legal basis for a trial. Most cases never actually go to trial. Civil trials usually "settle" before reaching trial, and most criminal trials are headed off through **plea bargaining.** In the event that a case does reach trial, jury selection can mark a pivotal phase. Jurors are drawn from citizens registered to vote, holding driver's licenses, or another form of official Texas identification, with some narrow exceptions. Attorneys for each side are allowed an unlimited number of **challenges for cause** to prevent potentially biased jurors from serving as well as a limited number of **peremptory challenges,** which require no explanation for dismissing a potential juror. Juries in Texas must be unanimous in their decision to convict in criminal trials. When unanimity does not occur, the result is a **hung jury,** and a new trial must be held if the prosecution wishes to pursue the case.

LearningOutcome 9–4 Compare the most common methods of judicial selection in the United States with the methods Texas uses to select judges. Texas is one of only seven states that select judges through partisan elections. Much more common in other states are nonpartisan elections and, the most popular method of selecting judges, the **merit (Missouri) plan.** In the latter system, governors appoint judges from a list of nominees selected by a special commission to fill judicial vacancies. These appointees are then subjected to a retention election during the next election cycle at which voters may vote for them to continue or be dismissed. The merit system is intended to make the judicial appointment process less political and ensure the appointment of more qualified judges, however, there is no clear evidence indicating that it achieves either of these goals. Criticism of Texas's partisan election system are straightforward. Judges are supposed to be neutral in cases and not "legislate from the bench", but it is difficult to maintain the pretense of neutrality when judicial candidates run openly on partisan and ideological credentials. Low voter turnout, lack of voter knowledge about judicial candidates, and the corrosive influence of campaign contributions further undermine public confidence in Texas's justice system, even among legal practitioners and raises the question of whether justice is "for sale." Many of the largest campaign contributors are those likely to have cases before the judges to whom they have contributed. The judiciary also under-represents Texas's minority groups in its ranks, as well as women. Yet there has been no significant movement to overhaul Texas's system of partisan elections which aspires, however imperfectly, to the ideal of citizen control of government institutions.

indictment or **true bill** A formal written accusation issued by a grand jury against a party charged with a crime when it has determined that there is sufficient evidence to bring the accused to trial. **212**

information In the context of criminal justice proceedings, a written accusation filed by the prosecutor against a party charged with a minor crime. It is an alternative to an indictment and does not involve a grand jury. **213**

merit (Missouri) plan A method of selecting judges on the basis of the supposed merit of the candidates rather than political considerations. The governor fills court vacancies from a list of nominees submitted by a judicial commission, and these appointees later face retention elections. **214**

no bill A grand jury's refusal to return an indictment filed by the prosecutor. **212**

original jurisdiction The authority of a court to consider a case in the first instance. The power to try a case, as contrasted with appellate jurisdiction. **203**

peremptory challenge A challenge made to a prospective juror without being required to give a reason for removal. The number of such challenges allotted to the prosecution and defense is limited. **214**

petit jury Trial jury for a civil or criminal case. **213**

plea bargaining Negotiations between the prosecution and the defense to obtain a lighter sentence or other benefits in exchange for a guilty plea by the accused. **209**

preponderance of the evidence The amount of evidence necessary for a party to win in a civil case. Proof that outweighs the evidence offered in opposition to it. **203**

ANSWERS TO STUDY TOOLS QUIZ

1. b. (LearningOutcome 9–1)
2. c. (LearningOutcome 9–1)
3. b. (LearningOutcome 9–1)
4. a. (LearningOutcome 9–1)
5. b. (LearningOutcome 9–2)
6. b. (LearningOutcome 9–2)
7. a. (LearningOutcome 9–2)
8. c. (LearningOutcome 9–2)
9. a. (LearningOutcome 9–3)
10. b. (LearningOutcome 9–3)
11. c. (LearningOutcome 9–3)
12. a. (LearningOutcome 9–4)
13. a. (LearningOutcome 9–4)
14. c. (LearningOutcome 9–4)
15. c. (LearningOutcome 9–4)

10 Law and Due Process

KEY TERMS

adversary system The legal system in which two contesting parties present opposing views and evidence in court. **234**

arraignment An accused person's initial appearance before a magistrate, in which the charges against the accused and his or her basic rights are explained. **231**

bail The security deposit required for release of a suspect awaiting trial. **232**

charter The organizing document for a corporation or a municipality. **223**

civil law The branch of law that spells out the duties that individuals in society owe to other persons or to their governments. **222**

closed shop A workplace in which the employer is limited to hiring individuals who were members of a particular labor union before they are hired. **223**

compulsory process A procedure to require witnesses to appear in court. **234**

criminal law The branch of law that defines and governs actions that constitute crimes. **222**

deterrence The discouragement of criminal behavior by threat of punishment. **236**

due process of law The requirement that the government use fair, reasonable, and standard procedures whenever it takes any legal action against an individual. **230**

eminent domain The power of a government to take land for public use from private citizens for just compensation. **225**

exclusionary rule A criminal procedural rule requiring that illegally obtained evidence not be admissible in court. **230**

FBI index crimes Crimes used as a national barometer of the crime rate. **227**

felony A serious crime punishable by state institutions. **226**

liability insurance Insurance against negligence claims such as those arising from auto accidents. **224**

libel A published report of a falsehood that injures a person's reputation. **224**

misdemeanor A minor crime punishable by a county jail sentence or a fine. **226**

mistrial A trial not completed for legal reasons. **235**

negligence Failure to act with the prudence or care that an ordinary person would exercise. **224**

no-fault insurance An insurance plan allowing the insured to collect from the

SUMMARY

Learning Outcome 10–1 Give examples of major types of civil law cases, and describe important controversies in civil law. Law divides into civil law and criminal law. Civil law deals largely with private rights and individual relationships, obligations, and responsibilities. Civil lawsuits are brought by plaintiffs who seek a remedy, or relief, for a violated right or perceived wrong. Courts apply civil law according to the English common law tradition, much of which is now formalized in statutory law that has been passed by legislative bodies. Judges follow the principle of *stare decisis,* meaning their decisions are based on precedents. The range of topics covered by civil law encompasses areas as diverse as family law, property law, estate law, corporate law, and personal injury (tort) law. In Texas, major areas of civil law that have risen to the level of political controversy include tort reform, concerning the ease with which individuals may initiate lawsuits and collect monetary damages, and the government's power of eminent domain.

Learning Outcome 10–2 Identify the major types of crime and the major factors that contribute to who becomes a criminal. Criminal law deals with enforcement of public morality as defined by government and punishes its violators with fines, imprisonment, and the death penalty. The overwhelming majority of criminal cases are prosecuted in the states, where the government is always the prosecution and the criminal the defendant. Crimes can generally be divided into serious crimes, felonies and less serious crimes, misdemeanors. The former is punishable by considerable prison time and even death for capital crimes, while the latter is usually only punishable by fines or mild jail sentences. Other categories of crime include white-collar crime and so-called "victimless" crimes such as drug use and gambling which some argue only affect the criminals themselves. FBI index crimes actually indicate that crime has decreased dramatically since the early 1990s though most Americans seem to think it has increased. There is a vast literature is devoted to the study of crime's causes, but what all criminals seem to have in common is an aggressive rejection of societal values and often a feeling of victimization. They tend to come from neighborhoods with weak communities and broken family structures and suffer from the accompanying stress that this involves. Crime is primarily an urban phenomenon and is disproportionately perpetrated by young, minority men.

Learning Outcome 10–3 Describe how the due process of law applies to searches and arrests in criminal cases. Texas and U.S. law provide for due process of law, the requirement that the government use fair, reasonable, and standard procedures whenever it takes any legal action against an individual. The Fourth Amendment of the U.S. Constitution protects criminal suspects against "unreasonable searches and seizures." This has been generally been interpreted to mean that law enforcement officers must have probable cause, and in many circumstances a warrant, to detain a suspect or search his or her property. When the government violates this requirement the courts use the exclusionary rule, under which evidence acquired in violation of the Fourth Amendment cannot be admitted in federal courts. This rule applies to the states, though there are exceptions to its use. Upon taking a suspect into custody, government officials must also inform suspects of their *Miranda* rights, informing them of their right to remain silent, their right to an attorney, and that any information they provide may be used against them in a court of law.

Learning Outcome 10–4 List the major steps that take place before a criminal trial and how they relate to the rights of the accused. Due process entails several important events before a criminal suspect ever reaches trial. After being arrested and jailed, an arraignment is held before a magistrate in which formal charges are brought against the accused, the suspect is reminded of his rights, bail is set, and the suspect is informed of the right to an examining trial. The Sixth Amendment guarantees the right to an attorney and the government must provide legal counsel at its own expense for criminal defendants who cannot afford their own. In Texas, this function is sometimes performed by private attorneys on a case-by-case basis, but many larger cities have a system of permanent public defenders dedicated to this task. Felony cases are usually presented to a grand jury, the purpose of which is to determine whether the prosecution has enough evidence for a *prima facie* case. In practice, grand juries typically serve as a rubber stamp for the prosecution. In particularly violent cases or cases surrounded by publicity the defendant may file for a change of venue in the hopes of receiving a more fair trial.

LearningOutcome 10–5 Explain the processes involved in a trial, and describe the adversary system. Due to crowded dockets and the risk of conviction, both prosecutor and defendant have strong incentives to reach a plea bargain; the prosecutor offers the deal of reduced charges, probation, or a lighter sentence in return for the defendant's agreement to plead guilty. If a case actually makes it to trial, criminal defendants have the right to a trial by a jury of their peers. Particularly important is the process of jury selection (*voir dire*) in which lawyers on both sides attempt to eliminate perceived unfavorable jurors in hopes of securing a jury more likely to be sympathetic at trial. The American (and Texas) trial system is an adversary system. This means the two parties, prosecution and defense, use whatever evidence they can gather and argue to their utmost within the rules of law in an attempt to win a final judgment. The judge is supposed to act as a neutral umpire enforcing the rules of procedure and evidence to ensure a fair outcome, and instructs the jury how to apply the law in the case once evidence has been provided. The jury then deliberates and delivers a verdict. If it cannot agree on a verdict, a mistrial will be declared and a new trial may be necessary. Following a guilty verdict, the judge determines the sentence. Defendants found guilty may appeal their sentence to the appropriate court of appeals.

LearningOutcome 10–6 Define and evaluate the functions of correctional institutions. Texas correctional facilities are intended to serve several functions. How successfully they do so is debatable. Punishment is meant to serve as a substitute for private revenge. The death penalty is the ultimate form of punishment and Texas leads the country in the number of executions per year. Deterrence is the theory that punishment of criminals serves as an example and prevents others from committing crimes. Isolation is based on the simple notion that criminals must be incarcerated to keep them from committing additional crimes. Rehabilitation is another ideal goal of correctional facilities and aims to reform criminals so that they can be released as useful members of society once they have served their sentences. However, since a majority of crimes are committed by recidivists (repeat offenders) suggests that Texas's present prison system fails to do this. It is even argued that the brutality of prison life actually produces even more hardened criminals. Texas has one of the largest percentages of its population in prison, yet it still experiences one of the nation's highest crime rates. Thus, the public policy challenge of how to manage the classic problem of crime and punishment remains unanswered in Texas.

ANSWERS TO STUDY TOOLS QUIZ

1. c. (LearningOutcome 10–1)
2. b. (LearningOutcome 10–1)
3. a. (LearningOutcome 10–1)
4. c. (LearningOutcome 10–2)
5. c. (LearningOutcome 10–2)
6. a. (LearningOutcome 10–3)
7. b. (LearningOutcome 10–3)
8. b. (LearningOutcome 10–4)
9. a. (LearningOutcome 10–4)
10. c. (LearningOutcome 10–5)
11. c. (LearningOutcome 10–5)
12. b. (LearningOutcome 10–6)
13. c. (LearningOutcome 10–6)

individual's insurance company regardless of fault. **224**

parole Early release from prison under official supervision. **237**

personal recognizance A defendant's personal promise to appear. **232**

plaintiff The party initiating a civil lawsuit. **222**

precedent A court decision that furnishes an example or authority for deciding subsequent cases involving identical or similar facts and legal issues. **222**

prima facie **case** A case in which there is sufficient evidence to convict if unchallenged at trial. **223**

probable cause Sufficient information to convince a reasonably cautious person that a search or arrest is justified. **230**

probate The procedure for proving the validity of a will. **223**

probation A judge's sentence of an offender to serve without confinement but under specific restrictions and official supervision. **235**

punitive damages Judgments in excess of actual damages intended to punish a defendant in a civil suit. **224**

recidivist A criminal who commits another crime after having been incarcerated. **237**

rehabilitation The effort to correct criminals' antisocial behavior. **237**

remedy The relief or compensation given to an innocent party to enforce a right or address the violation of a right. **222**

right-to-work law A law that bans unions from collecting dues from workers who have not actually joined the union. **223**

slander A public utterance that holds a person up for contempt or ridicule. **223**

stare decisis A common law principle under which judges are obligated to follow the precedents established by prior court decisions. **222**

tort A private or civil injury or wrong other than a breach of contract. **224**

tort reform Efforts to limit liability in civil cases. **224**

union shop A workplace in which management requires all new employees to join a union or pay union dues as a condition of employment. **223**

voir dire The initial questioning of jurors to determine possible biases. **234**

white-collar crime Nonviolent crimes usually committed by more prosperous individuals than those who commit street crimes. **228**

11

Public Policy in Texas

KEY TERMS

ability-to-pay taxes Taxes apportioned according to taxpayers' financial capacity. **246**

accountability The responsibility for a program's results. **251**

ad valorem tax A tax assessed according to value, such as the tax on real property and personal property. **245**

affirmative action Positive efforts to recruit ethnic minorities, women, and the economically disadvantaged. **259**

Affordable Care Act The full name of the legislation is the Patient Protection and Affordable Care Act of 2010. **262**

appropriations process The process by which a legislative body legally authorizes a government to spend specific sums of money to provide various programs and services. **249**

benefits-received tax A tax assessed according to the services received by the payers. **246**

broad-based tax A tax designed to be paid by a large number of taxpayers. **246**

Children's Health Insurance Program (CHIP) A state program that provides health insurance for children of low-income families. **262**

community college approach A higher-education policy based on open admissions, maximizing accessibility, and incorporating technical, compensatory, and continuing education among the traditional academic course offerings. **258**

general-obligation bonds Bonds to be repaid from general taxes and other revenues. **248**

general sales tax A tax collected on the retail price of most items. **244**

gross-receipts tax A tax on the gross revenues of certain enterprises. **244**

hidden taxes Taxes included in the retail prices of goods and services. **244**

income redistribution The public policy goal of shifting income from one class of recipients to another. **264**

individual mandate The requirement that individuals get health insurance or pay a tax penalty to the federal government. **262**

K–12 systems School systems in which students progress from kindergarten to the twelfth grade. **250**

SUMMARY

LearningOutcome 11–1 **Detail the major sources of revenue for the state, and summarize the debate over progressive and regressive tax rates.** Although the Texas state budget is enormous in absolute terms, Texas ranks toward the bottom of all fifty state governments in per capita spending. Though the biggest portion of state revenue comes from state taxes, federal funding counts for over a third of its income. General sales taxes, selective (excise) taxes, gross receipts taxes are the major source of state-generated revenues. When Texas's economy was more narrowly dependent on oil, severance taxes on the production of oil and natural gas accounted for a much larger share of state income. Local governments in Texas primarily rely on ad valorem taxes on real or personal property, but most also have additional sales taxes which are capped by state law at a maximum of 2 percent. Two vexing issues in the politics of taxation concern the nature of tax rates and the tax base, and the relative burden of the tax system on lower- and upper-income individuals. Tax rates set too low may not collect enough revenue, but tax rates set to high may discourage the economic activity that provides taxable revenue in the first place. Having a broad tax base through the use of broad-based taxes is important. But regulatory taxes and benefits-received taxes that are frequently used to discourage unpopular activities or base taxation on use of a resource also play an important role. Finally, who bears the greatest burden in paying taxes? A tax is said to be progressive if the effective tax rate goes up as income increases such as the federal income tax. A tax is said to be regressive if the effective tax rate goes up as income decreases, such as general sales taxes.

LearningOutcome 11–2 **Explain how the legislature appropriates funds, and describe the major purposes of state spending.** Appropriations refers to the process by which the state legislature authorizes the government's budget and targets spending on various programs and services. It is among the most important functions of the legislative branch. The major sources of revenue are state and federal tax revenue, and borrowing. However, Texas enjoys relatively low public debt compared to other states because of the legal requirement that the legislature pass a balanced budget. Because appropriations determines the "who gets what, when, and how" of state spending, it is a highly politicized affair. Interest groups and lobbyists swarm the legislature when it is in session seeking to obtain or preserve programs beneficial to them. Legislators themselves jockey for position and engage in logrolling or vote-trading, to secure funding for the constituents they represent and to bolster their own political careers. The main areas of state spending, from largest to smallest, are education, health and human services, transportation, and public safety and criminal justice.

LearningOutcome 11–3 **Discuss the systems that govern public K–12 and higher-education institutions in Texas, and describe major political issues dealing with education.** The governing institutions overseeing public school administration in Texas are the State Board of Education (SBOE), which oversees elementary and high schools, and the Texas Higher Education Coordinating Board (THECB), which coordinates policies governing colleges and universites. The SBOE consists of fifteen members elected from single-member districts for four-year overlapping terms. The THECB is composed of eighteen members, who are appointed by the governor, confirmed by the Senate, and serve six-year terms. Politically charged issues in K–12 education include attempts to hold schools and teachers accountable for students' academic performance, an ongoing effort to achieve school finance reform equalizing funding for public school systems following a 1987 Texas Supreme Court decision requiring greater equality, and skirmishes between secularists and faith-based interest groups and their

county treasurer In many counties, the official who is responsible for receiving, depositing, and disbursing funds. **284**

district attorney A county officer who prosecutes criminal cases and also handles civil matters in many counties. **285**

district clerk The recordkeeper for the district court in counties with a population exceeding eight thousand. **285**

extraterritorial jurisdiction (ETJ) In Texas, a buffer area that may extend beyond a city's limits. **280**

general-law city A city, usually with a population of five thousand or less, with a structure and organization prescribed and limited by state law. **272**

general-purpose government A municipal or county government that provides a wide range of public services. **271**

home-rule city A city with a population greater than five thousand that has exercised its legal option to write its own charter using any organizational structure that complies with state law. **272**

long ballot The listing of a large number of independently elected offices on an election ballot. **286**

mandate A federal or state requirement that a lower level of government provide a certain service or meet specified standards, often as a condition for receiving financial aid. **280**

mayor-council system A form of municipal government consisting of a mayor and a city council. **270**

merit system An employment and promotion system based on qualifications and performance rather than party affiliation or political support. **286**

public debt Money owed by government, ordinarily through the issuance of bonds. **279**

pure at-large system An electoral system in which candidates for city council run citywide and the top vote-getters are elected to fill the number of open seats. **276**

recall election An election that permits voters to remove an elected official before the official's term expires. **273**

sheriff The chief county law enforcement officer. **283**

single-member districts Election districts in which one candidate is elected to a legislative body by voters who live in a particular geographical area. **276**

spoils system A system that gives elected officials considerable discretion in employment decisions. **286**

strong-mayor form A form of municipal government in which substantial authority over appointments and budgets is lodged in the mayor's office. **274**

tax abatement A tax reduction or exemption granted by a local government to an industry or business in exchange for a perceived benefit to the community. **280**

tax assessor-collector A county financial officer who collects various county taxes and fees, and registers voters. **284**

term limits Restrictions on the number of times that a politician can be reelected to an office or the number of years that a person may hold a particular office. **277**

weak-mayor form A form of municipal government in which an elected mayor and city council share administrative responsibilities. **275**

LearningOutcome 12–4 Identify the major county officials, and describe the controversies resulting from the ways in which counties are organized. Counties are larger geographic, general-purpose governments established by the state constitution and legislature. Their governance structure is more rigidly defined than that of general-law cities, and they serve as administrative arms of the state government, though state supervision of county governments is relatively slight. Texas is organized into 254 counties whose primary governing body is the **county commissioners court,** presided over by an elected **county "judge"** who is actually an administrative, not judicial, figure. A variety of other elected officials such as **county sheriffs, constables, tax assessor-collectors,** and **district attorneys** perform more specialized functions. County governments perform many functions, some of which often overlap with municipal functions. These include law enforcement, civil and criminal courts, registering motor vehicles and recording land titles and deeds, collecting some state taxes, and recording births, deaths, and marriages. Because the structure of county governments reflects the needs of the 19th century, they are criticized for their lack of flexibility, decentralization of authority that makes it difficult for voters to hold elected officials accountable, and use of **the spoils system** in hiring employees. The spoils system has its defenders has its defenders, however, who insist that the potential for corruption is counterbalanced by the authority it gives elected officials and the perils of too much job security that come with employees hired under **the merit system,** which a number of large counties have adopted.

LearningOutcome 12–5 Consider the uses of special districts and the danger that voters will not be able to monitor them effectively. *Special districts* are local governments that provide a single service or cluster of services not provided by general-purpose county or municipal governments. These districts may include airport and hospital authorities, library and utility districts, and regional authorities responsible for managing rivers and environmental conditions. Special districts are usually governed by elected multimember boards. They are distinct from *dependent agencies* that are closely related to general-purpose governments and do not enjoy as much independence. Studies have called into question whether special districts actually deliver more efficient service than general-purpose districts, though that is their intent. Another entity that is intergovernmental rather than strictly governmental are *councils of government (COGs),* advisory bodies consisting of representatives from various local governments who come together for the purposes of regional planning and cooperation.

ANSWERS TO STUDY TOOLS QUIZ

1. c. (LearningOutcome 12–1)
2. a. (LearningOutcome 12–1)
3. a. (LearningOutcome 12–1)
4. b. (LearningOutcome 12–2)
5. c. (LearningOutcome 12–2)
6. b. (LearningOutcome 12–2)
7. c. (LearningOutcome 12–3)
8. b. (LearningOutcome 12–3)
9. c. (LearningOutcome 12–3)
10. b. (LearningOutcome 12–4)
11. a. (LearningOutcome 12–4)
12. a. (LearningOutcome 12–4)
13. b. (LearningOutcome 12–4)
14. c. (LearningOutcome 12–5)
15. c. (LearningOutcome 12–5)